Mathematica
in Action

Mathematica in Action

Stan Wagon
Macalester College

W. H. Freeman and Company
New York

Mathematica is a registered trademark of Wolfram Research, Inc.
Macintosh is a trademark of Apple Computer, Inc.
NeXT is a trademark of NeXT Computer, Inc.

Library of Congress Cataloging-in-Publication Data

Wagon, S.
    Mathematica in action / by Stan Wagon.
       p.   cm.
    Includes bibliographical references and index.
    ISBN 0-7167-2229-1 ISBN 0-7167-2202-X (pbk.)
    1. Mathematica (Computer program) 2. Mathematics—Data
processing. I. Title.
    QA76.95.W34 1991
    510'.285'536—dc20   90-48635
                                         CIP

Copyright © 1991 by W. H. Freeman and Company

Printed in the United States of America

1 2 3 4 5 6 7 8 9 0 RRD 9 9 8 7 6 5 4 3 2 1

Contents

Preface

This book is an example-based introduction to techniques, both elementary and advanced, of using *Mathematica*, a revolutionary tool for mathematical computation and exploration. By integrating the basic functions of mathematics with a powerful and easy-to-use programming language, *Mathematica* allows users to carry out projects that would be extremely laborious in traditional programming environments. *Mathematica in Action* illustrates this power by using animations, 3-dimensional graphics, high-precision number theory computations, and a variety of other methods to attack a diverse collection of problems. Indeed, so much can be done that it may take a little time for our imaginations to catch up with the possibilities.

It is my hope that this book will serve a mathematical purpose as well, and I have interspersed several unusual or complicated examples among examples that will be more familiar. Thus the reader may have to deal simultaneously with new mathematics and new *Mathematica* techniques. Rarely is more than a knowledge of undergraduate mathematics required, however.

An underlying theme of this book is that a computational way of looking at a mathematical problem or result yields many benefits. For example:

- Well-chosen computations can shed light on familiar relations and reveal new patterns.

- One is forced to think very precisely about the problem; any gaps in understanding must be eliminated if a program is to work.

- Dozens (or even hundreds) of cases can be examined, perhaps showing new patterns or phenomena.

- Methods of verifying the results must be worked out, again adding to one's overall understanding of a problem.

- Different proofs of the same theorem can be compared from the point of view of algorithmic efficiency.

My favorite example of the last point arose from an attempt to illustrate the theorem that the sum of two algebraic numbers is algebraic. I wanted a routine that took an algebraic expression, such as $\sqrt{\sqrt{2}+\sqrt{3}}+5^{1/3}$, and returned a polynomial having the input as a root. At first I programmed this using traditional proofs of facts such as the aforementioned result about sums of algebraic numbers. Then, as I learned about them, I implemented more advanced proofs, which led to better algorithms. Finally the connection with the resultant of two polynomials was pointed out to me; because the resultant function is available in *Mathematica*, this led to an extremely fast implementation, at least compared with my early attempts (see Chapter 10). This does not mean that the proof using resultants is necessarily the best to present to undergraduates, but it does instill a certain respect for the diversity of proofs of a theorem.

As the computations become more involved than the calculator computations that we are all familiar with, users may need a way to verify that results are correct. Fortunately, *Mathematica* provides the tools appropriate for such verification. For example, *Mathematica* might evaluate an integral symbolically, returning an answer in a form such that differentiating the answer does not yield an expression identical to the integrand. One approach to verification would be to compare a dozen or so numerical values of the two presumably equal functions.

There are many types of errors that can be made. The great majority of my mistakes happened when I pushed ahead in a computation without pausing sufficiently to think. When creating a complex animation or 3-dimensional image, one is always eager to see the graphics on the screen; this leads to haste and, often, to an inaccurate algorithm. For example, the brachistochrone routines that occur in Chapter 2 required several passes before they were right. I finally realized that it was essential to double-check the animation routine carefully using numerical integration. Another interesting error occurred when I was animating the rotation of a Reuleaux triangle inside a square (Chapter 2). It seemed as if the centroid of the triangle rotated along a circle. This assumption led to an animation that looked exactly right. But it was wrong! In reality the "circle" was composed of parts of four ellipses (see Figure 2.11), and my erroneous assumption led to an error of about one pixel in the images.

The eleven chapters of *Mathematica in Action* are written so that an experienced *Mathematica* user can browse anywhere. However, there is a natural progression from elementary to advanced techniques and the novice is encouraged to read the chapters in order.

Chapter 0 contains a brief review of *Mathematica*'s syntax and built-in functions.

Chapter 1 introduces some techniques of elementary number theory, with emphasis on the prime numbers. Although the generation of graphics is not discussed in detail until Chapter 2, some basic plotting routines are presented in Chapter 1.

Chapter 2 introduces graphics through several 2-dimensional routines that explore many of the facets of the cycloid curve. This chapter also introduces animations, which can be created by simply using a Do loop to generate the individual frames. The animations range from the simple (such as rolling a wheel to generate the cycloid) to the complex (such as a simulation of a bead falling down an inverted cycloid under the influence of gravity). Some symbolic differentiation and integration and some numerical integration appear in this chapter.

Chapter 3 discusses the plotting of surfaces that arise as graphs of $f(x, y)$. There are many complications in 3-dimensional plotting—choice of a viewpoint, illumination options, axis placement, and so forth—and these are discussed in detail.

Chapter 4 contains some 2-dimensional graphics applications that require more advanced techniques than those in Chapter 2. A large part of the chapter is devoted to exploring the dynamics of the quadratic map through both simple plots and animations and more complicated graphics, such as orbit diagrams and shaded surfaces.

Chapter 5 continues the discussion of 2-dimensional graphics, focusing on problems that involve complex numbers and fractals. Examples include the use of iterated function systems to generate lifelike images, such as Barnsley's fern, and mathematical images, such as Julia sets for complex maps.

Chapter 6 contains yet another approach to certain 2- and 3-dimensional graphics applications, one that uses an imaginary turtle to trace out lines in space. Space-filling curves are discussed in detail, including a 3-dimensional version.

Chapter 7 focuses on techniques for producing 3-dimensional images. Included are alternative ways to view graphs of functions $z = f(x, y)$, the generation of parametric surfaces (such as a torus or Möbius strip), ways to combine graphics images (for example, a graph of a function with a family of space curves), and an illustration of a complicated polyhedron obtained by generalizing the Koch snowflake idea to three dimensions.

In Chapters 8 and 9 graphics takes a backseat to high-precision integer computations. These chapters explore various algorithms of number theory, from the ancient ideas of the Euclidean algorithm, the Chinese remainder theorem, and Egyptian fractions, to modern ideas such as quadratic reciprocity, primes in imaginary number fields, and nondeterministic primality certificates. Chapter 8 is a prerequisite for Chapter 9. The thorny problem of protecting variable names in packages is discussed in the section on linear Diophantine equations. Chapter 9 includes two routines that are much longer than the others in this book. The first gives a complete solution to the problem of solving $x^2 \equiv a \pmod{n}$ for any positive integers a and n; the second finds all representations of an integer as a sum of two squares. Long routines demand an organized approach to the many subroutines that are used in order to guarantee accuracy and make debugging feasible.

Chapter 10 contains some miscellaneous applications starting with a very simple animation to illustrate the formation of the derivative of a function, and including programs that illustrate the following theorems:

1. The path generated by a billiard ball on an elliptical billiard table surrounds an ellipse or a hyperbola (except for periodic or degenerate cases).

2. The Art Gallery Theorem: When guards are to be placed in an n-sided polygon so that each point of the polygon is seen by a guard, Floor($n/3$) guards are always sufficient and sometimes necessary.

3. The rational numbers are countable.

4. The algebraic numbers form a field.

5. There is a formula—the Riemann–van Mangoldt formula—that represents the number of primes less than an integer as an exact function of the complex zeros of the Riemann zeta function.

Mathematica comes in two pieces: the kernel, which is identical on all systems, and the front end, the capabilities of which vary from computer to computer. The front end on the Macintosh supports many features that make *Mathematica* especially powerful, such as the Notebook format and the ability to generate animations. Although some of these features exist on other front ends, there are certain details in this book that will apply only to the Macintosh. However, the majority of the material is kernel oriented and so should apply to all implementations. All the examples were developed on a Macintosh SE/30 with 8 megabytes of memory. But all the computations, even the memory-intensive ones, can be carried out on machines with less memory, provided some of the parameters, such as those governing the resolution of a graphics image, are modified appropriately. The general rule is to start by setting the parameters so that a rough image is generated quickly, using very little memory, and then increasing the resolution to the limits of the hardware.

The material in this book was developed using the Enhanced Macintosh Version 1.2. Version 2.0 of *Mathematica* will contain many new features. All the code here should be compatible with Version 2.0, although there will undoubtedly be improved ways of doing certain things. Examples: the `GuassianFactors` routine of Chapter 9 has been incorporated into Version 2.0 via a `GaussianIntegers->True` option to `Factor-Integer`; the function `PrimePi` discussed in Chapter 1 (it returns $\pi(x)$) is built into Version 2.0.

To obtain all the code in this book on a Macintosh disk, send $5.00 to the author.

I am grateful to the many people who have shared with me their expertise in mathematics and in *Mathematica*. Special thanks to the following: Joe Buhler, Gerald Goodman, Branko Grünbaum, Eric Halsey, Joan Hutchinson, Victor Klee, Doug Lind, Joe O'Rourke, Moshe Rosenfeld, Marion Scheepers, Jeffrey Shallit, and Ilan Vardi. The staff of WRI, in particular, Paul Abbott, Joe Grohens, Brad Horn, Jerry Keiper, Shawn Sheridan, and Stephen Wolfram, were extremely helpful with encouragement and technical advice. And I am also indebted to Jerry Lyons, my editor at W. H. Freeman, and the manuscript reviewers Michael Frame, David Graves, and Anne Hudson for their excellent work. Nevertheless, the endless cutting and pasting has probably caused some inaccuracies to creep into the code, for which I apologize. I would be happy to hear from readers regarding errors. And I am always interested in learning about interesting *Mathematica* projects carried out by others. Happy coding!

Stan Wagon
Department of Mathematics
Macalester College
Saint Paul, Minnesota 55105

wagon@macalstr.edu

Mathematica
in Action

0

A Brief Introduction

T his brief chapter contains a summary of some notational features and built-in functions of *Mathematica*, for the help of the reader who has not had much experience with the program. It is very brief. Some of the points alluded to here are discussed more fully elsewhere in the book. For a detailed description of commands and usages beyond what is discussed in this book, see the *Mathematica* book by Stephen Wolfram [Wol]. More advanced users should consult *Programming in Mathematica* by Roman Maeder [Mae].

About the illustration overleaf:

The butterfly curve is the image (rotated 90°) of the polar function $r = e^{\cos\theta} + 2\cos 4\theta + \sin^5(\theta/12)$ (see [Fay]). It was generated by the following command (after the package **Graphics.m**, where `PolarPlot` lives, was loaded).

```
PolarPlot[(s = t-Pi/2; Exp[Cos[s]] - 2 Cos[4 s] + Sin[s/12]^5),
          {t, 0, 75.39},
          MaxBend->1, PlotDivision->50, Axes->None,
          PlotStyle->Thickness[.0005]]
```

To understand this curve better, generate the following sequence of plots.

```
PolarPlot[Exp[Cos[t]], {t, 0, 2 Pi}]
PolarPlot[-2 Cos[4 t], {t, 0, 2 Pi}]
PolarPlot[Exp[Cos[t]] - 2 Cos[4 t], {t, 0, 2 Pi}]
Plot[{-2 Cos[4 t], -Sin[t/12]^5}, {t, 0, 75.35},
    PlotStyle->Thickness[.0005]]
PolarPlot[-2 Cos[4 t] - Sin[t/12]^5, {t, 0, 75.39}]
```

0.1 Notational Conventions ▰▰▰▰▰▰

The *Mathematica* kernel accepts input cells and returns output cells. During a session these cells are labelled with *In[1]*, *Out[1]*, *In[2]*, and so on. In this book we will suppress these labels, but the input cells are printed in boldface. On most front ends input cells are executed by either the enter key or the shift-return key.

Built-in *Mathematica* functions always begin with capital letters. It is good practice for user-defined variables and functions to begin with lower-case letters.

Function arguments are always enclosed by square brackets, [ ]. Round brackets, ( ), are used to group objects together, that is, to establish priority of operations. The standard arithmetic operations are: +, -, *, /, and ^. A space is interpreted as a multiplication. Sometimes, even a space is unnecessary: 2a and 2Sin[x] work as expected (but xy ≠ x*y). Variable names cannot begin with numbers, but otherwise numbers can occur and there is no restriction on the length of a name.

Lists are enclosed by braces, { }. List elements are accessed via double square brackets. Thus if list is {a,b,c}, then list[[3]] returns c. Matrices are lists of lists (rows). Matrix multiplication and dot products are via the dot: {{1,2},{3,4}}.{5,0} is {5,15}. Some of the built-in matrix commands are MatrixPower, Inverse, Transpose, Det, Eigenvalues, and IdentityMatrix.

Comments are delimited by (* *).

One can refer to output later on in a *Mathematica* session by Out[n] or by %n, both of which refer to the *n*th output cell. The symbol % refers to the last output produced; %% refers to the second-last output, %%% to the third-last, and so on.

n++ abbreviates n = n + 1; similarly n-- abbreviates n = n - 1. n += i abbreviates n = n + i; similarly for n -= i, n *= i, and n /= i.

@ can serve as an abbreviation for []. Sin@Pi and Print@x abbreviate Sin[Pi] and Print[x], respectively. However, @ is less precise than square brackets and should be used sparingly, if at all. One situation where this abbreviation is useful is when several Print statements are inserted during debugging.

Iterators occur often, especially in Do loops and when lists are built using the Table command. An iterator has the form {i, n0, n, step}. The default step size is 1, and an iterator of the form {i, 200} abbreviates {i, 1, 200, 1}.

There are three usages of the equal sign. An ordinary assignment of one value to a variable is via, for example, a = 3; one can also use {a, b} = {3, 7}, for example, to handle two (or more) assignments. A delayed assignment is identified by :=; f := x^2, for example, means that whenever f is called, it will be replaced by x^2 for the current value of x. This is most often used in the definition of functions via dummy variables, as in f[t_] := t^2; the underscore indicates that the right-hand rule is to replace any occurrence of f[*expr*]. Finally, in an equation (for example, as might occur in Solve[x^5 + x == 7, x] or If[n == 100, ...]), equality is denoted by ==.

0.2 Built-in Functions ▬▬▬▬▬

Pi, I, Infinity, E, EulerGamma, and GoldenRatio are built-in constants. To turn a symbolic value into a numerical value, use the function N[]; for example, N[Pi] returns 3.14159. Degree, the value of 1 degree in radians, is also built in. Thus N[i Degree] returns the radian value of *i* degrees.

Log refers to $\log_e$. Log[b,x] is used for $\log_b x$.

Exp[z] denotes e^z.

Sin, Cos, Tan, Cot, Sec, Csc, ArcSin, ArcCos, ArcTan, ArcSec, and so on are the common trigonometric functions; the default angular measure is radians.

! has other uses (e.g., logical negation), but immediately following a number it refers to the factorial of the number (or the Gamma function of the number minus 1).

Some of the 2-dimensional plotting commands are Plot, ListPlot, ParametricPlot, ContourPlot, and DensityPlot.

The logical connectives are && (and), || (or), ! (not), and Xor (exclusive or). Logical constants are True and False.

0.3 Using Functions

This section briefly presents some advanced techniques for using functions that will be useful to anyone writing progams in *Mathematica*. Although we sometimes think of them as the same, there are several distinct ways in which functions are used. We can apply a function to one or more arguments in the traditional way [$f(x)$ or $f(x, y)$]. We can map a function of, say, one variable onto each element of a set to form $\{f(x) : x \in X\}$, which logicians denote by $f''X$. We can also apply a function of, say, two variables to a single set consisting of a two-element list, where the elements of the list are to be treated as arguments; that is, we can interpret $f(\{x, y\})$ as $f(x, y)$. *Mathematica* has the means to perform all these types of transformations, as well as several higher-level forms of function application.

The following all return $f(x)$: `f[x]`, `f@x`, and `x//f`. The first form is the standard prefix notation for function application. The second is useful to avoid the buildup of brackets; for example, `Print[x]` can be abbreviated to `Print@x`. This shortcut can be dangerous, because there are no brackets to indicate what is being acted on by f. The `//f` form, called postfix notation, is useful when the emphasis is on the argument, not the function. Thus, `A//MatrixForm`, `Sqrt[2 + Pi]//N`, and (*expr*; *expr*)`//Timing` are common uses. In this form the function applies to everything that precedes it. Another special form that reduces brackets is `~f~` for a function of several variables; for example, `X ~Union~ Y` returns $X \cup Y$.

The set-image $\{f(x) : x \in X\}$ is returned by the `Map` function, which takes two arguments as follows: `Map[f, set]`. Thus `Map[Sin, X]` returns the set consisting of the sines of values in `X`. `Map` can be abbreviated via `/@`. Thus if, say, `turtle` is a user-defined function, then `turtle /@ X` returns the set of `turtle[x]` for each x in the list X.

Some built-in functions have an attribute called `Listable`.

```
??ArcTanh
ArcTanh[z] gives the hyperbolic arc tangent of z.
Attributes[ArcTanh] = {Listable, Protected}
```

Listable functions are automatically mapped over sets given as arguments. That is, a listable function ignores all braces in an argument, applies to the numbers or symbols at any depth, and returns a list that includes the original braces. For example, if f is listable and X is a set of numbers, then f[X] automatically returns Map[f, X].

To transform a list into an argument list, one "applies" a function: Apply[Plus, {x, y}] returns Plus[x, y], which is just x + y. An abbreviation for Apply[f, X] is f @@ X.

Three more subtle operations are Thread, Inner, and Outer. "Threading" a function causes it to match corresponding entries in lists. Thus:

```
Thread[f[{a, b, c}, {x, y, z}]]
{f[a, x], f[b, y], f[c, z]}
```

Inner is a generalization of the familiar dot product. In the command Inner[f, {·}, {·}, {·}, g], f plays the role of multiplication and g the role of addition in dot product. If g is omitted, it is assumed to be addition.

```
Inner[f, {a, b, c}, {x, y, z}]
f[a, x] + f[b, y] + f[c, z]

Inner[f, {a, b, c}, {x, y, z}, g]
g[f[a, x], f[b, y], f[c, z]]

Inner[f, {a, b, c}, {x, y, z}, List]
{f[a, x], f[b, y], f[c, z]}
```

Because List is a function that makes a list out of its arguments, Inner[f, {a, b, c}, {x, y, z}, List] yields the same result as the Thread command displayed above.

The Outer command is very powerful: it applies a function to all combinations from a sequence of lists.

```
Outer[f, {a, b, c}, {d, e, f}]
{{f[a, d], f[a, e], f[a, f]}, {f[b, d], f[b, e], f[b, f]},
  {f[c, d], f[c, e], f[c, f]}}
```

One nice use of this function is to generate all sequences of 0s and 1s.

```
Outer[List, {0, 1}, {0, 1}, {0, 1}]
{{{{0, 0, 0}, {0, 0, 1}}, {{0, 1, 0}, {0, 1, 1}}},
  {{{1, 0, 0}, {1, 0, 1}}, {{1, 1, 0}, {1, 1, 1}}}}
```

Several of the preceding ideas can be combined to write an efficient routine for generating all 0-1 sequences of length n. The function Flatten[·, n - 1] reduces the nesting of the final list appropriately.

```
sequences[n_] := Flatten[Apply[Outer,
         Prepend[Table[{0, 1}, {n}], List]], n - 1]
sequences[3]
{{0, 0, 0}, {0, 0, 1}, {0, 1, 0}, {0, 1, 1}, {1, 0, 0},
  {1, 0, 1}, {1, 1, 0}, {1, 1, 1}}
```

Two more nontraditional ways of applying functions are provided by Nest and NestList, which are useful in any sort of iterative work. Nest[f, x, n] returns the result of n iterations of the function f on starting value x. NestList[f, x, n] returns the complete list of n iterates together with the starting value: $\{x, f(x), f(f(x)), f(f(f(x))), \ldots\}$. These two functions are used extensively in Chapter 4.

Very often one wishes to use one of the preceding methods of function application on a user-defined function. This can be done by first defining the function and then using, for example, Map[userfunction, list]. But this can be inconvenient when the function is simple; there is a way of succinctly giving *Mathematica* a function definition at the time it is needed. Such functions are called *pure functions* and use the generic variable #; the definition must be followed by an &, which indicates that a pure function is being used. Thus #^2 & denotes the squaring function. So, for example, if one wishes to iterate the function $4x(1-x)$ eight times on the starting value 0.5, it can be done by: Nest[4#(1 - #) &, 0.5, 8].

0.4 Getting Information

Mathematica comes with many packages for doing specialized tasks; two of the most important are **IntegralTables.m** and **Series.m**. To read in a package, execute, for example, <<Series.m.

To find out some information about a built-in command or to find out what *Mathematica*'s state of knowledge about a user-defined function is, execute, for example, ??PowerMod (same as: Information[Power-Mod]). To see a short usage statement, execute ?PowerMod.

The function names in *Mathematica* are very descriptive and therefore easy to remember; but long names can be bothersome to type in.

Typing (and possible typing errors) can be avoided by the very useful command completion feature, which works for both built-in and user-defined functions and variables. On a Macintosh or NeXT computer, command completion is invoked by typing ⌘-K (command-K) after a string of characters. Thus typing `Plot` followed by ⌘-K yields a list of commands beginning with `Plot`; `PlotJ` followed by ⌘-K causes the unique command `PlotJoined` to appear on the screen. Also useful is the template feature ⌘-I, which completes the command and inserts arguments in the proper place for easy substitution. Thus the result of `Plot` ⌘-I is `Plot[f, {x, xmin, xmax}]`.

> `Short[`*expr*`]` outputs an abbreviated version of an expression; for example, the short form of a list of 100 items is an expression that shows a few terms at the beginning and end and indicates how many are missing.

> `TableForm[`*list*`]` outputs a list in the form of a table, which is often much easier to read.

> `MatrixForm[`*list*`]` outputs a list of lists (rows) in the form of a matrix.

> `FullForm[`*expr*`]` outputs the internal form of an expression; examining these gives one a feeling for the internal workings of *Mathematica*.

0.5 Removing Information

`Clear`, `ClearAll`, `Unset`, and `Remove` are the functions used to get rid of information. `Unset[i]`, which abbreviates to `i = .`, simply removes any value assigned to `i`. This is useful if, for example, you wish to use `i` in an iterator, but have already assigned a value to `i`. Note that assignments remain in force throughout a *Mathematica* session, even when computations take place in a new file. `Clear` clears out function definitions as well as assigned values. `Remove` is more thorough than `Clear`, as it removes the name of the symbol completely from *Mathematica*'s memory of the session. Some other reasons to get rid of information are (1) to redefine a function by clearing the prior definition as necessary depending on the nature of the changes and (2) to free up memory by clearing values. A simple way to clear all definitions in a *Mathematica* session is by using

`ClearAll["Global`*"]`. Following this by a Clear Kernel History command (Action menu on a Macintosh) frees up even more memory by clearing, among other things, the `Out[n]` pointers. However, none of these actions returns *Mathematica* to the exact same state it has when started; when memory starts getting low, it is best to quit the session and restart.

Computations can be aborted by ⌘-period. However, not all procedures react instantaneously to this interrupt, and sometimes more drastic measures are necessary—namely, quitting and restarting the program.

0.6 Customizing *Mathematica*

A user can customize his or her version of *Mathematica* by using the **init.m** file, which can be found among the packages accompanying the program. Any instructions placed in that file will be executed whenever a *Mathematica* session is started. For example, I have found it useful to use `pi` to denote `N[Pi]`. The reason for this is that in graphics or numerical applications one may not want the symbolic value of π, but its numerical value instead, so as to avoid the buildup of long symbolic strings. A line of the form `pi = N[Pi]` placed in **init.m** means that this abbreviation can be used all the time. One could also use **init.m** to load certain packages that will be used very often, either one of *Mathematica*'s packages or one that contains a library of routines that the user has developed. Finally, the user may find it convenient to assign the `Listable` attribute, discussed earlier in this chapter, to certain functions that do not already have this attribute. That way the functions can be used on sets and the braces will be ignored. This can be done by placing a command such as the following into **init.m**.

```
SetAttributes[{PowerMod, EulerPhi, JacobiSymbol}, Listable]
```

0.7 Bugs

Mathematica is a massive program, with versions for many different computers. The program is now maturing, but bugs do exist. Often, the user can fix them by adding an appropriate statement to the **init.m** file.

Bugs that cause incorrect graphics output are harder to fix. The serious Macintosh-based user—that is, one who wants perfect, publication-quality images—should consider getting *Adobe Illustrator*. *Illustrator* is a complicated program to use, more so than the first-generation drawing progams. But it is worth learning, because *Mathematica* can transform its images into *Illustrator* format, thus allowing the user to modify images by adding labels, arrows, or text, or by subtracting any unwanted parts of an image.

1 Prime Numbers

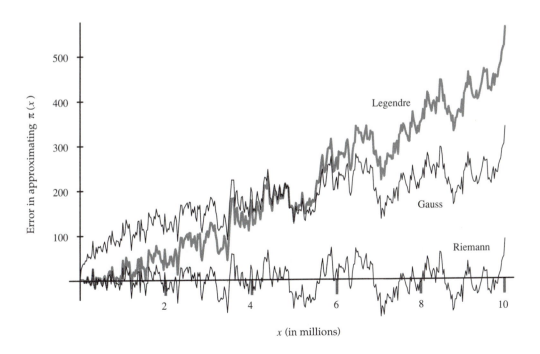

T his chapter uses number theory to introduce a variety of elementary and advanced features of *Mathematica*; please read it even if you are not interested in number theory. We will see how to use *Mathematica* as a supercalculator, and also how to write short programs. Several important general techniques are introduced, as well as different approaches to graphing data. Only a little bit of number theory is assumed—not much beyond modular arithmetic and the definition of a prime number. The proofs of the elementary results quoted are simple and can be found in any number theory text (e.g., [Ros]).

About the illustration overleaf:

This graph compares the errors in Legendre's, Gauss's, and Riemann's approximations to $\pi(x)$, the number of primes below x. The latter two are based on the LogIntegral function, which is built into *Mathematica*. Note the remarkable accuracy of Riemann's approximation; for example, $\pi(10,000,000) = 664,579$ and $R(10,000,000) = 664,667$. The graph was produced by first generating the data values and then using the ListPlot command. The labels were added in *Adobe Illustrator*.

1.1 Recognizing Large Primes ▰▰▰▰▰

Let's start by using *Mathematica* as a guide for a tour through the realm of prime numbers. Because there is no limit on the number of digits that can be used in a computation in *Mathematica*, we can explore farther than is usual. *Mathematica* is an interpreted environment, just like BASIC, and we can use it as a calculator to execute single commands. But it is as simple to execute a sequence of lines (i.e., a program) as a single line, and we will see several short programs in this chapter.

Integer arithmetic in *Mathematica* is done to full precision. Thus we can check Wilson's theorem that for p prime, $(p-1)! \equiv -1 \pmod{p}$, using the built-in Mod and Factorial functions (throughout this chapter p denotes a prime number).

```
Mod[100!, 101]        Mod[90!, 91]
100                    0
```

The function Mod[a, n] returns the value of a modulo n. In fact, Wilson's theorem characterizes the primes; that is, n is prime if and only if $(n-1)! \equiv -1 \pmod{n}$. The motivation behind the "if" direction is clear: if n is not prime and $n > 4$, then n divides $(n-1)!$. For example, $90! \equiv 0 \pmod{91}$ because $90!$ is divisible by 7 and 13, the prime divisors of 91. (Exercise: Make this argument rigorous; you will have to treat 4 as a special case.) Wilson's theorem does not yield a workable primality test, however, because it takes $n-1$ modular multiplications to test n; if n has 50 digits, this is not a feasible computation. Exercise: After learning a little bit about programming, write a routine that uses the converse of Wilson's theorem to check primality. (One solution—using Nest, which is discussed in detail in Chapter 4—is given in the Appendix.)

We can also examine Fermat's Little Theorem that $a^{p-1} \equiv 1 \pmod{p}$ when a is not divisible by p.

```
Mod[2^100, 101]
1
```

When computing powers in modular arithmetic, the PowerMod function should be used instead of the Mod function. Briefly, PowerMod implements a very efficient way of computing powers using only a few multiplications; it generalizes the fact that, say, a^{16} can be computed using only four multiplications: $(((a^2)^2)^2)^2$. (The naive approach uses 15 multiplications.) PowerMod[a, b, n] returns a^b (mod n) and works for negative b as well, in which case it returns the appropriate power of a's inverse modulo n.

```
PowerMod[2, 100, 101]
1
```

```
PowerMod[17, -1, 10001]
5883
```

We can check that the inverse of 17 is in fact 5,883 as follows. Note that a space between expressions is interpreted as multiplication.

```
Mod[17 %, 10001]
1
```

It would be wonderful if the converse of Fermat's Little Theorem were true—that is, if a number n were prime if and only if, say, $2^{n-1} \equiv 1$ (mod n)—for then, because of the speed of PowerMod, one would have a very fast test for primality. Let's use *Mathematica* to find out if this converse is true. We will use programming techniques (For and Do loops) familiar to users of languages such as BASIC, although such an approach is neither the best nor the fastest way to program in *Mathematica*. The For loop (which takes four arguments, the last of which is the command or compound expression to be iterated) and an If command (which takes two arguments) are used as follows. We use the built-in prime query command PrimeQ (more on this later) to check for primality. And we check only odd values of n.

```
For[n = 3, n < 3000, n = n + 2,
If[PowerMod[2, n - 1, n] == 1 && !PrimeQ[n], Print[n]]]
341
561
645
1105
1387
1729
1905
```

```
2047
2465
2701
2821
```

So we see that up to 3,000, there are 11 composite numbers n that mimic prime numbers in that they satisfy $2^{n-1} \equiv 1 \pmod{n}$. A Do loop would be more appropriate than a For loop here. Do takes two arguments, a command to be iterated and an iterator. Using Do, the preceding program becomes:

```
Do[If[PowerMod[2, n - 1, n] == 1 && !PrimeQ[n], Print[n]],
    {n, 3, 3000, 2}]
```

In any event, the numbers on the list just formed are composite (called 2-pseudoprimes), as can be seen explicitly with FactorInteger.

```
FactorInteger[2701]
{{37, 1}, {73, 1}}
```

The three built-in functions that are most relevant to prime numbers are PrimeQ, Prime, and FactorInteger. PrimeQ (used earlier in the For loop) is a function that returns the logical value True or False according as its argument is or is not prime; it works on arbitrarily large integers.

```
PrimeQ[1000001]
False
```

```
PrimeQ[10^100 + 1]
False
```

How does PrimeQ work? Checking all potential divisors of a 100-digit number is, for mortals, a nonterminating task. *Mathematica* uses an approach that is very fast, though it has not been proved to be infallible. As we have just shown, the 2-pseudoprime test fails quite often. That is, it may report that a number is prime when it is not; however, if it reports that a number is composite, then it definitely is composite. There are refinements that reduce the number of false positives, and *Mathematica* uses one of these refinements that, it is conjectured, totally eliminates the false positives. The so-called strong 2-pseudoprime test works for numbers below 25 billion with only 13 exceptions (99.999999948% accuracy). When an additional test based on Lucas pseudoprimes is added, these exceptions disappear; thus it seems plausible that these two tests combine to form a fail-safe primality test. This is what *Mathematica* currently uses; that is, `PrimeQ[n]` returns `True` if n passes a strong pseudoprime test and a Lucas pseudoprime test, and `False` (definitely a correct answer) otherwise.

There remains the possibility that some composite number sneaks by this two-test test, but at least it is known that there are no such false positives below 25×10^9; thus `PrimeQ` can be used with absolute confidence on numbers having at most 10 digits. For the precise definitions of these tests and the results of various computations relating to them, see [PSW]. The field of primality testing is changing rapidly, and it is now possible, using the theory of elliptic curves and an algorithm due to A. O. L. Atkin and F. Morain (building on earlier work of S. Goldwasser and J. Kilian), to come up with a certificate (i.e., a proof) that a given number of a few hundred digits is prime. This method has been programmed in *Mathematica* by Ilan Vardi and may be included in a future release.

A brief description of `PrimeQ`'s method of attack can be found by executing `??PrimeQ`.

```
??PrimeQ
PrimeQ[expr] yields True if expr is a prime number, and yields
    False otherwise. In the current version of Mathematica, the
    algorithm used for large integers is probabilistic, but
    very reliable (pseudoprime test and Lucas test).
Attributes[PrimeQ] = {Listable, Protected}
```

`PrimeQ` is a bare-bones test in that it does not first check the input for divisibility by small primes (although it does do a quick check for divisibility by 2). Thus it takes just as long to show that $10^{100} + 5$ is composite as it does to test $10^{100}+1$ (try it!). One can easily modify `PrimeQ` to `primeQ`, which does invoke a divisibility test. One such modification, which speeds things up for inputs larger than about 10^{40}, is given in the program `primeQ` in the Appendix. Recall that *Mathematica* distinguishes between upper- and lower-case letters: All built-in functions begin with an upper-case letter. As a general rule, it is best to use only lower-case letters for functions you define.

Unlike primality testing, which is widely believed to be solvable in polynomial time[1] (in fact, this is a consequence of the Extended Riemann Hypothesis; see [Wag]), factoring is thought to be inherently difficult. The best known algorithms take hours or days to factor 80-digit numbers. Thus any program that requires the factorization of integers beyond about 10^{20} can be expected occasionally to run into values that take a long time. *Mathematica*'s factoring routine took just about a minute to perform the following factorization.

```
FactorInteger[2^67 - 1]
{{193707721, 1}, {761838257287, 1}}
```

`FactorInteger` returns a list of pairs, each of which consists of a prime number and an exponent.

Numbers of more modest size are handled easily. The `Timing[]` command returns a pair: the time needed for a computation and the result of the computation. Although square brackets are the standard way of applying a function, there are other ways. A function preceded by `//` can be placed after its argument, which is sometimes convenient. For example, it is easier to insert and delete `Timing` commands this way.

```
FactorInteger[1000001] //Timing
{0.2 Second, {{101, 1}, {9901, 1}}}
```

Mathematica can factor integers and polynomials; for the latter, the function `Factor[]` is used, for the former, `FactorInteger[]`.

Let's return to `PrimeQ` and see how a `While` loop can be used to find the first prime beyond a given input value. `While` takes two arguments, a logical expression and a statement (or compound statement) that will be executed until the first argument yields `False`. The following

---

[1]A computational problem is said to be *solvable in polynomial time* if there is an algorithm that solves the problem and, for some fixed positive integer d, the algorithm halts in fewer than n^d steps on any input having length n. When d is not too large, such algorithms run quickly, at least when compared with algorithms that take an exponential amount of time.

commands show that $10^{30} + 57$ is, almost surely, the first prime beyond 10^{30}. In Chapter 8 we will present a method that, for certain primes, can provide a certificate that guarantees primality. Such a certificate appears as the chapter cover for Chapter 8, thus guaranteeing that $10^{30} + 57$ is indeed prime. Because PrimeQ's falses are definitely correct, we can state unequivocally that $10^{30} + 57$ is the first prime past 10^{30}.

```
n = 10^30 + 1
While[!PrimeQ[n], n = n + 2]
n
1000000000000000000000000000057
```

This bit of code can be easily turned into a function that produces the first prime past its input.

```
FirstPrimeAbove[n_] := Block[{k},
    k = n;
    While[!PrimeQ[k], k = k + 1];
    Return[k]]
```

The underscore indicates that n is a dummy variable and that the sequence of commands is to apply to any expression used as an argument in FirstPrimeAbove. The use of := means that this is a delayed assignment, to be consulted whenever the expression FirstPrimeAbove appears. The Block command ensures that k (and any other variables that might be included in the list of variables to be blocked) doesn't interfere with any other uses of k (and vice versa); the use of Block is not essential, but it is a good idea to use it in programs that might be used by others. Block takes two arguments, a list of variables to be blocked and a compound statement forming the body of the function definition. A sequence of statements is turned into a compound statement if semicolons are used to separate the commands. If there are no variables to be blocked, then the compound statement forming the body must be grouped within (). A semicolon has another feature; namely, used at the end of a statement, it suppresses output. This can be important when one wishes to execute an assignment of the form x = *expr* where *expr* is, say, a long list. Without the semicolon the list would be formatted and displayed, and this can take a long time; a terminal semicolon causes the assignment to be made without the display of any output.

```
FirstPrimeAbove[234436]
234457
```

```
FirstPrimeAbove[10^30]
1000000000000000000000000000057
```

Even this short program can be shortened and improved. First note that it would not do to eliminate k entirely by replacing k with n throughout, because when the function is called with input 4, it would replace all occurrences of n by 4, and so would attempt to execute 4 = 4 + 1. This would lead to an error, since the value of 4 can't be changed. However, there are other shortcuts. First of all, there is an abbreviation for the command n = n + 1, which occurs often in While, Do, and For loops, namely, n++. Another shortcut comes from making initializations directly in the list of variables to be blocked. However, they must be to values directly obtainable from the parameter list; "initializations" of the form {k = n, w = 0, t = {}, r = Log[k]} can lead to errors, since the assignment to r is not a strict initialization from the parameters. Finally, if this function is going to be used on large inputs, then the call to PrimeQ should be replaced by a call to primeQ, which, as previously discussed, saves time by checking for division by small primes. At first glance it might seem worthwhile to jump by 2 instead of by 1, provided we arrange to start the search on an odd number. However, it turns out that it is faster to have PrimeQ do the parity check than to add 2 to the counter. (Exercise: Run some timing experiments to compare the speed of the following definition when k++ is replaced by k += 2.) Finally, a compound statement automatically returns the value of the last command in the list, so the Return can be omitted in this case (but there can be no ; after the final k as that would cause nothing to be returned).

```
FirstPrimeAbove[n_] := Block[{k = n},
        While[!primeQ[k], k++];
        k]
```

EXERCISE How does a loop of the form While[!PrimeQ[k++]] behave? In other words, what is the value of k at the end of the loop? (Hint: The assignment x = y returns the value y.)

Before using the preceding program, we must load primeQ. That done, we can attack a fairly large number, if we are willing to wait a few minutes for an answer. Exercise: Compare the performance of FirstPrimeAbove using primeQ with the same routine using the built-in PrimeQ.

```
FirstPrimeAbove[10^100]
1000000000000000000000000000000000000000000000000000000000000000\
  00000000000000000000000000000000000000267
```

1.2 Public-Key Encryption

The function FirstPrimeAbove is useful in a demonstration of the RSA public-key cryptosystem scheme. The way the scheme works is that a user (Alice) generates two large primes p and q, which she keeps secret, and an exponent $e < pq$ (which is relatively prime to $p-1$ and $q-1$). Then n $(= pq)$ and e are made public. If Bob wishes to send a message m (which, for now, is assumed to be translated into an integer less than n), he codes it as m^e modulo n and sends the result over a completely public channel. Alice then decodes by taking the encoded message and raising it to the power d modulo n where d is the inverse of e modulo $(p-1)(q-1)$. Because Alice is the only person in the world who knows p and q (this assumes that factoring, say, 200-digit numbers of the form pq is indeed an essentially impossible problem), she is the only one who has access to d. An explanation of why this works, in particular, why $p-1$ and $q-1$ are used, can be found in most number theory texts (e.g., [Ros]); a nontechnical introduction can be found in [Gar].

```
p = FirstPrimeAbove[12400123056421444]
q = FirstPrimeAbove[24760095346677660]
24760095346677671
```

The preceding pair of commands yields as output only the result of the final computation.

```
n = p q
307028229187532010914295627450751
```

Remember that a space between expressions is interpreted as multiplication. We will also need a random exponent that must be relatively prime to $(p-1)(q-1)$.

```
exponent = 230959
GCD[exponent, (p-1)(q-1)]
1
```

Now, suppose Bob wishes to send the following message to Alice.

```
message = 29677666357357111357;
```

Of course, most people with secret messages would be more interested in messages of the form "Sell all shares of the company now." The details of transforming such a message to an integer are somewhat dull, and the Appendix contains two short programs, encode and decode, that do such transformations. Scanning those programs will give you an idea of some of the string manipulation functions in *Mathematica*.

Now, we can encode easily, using PowerMod.

```
PowerMod[message, exponent, n]
26737620354107569160971 6691173238
```

To decode, Alice needs to use the decoding inverse d. Again PowerMod can be used with exponent -1.

```
d = PowerMod[exponent, -1, (p - 1)(q - 1)]
18925468956950363243475 7701777439
```

To decode, Alice raises the coded message to the dth power modulo n. One can refer to the values of previous output lines later on in a *Mathematica* session as follows: %15 refers to the 15th output cell, %% refers to the second-preceding output. So we can refer to previous results without having to constantly store them in variables. Of course, if one has generated some data in a time-consuming computation, one should save it immediately, either by saving the notebook containing the output or by saving the value of the variable or output cell to a file. Periodic saving of notebooks is always a good idea, as system crashes due to infinite loops or the exceeding of memory limits are always possible. Anyway, to decode, Alice would do the following exponentiation, which returns the original message.

```
PowerMod[%%, d, n]                    (%% refers to 26737... )
2967766666357357111357
```

After loading encode and decode, we can deal with coherent messages, provided they are shorter than the length of n.

```
PowerMod[encode["Sell shares now"], exponent, n]
6069506438608865473682511731 3919

decode[PowerMod[%, d, n]]
Sell shares now
```

To turn this into a secure system, one should let p and q have about 100 digits each. It would take a few minutes to generate them, but then the various exponentiations needed to code and decode are quite fast.

1.3 The Distribution of the Primes ▬▬▬

Prime[n] gives the nth prime. (On a Macintosh the value of n must be less than 100,000,000; the 100,000,000th prime is just over 2,000,000,000.)

```
Prime[10^8]
2038074743
```

The most common way of generating a list is with the Table command. This command takes two arguments, a statement or compound statement, and an iterator. We now generate a list of the first 100 primes.

```
Table[Prime[n], {n, 100}]
{2, 3, 5, 7, 11, 13, 17, 19, 23, 29, 31, 37, 41, 43, 47, 53,
59, 61, 67, 71, 73, 79, 83, 89, 97, 101, 103, 107, 109,
113, 127, 131, 137, 139, 149, 151, 157, 163, 167, 173, 179,
181, 191, 193, 197, 199, 211, 223, 227, 229, 233, 239, 241,
251, 257, 263, 269, 271, 277, 281, 283, 293, 307, 311, 313,
317, 331, 337, 347, 349, 353, 359, 367, 373, 379, 383, 389,
397, 401, 409, 419, 421, 431, 433, 439, 443, 449, 457, 461,
463, 467, 479, 487, 491, 499, 503, 509, 521, 523, 541}
```

We may now find that it would have been convenient to store this list as the value of a variable, primes, say. We could do this easily by primes = %; but let's go back and recompute the table, this time putting a semicolon at the end of the command to suppress the display of the output.

```
primes = Table[Prime[n], {n, 100}];
```

We can check that this worked properly without looking at the entire list by using a command that shows a shortened form of an expression.

```
Short[primes]
{2, 3, 5, 7, 11, 13, 17, 19, <<88>>, 509, 521, 523, 541}
```

As usual, we could have generated this table in many other ways. Prime is a listable function (execute Attributes[Prime] to see this); this means that when it is applied to a list (or a list of lists, or a list of lists of lists, etc.), it brings itself inside all the braces to apply to the innermost integers. Another convenience in list generation is the Range function, which works much like the iterators just discussed, in that it produces the iteration values as a list.

```
Range[10]
{1, 2, 3, 4, 5, 6, 7, 8, 9, 10}
```

```
Range[3, 70, 5]
{3, 8, 13, 18, 23, 28, 33, 38, 43, 48, 53, 58, 63, 68}
```

So, we can simply apply Prime directly to the appropriate list. That is, the command Prime[Range[100]] suffices to generate a list of the first 100 primes.

The function $\pi(x)$ is the number of primes less than or equal to x. In Version 1.2, this function is not built in, so we must write a program to compute it. Again, we have relegated the code to the Appendix. Essentially, it is just the inverse of the Prime[] function; that is, Prime[n] returns p if and only if $\pi(p) = n$. We use the name PrimePi[] for this function. We'll use $\pi(x)$ to demonstrate some of the 2-dimensional plotting capabilities of *Mathematica*. The following command assumes that PrimePi has been loaded.

`Plot[PrimePi[x], {x, 1, 200}]`

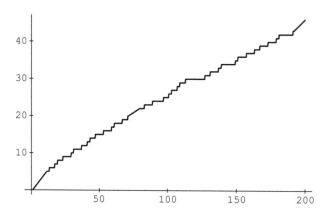

FIGURE 1.1 The graph of $\pi(x)$ generated by `Plot`.

The `Plot` command is meant for continuous functions such as `Sin[x]` or `x^2 Sin[1/x]`. For example, here is a graph of $x^2 \sin(1/x)$, together with the graphs of $\pm x^2$.

`Plot[{x^2 Sin[1/x], x^2, -x^2}, {x, -.1, .1}]`

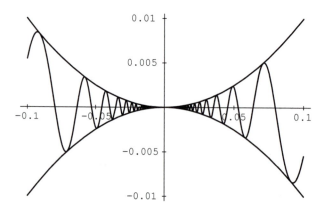

FIGURE 1.2 The graphs of $x^2 \sin(1/x)$, x^2, and $-x^2$ generated by `Plot`.

`Plot` uses an adaptive algorithm that seeks enough points to smooth out the function. There are options that control the degree of smoothness sought (MaxBend, PlotDivision, PlotPoints), and these options can be tweaked to generate a nicer version of the graph of $\pi(x)$, with each prime step clearly shown. But because we know π is a step function, it's best to use another approach. The command ListPlot plots a list of pairs as points. To use it here, we must add extra pairs to the list to get a nice-looking step function with vertical lines at the primes. (Of course, the true graph of π is disconnected with jumps at primes. This true graph could be produced using other graphics operations; see the Cantor function example in Chapter 4.) First we recompute our data so as to add the x values to the data points.

```
Table[{x, PrimePi[x]}, {x, 200}];

Short[%]    (* % works even if preceding output wasn't shown *)
{{1, 0}, {2, 1}, {3, 2}, <<195>>, {199, 46}, {200, 46}}
```

But now we must throw in additional points of the form $(p, \pi(p)-1)$, so that each prime is associated to two y values, $\pi(p)$ and $\pi(p)-1$. We can do this by using Join or Union. The difference is that Union sorts and removes duplications. First we generate the table and have a brief look at it.

```
Short[Table[{Prime[n], n - 1}, {n, PrimePi[200]}]]
{{2, 0}, {3, 1}, {5, 2}, <<41>>, {197, 44}, {199, 45}}
```

Now we take the union of the table with our previous table. The Take command allows us to see the first 10 elements of a list; we are thus able to confirm that all is going according to plan.

```
primepoints = Union[%, %%]
Take[primepoints, 10]
{{1, 0}, {2, 0}, {2, 1}, {3, 1}, {3, 2}, {4, 2}, {5, 2},
 {5, 3}, {6, 3}, {7, 3}}

ListPlot[primepoints, PlotJoined->True]
```

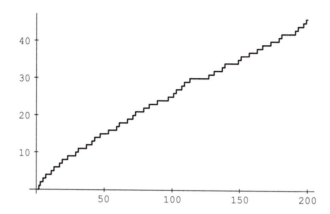

FIGURE 1.3 The graph of $\pi(x)$ generated by ListPlot.

The default line thickness of the graph will be too thick for some purposes. There are two ways of making the lines in a plot thinner. One can redo the plot with the option PlotStyle->Thickness[0.0005] added. The number 0.0005 refers to the ratio of the line width of the graph to the width of the entire plot. But since this is such a common adjustment—for example, if you scale a graphics image, say a surface, to a much larger size, all line thicknesses are scaled up as well—a quick way of making the lines thinner is available on some front ends.

Let's look briefly at an alternative way of generating the data points for this graph. The following command generates a pair of lists, the domain and range of π on $\{1, \ldots, 100\}$.

```
{Range[100], PrimePi[Range[100]]};
```

This can be interpreted as a 2×100 matrix, and its transpose is exactly the set of pairs we want. We must then add in the additional points as we did above, so we define another list and take the union of the transposes of the two lists. Square brackets get tiresome and there are some ways of avoiding them. For example, ~f~ placed between two arguments a and b yields f[a,b]. Exercise: Verify that the following yields a list identical to primepoints.

```
Transpose[{Range[200], PrimePi[Range[200]]}]  ~Union~
Transpose[{Prime[Range[PrimePi[200]]], Range[0, PrimePi[200]-1]}];
```

The steps of $\pi(x)$ are less noticeable for larger ranges, and then it is appropriate to use the built-in adaptive routine Plot. Here is a view of the growth of the primes under one million.

```
Plot[PrimePi[x], {x, 1, 10^6}, PlotStyle->Thickness[.0005]]
```

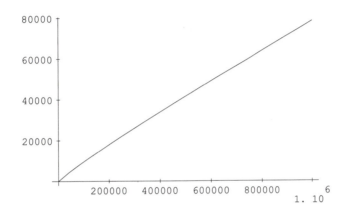

FIGURE 1.4   The rate of accumulation of the primes under 1,000,000.

Note how straight this curve is. Only a slight curvature visible at the lower end gives some indication of the nonlinearity of $\pi(x)$. The primes do become less dense (that is, $\pi(x)$ is concave downward), but it is hard to see in a graph. The smoothness of $\pi(x)$ is noteworthy, since the primes seem, at first glance, to show up randomly among the integers. As Don Zagier has observed [Zag]: "The smoothness with which this curve climbs is one of the most astonishing facts in mathematics."

We can compare $\pi(x)$ with the various approximations discovered by Legendre, Gauss and Riemann. The celebrated Prime Number Theorem states that $\pi(x)$ is asymptotic to $x/\log x$. This means that the ratio of $\pi(x)$ to $x/\log x$ approaches 1 as x approaches infinity. (We use log to denote $\log_e$, to conform with *Mathematica*'s usage; that is, Log[x] = $\log_e x$, and Log[10,x] and Log[2,x] are used for bases 10, 2, and so on.) Here is a view of this approximation. Note how PlotStyle is now set to be a list of two lists: the first is a list of options for the first graph and the second is a list of options for the second graph. The following command will generate an error message because of the attempt to evaluate the reciprocal of log 1. But the desired graph will still be produced. The numbers in Dashing refer to the alternating lengths in a dashed line.

```
Plot[{PrimePi[x], x/Log[x]}, {x, 1, 50000},
  PlotStyle->{{Thickness[.0005]},
              {Thickness[.0001], Dashing[{.02, .04}]}}]
Power::infy: Infinite expression -- encountered.
Plot::notnum:

     x
  ------ does not evaluate to a real number at x=1..
  Log[x]
```

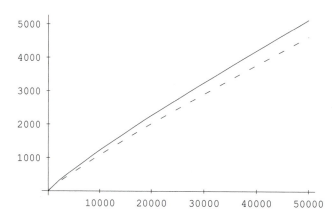

FIGURE 1.5   The graphs of $\pi(x)$ and $x/\log x$ generated by Plot.

EXERCISE Generate a table of $\pi(x)/(x/\log x)$ as x goes from 10 to 10^9.

There are much better approximations to $\pi(x)$. Legendre discovered (empirically) that $x/(\log x - 1.08366)$ is better than $x/\log x$. Gauss, also working empirically (the Prime Number Theorem was not proved until 1896), found that the following integral is an excellent approximation: $\int_2^t 1/\log t\, dt$; this integral (taken from 0 to t instead—the singularity at $t = 1$ is easily dealt with) is called the logarithmic integral of x, usually denoted by li(x). Riemann's approximation is the following:

$$R(x) = \sum_{n=1}^{\infty} \frac{\mu(n)}{n}\, \mathrm{li}(x^{1/n})$$

where μ denotes the Möbius function ($\mu(n) = 0$ unless $n = p_1 p_2 \cdots p_r$, in which case $\mu(n) = (-1)^r$). Let's see how these functions compare as approximations to $\pi(x)$.

Legendre's approximation is simply translated into x/(Log[x] - 1.08366). Gauss's approximation uses the logarithmic integral, which is built in as LogIntegral[x]. For Riemann's we must write our own code and again we relegate this to the Appendix. For more information on these approximations, see [Rie, Zag].

Now let's do a major computation and compare the approximations of Legendre, Gauss, and Riemann on the same graph, for x up to 10 million. Even for supercomputers, the computation of $\pi(x)$ for large values of x is difficult; the largest value known (see [LMO]) is only $\pi(4 \times 10^{16})$. We cannot simply plot the functions the way we did for $x/\log x$, because all the graphs would coincide with each other. Instead we plot the differences between the approximations and $\pi(x)$. We could use the Plot function to do this, as it can display several plots on the same set of axes, as follows:

```
Plot[{x/(Log[x] - 1.08366) - PrimePi[x],
    LogIntegral[x] - PrimePi[x],
    RiemannR[x] - PrimePi[x]}, {x, 1, 10^7}]
```

One problem with this approach is that PrimePi would be called more often than is necessary. Another problem is that these graphs change direction rapidly and Plot, in its attempt to draw a smooth curve, may end up sampling too many points. Again, it is better to use List-Plot to connect the dots in tables of data that are computed in advance. Here is the code used to generate this chapter's cover diagram, shown again in Figure 1.6; comments on the code follow. The actual chapter cover picture was further massaged in *Adobe Illustrator*.

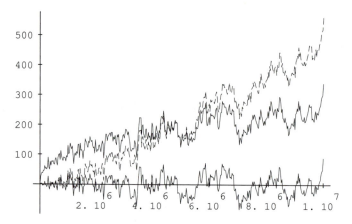

FIGURE 1.6 The error in the approximations to $\pi(x)$ found by Legendre, Gauss, and Riemann, graphed using `ListPlot`.

```
step = 25000;
domain = Range[0, 10^7, step];
options = {PlotJoined->True};

primepilist = Table[PrimePi[x], {x, 0, 10^7, step}];
Print["Done primepi"];
legendre = Table[x/(Log[x] - 1.08366), {x, 0., 10^7, step}];
Print["Done legendre"];
gauss = LogIntegral[Range[0., 10^7, step]];
Print["Done gauss"];
riemann = Table[If[Mod[x, 500000] == 0, Print@x]; RiemannR[x],
                {x, 0, 10^7, step}];

legendre = Transpose[{domain, legendre - primepilist}];
gauss    = Transpose[{domain,  gauss  - primepilist}];
riemann  = Transpose[{domain, riemann - primepilist}];

Show[{ListPlot[legendre, options,
          PlotStyle->{Thickness[1.5/420], GrayLevel[0.5]}],
      ListPlot[gauss, options, PlotStyle->Thickness[.5/420]],
      ListPlot[riemann, options, PlotStyle->Thickness[.5/420]]}]
```

Here are some comments on the program. The first two definitions are simply for convenience and to avoid retyping. They also make it easy to change the step size—when debugging it is useful to produce a plot with minimal computation, that is, with parameters that yield only a few data points. The various `Print` statements are included for ease of monitoring the computation. That way, if a bug occurs, we will have some idea of where it is. Note the compound statement that is the first argument of `Table` in the definition of `riemann`. The `If` command is executed, but the compound statement returns the value of `RiemannR[x]`, as desired.

We avoid recomputing values of $\pi(x)$ by computing a table once and subtracting it from tables of the other three functions. The basic arithmetic operations (`+`, `-`, `*`, `/`, `^`) are listable, so, for example, `{4, 5, 6} ^ {2, 3, 4}` yields the pointwise result `{16, 125, 1296}`. Matrix exponentiation and multiplication and dot products are accomplished by the `MatrixPower` command and the dot (e.g., `{4, 5, 6} . {2, 3, 4}` yields 47). The subtraction step is combined with the adjunction of the domain values by the transpose trick, and the results are displayed by showing them with three different plot styles. *Mathematica* will display each plot individually, and then all the plots on a single set of axes. This computation can take up to a half hour on a Macintosh (six minutes on a Mac IIfx).

Because `LogIntegral` is listable, gauss is defined using `Range` as opposed to `Table`.

Although one of the joys of working in *Mathematica* is that one does not have to worry about data types, there are a few points to note. *Mathematica* distinguishes between a true integer, say 10, and 10., which is an approximate real number. Because of its symbolic manipulation features, *Mathematica* will not evaluate certain functions unless forced to. For example, `10^(1/3)` does not return the same value as `10.^(1/3)`: the latter returns an approximate real; the former returns the expression `10^(1/3)`. The advantage is that cubing the expression yields the exact integer 10; cubing the approximate real yields a number that looks like 10, but subtracting 10 from it will show the roundoff error. One can force evaluation of a symbolic expression with the `N[]` command. `N[x]` returns an approximate real; `N[x, a]` returns the real with a significant digits.

When doing computations that need only approximate real numbers (such as plotting a function), it is good practice to use approximate reals in various initializations and iterators. This also avoids the buildup of long symbolic expressions. For example, if a plot of the first 100 iterates cos(1), cos(cos(1)), cos(cos(cos(1))), and so on was desired, it would be bad to first generate a table of values using the exact integer 1, for then the hundredth value will be a long unevaluated string. Using 1. instead will yield real numbers at each stage. This explains why the decimal points are used at two points in the program that generated Figure 1.6. We wish real approximations to values of LogIntegral and Log, and if the Range and iterator were defined using 0 instead of 0., legendre and gauss would consist only of symbolic values. (The user-defined functions PrimePi and RiemannR do not return symbolic values.) These symbolic values would have been evaluated eventually by the plotting command, but it's better to specify exactly what is wanted.

Note how Gauss's approximation is worse than Legendre's for a while, but is better beyond $x = 5{,}000{,}000$. Note also the phenomenal accuracy of Riemann's $R(x)$: it differs from $\pi(x)$ by no more than 88 on the entire range.

Riemann's function both over- and underestimates $\pi(x)$. It seems as if li(x) overestimates. Let's make one more graph, taking li$(x) - \pi(x)$ a little bit farther, to 2×10^9.

```
ListPlot[Table[{x, LogIntegral[x] - PrimePi[x]},
              {x, 0., 2 10^9, 2 10^7}], PlotJoined->True]
```

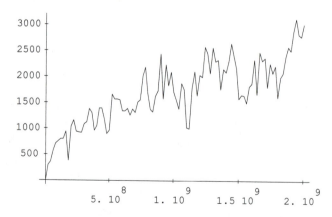

FIGURE 1.7 The error in the logarithmic integral approximation to $\pi(x)$.

Even on this hundredfold expansion of the range, $\mathrm{li}(x)$ overestimates $\pi(x)$. This computation is in sharp contrast with the spectacular result of Littlewood, which states that $\mathrm{li}(x) - \pi(x)$ is not always positive; in fact, it crosses the x-axis infinitely often. The first crossing is called the *Skewes number*, after S. Skewes who proved that it was less than $10^{(10^{(10^{34})})}$. It is now known that the Skewes number is less than 10^{371} (due to H. te Riele [teR]; for a further discussion of the Skewes number see [Boa]). This remarkable phenomenon—that millions of hours of computation might lead to overwhelming evidence in favor of a conclusion that is, in fact, false—is a striking warning against basing conclusions solely on numerical evidence. The Riemann Hypothesis, a conjecture about the zeros of a complex function called the Riemann zeta function that is considered by many to be the most important unsolved problem in mathematics, is equivalent to the assertion that for some constant c, $|\mathrm{li}(x) - \pi(x)| \leq c\sqrt{x} - \log x$. The zeta function is discussed further in Chapter 10. Exercise: Compare the graph of $|\mathrm{li}(x) - \pi(x)|$ with that of $c\sqrt{x}\log x$ for various values of c.

The prime number theorem has an extension that explains the growth of the sequence of primes in the congruence classes modulo some integer. Let $\pi_n(x, m)$ be the number of primes $p \leq x$ such that $p \equiv m \pmod{n}$. Then the famous theorem of Dirichlet on primes in arithmetic progressions guarantees that each congruence class contains infinitely many primes (provided $\gcd(m, n) = 1$); that is, each function $\pi_n(x, m)$ approaches infinity as x approaches infinity. Moreover, when n is prime, then the $p-1$ classes are uniformly distributed. The Appendix contains a routine, `PrimePiModn[y, n]`, that computes this function up to the yth prime. The program outputs a list of the primes in each residue class modulo n, pairing each prime with the count up to that point. This is not the most efficient way to tabulate this data, but it makes it easy to graph. The `TableForm` command makes the output easier to read. Note that 23 is the first prime congruent to 1 modulo 11, 2 is the first prime congruent to 2 modulo 11, and so on.

```
PrimePiModn[40, 11] // TableForm
{{23, 1}, {67, 2}, {89, 3}}
{{2, 1}, {13, 2}, {79, 3}, {101, 4}, {167, 5}}
{{3, 1}, {47, 2}, {113, 3}, {157, 4}}
{{37, 1}, {59, 2}, {103, 3}}
{{5, 1}, {71, 2}, {137, 3}}
```

```
{{17, 1}, {61, 2}, {83, 3}, {127, 4}, {149, 5}}
{{7, 1}, {29, 2}, {73, 3}, {139, 4}}
{{19, 1}, {41, 2}, {107, 3}, {151, 4}, {173, 5}}
{{31, 1}, {53, 2}, {97, 3}, {163, 4}}
{{43, 1}, {109, 2}, {131, 3}}
```

Because `ListPlot` displays only a single function, we need to gather the ten listplots into a table and show them all at once. This can be done as follows, where `list` is used to avoid recomputation of the master list.

```
list = PrimePiModn[500, 11]
Show[Table[ListPlot[list[[m]], PlotJoined->True], {m, 10}]]
```

However, this approach will cause the ten individual graphs to be displayed. We can use the following technique to avoid this. The `Display-Function` option to `Show` can be set to be `Identity`, which suppresses the display. Now, when the ten plots are passed to `Show`, we can set `DisplayFunction` to its default value `$DisplayFunction`. All this will have the effect of displaying only the combined plot on the screen.

```
list = PrimePiModn[669, 11]
Show[Table[
  ListPlot[list[[m]], PlotJoined->True, DisplayFunction->Identity],
  {m, 10}], DisplayFunction->$DisplayFunction]
```

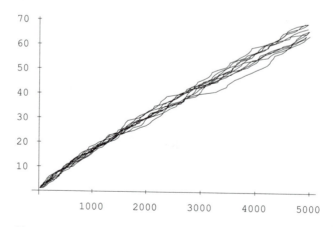

FIGURE 1.8 The graphs of $\pi_{11}(x, i)$ for $i = 1, 2, ..., 10$.

Note that the division of primes into the mod-11 classes is approximately uniform, as predicted by the theory.

EXERCISE All primes except 2 are congruent to 1 or 3 modulo 4. Generate a graph that compares the two prime counts $\pi_4(x, 1)$ and $\pi_4(x, 3)$. Find the first point at which the 1-count is greater than the 3-count. Do not use the `PrimePiModn` routine, but write a routine from scratch that keeps track of the two counts at each prime p. This will be more efficient, and time and space are important since the value sought is large. (A solution is in the Appendix.)

1.4 Recursion and Caching

To conclude this chapter, we'll use Euclid's proof that there are infinitely many primes to illustrate some aspects of the use of recursion in *Mathematica*. Euclid considered the sum of 1 and the product of the first n primes and concluded that this number is either prime or has a prime factor greater than the first n primes. Therefore there are infinitely many primes. Let's use `euclid[n]` for the product of the first n primes (though we'll use the term *Euclid number* for the first integer past this product). It is easy to program this recursively, but care is necessary.

```
euclid[n_] := euclid[n-1] Prime[n]
euclid[1] = 2;
Table[euclid[n] + 1, {n, 20}]
{3, 7, 31, 211, 2311, 30031, 510511,
    9699691, 223092871, 6469693231, 200560490131,
    7420738134811, 304250263527211, 13082761331670031,
    614889782588491411, 32589158477190044731,
    1922760350154212639071, 117288381359406970983271,
    7858321551080267055879091, 557940830126698960967415391}
```

This works, but each entry in the table requires the recomputation of all preceding values, and this is very inefficient. To see the inefficiency, use the following code to compute a table of the first eight values of `euclid[n]`.

```
euclid[n_] := (Print[n]; euclid[n - 1] Prime[n])
euclid[1] = 2;
```

When a similar recursion is used to compute Fibonacci numbers, the computational buildup is much worse and the program is incapable of computing even the 30th Fibonacci number in a reasonable period of time. Of course, a better way to deal with this is to make a table of all previous values, so that they need not be computed again. The preceding definition of euclid[] contains the explicit value of euclid[1] as a base to the recursion. We wish to add all new values to this list as they are computed, since *Mathematica* will scan this list before applying the recursion rule. It turns out there is an especially elegant way to do this. First, clear out the old value of euclid; this can be done by either Clear[euclid] or euclid = .. This is not essential here, but sometimes it is important when function definitions are changed dramatically. A short way of clearing out all previously defined variables in a session is by the single command ClearAll["Global`*"].

Now, consider the following definition.

```
euclid[n_] := euclid[n] = euclid[n - 1] Prime[n]
euclid[1] = 2;
```

Recall that an assignment statement returns the value being assigned. So the statement euclid[n] = euclid[n - 1] Prime[n] returns the correct value. But it has the additional effect of appending a value to the internal list of *Mathematica*'s knowledge about euclid. To see this, type ??euclid after executing the preceding definition and computing euclid[8]. This technique, called caching, speeds up the computation of the table dramatically and is useful in many recursions (though in a specific computation some experimenting may be necessary to see if caching is worthwhile).

Now, let's find the prime Euclid numbers. If we make euclid into a listable function, then we can apply it to a list of numbers. Since PrimeQ is already listable, the following code shows the prime values.

```
Attributes[euclid] = {Listable}
PrimeQ[euclid[Range[20]] + 1 ]
{True, True, True, True, True, False, False, False, False, False,
 True, False, False, False, False, False, False, False, False,
 False}
```

Finally, we can generate the indices of the prime Euclid numbers using `Select`. This command takes two arguments, a list and a function, and returns the sublist consisting of elements of the list for which the function is true. Thus the following command returns the prime Euclid numbers.

```
Select[euclid[Range[20]] + 1, PrimeQ]
{3, 7, 31, 211, 2311, 200560490131}
```

Suppose we wanted the indices of the prime Euclid numbers, rather than the numbers themselves. Then we wish to select from, say, $\{1, \ldots, 40\}$ those indices for which the corresponding Euclid number is prime. We need to define the appropriate logical function, but rather than setting it up as a separate definition, it can be done using `Function` as follows. `Function[x, ...x...]` is one way of defining a function right where it is needed.

```
Select[Range[40], Function[x, PrimeQ[euclid[x] + 1]]]
```

This works, but is a bit unwieldy. It can be done without introducing a new variable by using a "pure function." *Mathematica* reserves the symbol `#` as a generic variable that can be used to define functions, provided the `&` symbol follows the definition. Thus `#^2 &` refers to the squaring function. This is a very useful concept, and is used in this book often in conjunction with the `Map` and `Scan` commands. Its use with `Select` is as follows.

```
Select[Range[40], PrimeQ[euclid[#] + 1] &]
{1, 2, 3, 4, 5, 11}
```

The prime Euclid numbers quickly become rare, and it is not known whether infinitely many exist (see [Guy, Rib]). Exercise: Find the next prime Euclid number. Remember that `primeq` is faster than `PrimeQ`.

EXERCISE Produce a similar program (i.e., use recursion) for the Fermat numbers: $2^{(2^n)} + 1$. It was once thought they were all prime. It is now thought that except for the first few, they are all composite! See [Guy, Rib].

2 Rolling Circles

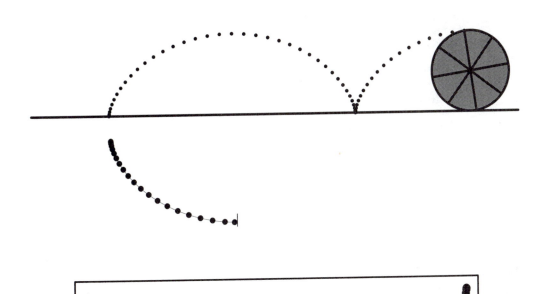

The principal goal of this chapter is to introduce the 2-dimensional graphics capabilities of *Mathematica*. Two-dimensional images can be created with the built-in plotting commands or with various more primitive graphing commands or with a combination of the two. We will see how to generate a sequence of images that can be animated to illustrate the way different types of cycloidal curves are generated. And we will create an animation that simulates how gravity affects a bead sliding down a curve. We will also answer various questions about the cycloid that require both symbolic (i.e., indefinite) and numerical (i.e., definite) integration.

About the illustration overleaf:

The cycloid, which is the path traced out by a point on the circumference of a rolling circle, has many amazing properties, one of which is that it is a tautochrone. This means that the time needed for a bead starting from rest to slide down to the bottom of the cycloid is independent of the starting position on the cycloid. The lowest image overleaf compares the motion of a bead (shown at $1/100$-of-a-second intervals) starting in the middle of the cycloid with the motion of one starting at the top. The top two images show that the usual method of generation of a cycloid corresponds exactly to the motion of a particle falling down a cycloid: the spacing of the dots in the two images is identical. These images were created by programs that will be discussed in this chapter.

2.1 Discovering the Cycloid

Everyone knows what happens to the center of a wheel that is rolling along a straight road: it travels in a straight line. But what about a point on the circumference of the wheel? The path traced out by such a point on a rolling wheel is known as the cycloid, and it is one of the most fascinating curves in mathematics. In this chapter we'll create some movies that show exactly how this curve and some of its relatives are formed. To get a quick image of a cycloid, recall that the point obtained by rotating a point (x, y) clockwise about the origin through θ radians is the point

$$\begin{pmatrix} \cos\theta & \sin\theta \\ -\sin\theta & \cos\theta \end{pmatrix} \begin{pmatrix} x \\ y \end{pmatrix}$$

whose coordinates are $x\cos\theta - y\sin\theta$ and $x\sin\theta + y\cos\theta$. Now, imagine a circle of radius 1 centered at the point $(0, 1)$, with bottom point P. If the circle rolls to the right so that its center moves θ units of length, then P becomes θ units distant from the bottom, measured along the arc of the circle, and it follows that θ radians is the amount of angle through which P has rotated about the center (recall the formula $s = r\theta$). Thus we can consider the rolling motion as composed of two separate motions, a clockwise rotation of θ radians about the fixed center $(0, 1)$ and a slide of θ units to the right.

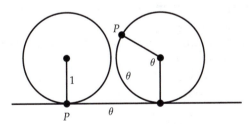

FIGURE 2.1 As a circle rolls θ units rightward, a point on its circumference rotates through θ radians.

With the additional assumption that the rolling speed is such that the center moves rightward at a speed of 1 unit per second, we can easily get the parametric equation of the cycloid in terms of the time parameter t. Let's use *Mathematica* to help. First we define a function that rotates a point about a center. Note the use of the dot for matrix-vector (or matrix-matrix) multiplications; the addition and subtraction are needed because the center is not necessarily (0, 0).

```
rotate[point_, t_, center_] := center +
     {{Cos[t], Sin[t]}, {-Sin[t], Cos[t]}} . (point - center)
```

Now we can obtain the position of the tracing point at time t by first rotating the point and then sliding it to the right.

```
rotate[{0, 0}, t, {0, 1}] + {t, 0}
{t - Sin[t], 1 - Cos[t]}
```

This last expression is a parametric representation of the cycloid. Since we'll need this function throughout the chapter, let's define it as `cycloid`. Then we can use the `ParametricPlot` command to graph it. We set the `AspectRatio` to the ratio of the vertical range to the horizontal so that the graph's scale is true; *Mathematica*'s default aspect ratio is the reciprocal of the golden ratio.

```
cycloid[t_] := {t - Sin[t], 1 - Cos[t]};
ParametricPlot[cycloid[t], {t, 0, 4 Pi}, AspectRatio->2/(4 Pi)]
```

As you might guess from the graph in Figure 2.2, the speed of the tracing point varies in time; in fact, this point has 0 speed at the cusps and maximum speed at the top of the curve. This is because at the top the speed due to the rotation is added to the sliding speed, whereas at the bottom the rotation speed cancels the sliding speed exactly. An animation will make this clear. So let's turn to the problem of generating, say, 60 images that show a circle rolling with a point on its circumference tracing

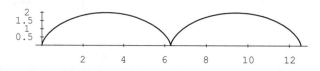

FIGURE 2.2 The path traced by a point on the circumference of a rolling circle.

out the cycloid. The idea is to run a Do loop to generate the images, each of which will consist of a base line on which the circle rolls, the circle at its proper position (in ¼₀-of-a-second increments), a spoke on the circle to identify the special point and aid visualization of the rolling, and a trace of dots left by the special point. Not all front ends for *Mathematica* support animations; however, many animations, including all the ones in this chapter, can be compressed into a single image that is equally instructive.

```
cycloid[t_] := {t - Sin[t], 1 - Cos[t]};
baseline = Line[{{-2, 0}, {10.5, 0}}];
pi = N[Pi];
dots = {PointSize[.006]};
Do[ AppendTo[dots, Point[cycloid[t]]];
    Show[Graphics[{{GrayLevel[.5], Disk[{t, 1}, 1]},
                   Line[{{t, 1}, cycloid[t]}],    (* spoke *)
                   baseline,
                   dots}],
        AspectRatio->3/12,
        PlotRange->{{-1.5, 10.5}, {-.5, 2.5}}],
    {t, 0., 59/40 2 pi, 2 pi/40}]
```

The heart of the program is the Show command within the Do loop. This command is used to show various graphics objects such as points, lines, disks, circles, and filled polygons. For example, Point[{x,y}] represents the point at (x, y), Line[{{x,y}, {a,b}}] represents a line from (x, y) to (a, b), and Disk[{x,y}, r] represents a filled disk at center (x, y) with radius r [default is black (GrayLevel[0]); disk and circle were added in version 1.2, but the disk primitive can be simulated in version 1.1 with Point]. The Graphics command turns these primitives into graphics objects. Graphics requires its first argument to be a list of graphics primitives; additional arguments can be various options, none of which is used above. Rather, the options AspectRatio and Plot-Range are set in the Show command. Note that the first object in the list sent to Graphics is itself a list of a GrayLevel command and a Disk command. This has the effect of restricting the GrayLevel to the objects in its list. Similarly, dots is built up from the single PointSize[.006] primitive (0.006 is the proportion of the output window that is to be a point's diameter) to a list of the dots in the image. The items will be shown in the order in which they appear in the list; `dots` is shown last so the black dots appear on top of the gray disk. Note the use of reals in the `Do` loop's iterator.

The initialization of dots is essential because of the subsequent `AppendTo` (`AppendTo[x,y]` appends `y` to the list `x`; `Append[x,y]` simply returns the list `x` with `y` appended, but does not change `x`). If `dots` had not been initialized, there would be nothing to append to, and an error message would result.

Here are two very important points.

- When building up a computation that starts with a symbolic value such as `Pi` or `Sqrt[3]`, but does not really need symbolic values, it is best to first turn these into numbers. Otherwise long symbolic strings will build up. This explains the `pi = N[Pi]` command.

- The use of `PlotRange` is important, and in 2-dimensional graphics you should use either `All` or a particular range as a value of `PlotRange`. Otherwise, *Mathematica* will use its default; this usually causes all the graphics to be shown, but occasionally *Mathematica* clips images to what it decides is the region of interest. This is a useful feature for commands such as `Plot[Sec[x], {x, -5, 5}]`, which causes a nice graph to be drawn without the user having to worry about the singularities. But for graphics where strict control is wanted, this default must be overridden by setting `PlotRange` to either `All` or a specific range. The latter is often best for animations, where one wants an identical range for each image. (Exercise: Run the above animation without the `PlotRange` option.)

The actual 60-frame movie (some stills are shown in Figure 2.3) is an effective mechanism for showing how the cycloid is formed; the positions of the dots in the final image reveals the speed change: the spacing of the dots at the top of the cycloid indicates a faster speed than near the cusp. Depending on the memory of your system, you may wish to generate fewer images: just change the 59 in the iterator to a smaller value. Animations take up a lot of memory. An important way to conserve memory and disk space is by converting the images to Bitmap PICT format. On the Macintosh this is done by simply selecting all the images and applying the Convert to Bitmap PICT command in the Graph menu. *Mathematica*'s graphics output is always in the PostScript language, which yields high

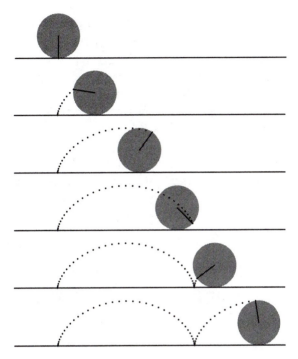

FIGURE 2.3 Six stills from the rolling wheel movie.

resolution on a variety of printers. But there is no need to use PostScript if the images are only to be displayed on a screen. Highly memory-intensive animations, such as surface rotations, may have to be generated (and converted to bitmaps) in pieces. The whole movie can be spliced together and displayed when the kernel is turned off (which frees up lots of memory).

Cycloids are relevant to the following old puzzle: If a train is moving forward at 80 miles per hour, is there any point on the train that is moving backward with respect to the ground? The answer is yes, and an animation will make this clear. Imagine that we wish to study the path traced by a point at the end of a spoke that extends beyond the rolling circle (as indeed, the flange of a train wheel extends below the track!). It is routine to modify the preceding program to generate such an animation. If the radius of the spoke is r, then the equation of this generalized cycloid is simply $(t-r\sin t, 1-r\cos t)$, as can be easily seen by reworking the discussion at the beginning of this chapter. So we simply have to add r to the definition of `cycloid[t]`. If this change is made with $r = 1.3$, then an animation results for which the last frame is as in Figure 2.4. Such curves are called *trochoids*.

These movies can be spiced up by adding a circle around the disk to give it better definition and more spokes to enhance the rolling effect. The Appendix contains a single program that generates a trochoid animation for arbitrary values of r. In order to accommodate extra-large values of r, `AspectRatio` and `PlotRange` are made to depend on r. Figure 2.5 shows two different final images from that program.

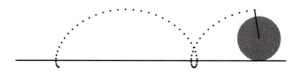

FIGURE 2.4 The trochoid traced by a point outside a rolling circle. Note that below the level of the rail, the horizontal speed of the point is negative; this shows that the bottom of a train's wheel moves backward.

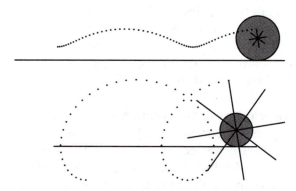

FIGURE 2.5 The final frames of trochoid animations with spoke length 0.4 and 3. A program in the Appendix (Trochoid Animation Generator) generates movies for arbitrary radius.

Finally, it is amusing to generate an animation of all the trochoids as the spoke length varies from 0 to, say, 2. Here is a program that does it.

```
Do[ParametricPlot[{t - r Sin[t], 1 - r Cos[t]},
                                    {t, 0, 2 Pi 58/40},
        PlotRange->{{-1, 8.6},{-1.2, 3.2}}, AspectRatio->4.4/9.5],
    {r, 0, 2, .1}]
```

In Chapter 7 (Figure 7.3) we will show how to glue all these curves together to form a parametric surface in 3-space.

2.2 The Derivative of the Trochoid ▪▪▪▪▪▪

One can analyze the velocity vector of the cycloid using calculus. Let's use a radius of 1.3 to illustrate. Of course, these techniques can be used on much more complicated curves.

```
trochoid[t_] := {t - 1.3 Sin[t], 1 - 1.3 Cos[t]}
velocity = trochoid'
{1 - 1.3*Cos[#1], 1.3*Sin[#1]} &
```

There are several approaches to taking derivatives. In general, if `f` is an expression that is a function of `x` (and perhaps other variables), then the partial derivative of `f` with respect to `x` is given by `D[f, x]`. If `f` is defined to be a function via, say, `f[y_] := ... y ...`, then the derivative can be obtained by `D[f[x], x]`. But, returning to the case where `f` is an expression involving `x`, one could not define the derivative by `g[x_] := D[f, x]`, for then `g[3]` would be `D[f, 3]`; this is just a variation of the common calculus error of substituting a value for the variable before differentiating. One could define `g[t_]` to be `D[f, x] /. x -> t`, using the substitution operator to make sure differentiation precedes substitution. But then one would have to make sure that `x` was not being used elsewhere in the session. Alternatively, one could use `g[x_] = D[f, x]`. The use of = rather than := means that the right-hand side will be evaluated immediately; the use of `x_` means that the proper substitution will take place for any argument of `g`. However, *Mathematica* understands the familiar `f'` notation for functions of one variable. The result is a pure function (this concept is described in Chapter 0 and at the end of Chapter 1), which can be applied to any number or variable. This explains the mysterious-looking output to the definition of velocity just given: & indicates a pure function, and #1 plays the role of the argument.

Now we can generate a parametric plot of the velocity of the trochoid. In the following command we could have bypassed `velocity` and simply asked for a plot of `trochoid'[t]`, but this would be slower, since it would require that the derivative of `trochoid` be taken over a hundred times, when once is sufficient. Warning: `Plot[D[f, t], {t, 0, 1}]` does not work; see the discussion of `Release` in Chapter 3.

```
ParametricPlot[velocity[t], {t, 0, 2 Pi}, AspectRatio->1]
```

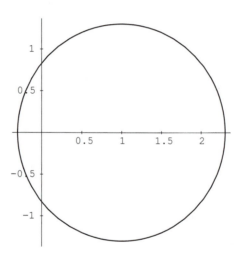

FIGURE 2.6 The velocity vectors of the trochoid lie on a circle.

To clarify the relationship between the trochoid and the circle that is the image of its velocity, let's draw velocity vectors as vectors starting at the corresponding point on the trochoid. First we make a table of pairs, corresponding to line segments from a point on the trochoid to the point at the end of the velocity vector located on the trochoid. Then we use the `Map` command to turn each pair into a line, and the `Graphics` and `Show` commands to display the lines. `Map` takes two arguments, the first a function and the second a list; then `Map` returns the list obtained

by applying the function to each element of the second argument. Thus
Map[PrimeQ, {2,3,4}] returns {True, True, False}.

```
vectors = Table[
        {trochoid[t], trochoid[t] + velocity[t]}, {t, 0, 8, .3}];
Show[Graphics[{Thickness[.0005], Map[Line, vectors]}],
    AspectRatio->4/8]
```

FIGURE 2.7   The velocity vectors of the trochoid with spoke-length 1.3.

Now we can redraw these vectors at the origin (which corresponds to
the derivative function of motion in the plane). This clarifies the circular
nature of the velocity of the trochoid.

```
Show[Graphics[Table[
        Line[{{0,0}, velocity[t]}], {t, 0, 2 Pi, .3}]],
    AspectRatio->1]
```

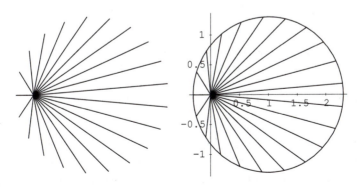

FIGURE 2.8 Placing the trochoid's velocity vectors at the origin clarifies the circular nature of its derivative.

Finally, we can combine this plot with the velocity curve via Show[%, %1].

2.3 Circles Rolling on Circles ▬▬▬▬

So far we have been discussing the result of rolling a circle on a straight line. Rolling a circle around (or inside) another circle yields additional types of cycloidal curves. The Appendix contains a program, Epicycloid and Hypocycloid Animation Generator, that generates animations for these curves where the radius can be either positive (outside, *epicycloid*) or negative (inside, *hypocycloid*). Figure 2.9 shows the last frame of some of these animations. The case $r = 1$ corresponds to the well-known puzzle about rolling a penny around another penny: How many times does the rolling penny rotate about its center? The animation makes it clear. The case of a circle of half the radius rolling around the inside is interesting as the resulting motion is on a straight line (an observation of Copernicus); this is in fact the basis of a mechanical device for turning circular motion into straight line motion, and vice versa. The program could easily be modified to show the curves generated by points at the end of rays that are longer or shorter than the radius of the rolling circle (called epitrochoids and hypotrochoids).

EXERCISE Repeat all the commands of this chapter for some of the circular cycloids, starting with matrix manipulations to discover the parametric equations.

EXERCISE Create an animation that shows a circle of radius 1 rolling along a series of linked, upward-opening semicircles of radius 2. This provides the answer to the puzzle: Along what sort of curve should a circle roll in order that a point on its circumference lies on a straight line?

The three-cusped hypocycloid, $r = -1/3$ in the hypocycloid generating program, has an interesting feature related to the Kakeya needle problem, which is the problem of finding small regions in which it is possible to turn a needle around. The tangents to the three-cusped hypocycloid, when cut off at the curve, all have the same length, and so the interior of

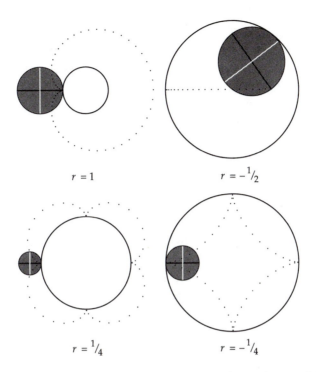

$r = 1$ $r = -\frac{1}{2}$

$r = \frac{1}{4}$ $r = -\frac{1}{4}$

FIGURE 2.9 Images from animations that generate the path traced by a particle on a circle rolling around or inside another circle.

this hypocycloid provides one example of a region in which a needle can be turned. For more on this problem see [CS].

EXERCISE Generate a needle-turning animation as follows.

1. Use the hypocycloid animation program to generate the parametric representation $f(t)$ of the three-cusped hypocycloid. (Hint: Clear theta, execute r = -1/3, and then execute the relevant lines from the program.)

2. Verify that the line connecting $f(t)$ and $f(t+\pi)$ is tangent to the curve at the point $f(-2t)$ and that it has the same length for all values of t. (Hint: If working by hand, it is easier to work with f in the form $f(t) = e^{it} + \frac{1}{2}e^{-2it}$.)

3. Generate the animation by using `ParametricPlot` to generate and store the hypocycloid plot and a Do loop to show it repeatedly in combination with the tangent lines; place a point at one end of the needle to orient it.

One can roll noncircular wheels over appropriate roads. Figure 2.10 contains the final image from an animation that shows a square rolling smoothly over a specially constructed road. In this case the road is a series of truncated catenaries ($y = -\cosh x = -(e^x + e^{-x})/2$). The ride is smooth in the sense that the center of the square moves horizontally, and its center is always directly above the point of tangency. This animation was inspired by an exhibit at San Francisco's Exploratorium. It is not too difficult to show, by deriving a simple differential equation, that $-\cosh x$, truncated at $x = \pm \operatorname{arcsinh} 1$, is indeed the curve on which a square will roll. See [HW], which contains many other examples of curves rolling on other curves. Once this is known, it is straightforward to construct the animation, in part because the arc length function for cosh is sinh. To generate the entire animation, run the Rolling Polygons program in the Appendix, with input value 4. Exercise: Why is it that in the case of a triangular wheel, a physical model that illustrates the rolling on the appropriate sequence of linked catenaries would be impossible to construct?

Another type of noncircular rolling arises from the Reuleaux polygon, which refers to the shape enclosed by three 60° arcs around an equilateral triangle, where each arc is drawn radially from one of the vertices. This region has constant width equal to the side of the triangle and so can roll along a road or inside a square. The Appendix contains a program that generates an animation of the rolling of a Reuleaux polygon inside a square, the final frame of which is shown in Figure 2.11. The animation

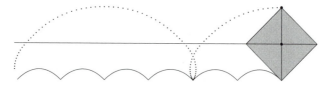

FIGURE 2.10 A square will roll smoothly on a road made up of catenaries, that is, a road with bumps in the shape of the graph of the hyperbolic cosine.

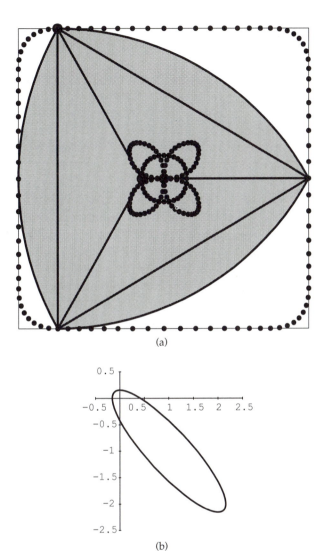

(a)

(b)

Figure 2.11 (a) A Reuleaux triangle can be rotated inside a square. A drill bit in the shape of a Reuleaux triangle yields a device that drills square holes. (b) Despite appearances, the curve traced by the centroid of the triangle is not a circle! Rather it is made up of pieces of ellipses, where each piece is congruent to the second-quadrant portion of the ellipse illustrated.

also shows the paths traced out by one of the vertices, the centroid of the triangle, and the center of the square.

The method used to program the animation was as follows. An arc function was defined to draw piecewise linear approximations to 60° arcs from a specified center; this function was used in each frame to form a single `Polygon` object: the Reuleaux triangle. The positions of the three vertices in each image were determined by first rotating the triangle t radians about the centroid and then translating this rotated triangle so that it would fit inside the square. The translation was obtained from the x-coordinate of one of the (rotated) vertices and the y-coordinate of another. The choice of vertices varies, however, as the rotation proceeds. Once the animation was completed, the dots were added in the usual way by accumulating a list and showing it in each frame.

As often happens, programming an animation leads to interesting mathematical questions, and often the symbolic power of *Mathematica* can lead to the answers. In this example, it came as a surprise to the author that the path traced out by the centroid as the Reuleaux triangle rotates within the square is not a circle. Easy exercise: As the Reuleaux triangle makes one complete revolution inside the square, how many revolutions does the centroid make around the circle-like path that it generates? Harder exercise: Use the symbolic power of *Mathematica* to obtain the explicit functions of t that govern the motion of the centroid of the triangle. It turns out that the circle-like path is in fact made up of pieces of four congruent ellipses! Reuleaux himself considered the paths traced by the centroid and various other points in the triangle; see [Reu, §27].

2.4 The Cycloid and Gravity ▰▰▰▰▰▰▰▰

The cycloid has several amazing properties. For example, the time it takes a ball placed on an inverted cycloid to roll to the bottom is independent of the starting position (thus the cycloid is called a *tautochrone*; this property was discovered by Huyghens in 1673). In other words, even if a ball is placed very near the bottom, its acceleration will be so slow that it will reach the bottom at *exactly* the same time as a ball placed at the top. Throughout this chapter the effect of friction is ignored; in fact, the use of the word "rolling" is a misnomer: in the absence of friction there will not be any rolling. But there is a more important reason to avoid rolling balls. The theory demands that the descending object have its center of gravity on the curve being studied. A ball of positive radius rolling down a cycloid is affected by gravity as if it were an infinitely small ball rolling down a curve parallel to the cycloid. Thus to present the properties of the cycloid correctly, one should consider beads sliding down a thin, rigid wire shaped like a cycloid.

We wish to create an animation to demonstrate the tautochrone effect on a cycloidal wire (see the cover illustrations for this chapter), but first let's use the integration abilities of *Mathematica* to prove that the descent time is independent of the starting position. Consider a bead sliding down a curve with parametric representation $\boldsymbol{f}(t) = (x(t), y(t))$, connecting two points $\boldsymbol{f}(t_0)$ and $\boldsymbol{f}(t_1)$. (We assume that the curve has no loops and proceeds smoothly from top to bottom.) Then an easy argument based on potential and kinetic energy [TF, §8.9] shows that the velocity of the bead when it is at the point (x, y) on the curve is $\sqrt{2g(y_0 - y)}$, where g is the gravitational constant (32 feet/sec^2, or 980 cm/sec^2) and y_0 is the starting y-coordinate. It follows by standard calculus that the time needed to reach the bottom is

$$\int_{t_0}^{t_1} \sqrt{\frac{x'(t)^2 + y'(t)^2}{2g[y_0 - y(t)]}}\, dt$$

Therefore we can express the time required for a bead starting from the point on the cycloid given by parameter t_0 to reach the bottom as an integral. The calculus and algebra to get the integral are straightforward, but it is instructive to try to use *Mathematica* to generate the integrand in the case of a cycloid.

```
cycloid[t_] := {t - Sin[t], Cos[t] - 1}   (*upside-down cycloid*)
norm[u_] := Sqrt[u.u]
norm[cycloid'[t]]/Sqrt[2g(cycloid[t0][[2]] - cycloid[t][[2]])]
                        2          2
     Sqrt[(1 - Cos[t])  + Sin[t] ]
    ---------------------------------------
    Sqrt[2] Sqrt[g] Sqrt[-Cos[t] + Cos[t0]]
```

Expanding the numerator of this integrand is a good idea because of the $\sin^2 + \cos^2$ term that will result. The `ExpandAll` command expands all levels of an expression. However, the $\sin^2 + \cos^2 = 1$ identity is not built into *Mathematica*. (There is a trigonometric simplification package that contains routines for simplifying trigonometric expressions in a variety of ways.) We can apply the identity by using a substitution as follows.

```
ExpandAll[%] /. Cos[w_]^2 + Sin[w_]^2 -> 1
          Sqrt[2 - 2 Cos[t]]
-------------------------------------------
Sqrt[2] Sqrt[g] Sqrt[-Cos[t] + Cos[t0]]
```

So we see that the time for a bead to fall from an initial point to the bottom of the cycloid is given by

$$\frac{1}{\sqrt{g}} \int_{t_0}^{t_1} \sqrt{\frac{1 - \cos t}{\cos t_0 - \cos t}}\, dt$$

We'll now show that this integral is independent of t_0, which proves that the cycloid is a tautochrone. The integral has a singularity at its lower limit, so it is better to attack it by indefinite integration (for which the integration package **IntegralTables.m** must first be loaded via `<<IntegralTables.m`). The output of the following command has been formatted into standard mathematical notation.

```
Integrate[Sqrt[(1 - Cos[t])/(Cos[t0] - Cos[t])], t]/Sqrt[g]
```

$$\frac{1}{\sqrt{g}} \arctan \sqrt{\frac{-1 + \cos t_0 + \frac{\sin^2 t}{(1+\cos t)^2} + \frac{\cos t_0 \sin^2 t}{(1+\cos t)^2}}{2}} \qquad (*)$$

The preceding can be simplified with the help of the identity $\arctan r = \arccos(1/\sqrt{r^2 + 1})$ (valid when $r \geq 0$). The following is the result of (1) using this identity on (∗) exactly as was done earlier for $\sin^2 + \cos^2 = 1$, (2) simplifying via `Simplify`, (3) applying the `Cos[w_]^2 + Sin[w_]^2 -> 1` rule as before, and, finally, (4) executing `MapAll[Factor, %]` for a final simplification.

```
            Sqrt[1 + Cos[t]]
  2 ArcCos[------------------]
           Sqrt[1 + Cos[t0]]
  ---------------------------

           Sqrt[g]
```

A further simplification is possible using a half-angle identity for cosine. Note that using `Sqrt[1 + Cos[x_]]` as the left side of the substitution rule would not work because the denominator gets interpreted as *expr^(-1/2)*, not *expr^(1/2)*. Remember: The way to learn about *Mathematica*'s internal forms is to use the `FullForm` command.

`% /. Cos[x_] -> Cos[x/2]^2 - 1`

$$\frac{2}{\sqrt{g}} \arccos\left(\frac{\cos\frac{t}{2}}{\cos\frac{t_0}{2}}\right) \qquad (\ast\ast)$$

EXERCISE Use the derivative operator to verify that (∗∗) is indeed an antiderivative of the function that was integrated to produce (∗).

Formula (∗∗) completes the proof that the cycloid is a tautochrone, since substituting, in turn, π and t_0 for t and subtracting yields the value $\pi/\sqrt{g}$ for the definite integral, no matter what t_0 is. Thus the time needed for a ball to reach the bottom of the cycloid, from any starting position on the cycloid, is $\pi/\sqrt{g} \approx 0.155057$ seconds. Another useful feature of (∗∗) is that it can be inverted, which yields the parameter t that corresponds to the position of a rolling ball after time seconds, which will be useful when we program the animation. We can use *Mathematica* to do the inversion.

`Solve[% == time, t]`

```
            t0        Sqrt[g] time
  2 ArcCos[Cos[--] Cos[-----------]]                    (∗∗∗)
              2             2
```

In particular, a bead starting at the top of the cycloid (i.e., $t_0 = 0$) will, after time seconds, be at the point cycloid[time Sqrt[g]]. In other words the progress of the falling bead is *linear* in the cycloid-generating parameter: If we turn Figure 2.3 upside down, then the dots correspond exactly to the positions at equal time intervals of a bead falling down a cycloid!

It is natural to wonder if the cycloid is the only tautochrone. It is. A proof of this, based on Laplace transforms, can be found in [BdP, §6.5, Ex. 10].

Because position is expressed by the straightforward formula (∗∗∗), it is easy to create an animation that shows a bead falling down a cycloid.

```
pi = Pi//N
cycloid[t_] := {t - Sin[t], -1 + Cos[t]}
cycloidplot = ParametricPlot[cycloid[s], {s, 0, pi},
    Axes->None, PlotStyle->Thickness[.0005], MaxBend->5,
    DisplayFunction->Identity];
showframe := Show[cycloidplot,
    Graphics[{Thickness[.0004],
            Disk[posn, radius],
            {Thickness[.002], Line[{{pi,-2.1}, {pi,-1.8}}]}}],
        PlotRange->{{-.2,  2 pi + .2}, {-2.2,  .2}},
        AspectRatio->2.4/(2 pi + .4),
        DisplayFunction->$DisplayFunction];
t0 = N[Input["Enter initial t-value for start time on
            cycloid:  0 ≤ t < Pi"]];
radius = .07;
g = 980 2 pi /15;
inc = 1./100;
Do[ t = 2 ArcCos[Cos[t0/2] * Cos[Sqrt[g]*time/2]];
    posn = cycloid[Min[t, pi - radius/2]];
    showframe,
   {time, 0, pi/Sqrt[g], inc}]
```

The output of this program, compressed into a single image, is shown in Figure 2.12. Here are some comments on the code.

g is the gravity constant, which is scaled to screen units, approximately 15 centimeters for the width of the image, 2π in this case.

This allows the animation to be set up to coincide exactly with a real-world falling bead by setting the number of frames per second to be, in this case, 200.

cycloidplot is introduced so that the cycloid curve is not recomputed for each image of the animation; DisplayFunction-> Identity suppresses the display, whereas DisplayFunction-> $DisplayFunction in the Show command resets Display-Function to its default value.

showframe abbreviates the code needed to display an image. The Line is used to place a vertical stop bar at the bottom of the cycloid. The Thickness setting for Line affects only the line; the thinner setting applies to the disks.

radius is the radius of the falling bead.

posn gives the position on the cycloid curve; the minimum is taken to force the bead to come to rest at the vertical bar at the bottom of the cycloid. (Exercise: Use the approximation $\sin x \approx x$ to verify that radius/2 is the right amount to subtract.)

inc is the time increment. Decreasing the time increment yields more frames.

The output of the preceding program is not very informative. A comparison of two beads falling simultaneously but from different starting positions would be better. The Appendix contains a program, Cycloid as Tautochrone, which does this, and more. The program in the Appendix displays two beads: one falls from the top, the other starts at a user-specified start point. Moreover, it offers the user a choice of generating

FIGURE 2.12 Two composite images from animations that show a bead sliding down a cycloid, with starting values $t_0 = 0$ and $t_0 = 2$.

the entire animation or just a single graphic containing multiple images of the falling beads (as in the bottom image on the cover page for this chapter). To obtain such a still, a list accumulates the positions and, after the entire list is computed, Show is invoked.

Now we can turn to the more famous brachistochrone property of the cycloid: Among all curves connecting the points (0, 0) and $(\pi, -2)$, the cycloid is the quickest in that for any other curve, a falling bead will take longer than $\pi/\sqrt{g}$ seconds to reach the bottom. This problem has a rich history. When, in 1696, John Bernoulli posed it as a challenge to "the shrewdest mathematicians of the world," five solutions appeared: from John and his brother James, Leibniz, Newton, and l'Hospital. Newton published his solution anonymously, but John Bernoulli recognized that Newton's solution could have come from no one else, just as one "recognizes a lion from his claw marks." The problem had been considered earlier, notably by Galileo who, in 1630, built wooden models and discovered experimentally that a small ball rolls down an arc of a circle faster than on a straight line. In fact, it was Galileo who named the cycloid and brought it to public attention, though he did not consider it in the context of the brachistochrone problem (see [Whi] for more on the cycloid's history). An exquisite example of a cycloid made in 1775 out of sandalwood, olive wood, violet ebony, brass, and iron can be seen at the Museum of the History of Science in Florence, Italy (see Color Plate 1).

The program Cycloid as Brachistochrone in the Appendix is similar to the tautochrone program in that it generates either a complete animation or a single still. The program compares the cycloid with curves of the form $f(t) = \{t, -2(t/\pi))^d\}$, which connect (0, 0) and $(\pi, -2)$. Unlike the case for the cycloid, there is not a closed-form representation of the function giving the position of a bead falling down the curve f as a function of time. Thus we must somehow approximate the effect of gravity. Recall that an object with initial velocity v_0 falling under the force of gravity drops a distance of $v_0 t + \frac{1}{2}gt^2$ feet in t seconds. And if it is rolling down a plane inclined at an angle θ to the vertical, then the second term in the sum must be multiplied by $\cos \theta$. We have already mentioned that the speed of a sliding bead at (x, y) is $\sqrt{-2g(y - y_0)}$. Thus we can approximate gravity as follows. Choose a small time increment *inc*, and assume the bead travels from its current point on the curve along the tangent line to the curve at the current point so as to cover the distance

$\sqrt{-2g(y - y_0)}\, inc + \frac{1}{2}g(\cos\theta)\, inc^2$, where θ is the angle formed by the tangent and a vertical line. Let (x, y) be this point on the tangent line. Now comes the problem of finding a point on the cycloid that corresponds in some way to (x, y). We do this by considering the line perpendicular to the tangent at (x, y) and using the built-in root-finder to get the point where this line intersects the curve defined by f. This method works reasonably well; Figure 2.13 shows various stills produced by this program.

EXERCISE What is the curve of fastest descent connecting $(0, 0)$ to $(1, -1)$? Generalize: Given two points P and Q in the plane, describe exactly the curve of fastest descent that connects them. (Hint: These curves are all arcs of appropriately scaled cycloids.) Redo the brachistochrone program to compare descents down the fastest curve with those down other curves descending from $(0, 0)$ to $(1, -1)$, such as straight lines, polynomials, or, to duplicate an experiment of Galileo, a quarter-circle. (Solution: The cycloid $a(t - \sin t, -1 + \cos t)$ with $a = 0.572917$ and t ranging from 0 to 2.412011 is the fastest curve from the origin to $(1, -1)$.)

The images of Figure 2.13 are inconclusive in the cases of degrees 2 and 3, as the descent time seems to be identical for these curves and the cycloid. But it does look as if steeper curves require more time, at least past degree 3. In order to get more exact results (which will also serve as a check on the accuracy of the gravity simulation in the brachistochrone program), we turn to numerical integration to compute exactly the time needed for the descent down f as the degree varies upward from 1. The time of descent is given by the integral at the beginning of the chapter, so we could first try to feed this directly to the built-in numerical integration routine as follows:

```
NIntegrate[Sqrt[(1 + f'[t]^2) / (-f[t])], {t, 0, Pi}]]
```

However, the integrand is infinite at $t = 0$, and although *Mathematica* can integrate over some singularities, it does not handle this one. (Exercise: Try integrating $x^{-1/2}$ from 0 to 2. What happens if the exponent moves closer to 1?) We get around the singularity problem in this case by integrating from a small positive value to π and estimating the omitted part. It is clear that the time taken to slide to a point on the curve lies between the time needed to drop straight down the y-axis to the correct

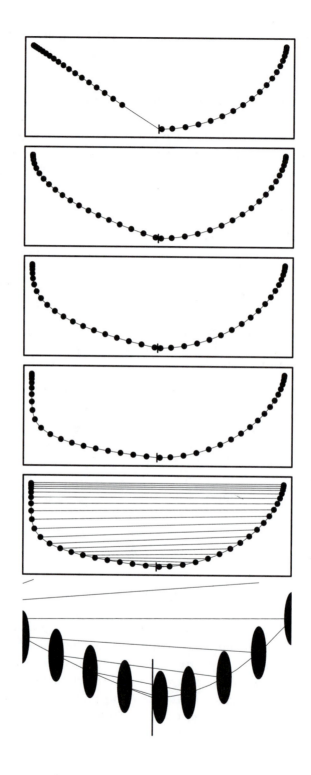

y-coordinate and the time needed to slide to the point along a straight line connecting the origin to the point. So we can bound the error by the difference between these two times. We leave it as an exercise for the reader to verify that the straight-line time from $(0, 0)$ to a point $P = (x, y)$ is $|P|\sqrt{2/(-gy)}$. Thus the error is bounded by error[d], defined as follows:

```
pi = Pi//N
f[t_] := -2 (t/pi)^(1/degree)
g = 980 2 pi /15
norm[p_]   := Sqrt[p.p]
error[d_] := norm[{d,f[d]}] Sqrt[2/(-g f[d])] - Sqrt[2 f[d]/-g]

degree = 2
error[0.001]
0.00000517678
```

Naturally, the error is less if 0.001 is replaced by a smaller value, but this would make more work for the numerical integrator. Since the error decreases as the degree increases, 0.001 is a good point to begin the integration. We define a function to give the time as the degree varies, with a special case for the straight line. Note the use of the conditional, /; n != 1; this is necessary so that when $n = 1$, the specific definition is used, rather than the general definition via integration.

FIGURE 2.13 Comparison of a bead sliding down the cycloid (right) with one sliding down curves of degree 1, 2, 3, 6, and 10. The first four images were generated by the program Cycloid as Brachistochrone in the Appendix. The degree-10 image was enhanced with lines connecting simultaneous images of the bead; this shows how the extra vertical speed gained by the initial steepness is eventually overcome. The final image is a blowup (slow-motion replay) of the region where the cycloid's vertical position overtakes that of the polynomial. It was generated from the image preceding it by Show[%, PlotRange->{{1.8,4.4}, {-2.1,-1.7}}, AspectRatio->0.6]

```
t = .    (* Clears t so it can be used as a dummy variable *)
time[n_] := (degree = n;
    Sqrt[2 f[.001] / -g] +    (* Time to fall straight down *)
    NIntegrate[Sqrt[(1 + f'[t]^2) / (-f[t])] / Sqrt[2g],
               {t, .001, Pi}])  /; n != 1
time[1] := norm[{pi, -2}] / Sqrt[g]

TableForm[Table[{n, time[n]}, {n, 8}]]
1        0.183812
2        0.156573
3        0.157058
4        0.158683
5        0.160206
6        0.161508
7        0.162607
8        0.163542
```

Thus we see that in the family of curves being considered, the curve of degree 2 is the fastest among those with integer degree. Moreover, this curve needs only about a thousandth of a second more than the cycloid; this explains why the image for the parabola in Figure 2.13 is inconclusive as to which is faster. This provides confirmation that the gravity simulation used to generate Figure 2.13 is accurate.

EXERCISE Find, to two decimal places, the degree that yields the fastest curve in the family f. (This can be done with a single Table command, though it would be better to do it via a loop having the form While[newtime < oldtime, ... to avoid computing past the minimum. And the lower limit of integration may have to be decreased further to get enough accuracy. Use error to determine an appropriate lower bound.)

EXERCISE Find the equation of the circle through (0, 0) whose bottom point is at $(\pi, -2)$. Then use NIntegrate to compute the descent time for the arc of this circle connecting (0, 0) to $(\pi, -2)$. The answer to this exercise explains why Galileo thought that such an arc was the curve of fastest descent.

EXERCISE Find the equations of the family of polynomials of the form $a(t-b)^d + c$ passing through (0, 0) and $(\pi, -2)$ and having a horizontal tangent at $(\pi, -2)$ and compute the descent times for various members of this family.

We can easily generate a plot of the descent time versus the degree. When the degree is near 1, the method of approximating the integral near the singularity at 0 by the free-fall time does not work as well as for larger degrees. The simplest solution is to decrease the lower limit of the integration to 0.0001 and use the straight-line descent time rather than the free-fall time (checking via the `error` function that this is acceptable). The plot could be speeded up by considering only degrees greater than 2, in which case a lower limit of 0.01 is adequate, or by inserting an `If` statement to make the lower limit vary with the degree.

```
a = .0001
time[n_] := (degree = n;
      norm[{a, f[a]}] Sqrt[2 / (- g f[a])] +
                                (* straight-line descent time *)
      NIntegrate[Sqrt[(1 + f'[t]^2) / (-f[t])] / Sqrt[2g],
            {t, a, Pi}])
Plot[time[n], {n, 1, 15}, Axes->{0, 0.155}]
```

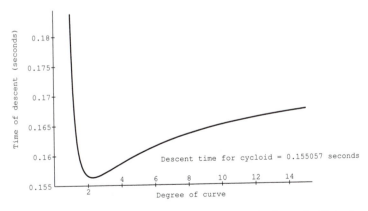

FIGURE 2.14 A plot of the time it takes a bead to slide from (0, 0) to $(\pi, -2)$ along the curves $\{t, -2(t/\pi)^d\}$ for d between 1 and 20. The fastest curve in this family is the one of degree 2.274. . . , for which the descent time is 0.156354. . . seconds. The cycloid, however, has a descent time of 0.155057. . . seconds.

EXERCISE Show that for a bead sliding down the cycloid, if θ is the angle made by the tangent to the cycloid at the point (x, y), then $(\cos\theta)/v$ is constant where v is the speed of the bead at the point (x, y). The fact that the cycloid is the unique curve with this property is the main point of the proof that it is the solution (and the only solution) to the brachistochrone problem (see [Lyu, §19] or [Bli]).

EXERCISE Show (mathematically, not by computation) that the limiting value of the descent time as the degree approaches infinity is $0.1762\ldots$ seconds.

3 Surfaces

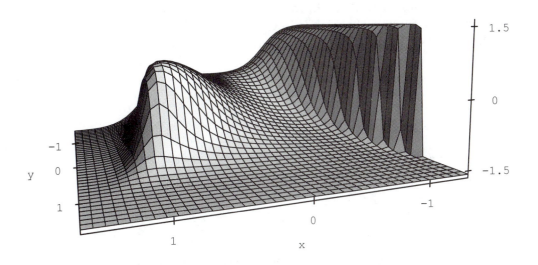

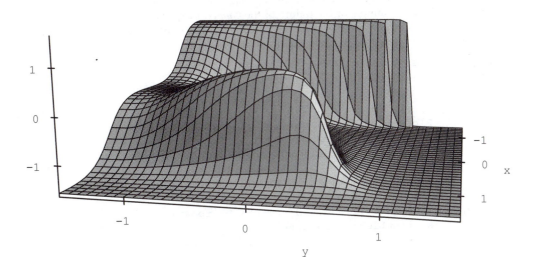

This chapter introduces 3-dimensional graphics via the problem of visualizing the surface that is the graph of a function $z = f(x, y)$. The basic tools are contour plots, density plots, and 3-dimensional surface plots. Surface plotting can be quite complicated, as there are many issues that do not arise in 2-dimensional graphics: viewpoint selection, lighting options, axes placement, and so on. The surface plotting techniques described in this chapter are only the beginning, as *Mathematica* has additional tools for dealing with, for example, space curves or parametric surfaces, a discussion of which is in Chapter 7. These advanced tools can be helpful even when dealing with ordinary functions $f(x, y)$.

About the illustration overleaf:

Two views of the graph of $z = 3xe^y - x^3 - e^{3y}$ over the entire x-y plane (the tangent function is used to compress the entire plane to a square). This function (due to I. Rosenholtz and L. Smylie [RS]) is an example of the failure of the *only-critical-point-in-town test*, which is valid for functions of one variable. The function shown has only one critical point, but the local maximum is not an absolute maximum.

```
f[x_, y_] := 3 Exp[y] x - x^3 - Exp[3 y]
g[x_, y_] := ArcTan[f[Tan[x], Tan[y]]]

Plot3D[g[x, y], {x, -1.57, 1.57}, {y, -1.57, 1.57},
        PlotPoints->40, ViewPoint->({.5, 1.5, .2}),
        Lighting->True, AmbientLight->GrayLevel[.1],
        Ticks->{Automatic, Automatic, {-1.5, 0, 1.5}},
        AxesEdge->{{1, -1}, {1, -1}, {-1, 1}},
        AxesLabel->{"x", "y", None}, Boxed->False]

Show[%, ViewPoint->{2, .5, .3}, Ticks->Automatic,
        AmbientLight->GrayLevel[0],
        AxesEdge->{{1, -1}, {1, -1}, {1, -1}}]
```

3.1 Using Two-Dimensional Tools

We begin our study of 3-dimensional plotting with a detailed analysis of a single example: the function $(x^2 + 3y^2)e^{1-x^2-y^2}$. We begin by defining the function so that we can refer to it simply as f.

```
f[x_, y_] := (x^2 + 3 y^2) Exp[1 - x^2 - y^2]
```

Before drawing surfaces, let's see how 2-dimensional plotting commands can give us information about f. The ContourPlot function produces contour lines in the plane.

```
ContourPlot[f[x, y], {x, -2, 2}, {y, -2.5, 2.5}]
```

Recall that a critical point of $f(x, y)$ is a point at which both partial derivatives equal 0. The local maxima and minima of a function are found among its critical points; a critical point that is neither a maximum nor a minimum is called a saddle point. In a contour plot the maxima and minima show up as centers of closed, circlelike curves. Thus the contour plot in Figure 3.1 seems to be showing five critical points; because the

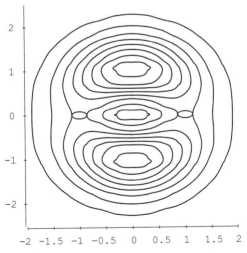

FIGURE 3.1 A contour plot (with default settings for the options) for the function $(x^2 + 3y^2)e^{1-x^2-y^2}$.

curves are not labelled, we cannot yet distinguish maxima from minima. Before addressing this problem, let's generate a finer contour plot, so as to resolve the incipient critical points at $(\pm 1, 0)$. There are many options that can be given to `ContourPlot`; `Options[ContourPlot]` shows the possibilities. The most important are `PlotPoints` and `Contour-Levels`. The first (default is 15) controls the number of points in the curves: a higher value yields smoother contours; the second (default is 10) controls the number of contour levels. But be aware that contour plots and surface images can be inherently difficult to obtain for functions that are especially pathological. Exercise: Try to generate a contour plot of `Tan[x/y]` over the unit square.

```
ContourPlot[f[x, y], {x, -2, 2}, {y, -2.5, 2.5},
    AspectRatio->4/5, PlotPoints->40, ContourLevels->15]
```

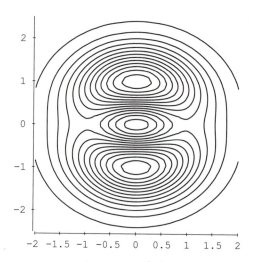

FIGURE 3.2 A contour plot of $(x^2 + 3y^2)e^{1-x^2-y^2}$ with `ContourLevels` set to 15 and `PlotPoints` set to 40.

As an aside, note that `ContourPlot` can be used to generate plots of a single curve of the form $f(x, y) = c$ in the x-y plane. Simply restrict the range to a single value, and the number of curves to 1.

```
ContourPlot[f[x, y], {x, -2, 2}, {y, -2.5, 2.5},
    PlotRange->{.5, .5}, PlotPoints->40, ContourLevels->1]
```

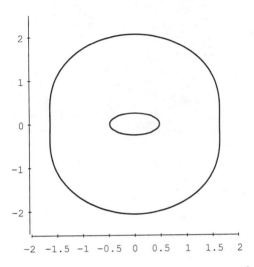

FIGURE 3.3 The graph of the equation $(x^2 + 3y^2)e^{1-x^2-y^2} = 0.5$.

The contour plot in Figure 3.2 shows the apparent extrema at $(\pm 1, 0)$; it now seems that those two points are saddle points. We will confirm this in a moment, but first let's discuss another way to view a surface without leaving the x-y plane. A density plot is similar to a contour plot, except that instead of curves, shades of gray are used to tie together points with common f-values. A density plot can be generated much more quickly than either a contour plot or a surface image. The information gained is similar to a contour plot, though less detailed. One advantage is that one can distinguish at a glance the high points from the low points: The gray levels go from black (`GrayLevel[0]`) for the lowest f-values to white (`GrayLevel[1]`) for the highest f-values. Here too, `PlotPoints` can be increased to get finer resolution (the default value is 15).

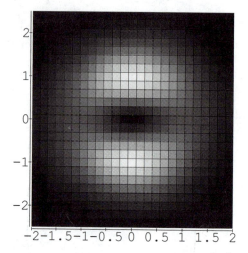

FIGURE 3.4 A density plot of the function $(x^2 + 3y^2)e^{1-x^2-y^2} = 0.5$; low points are black and high ones, white.

```
DensityPlot[f[x, y], {x, -2, 2}, {y, -2.5, 2.5}, PlotPoints->25]
```

The density plot indicates that there is a local minimum at the origin, surrounded above and below by two maxima. And the points (±1, 0) still look like saddle points, because each seems to be a maximum in the horizontal direction and a minimum in the vertical direction. In the next section we will confirm the critical point behavior of f both by looking at the surface and by taking derivatives symbolically. But keep in mind that ordinary 1-dimensional plotting of cross-sections can be used to obtain information about surfaces. The following plotting command shows the three critical points on the y-axis. Exercise: Plot some cross-sections (vertical, horizontal, 45°) that illuminate the behavior of f near (1, 0).

```
Plot[f[0, y], {y, -2.5, 2.5}]
```

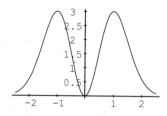

FIGURE 3.5 The cross-section of $z = f(x, y)$ corresponding to $x = 0$.

3.2 Plotting Surfaces

Now let's take a look at the actual surface $z = f(x, y)$ in $\mathbb{R}^3$, using the Plot3D command.

```
Plot3D[f[x, y], {x, -2, 2}, {y, -2.5, 2.5}]
```

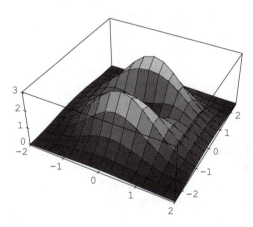

FIGURE 3.6 The surface $z = f(x, y)$ generated by Plot3D with all its default settings.

The surface image confirms the information obtained from the contour and density plots. Note, however, that it is not always the case that a surface is preferable to a contour plot. First of all, the surface is more work: more computation is involved and usually it takes several attempts before a satisfactory viewpoint is found (more on that shortly). But also there are times when the contour plot is inherently better. As noted by Wolfram (the *Mathematica* book, p. 136), "One point to realize is that irregularites become obvious in Plot3D and ContourPlot in somewhat complementary circumstances. Plot3D gives an irregular surface if your function varies too rapidly. ContourPlot, on the other and, gives a regular pattern of contour lines when your function varies rapidly, but can give irregular contour lines when the function is almost flat."

There are many options to the Plot3D command; Options[Plot3D] shows them all, along with their default values. PlotPoints is familiar and can be used to generate very fine renderings (see the chapter cover, which uses a setting of 40; the default is 15). But of course such renderings can take a lot of time to generate, and one should explore the surface extensively with a low setting of PlotPoints to find the best viewpoint. We'll discuss only some of the most important options here; see the *Mathematica* book for details on the others. The default value for Boxed is True and for Axes is Automatic. One can set these to False or None to eliminate the bounding box or axes, respectively. AxesLabel is used to add labels to the axes; AxesEdge is used to specify the edges of the bounding box that should contain the axes. The side lengths of the bounding box can be controlled by the BoxRatios option (default is $\{1, 1, 0.4\}$). For example, the following command shows the surface so that the units on the three axes have the same length in $\mathbb{R}^3$; of course, their perceived length in the plane projection will be different.

```
Plot3D[f[x, y], {x, -2, 2}, {y, -2.5, 2.5},
    BoxRatios->{4, 5, 3}, PlotPoints->25,
    AxesEdge->{Automatic, {+1, -1}, Automatic},
    AxesLabel->{None, "y", None}]
```

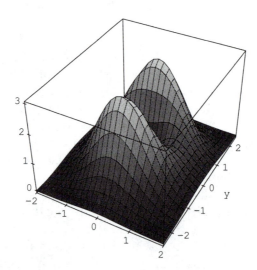

FIGURE 3.7 A BoxRatios setting of $\{4, 5, 3\}$ yields a true scale on the axes.

ViewPoint is perhaps the most important option as it gives the point in 3-space from which the surface is seen. The coordinate system for the viewpoint, however, is *not* the coordinate system of the plot, but is based on the ratios of the bounding box. Precisely, the largest side of the bounding box (y in the current example) is scaled to have length 1 (running from –0.5 to 0.5), with the two other directions scaled correspondingly. In our example, then, the box would have x running from –0.4 to 0.4 (because one half of ⁴⁄₅ is 0.4), y from –0.5 to 0.5, and z from –0.3 to 0.3 (see Figure 3.8). Now, it is this set of coordinates that is used to determine the viewpoint. Thus, still in our example, a viewpoint of $\{0.8, -1, 0.6\}$ places the viewer's eye on the line connecting the center of the box (which always has viewing coordinates $\{0, 0, 0\}$) to the (+, –, +) corner, at a distance from the center of twice the distance to the corner.

This is independent of the coordinates of the surface, which might all be numbers between 5,000 and 6,000; a viewpoint of $\{2, 2, 2\}$ always yields a view from above, in front of, and to the right of the surface. The default viewpoint is $\{1.3, -2.4, 2\}$. If we look at the graph of f from $\{2, 0, 0\}$, that is, from front center, halfway up, then the equality of axes scales due to our BoxRatios setting becomes evident. Note how the option settings remain active when % is used to regenerate the image with a new viewpoint. In Figure 3.9(b) and (c) the viewpoint is raised to the level of the top of the box and higher. These commands also

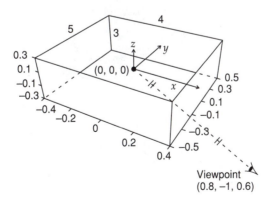

FIGURE 3.8 The coordinates of the bounding box and viewpoint for a surface plot with x between –2 and 2, y between –2.5 and 2.5, and z between 0 and 3.

illustrate the use of `Ticks` to control the selection of tick marks; this improves legibility.

(a) `Show[%, ViewPoint->{1.6, 0, 0},`
     `AxesEdge->{{-1, +1}, Automatic, Automatic},`
     `Ticks->{{0, -1, -2}, Automatic, Automatic}]`

(b) `Show[%, ViewPoint->{1.6, 0, 0.3},`
       `AxesEdge->{None, {+1, -1}, None}]`

(c) `Show[%, ViewPoint->{1.6, 0, 0.7}, Boxed->False, Axes->None]`

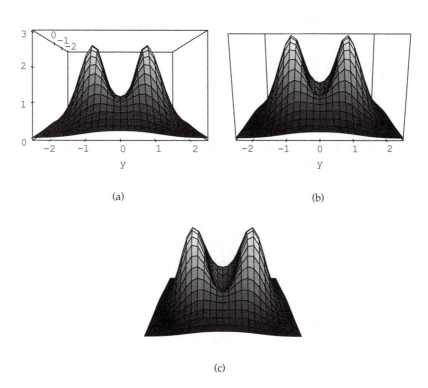

FIGURE 3.9 (a) `BoxRatios` = $\{4, 5, 3\}$, `ViewPoint` = $\{1.6, 0, 0\}$; note the equal spacing of the units on the y- and z-axes. (b) `BoxRatios` = $\{4, 5, 3\}$, `ViewPoint` = $\{1.6, 0, 0.3\}$; this viewpoint is exactly level with the top of the bounding box, whose z-coordinate runs from –0.3 to 0.3. (c) `BoxRatios` = $\{4, 5, 3\}$, `ViewPoint` = $\{1.6, 0, 0.3\}$, `Boxed` = False; this viewpoint improves the view of the hole in the center.

The default shading of a surface generated by Plot3D is from black to white with increasing height. One can eliminate shading entirely by turning Shading off. However, on the Macintosh implementation there is a menu command (Show Filled Areas) that does this directly, without recomputing the surface, so it generally makes sense to generate the shading and toggle it off and on via this command as desired.

The default setting of Lighting is False; a True setting causes the surface to be illuminated by three light sources, positioned above and to the right of the surface and shining with red, blue, and green light, respectively. One consequence of using illumination is that some regions in shadow may turn out black, a problem that can be avoided by setting AmbientLight to, say, GrayLevel[0.15]; this adds a little bit of light to the entire surface uniformly. One can specify the directions of the light sources, or eliminate them entirely by LightSources->{}. Note that LightSources and AmbientLight have an effect only if Lighting is turned on. The following five commands in succession generated the images of Figure 3.10. Of course, if you have a color monitor, then there are many more possibilities as all the GrayLevel settings can be replaced by red-green-blue settings.

(a) `Show[%, Lighting->True]`

(b) `Show[%, AmbientLight->GrayLevel[0.15]]`

(c) `Show[%, Shading->False, Axes->Automatic,`
`       AxesLabel->{"x", "y", None}]`

(d) `Show[%, Shading->True, LightSources->{},`
`       AmbientLight->GrayLevel[0.5]]`

(e) `Show[%, AmbientLight->GrayLevel[0.3],`
`       LightSources->{`
`               {{-1, 0, 0}, RGBColor[1, 0, 0]},`
`               {{-1, 0, 0}, RGBColor[0, 1, 0]},`
`               {{-1, 0, 0}, RGBColor[0, 0, 1]}}]`

The positioning of the light sources takes place in yet another co-ordinate system. (Note that generating 3-dimensional graphics is much more complicated than 2-dimensional graphics; this is the third coordinate system related to this surface.) This one is really a 2-dimensional system, based on the viewing plane. In other words, one is really specifying only the direction of the light sources, not their actual placement in three dimensions. The lighting origin is the center of the projected image, with x and y oriented as usual and z increasing toward the viewpoint. Thus a setting of $\{1,1,1\}$ corresponds to a light source shining from the upper right front. The illumination of a polygon is determined by its orientation only; there are no shadows. In essence, it is as if light sources shining in the specified directions are placed uniformly throughout $\mathbb{R}^3$. In Figure 3.10(e), the sources have all been placed at the far left, in the direction of the negative y-axis. To see the default settings, execute `Options[Plot3D]`.

There is an additional way of shading a surface, and that is by a user-defined function that varies with x and y. `Plot3D[{f[x,y], GrayLevel[s[x,y]]},...]` causes the function `s[x,y]` to govern the shading; this overrides any lighting settings. Of course, the shading function's values must be between 0 and 1. Shading according to the value of x (scaled to run from 0 to 1) is a good way to bring out the dip in the surface (Figure 3.11(a)). Another use of shading is to show a fourth coordinate; this generates an image of a function from $\mathbb{R}^2$ to $\mathbb{R}^2$. Figure 3.11(b) is shaded according to the value of $|x^2 - y^2|$, suitably scaled.

(a) `Plot3D[{f[x, y], GrayLevel[1 + (x-2)/4]},`
`                                    {x, -2, 2}, {y, -2.5, 2.5},`
`        BoxRatios->{4, 5, 3}, Boxed-> False,`
`        PlotPoints->25,`
`        ViewPoint->{1.6, 0, 0.7},`
`        Axes->Automatic, AxesEdge->{None, {+1, -1}, None},`
`        AxesLabel->{None, "y", None}]`

(b) `Plot3D[{f[x,y], GrayLevel[.1 + .9 (Abs[(x^2 - y^2)]/6.25)]},`
`                                    {x, -2, 2}, {y, -2.5, 2.5},`
`        Boxed->False, PlotPoints->25]`

On the Macintosh, one can resize images by selecting them and dragging the handles. The commands on the Graph menu are very useful. For example, doubling the size of a shaded surface doubles all the mesh lines. To restore them to an appropriate thinness, use the Make Lines Thin command. Another nice feature of some front ends is the inclusion of a viewpoint selector, which allows the user to grab and rotate a wire frame to change the viewpoint; this is in the Prepare Input submenu of the Action menu.

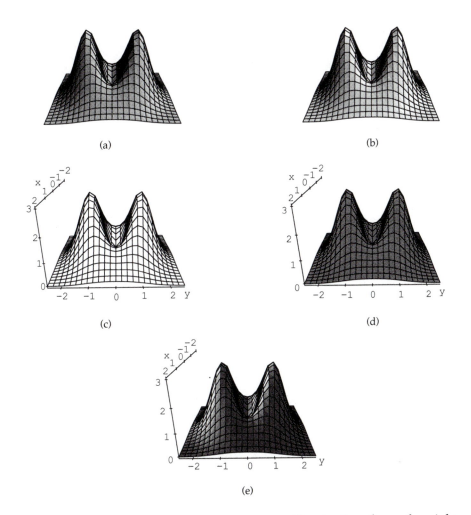

FIGURE 3.10 (a) Turning `Lighting` on causes illumination from the right. (b) Using a little ambient light turns the black left-facing slopes to dark gray. (c) Turning `Shading` off yields a plain grid, regardless of the lighting setting; the axes are restored in this image. (d) Eliminating the light sources allows `AmbientLight` to generate a uniform shading. (e) Moving the light sources to the left illuminates the left-facing parts of the image, but does not cast a shadow on the left side of the rightmost bump. As in (b), turning on some ambient light eliminates blackness.

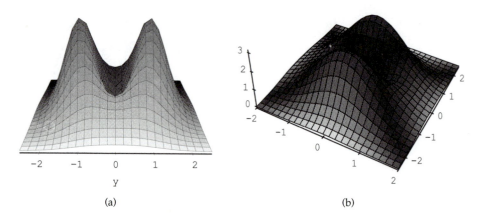

(a)   (b)

FIGURE 3.11 The result of shading the surface according to (a) the value of x, and (b) the value of $|x^2 - y^2|$.

The Macintosh and some other front ends have the the ability to animate a sequence of images; this allows the creation of movies that simulate the rotation of a surface or the fly-by of a surface along a specified path. This is precisely what the commands SpinShow and FlyBy do. These commands are activated by first executing the implementation group in the **Animation** file in one of the **Samples** folders included with *Mathematica* (not to be confused with the **Animation.m** package, which is entirely different). SpinShow generates a sequence of images of a 3-dimensional object, with the viewpoint moving around a circle centered at the viewing origin (or higher or lower on the viewing z-axis). Animating this sequence has the effect of spinning the surface. Of course, such movies take up a lot of memory, especially if the images are shaded and have a fine mesh. Remember that one way to save memory is to convert the images to Bitmap PICT format as discussed on page 44.

After defining SpinShow, you can see its options as follows.

```
Options[SpinShow]
{SpinOrigin -> {0, 0, 1.5}, SpinTilt -> {0, 0}, SpinDistance -> 2,
  SpinSteps -> 15, SpinRange -> {0, 360*Degree},
  RotateLights -> False, Axes -> None}
```

The default number of frames is 15, and the default origin of the spin is 0.7 units directly above the viewing origin (measured in the coordinates of the bounding box). The following commands generate a nice movie of our sample surface.

```
surface = Plot3D[f[x, y], {x, -2, 2}, {y, -2, 2},
            PlotPoints->20, Shading->False, Boxed->False,
            BoxRatios->{4, 5, 3}]

SpinShow[surface, SpinOrigin->{0, 0, .7}, SpinDistance->1,
        SpinTilt->{Pi/8, 0}, SpinSteps->20]
```

Unlike the animations in Chapter 2, it is impossible to compress this movie into a single frame!

Let's wrap up our analysis of f by doing some partial differentiation. The Solve command can by no means be used on any system of equations, but it does work on simple systems, such as the one obtained by setting the gradient of f equal to 0. It's easy to write a routine that we can use again later in this chapter. We must block x and y so that they can be used as dummy variables for differentiation.

```
CriticalPoints[f_] := Block[{x, y},
      Solve[{D[f[x, y], x], D[f[x, y], y]} == {0, 0}, {x, y}]]
cps = CriticalPoints[f]
{{x -> 0, y -> 1}, {x -> 0, y -> -1}, {x -> 1, y -> 0},
  {x -> -1, y -> 0}, {x -> 0, y -> 0}}
```

The output of Solve is a set of rules. A check is therefore easily accomplished by substituting these rules into the gradient as follows:

```
{D[f[x, y], x], D[f[x, y], y]} /. cps
{{0, 0}, {0, 0}, {0, 0}, {0, 0}, {0, 0}}
```

Now we may as well write a routine to apply the second derivative test to a function at a critical point. Repeated derivatives are obtained by, for example, D[f[x,y], x, y] for f_{xy}.

```
SecondDerivTest[f_, {a_, b_}] := Block[{x, y, dxx, disc},
    dxx = N[D[f[x,y], x, x] /. {x -> a, y -> b}];
    disc = N[(dxx D[f[x, y], y, y] - D[f[x, y], x, y]^2) /.
                        {x -> a, y -> b}];
    Return["Local maximum"] /; dxx < 0 && disc > 0;
    Return["Local minimum"] /; dxx > 0 && disc > 0;
    Return["Saddle point"]  /; disc < 0;
    Return["Test fails"]    /; disc == 0]
```

```
SecondDerivTest[f, {0, 0}]
Local minimum
```

We can test all five critical points at once by mapping Second-DerivTest onto the set of critical points, which set is obtained by substitution. Map and the use of # and & to define a pure function are discussed in Chapter 0. In the following command we map three functions so as to get a table of the type of critical point, its location, and the function value there. TableForm puts the output into a nice form. Apply[f, list] yields the value of f when its arguments come from a list; thus Apply[f, {x, y}] returns f[x, y]. Apply can be abbreviated by @@; thus f@@# is the value of f at a generic point of the list that is the second argument of Map.

```
TableForm@
    Map[{SecondDerivTest[f, #], #, f@@#} &, {x,y} /. cps]
Local maximum    {0, 1}     3
Local maximum    {0, -1}    3
Saddle point     {1, 0}     1
Saddle point     {-1, 0}    1
Local minimum    {0, 0}     0
```

This completes the analysis of our sample function.

EXERCISE Write a routine to generate the equation of the plane tangent to the surface $z = f(x, y)$ at $(a, b, f(a, b))$.

3.3 Mixed Partial Derivatives Need Not Be Equal

We now present several interesting examples of graphs of $z = f(x, y)$. We begin with the well-known example of a function whose mixed partial derivatives at the origin are not equal:

$$f(x, y) = \begin{cases} \dfrac{xy(x^2 - y^2)}{x^2 + y^2} & \text{if } (x, y) \neq 0 \\ 0 & \text{if } (x, y) = 0 \end{cases}$$

The graph of this surface is shown in Figure 3.12. It was generated as follows; the axes were added in *Adobe Illustrator*. (It is possible to use *Mathematica* to add lines and curves to a surface; see Chapter 7.) Because f is not defined at the origin, a warning may appear. Exercise: Why is this warning more likely when `PlotPoints` is odd?

```
Plot3D[f[x, y], {x, -2, 2}, {y, -2, 2},
        Boxed->False, Lighting->True, PlotPoints->31, Axes->None]
f[x_, y_] := x y (x^2 - y^2) / (x^2 + y^2)
```

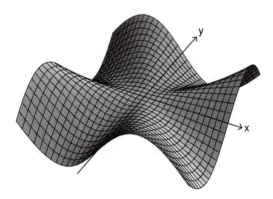

FIGURE 3.12 The graph of a differentiable function whose mixed partials at the origin do not have the same sign. Geometrically, this says that if you walk away from the origin straight along the x-axis, your shoes will tilt to an ever-steeper slope in the y direction ($f_{yx}(0,0) = +1$), whereas if you walk along the y-axis, your shoes tilt more and more steeply in the negative x direction [$f_{xy}(0,0) = -1$].

If we simply compare the two mixed partials of f, then we will see that they are the same. A short way to check this is as follows; note that the D operator can be used for second (and higher) derivatives.

```
D[f[x, y], y, x] == D[f[x, y], x, y]
True
```

This result is misleading, however, because the function has not been defined at the origin; thus the partials are being compared only where they equal the symbolic derivatives of the quotient defining f, that is, at all points except $(0, 0)$. For the analysis at the origin, first note that defining $f(0,0)$ to be 0 yields a continuous function whose partial derivatives exist and are continuous everywhere. The continuity is evident from the image of the surface, and because f vanishes on the axes, the partials at $(0, 0)$ both exist and are equal to 0. The fact that the partials approach 0 as (x, y) approaches the origin is evident from the flatness of the surface near the origin. Of course, one should verify these claims rigorously; we leave the details as an exercise. {The fact that the partials approach 0 as (x, y) approaches $(0, 0)$ is best proven by using `Simplify[D[f[x, y], x]]` to show that $|f_x(x, y)| \leq 2y$.} By the well-known criterion for differentiability, these observations imply that f is a differentiable function.

What about the second partial derivatives at the origin? Recall that the mixed partial $f_{xy}(0, 0)$ measures how f_x changes as one travels from $(0, 0)$ to nearby points *on the y-axis*. Now, $f_x(0, y)$ may be obtained as follows:

```
D[f[x, y], x] /. x -> 0
-y
```

Because the first partials are continuous, this result is valid even when $y = 0$; therefore $f_{xy}(0, 0) = -1$. A similar computation shows that $f_{yx}(0, 0) = +1$. This could have been done in one step as follows.

```
{D[D[f[x, y], x] /. x -> 0, y] /. y -> 0,
 D[D[f[x, y], y] /. y -> 0, x] /. x -> 0}
{-1, 1}
```

Now, there is a theorem that guarantees equality of mixed partials for "nice" functions. Precisely (see [TF, §16.8]), if f, f_x, f_y, f_{xy}, and f_{yx} are all defined and continuous in a neighborhood of (a, b), then $f_{yx}(a, b) =$

$f_{yx}(a, b)$. The hypotheses of this theorem must be violated for our example, and indeed, the mixed partials are not continuous. Recalling Wolfram's advice to use contour plots (or density plots) rather than surface renderings to see functions that are very steep (and, of course, a discontinuous function may be infinitely steep), we illustrate the discontinuity with a density plot.

```
Simplify[D[(D[f[x,y], x] /. x -> a), y] /. y -> b]
```

```
                  4       2 2      4
(a - b) (a + b) (a  + 10 a  b  + b )
-----------------------------------
          2    2 3
         (a + b )
```

```
g[a_, b_] :=
    ((a - b)*(a + b)*(a^4 + 10*a^2*b^2 + b^4))/(a^2 + b^2)^3
```

```
DensityPlot[g[a, b], {a, -2, 2}, {b, -2, 2}, PlotPoints->40];
```

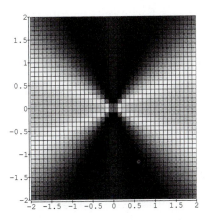

FIGURE 3.13 A density plot of the discontinous function f_{xy}.

EXERCISE Plot the surface of $z = f_{xy}$. (Chapter 7 will discuss some techniques to get good images of discontinuous surfaces.)

The density plot shows differing shades of gray emanating radially from the origin; that is, it seems that the function in question is constant on straight lines through the origin. We can easily verify the discontinuity by the following computation, which shows that f_{xy} vanishes on the 45° lines but takes on the value –1 on the y-axis.

```
g[0, a]                                          g[a, a]
-1                                               0
```

In fact, we can verify the more general behavior on straight lines through the origin with the help of `Simplify[g[a, m a]]`, which shows that the value of the mixed partial on such a line is the following, which is independent of a:

$$\frac{-(m-1)(m+1)(m^4 + 10m^2 + 1)}{(1 + m^2)^3}$$

EXERCISE Generate a density plot of the absolute value of f_{xy}, which will bring out the discontinuity even more strikingly.

We pause for a moment to discuss a subtlety concerning the plotting of derivatives. The density plot was generated in two steps: first the mixed partial derivative was defined as g, and then g was plotted. Can the derivative of a one-variable function $f(x)$ be plotted in one step via `Plot[D[f[x], x], {x, 0, 1}]`? Try it. You will discover that it doesn't work. The reason for the failure is that as x takes on values between 0 and 1, they are passed on to the function in the first argument; this asks *Mathematica* to evaluate, for example, `D[f[0], 0]`. The easy way to avoid this problem is to first define g to be the desired derivative, as was done for the density plot in Figure 3.13. There is another way around this; it is slower in this particular application, but is sometimes very useful, for example, when one wants a combined plot of each member of a table of functions. The idea is to force *Mathematica* to evaluate the first argument to `Plot`, rather than holding it unevaluated. The `Release` command does just this. Thus `Plot[Release[D[Sin[x], x]], {x, 0, Pi}]` yields a plot of the cosine function. Releasing an expression is useful when one wishes a list of functions to be plotted on the same set of axes. The following command does not work, because the x-values will be substituted into the `Table` expression before the table is generated.

```
Plot[Table[Sin[x] + t Cos[x], {t, 0, 1, .1}], {x, 0, Pi}]
```

But changing the order of evaluation via `Release` yields the desired plot.

```
Plot[Release[Table[Sin[x] + t Cos[x], {t, 0, 1, .2}]],
        {x, 0, Pi}]
```

We could plot the value of f_{xy} on straight lines as a function of the slope m, but let's illustrate the numerical minimizer by using it to find the line on which the value of the function is a minimum.

```
FindMinimum[Simplify[g[a, m a]], {m, 1}]
{-1.41421, {m->2.414210775170481322}}
```

This explains the blackness in the density plot along the line with slope $1 + \sqrt{2}$, as there the function takes its minimum value $-\sqrt{2}$.

The function f_{xy} is an example of a function that is continuous everywhere except at the origin. A simpler example is $xy/(x^2 + y^2)$, which we will discuss in Chapter 7 as an illustration of polar coordinates.

3.4 Failure of the
Only-Critical-Point-in-Town Test ▬▬▬▬▬▬

If a differentiable function of one variable has a local maximum and no other critical points, then that local maximum must be an absolute maximum. This is true because if the function was somewhere greater than the local maximum, then there would have to be a local minimum between the local maximum and the higher point; in short, the function would have to turn around somewhere in order to gain elevation. This leads to the only-critical-point-in-town test: If $f(x)$ has a single critical point and that point is a local maximum, then f has its global maximum there. This test fails for functions of two variables, however. One example is $f(x, y) = 3xe^y - x^3 - e^{3y}$. We can verify this symbolically as follows:

```
f[x_, y_] := 3 Exp[y] x - x^3 - Exp[3 y]
D[f[x, y], x]
     y      2
3 E   - 3 x
```

```
D[f[x, y], y]
     3 y       y
  - 3 E    + 3 E   x
```

```
Simplify[%/E^y]   (* Dividing by E^y eases the job of Solve *)
     2 y
  - 3 E    + 3 x
```

```
Solve[%%% == 0 && % == 0, {x, y}]
                              (2 I)/3 Pi              (4 I)/3 Pi
  {{y -> 0, x -> 1}, {y -> Log[E          ], x -> E            },

            (4 I)/3 Pi           (8 I)/3 Pi
   {y -> Log[E          ], x -> E           },
   {y -> -Infinity, x ->   0}}
```

Thus we see that the only real critical point is $(1, 0)$. Since $f(1, 0) = 1$ while $f(-2, -2) = 7.18\ldots$, f is indeed a counterexample to the only-critical-point-in-town test. Figure 3.14 shows two views of the surface. Here, x and y are replaced by $\tan x$ and $\tan y$ and then the arctangent of the resulting value is taken. This has the effect of compressing the graph over the entire x-y plane to a graph contained in the cube of side length π, centered at the origin.

```
Clear[g]
g[x_, y_] := ArcTan[f[Tan[x], Tan[y]]]
```

(a)
```
Plot3D[g[x, y], {x, -1.57, 1.57}, {y, -1.57, 1.57},
    PlotPoints->40, ViewPoint->({.5, 1.5, .2}),
    Lighting->True, AmbientLight->GrayLevel[.1],
    Ticks->{Automatic, Automatic, {-1.5, 0, 1.5}},
    AxesEdge->{{1, -1}, {1, -1}, {-1, 1}},
    AxesLabel->{"x", "y", None},
    Boxed->False]
```

(b)
```
Show[%, ViewPoint->{2, .5, .3}, Ticks->Automatic,
    AmbientLight->GrayLevel[0],
    AxesEdge->{{1, -1}, {1, -1}, {1, -1}}]
```

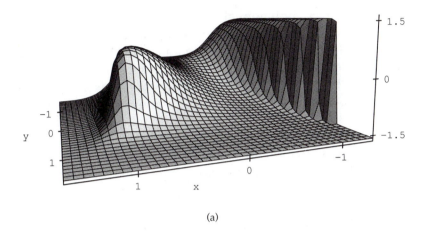

(a)

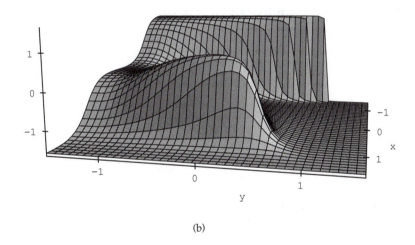

(b)

FIGURE 3.14 Front and side views of a counterexample to the only-critical-point-in-town test. The bump is a local maximum that is not an absolute maximum, yet there are no saddle points or critical points elsewhere on the surface. It looks as though there is a saddle point on the left boundary in image (b), but because of the compression of the entire x-y plane to a square, this represents a saddle point of f at infinity.

There are, in fact, polynomial examples. Exercise: Use the routines `CriticalPoints`, `SecondDerivTest`, and `DensityPlot` to verify that the fifth-degree polynomial $x^2(1+y)^3 + y^2$, due to B. Calvert and M. K. Vamanamurthy [CV], is a counterexample to the only-critical-point-in-town test. In [CV] it is shown that there are no counterexamples of degree 4 or less. A. M. Ash and H. Sexton [AS] observed that the only-critical-point-in-town test is valid for continuously differentiable functions $f(x, y)$ provided the inverse under f of any bounded subset of $\mathbb{R}$ is bounded. Another polynomial example of note is $-(x^2y - x - 1)^2 - (x^2 - 1)^2$ (due to R. Davies [Dav]); this function has two maxima (use `CriticalPoints` and `SecondDerivTest` to find them) with no minima or saddle points between them.

Here is a related example. The function $e^{-x}(xe^{-x} + \cos y)$ has infinitely many local maxima, but no local minima or saddle points. Of course, for functions of one variable any two maxima necessarily have a minimum between them. Note the use of `AxesLabel` and `Epilog`, which allows a message or graphic primitive to be superimposed on a plot; in this case `Text` is used to place some labels.

```
g[x_, y_] := (s = Exp[-x]; s (x s + Cos[y]))
```

(a)
```
Plot3D[g[x, y], {x, -0.5, 1.7}, {y, -14.1, 14.1},
       ViewPoint->{2.4, -1.3, 1.4},
       PlotPoints->40,
       AxesLabel->{"x", "y", None},
       Boxed->False]
```

(b)
```
Plot[Release@Table[g[x, t], {t, 0, Pi, Pi/9}], {x, -.5, 1.7},
     Ticks->{{-.5}, {-3, -2}},
     PlotRange->All,
     Epilog->
         {Text["y = Pi", {.5, 1}], Text["y = 0", {.5, -.65}]},
     PlotStyle->Thickness[.0005],
     AxesLabel->{"x", "z"}];
```

EXERCISE Use `D`, `Solve`, and the second derivative test routine given earlier in this chapter to give a rigorous analysis of the critical points of the function illustrated in Figure 3.15.

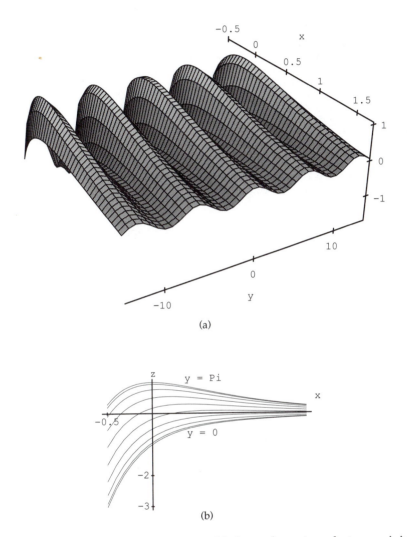

FIGURE 3.15 Two views of a function with lots of maxima, but no minima or saddle points. The ten cross-sections shown are between $y = 0$ (showing the lack of a saddle point) and $y = \pi$ (showing one of the maxima). Often ordinary 2-dimensional plots are the best way to visualize specific features of a surface.

4 Iterative Graphics

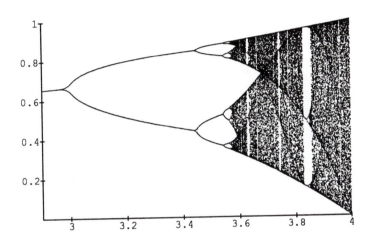

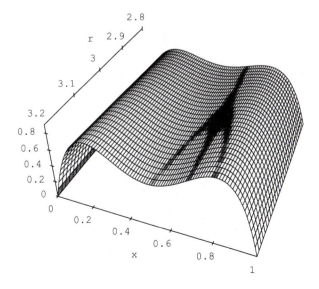

I n this chapter we return to two dimensions and discuss various techniques for producing complicated images in the plane, in particular, images based on some sort of iterative process. Examples range from mathematical roses and the Cantor set to tilings to illustrations of dynamical systems. *Mathematica* has several unusual built-in functions, such as Nest and NestList, that allow the efficient generation of a variety of complicated graphics.

About the illustration overleaf:

There are several ways to examine the dynamics of the quadratic map, defined by $f_r(x) = rx(1-x)$. Shown overleaf are two images that illustrate a certain bifurcation at $r = 3$. The first bifurcation in the orbit diagram shown at the top corresponds to the two outside tines of the three-tined fork on the surface. The surface was generated by the following command, which plots $g(x) = f_r(f_r(x))$, with additional viewing options set as explained in this chapter.

```
g[r_, x_] := r^2*(1 - x)*x*(1 - r*(1 - x)*x)
Plot3D[{z = g[r,x], GrayLevel[If[Abs[z -x] <=.0028, 0, 1]]},
                        {r, 2.8, 3.2}, {x, 0, 1}]
```

The orbit diagram was generated by OrbitDiagram[2.9, 4, 600, 120]; OrbitDiagram is a function that will be defined in this chapter.

Mathematica has several commands that can be used to program iterative processes. Some of them are analogous to commands from traditional programming languages, others are new and very powerful. Here is a summary of some of the iterative techniques that will be used in this chapter.

▪ If f is a listable function, then f[Range[m, n, s]] returns the list

$$\{f(m), f(m + s), f(m + 2s), \ldots, f(m + rs)\}$$

where $m + rs$ is the largest element of the arithmetic progression that is less than or equal to n. The Range command is an arithmetic-progression producer and was described in Chapter 1. For non-listable functions the same effect can be achieved by the command Map[f, Range[m, n, s]] or, using the built-in abbreviation for Map, simply f /@ Range[m, n, s]. Yet one more way of obtaining this list of *f* values is by Table[f[i], {i, m, n, s}].

▪ The familiar Do and For loops can be used. Either of the following two sequences would yield the same list as above, stored in S:

```
S = {}; Do[AppendTo[S, f[i]], {i, m, n, s}]
S = {}; For[i = m, i <= n, i += s, AppendTo[S, f[i]]]
```

This list-building approach is slower than the preceding methods, but there are times when these sorts of loops are necessary.

▪ Nest[f, x, n] is a built-in function that returns the result of *n* iterations of the function *f* on starting value *x*. Thus Nest[f, 1, 5] returns $f(f(f(f(f(1)))))$ when *f* is undefined, whereas Nest[Cos, 1., 30] returns 0.739087. Try the cosine example with the decimal point after the 1 omitted. This shows why it is often important to use N[] (or a decimal point) as a way of forcing numbers into floating-point form and thus avoiding the buildup of long symbolic strings.

▪ NestList[f, x, n] is a built-in function that returns the complete list of *n* iterates together with the starting value: $\{x, f(x), f(f(x)), f(f(f(x))), \ldots\}$.

```
NestList[Cos, 1., 30]
{1., 0.540302, 0.857553, 0.65429, 0.79348, 0.701369,
    0.76396, 0.722102, 0.750418, 0.731404, 0.744237,
    0.735605, 0.741425, 0.737507, 0.740147, 0.738369,
    0.739567, 0.73876, 0.739304, 0.738938, 0.739184,
    0.739018, 0.73913, 0.739055, 0.739106, 0.739071,
    0.739094, 0.739079, 0.739089, 0.739082, 0.739087}
```

When using `NestList` with a list-building function rather than a numeric function, the resulting list may have to be flattened. This occurs, for example, in the construction of the Cantor function later in this chapter.

Mathematica supports recursion (an example was presented at the end of Chapter 1), which is the principle underlying many iterative graphics objects. However, it is usually more convenient (i.e., faster, easier to program) to avoid direct recursion, and instead use commands such as `Nest` and `NestList` or repeatedly use a replacement rule. This chapter and the next have many examples for which recursion is the underlying principle, but they are implemented without explicitly defining a self-calling function.

4.1 Roses

A traditional way of introducing polar coordinates is via the family of n-leafed roses. The polar equation $r = \sin n\theta$ yields an n-leafed rose if n is odd (in which case θ need only run from 0 to π) and a $2n$-leafed rose if n is even (with θ running from 0 to 2π). The package **Graphics.m** contains a function, `PolarPlot`, that produces polar plots, but let's instead graph a rose with built-in functions by first defining a polar-to-rectangular conversion routine and then using `ParametricPlot`. We use the `N[]` function (in the equivalent "postfix" form: `//N`) to eliminate any symbolic values that might arise when θ is a rational multiple of π.

```
rect[theta_, r_] := {r Cos[theta], r Sin[theta]} //N
ParametricPlot[rect[theta, Sin[2 theta]], {theta, 0, 2 Pi},
                          Ticks->None, AspectRatio->1]
```

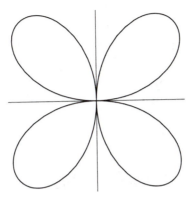

FIGURE 4.1 The 4-leafed rose generated by a polar coordinate plot of $r = \sin 2\theta$. An alternative way of generating this image is via `PolarPlot[Sin[2 theta], {theta, 0, 2 Pi}]`. (`PolarPlot` resides in the package **Graphics.m**.)

Now imagine starting at the origin and taking a walk along this rose, with steps corresponding to an increase in θ of $d°$. If d is relatively prime to 360, then we will return to the origin after exactly 360 steps. If d is $1°$, then the walk, where consecutive positions are joined by straight lines, will simply be a piecewise linear approximation to the 4-leafed rose. But Peter Maurer [Mau] observed that for larger values of d some surprisingly pretty patterns arise. Figure 4.2 shows the image of the walk when steps of length $71°$ are used; note that each point on the rose corresponding to an integer number of degrees is visited, but in a permutation of the usual order. To generate these walks, we'll make use of the built-in degree-to-radian conversion factor, a constant called `Degree`. The function `rose` computes the point on the rose with parameter θ equal to $i°$. We make `rose` listable so it can be applied to a set and then apply it to the set produced by the `Range` command, which produces the arithmetic progression $0, d, 2d, \ldots, 360d$. If we reduce this arithmetic progression modulo 360, then we can think in group theory terms: we are really looking at the subgroup of $\mathbb{Z}_{360}$ generated by 71, which in this case is the whole group. Because of the use of sine and cosine, there is no need to actually do the mod-360 reduction, but the group theory interpretation is important.

FIGURE 4.2 The 360 line segments that arise from a walk on a 4-leafed rose using steps of 71°.

```
rose[i_] := rect[i Degree, Sin[n i Degree]]
Attributes[rose] = {Listable}

n = 2
d = 71
walk = Line[rose[Range[0, 360 d, d]]]
Show[Graphics[{Thickness[.0005], walk}], AspectRatio->1]
```

Now, if the step size is not relatively prime to 360, the walk will return to the origin in fewer than 360 steps without having visited every integer-degree point of the rose. If $d = 30°$ for example, the walk will terminate in 12 steps (Figure 4.3). Exercise: Examine several other prematurely terminating cases. (Use the coset routine that follows, with the iterator m set to run only from 0 to 0.)

To fully cover the rose, we should superimpose *all* the walks starting at $0°, 1°, \ldots, \gcd(d, 360)-1°$. In other words, we should plot the subgroup generated by the step size together with all of its cosets. This can be done by applying rose to the fundamental arithmetic progression (start point $= m = 0$) as well as to $\gcd(d, 360)-1$ of its translates. Note that the final θ value of each coset walk is determined by the least common multiple of d and 360. Both gcd and lcm are built in. In the following routine all the coset walks are gathered into cosets by a Table command. Figure 4.4

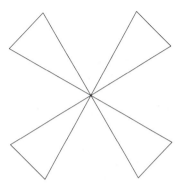

FIGURE 4.3 The result of a walk on the 4-leafed rose using 30° steps.

shows the result of using a step size of 180°. Exercise: What does the coset-superimposition image look like in the case of step size 30°?

```
n = 2; d = 180;
cosets = Table[Line[rose[Range[m, m + LCM[d, 360], d]]],
                                {m, 0, GCD[d, 360] - 1}]
Show[Graphics[{Thickness[.0005], cosets}], AspectRatio->1]
```

We can now write a general program that will work for any step size. Moreover, we can expand the scope by allowing divisions of the

FIGURE 4.4 The result of a walk (together with all cosets) on a 4-leafed rose using steps of 180°.

circle into "degrees" different from $1/360$. Of course, we cannot then use the built-in conversion factor. Recall that when n is odd, it is sufficient to consider values of θ in the interval $[0, \pi]$. Thus an additional If statement and an auxiliary variable zz have been added to MaurerRose to avoid duplication of the image in the case that n is odd and $z = 360$. Some images from this program are shown in Figure 4.5. Several interesting facts and suggestions for further explorations can be found in [Mau]. Exercise: Experiment with other values of the parameters. Exercise: Experiment with walks around other curves by changing the definition of rose (and deleting the definition of zz and changing zz to z in the lines following). An example is shown in Figure 4.5.

The definition of MaurerRose that follows has a few new features: a usage statement is included, which can be accessed by ?MaurerRose, and the z_Integer:360 in the argument list sets the argument z to be optional, with a default value of 360. In general, x_:*expr* is used for an argument that is to be given the default value *expr*. Note also the inclusion of the two definitions rect and rose within the body of MaurerRose; if, say, rose was located outside MaurerRose, it would not have access to the argument n.

```
MaurerRose::usage = "MaurerRose[n, d, z:360] shows the walk
    along an n- (or 2n-) leafed rose in steps of d degrees
    (including cosets). Varying z changes the size of a 'degree'."

MaurerRose[n_Integer, d_Integer, z_Integer:360] :=
    Block[{zz = If[!EvenQ[n] && z == 360, 180, z], cosets},

    rect[theta_, r_] := {r Cos[theta], r Sin[theta]} //N;

    rose[i_] := rect[i 2 Pi / z, Sin[n i 2 Pi / z]];
    Attributes[rose] = {Listable};

    cosets = Table[Line[rose[Range[m, m + LCM[d, zz], d]]],
                              {m, 0, GCD[d, zz] - 1}];

    Show[Graphics[{Thickness[.0005], cosets}], AspectRatio->1]]
```

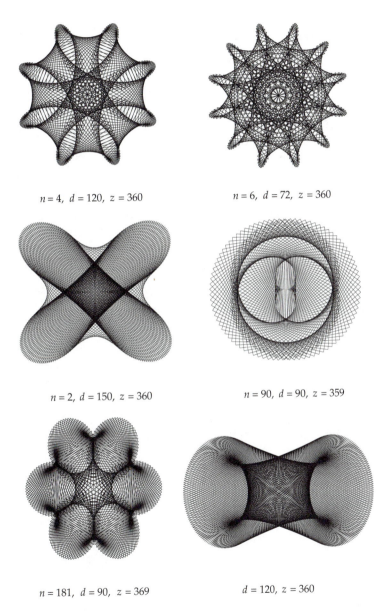

$n = 4,\ d = 120,\ z = 360$

$n = 6,\ d = 72,\ z = 360$

$n = 2,\ d = 150,\ z = 360$

$n = 90,\ d = 90,\ z = 359$

$n = 181,\ d = 90,\ z = 369$

$d = 120,\ z = 360$

FIGURE 4.5 Sample output from `MaurerRose`. In the lower right image, the function $(\theta, \sin n\theta)$ has been replaced by the polar coordinate function $\theta = \cos t$, $r = \sin t$.

Mathematica's animation feature can be used to clarify several aspects of these walks on roses. First, it is interesting to see how, in the case $\gcd(d, z) \neq 1$, the cosets build up to form the full image. Use a Do loop to generate a sequence of images so that the rth frame contains the cosets corresponding to m (the iterator in the definition of cosets) running from 0 to r, and then animate them. For example, in the case $n = 6$, $d = 72$, and $z = 360$ (see Figure 4.5), the full image is generated by a rolling pentangle. Animations can also provide a spectacular illustration of the effect of a change in the step size d. For a pretty example use a Do loop to show the images corresponding to $n = 2$ and $z = 360$, with d varying from 3 to 90 in steps of 3 (or try larger values of n). This will take some time to generate, and also a lot of space. You may have to generate the images in batches, convert each batch to Bitmap PICT to save memory, and run the animation only when the kernel is turned off.

4.2 The Cantor Function

Recall the formation of the Cantor middle-thirds set: Start with the unit interval [0, 1], remove the open interval ($1/3$, $2/3$); remove the middle thirds of the two remaining intervals, and so on. The set of points that survive this removal of countably many intervals is called the Cantor set C. It includes the endpoints of all the removed intervals, but contains much more. Indeed, C is an uncountable set, as can be seen by noting that C coincides with the set of numbers in [0, 1] having a base-3 expansion that contains no 1s. Some other interesting properties of C (see [GO]) are that it has Lebesgue measure zero and that it is nowhere dense and perfect (meaning C is closed, and every point of C is a limit point of C). Before turning to the Cantor function, let's generate the list of removed intervals, that is, the complement of C.

Observe that each removed interval (a, b) spawns two new removed intervals at the next stage; they are $(a-2w, a-w)$ and $(b+w, b+2w)$, where $w = (b-a)/3$. So we can define a function that turns a parent into its two children; the function applies to an interval (specified by its endpoints).

```
spawn[{a_Rational, b_Rational}] :=
    Block[{w = (b - a)/3}, {{a - 2w, a - w}, {b + w, b + 2w}}]
```

The use of _Rational means that this function will be applied only when the input is a pair of rationals. Thus it won't work on arguments such as {3.2, 4.6} or {0, 1}. The endpoints of the latter are rational, but not Rational; that is, an integer is not considered to be a rational, as can be seen by comparing FullForm[1] with FullForm[1/2]. The restriction to inputs of type Rational is valuable for several reasons: (1) the restriction is useful for debugging, as it prevents the function from being called inadvertently on an incorrect argument (and perhaps going into an infinite loop or worse); and (2) these declarations make code easier to read.

```
spawn[{1/3, 2/3}]                    spawn[{1/9,2/9}]
    1   2      7   8                     1    2      7    8
{{-,  -},  {-,  -}}                 {{--,  --},  {--,  --}}
    9   9      9   9                    27  27     27   27
```

Now, we wish to extend the definition of spawn so that it applies to a list of intervals and returns all the intervals spawned by each interval in the list. Because a single application of spawn to an interval returns a set of two intervals, the flattening function Flatten[·, 1] is used to reduce the set nesting by one level (with no second argument, Flatten eliminates *all* levels). We could use Union instead, but then there will be an unnecessary sort. Note the use of _List and the use of the If condition (via the postfix abbreviation /;). The latter is essential as it guarantees that this rule will not apply to $\{a,b\}$ when $\{a,b\}$ represents a single interval.[1] Actually, the order of definition in the present case will guarantee that things will work as planned even without this condition, but it is best to clarify the ambiguity: the object $\{x,y\}$ is interpreted as a single interval or a list of two intervals, depending on the size of x.

```
spawn[intervals_List] := Flatten[Map[spawn, intervals], 1] /;
        Length[intervals[[1]]] > 1
spawn[spawn[{1/3, 2/3}]]
```

---

[1] An alternative approach to the restriction is via

```
spawn[intervals:{_List..}] := Flatten[Map[spawn, intervals], 1],
```

which requires that the pattern to be matched consist of a list of lists; the double-dot pattern allows for repeating the preceding type.

```
  1   2      7   8       19  20      25  26
{{--, --}, {--, --}, {--, --}, {--, --}}
 27  27     27  27      27  27      27  27
```

To get the cumulative list of removed intervals up to level n, we use the NestList command, which iterates a function and returns the list of all iterations. Again, some flattening is necessary.

```
removedintervals[n_] :=
    Flatten[NestList[spawn, {{1/3, 2/3}}, n - 1], 1]
removedintervals[4]
   1  2     1  2     7  8     1   2     7   8      19  20      25  26
{{-, -}, {-, -}, {-, -}, {--, --}, {--, --}, {--, --}, {--, --},
   3  3     9  9     9  9     27  27     27  27      27  27      27  27


   1   2      7   8      19  20      25  26      55  56      61  62
{--, --}, {--, --}, {--, --}, {--, --}, {--, --}, {--, --},
 81  81     81  81      81  81      81  81      81  81      81  81


 73  74     79  80
{--, --}, {--, --}}
 81  81     81  81
```

The Cantor set is somewhat elusive. Base-3 notation (ternary) is one way of focusing more clearly on the set. Note that the endpoints of the removed intervals at level n correspond to multiplying the endpoints at the previous level by 0.1 (in base 3; these yield the intervals to the left of $\frac{1}{2}$ then adding 0.2 to these (to get those to the right of $\frac{1}{2}$). We can express the intervals in ternary as follows:

```
BaseForm[removedintervals[3]//N, 3]
{{0.1 , 0.2 }, {0.01 , 0.02 }, {0.21 , 0.22 }, {0.001 , 0.002 },
    3     3        3      3        3      3         3       3


 {0.021 , 0.022 }, {0.201 , 0.202 }, {0.221 , 0.222 }}
     3       3         3       3         3       3
```

We see that the first removed interval consists of ternary numbers beginning with a 1; the second level consists of ternary numbers having a 1 in the second position, but not the first; and so on. Any number having a 1 in its ternary expansion is in one of the removed intervals; this leads to the characterization of the Cantor set as consisting of those reals in the unit interval having no 1s in their ternary expansion.

A geometric way to think about it is to consider the Cantor set as consisting of all infinite branches down the full binary tree. To be precise, consider Figure 4.6, which was generated by code very similar to that of `spawn` and `removedintervals` (see Appendix; Exercise: Generate this image without consulting the Appendix). Any infinite sequence of 0s and 1s may be viewed as defining a unique point in the unit interval via the branch it defines in the tree structure of Figure 4.6. For example, the sequence 00100000... corresponds to $2/27$ (which, in ternary, is twice .00100000...); the sequence 0101010101... corresponds to a point in the intersection of a certain set of closed intervals, in this case, the point is just $1/4$ (= .020202... in ternary). A nonrepeating base-2 sequence leads to an irrational number.

The Cantor set can be used to define an important function called the Cantor function, denoted in this discussion by f. The traditional approach is to first define f on C by taking the base-3 expansion of a point in C having no 1s and converting it to a base-2 number by replacing all the 2s by 1s. This function has the same value at the two endpoints of any of the intervals in C's complement, and thus it can be extended to a monotonic, continuous function from [0, 1] to [0, 1]. Alternatively, it is not too hard to prove (see [Cha]) that f is the unique monotonic real-valued function on [0, 1] such that $f(0) = 0$; $f(x/3) = f(x)/2$, and $f(1-x) = 1 - f(x)$. The Cantor function has several interesting properties: (1) It is a continuous, monotonic function whose derivative is zero almost

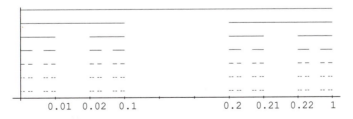

FIGURE 4.6 The Cantor set consists of those points that lie in the intersection of the sets represented at each level. The x-axis coordinates are in base-3 notation.

everywhere (i.e., everywhere except for a set of measure zero). (2) It is an example of a continuous function that maps a nowhere dense set (the Cantor set) onto the closed interval [0, 1]. (3) Slight modifications to it lead to a continuous function g and a measurable function h such that the composition $h \circ g$ is not measurable (on the other hand a continuous function of a measurable function is necessarily measurable). See [GO], or most texts on measure theory, for more details.

Our goal here is to use *Mathematica* to generate an accurate image of the graph of f. This can be done by considering only the values of f on the complement of C, which is dense in the interval. In other words, our goal is to graph the Cantor function on the set of removed intervals. Using the recursive characterization of f referred to earlier, we can do this as follows. First we define f assuming that the arguments will be endpoints of the removed intervals. Then we define a function connect that, given an interval, forms the Line object that connects the corresponding points on the graph of f. Finally, we generate the image by mapping the connecting function to the set of intervals generated by the removedintervals function. For convenience, the complete code is given below. Note the use of Range to specify tick marks. The horizontal tick marks in Figures 4.6–4.8 were changed to base-3 in *Adobe Illustrator*, although this could have been accomplished with the enhanced Ticks in Version 1.2, which allows such manipulations directly in *Mathematica*.

```
spawn[{a_Rational, b_Rational}] :=
    Block[{w = (b - a)/3}, {{a - 2w, a - w}, {b + w, b + 2w}}]
spawn[intervals_List] := Flatten[Map[spawn, intervals], 1] /;
                                 Length[intervals[[1]]] > 1
removedintervals[n_] :=
    Flatten[NestList[spawn, {{1/3, 2/3}}, n - 1], 1]

f[0] = 0;
f[x_] := f[3x]/2        /; x   <= 1/3;
f[x_] := 1 - f[1 - x]  /; 2/3 <= x;

connect[{a_, b_}] := Block[{y = f[a]}, Line[{{a, y}, {b, y}}]]

CantorFunction[levels_] := Show[Graphics[{Thickness[.001],
        Map[connect, removedintervals[levels]]}],
        Axes->{0, 0}, Ticks->{N[Range[0., 1, 1/9], 3], Automatic}]
```

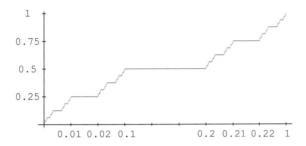

FIGURE 4.7 The graph generated by `CantorFunction[7]`, which uses a recursive definition of the Cantor function.

We conclude this discussion by mentioning a generalization of the Cantor function, one that can be used to create an instructive animation. Define f_r by modifying the recursive characterization of f as follows $(f = f_1)$:

$$f_r(0) = 0$$
$$f_r(1-x) = 1 - r f(x) \qquad \text{if } x < \tfrac{1}{3}$$
$$f_r(x/3) = f(x)/(r+1)$$

An example is given in Figure 4.8. Varying the parameter r generates a sequence of images that can be animated to show some surprising effects (see [Cha]); some code for doing this can be found in the Appendix.

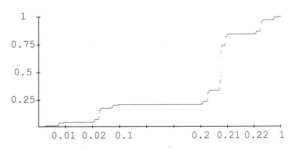

FIGURE 4.8 A generalized Cantor function with parameter r equal to 4. What happens as r gets larger?

EXERCISE Describe (with proof) the limiting behavior of the function $f_r(x)$ as r approaches infinity.

EXERCISE Use a technique similar to that used to generate the Cantor function to obtain the Sierpiński triangle pictured in Figure 4.9. [The solution can be found in the Appendix; other approaches are described in Chapter 5 (via iterating affine functions) and Chapter 6 (via a turtle graphics routine)].

FIGURE 4.9 The Sierpiński triangle, a 2-dimensional analog of the Cantor set.

4.3 Penrose Tiles

Tilings of the plane have both decorative and mathematical uses and have been studied for centuries. The notion of a tiling usually brings to mind a repetitive or periodic pattern of some sort: decorative tilings might use squares or hexagons, perhaps colored, whereas mathematical tilings of interest can involve more complicated polygons or curves, or even hyperbolic polygons, which can be used to tile the hyperbolic plane (a standard example of a non-Euclidean geometry). Non-Euclidean tilings can be portrayed in a Euclidean world, as exemplified by some woodcuts of M. C. Escher that are based on tilings of the hyperbolic plane. Because of the rich history of periodic tilings, it was a striking event when in the 1960s and 1970s, a completely new twist appeared and regions were discovered that could tile the plane only in a nonperiodic way. First some definitions: a set T of regions *tiles* the plane if the entire plane can be covered by copies of regions in T so that these copies have no interior points in common. By "copies," we mean congruent copies. A *symmetry* of a tiling is an isometry of the plane that leaves the tiling invariant, that is, maps each tile to a tile. A *periodic tiling* of the plane is one for which the symmetries include translations in at least two nonparallel directions. The terminology stems from the fact that a periodic tiling can be generated from a finite patch of itself by repetitively translating it in the two directions.

As examples, consider the tilings in Figure 4.10. The tiling by squares is nonperiodic: if F, a finite part of the tiling, generates the entire tiling by translations, then F has to contain some of the shifted squares; but then F cannot be translated upward. Of course, a square tile can be used to tile the plane periodically: just slide the singular row in the nonperiodic square tiling rightward. A set of tiles is called *aperiodic* if it tiles the plane, but it is not possible to use the tiles to tile the plane periodically. Note that a nonperiodic tiling can have symmetries; for example, the tiling of Figure 4.10(a) is invariant under some rightward translations.

Another nonperiodic tiling is illustrated in Figure 4.10(b). To obtain the entire tiling, start with an L-shaped 6-gon; rotate it 90°, double its size, and fill the doubled 6-gon with 4 tiles; then rotate this configuration 90°, double it, and fill it with four copies of the 4-L configuration. Continuing in this way yields a tiling of the plane. [Exercise: Write a routine defining `LTiling[n]`, which generates the nth iteration of the dissection illustrated in Figure 4.10(b).] This tiling is not periodic. Indeed, the tiling is not invariant under any translation. Briefly, this is because the associated tiling made up of tiles that are double the size would also be invariant under the same translation, as would be the tiling made up of quadruple-sized tiles, and so on. But once the size of the tiles is larger than the amount of translation, invariance is impossible. Of course, the L-shaped tile is not an aperiodic tile because it can be used to tile the plane periodically in several ways.

A very readable account of aperiodic tiles, with particular emphasis on the Penrose kites and darts, can be found in an essay by Martin Gardner [Gar, Chaps. 1, 2]; much more detail about nonperiodic tilings and

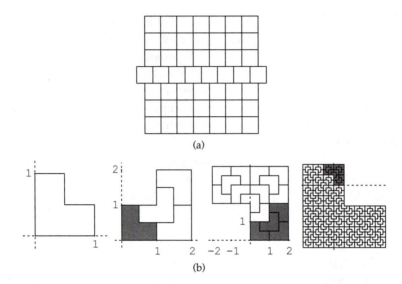

FIGURE 4.10 Two examples of nonperiodic tilings. Tiling (a) has translational symmetry in one direction, but no finite part of it can be repeated by translations to obtain the entire tiling. Shown in (b) are the zeroth, first, second, and fourth iterations of the function that rotates the L shape 90° and doubles it.

scores of other sorts of tilings can be found in the definitive study by Grünbaum and Shephard [GS].

In 1961, H. Wang conjectured that if a set of tiles could be used to tile the plane, then the tiles could be used to tile the plane in a periodic way (for motivation of this conjecture, see [GS, §11.3]). Wang's conjecture was refuted in 1966 by R. Berger's proof that an aperiodic set containing 20,426 tiles exists. The number was quickly reduced, and by 1971 the smallest known aperiodic set, discovered by Raphael Robinson, contained only 6 tiles. And it came as a surprise when Roger Penrose, in 1974, discovered two simple quadrilaterals, termed kites and darts, that form an aperiodic set.[2] The most noteworthy open question in the area is whether there is a single aperiodic tile, that is, a planar region that tiles the plane and is such that every tiling based on it is nonperiodic.

---

[2]Strictly speaking, the tiles together with certain color-matching conditions form the aperiodic set.

Penrose discovered two related aperiodic pairs: the kite and dart, and two rhombs, called Penrose rhombs. In this section we will focus on the kite-and-dart example, using an analysis due to R. M. Robinson based on triangles. This analysis is also relevant to the rhombs, which are discussed at the end of the section. A remarkable aspect of these discoveries is that tilings by Penrose rhombs and 3-dimensional generalizations thereof have played a role in explaining some interesting recent discoveries in crystallography [Nel, NH, Pen].

We use ϕ to denote the golden ratio, $\frac{1}{2}(1 + \sqrt{5})$, which is built into *Mathematica* as `GoldenRatio`; note that $\phi-1 = 1/\phi$ and $\phi^2 = \phi+1$. We also wish to generalize the notion of tiling by allowing tiles to have additional features, such as colored vertices or directed sides. Such tiles must be placed so that the colors and directions match at common vertices and sides. The use of colors and directions is most often inessential, in that the tiles can be transformed by cutting out notches and adding protrusions so that the additional conditions are forced to be satisifed by the way the tiles fit together (see [GS, Chap. 10]). Such modifications yield nonconvex tiles; however, it is known that an aperiodic set of three convex polygons exists (see [GS, Fig. 10.3.28]). In any event, in this section we will allow tiles to have colored vertices or directed sides, and in a tiling by such, it is assumed that the colors and directions match.

Now consider two types of isosceles triangles, 72°-72°-36° (type +1) and 36°-36°-108° (type −1), with their vertices colored black or white as indicated in Figure 4.11(a) and with the monochromatic side directed away from the longer of the other two sides (as indicated by an arrow in Figure 4.11). Such triangles have the property that each can be dissected into two smaller triangles, one of each type (though in some cases the colors are reversed and in one case the triangle is flipped), using lines as indicated in Figure 4.11(b). (Exercise: Verify that dividing these triangles using the proportions indicated in Figure 4.11(b) yields triangles of type +1 and −1.) Moreover, two type +1 triangles can be used to form a quadrilateral called a *kite* and two type −1 triangles can be joined to form a *dart*, as illustrated in Figure 4.11. But let's focus first on the triangles.

The dissections just mentioned allow us to start with a type +1 triangle, split it into 2 triangles, dissect the new type −1 triangle (to get 3 triangles); dissect the two smaller type +1 triangles (to get a total of 5 triangles), and so on (see Figure 4.12, where the directed sides are shown

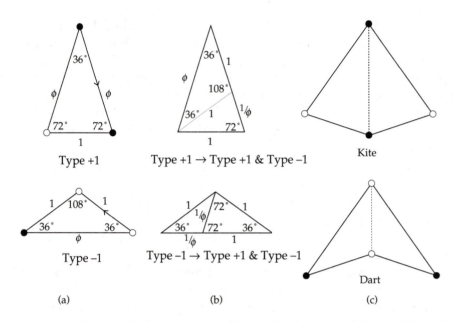

FIGURE 4.11 Type +1 and −1 triangles (a) can be dissected (b) to yield smaller triangles of the same type; two type +1 triangles can be combined to form the Penrose kite and two type −1 triangles form the Penrose dart (c).

by thicker lines). At each stage the total number of triangles will be a Fibonacci number, and the two preceding Fibonacci numbers will be the numbers of type +1 and type −1 triangles present. Now fix a type +1 triangle with sides 1, ϕ, and ϕ and a type −1 triangle with sides ϕ, 1, and 1. A tiling of the entire plane by these two triangles is called an *A-tiling*. We'll explain shortly how the repeated dissection idea can be used to generate *A*-tilings, but first we use *Mathematica* to perform the dissections illustrated in Figure 4.12.

```
phi = GoldenRatio //N;
toppoint = {1/2, Sin[72 Degree] phi} //N;
starttriangle = {toppoint, {1, 0.}, {0., 0.}, 1};

dissect[{p_, q_, r_, 1}] :=
            (newpoint = (phi q + p) * (2 - phi);
             {{r, newpoint, q, 1}, {r, newpoint, p, -1}})
```

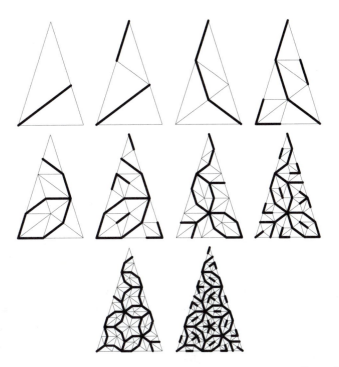

FIGURE 4.12 A nonperiodic tiling can be formed by repeatedly subdividing a 72°-72°-36° triangle. The number of tiles, the number of type +1 tiles, and the number of type –1 tiles in each triangle are consecutive Fibonacci numbers.

```
dissect[{p_, q_, r_, -1}] := (newpoint = (phi r + p)*(2 - phi);
        {{r, newpoint, q, -1}, {p, q, newpoint, 1}})

dissect[list_] := (type *= -1;
    Select[list, Last[#] != type &]
            ~Join~
    Flatten[Map[dissect, Select[list, Last[#] == type &]],1] /;
                                    TensorRank[list] != 1)

TriangleDissection[n_] := (type = 1;
    tiles = Nest[dissect, starttriangle, n] /.{p_, q_, r_, x_}->
            {Line[{q, r, p}], Thickness[.015], Line[{p, q}]};
```

```
Show[Graphics[{Thickness[.0005], tiles}],
      AspectRatio->toppoint[[2]],
      PlotRange->All])
```

```
Attributes[TriangleDissection] = Listable
```

The function `TriangleDissection[n]` performs n dissections of a type +1 triangle. The `Nest` command accumulates a list of triangles, where each triangle has its type appended as a fourth entry. The order of vertices in the triangles is very important: *each triangle is listed so that its first two vertices form the directed side.* The `dissect` function replaces each triangle of a certain type (which alternates with each call) by two smaller triangles, with vertices properly ordered. Note the use of `Select` to pick out the triangles of the current type and either leave them alone or dissect them. The `If`-condition involving `TensorRank` is not strictly necessary because of the ordering of the three cases of `dissect`, but it is a good idea to include it. `TensorRank` provides a way of distinguishing objects of different nesting levels; it is equivalent to `Length[Dimensions[]]`. The substitution following `Nest` replaces each triangle by three line segments, of which the directed line segment is the thickened one. The function is set to be listable so that Figure 4.12 can be generated by just `TriangleDissection[Range[10]]`.

We pause to discuss why these repeated dissections imply that infinitely many copies of two triangles having fixed side lengths (1, ϕ, ϕ) and (1, 1, ϕ) can be used to tile the entire plane (respecting the matching rules). Use the second triangle in Figure 4.12 (enlarged by the scaling factor ϕ) to locate the first three tiles. Now observe that the fourth triangle can be enlarged (by the scaling factor ϕ^2) and rotated so that it can be superimposed on the already placed three tiles. This gives the location of an additional five tiles. Then the sixth triangle can be expanded and rotated to cover the first eight tiles. One can continue in this way so as to cover the entire plane (or skip right to the tenth triangle and embed the first triangle in its interior; then repeat with the 19th tile, etc.). Note that this process definitely leads to a nonperiodic tiling, for if the tiling were periodic, the ratio of type +1 triangles to those of type −1 would be rational. However, the dissections that generate the triangular patches in Figure 4.12 imply that this limiting ratio is the limit of the ratio of consecutive Fibonacci numbers, which is the irrational number ϕ. Moreover, any tiling of the plane using these two triangles and matching the vertex colors and directed sides is nonperiodic (see [GS] for a proof), whence these triangles form an aperiodic set of tiles.

An *A*-tiling can be modified to yield a Penrose kite-and-dart tiling. A kite is the quadrilateral (with colored vertices) obtained by pasting together two type +1 triangles along their common directed edge and keeping the colors at the vertices intact [Figure 4.11(c)]. A dart is similarly obtained from two type –1 triangles. Then the kite and dart form an aperiodic set for tilings that match the colors of the vertices. One such tiling can be obtained by simply deleting the directed lines in an *A*-tiling. Using our sequence of approximations to an *A*-tiling, we can approximate a kite-and-dart tiling by deleting the directed lines from the even-indexed triangles in Figure 4.12. This is illustrated in Figure 4.13, where the kites have been shaded; the square region is a square inscribed in a large type +1 triangle.

The code to produce the kite-and-dart tiling follows; we assume that the definitions of `phi`, `toppoint`, `starttriangle`, and `dissect` have been retained. The only differences between `KitesAndDarts` and `TriangleDissection` are that 2n replaces n (so as to use only even-indexed

FIGURE 4.13 A Penrose tiling by kites and darts can be obtained by deleting the directed edge in all the triangles of a triangular *A*-tiling.

triangles) and the substitution rule is modified to yield polygons as well as lines and to delete the directed lines.

```
KitesAndDarts[n_] := (type = 1;
    tiles = Nest[dissect, starttriangle, 2 n] /.
        {{p_, q_, r_, -1} -> Line[{q, r, p}],
         {p_ ,q_, r_,  1} -> {GrayLevel[.5], Polygon[{q, r, p}],
                              GrayLevel[0],  Line[{q, r, p}]}}};
Show[Graphics[{Thickness[.0005], tiles}],
    AspectRatio->toppoint[[2]], PlotRange->All])
```

EXERCISE Generate the square image in Figure 4.13, by restricting the plot range to the largest square that can be inscribed in the triangle. Hint: The following command generates the x-coordinate of the lower left coordinate of the square.

```
First[x /. N[Solve[Tan[72 Degree] x == 1 - 2 x, x]]].
```

The first, third, and other odd-indexed triangles in Figure 4.12 are partial tilings where the type –1 triangle is larger than the type +1 triangle. Tilings of the plane that use such a pair, say a type +1 triangle with sides 1, ϕ, and ϕ and a type –1 triangle with sides $\phi + 1$, ϕ, and ϕ are called *B-tilings*, and the odd-indexed triangles in Figure 4.12 yield a *B*-tiling (in fact, many *B*-tilings), just as the even ones yield *A*-tilings. Note that two +1 triangles joined on their short side yield a rhombus, as do two type –1 triangles joined on their long side. These rhombs, with vertices suitably colored, from an aperiodic set of two tiles, called the Penrose rhombs. If the appropriate short and long sides in a *B*-tiling are deleted, then a tiling by these rhombs results. In our use of triangular approximations to the full planar tiling, the deletions must occur in the odd-indexed triangles. The following function generates tilings by Penrose rhombs as illustrated in Figure 4.14(a).

```
Rhombs[n_] := (type = 1;
            tiles = Nest[dissect, starttriangle, 2 n + 1] /.
        { {p_, q_, r_,  1} -> Line[{r, p, q}],
          {p_, q_, r_, -1} ->
            {{GrayLevel[.5], Polygon[{p,q,r}]}, Line[{p,q,r}]}};
    Show[Graphics[{Thickness[.003], tiles}],
    AspectRatio->toppoint[[2]], PlotRange->All])
```

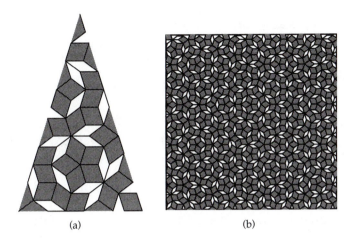

(a)   (b)

FIGURE 4.14 A Penrose tiling using two types of rhombs can be obtained by starting with a B-tiling and deleting the shortest sides in the type +1 triangle and the longest sides in the type −1 triangles. To get an approximation, we use the odd-indexed triangles in Figure 4.12. Remarkably, these tilings are related to recent discoveries in crystallography involving quasicrystals.

4.4 The Dynamics of the Quadratic Map ▬▬

The field of dynamical systems has seen phenomenal growth in recent years, in part because of the elementary and attractive nature of some of its basic concepts. One of the central examples concerns the behavior of the real quadratic function $rx(1-x)$, where r is a parameter. Let's denote this function throughout this section by f_r; it arises naturally as a model of the growth of a population under certain conditions (see [Gle]). Recall that a classical method for solving an equation of the form $g(x) = x$ is to choose a starting value x_0 and then iterate g on x_0 in the hope that the sequence of iterates will converge to a solution. For example, if we seek a solution of $\cos x = x$, we choose a starting value at random and iterate.

```
NestList[Cos, 1.5, 20]
{1.5, 0.0707372, 0.997499, 0.542405, 0.85647, 0.655109, 0.792982,
    0.701724, 0.76373, 0.722261, 0.750313, 0.731476, 0.74419,
    0.735637, 0.741403, 0.737522, 0.740137, 0.738376, 0.739563,
    0.738763, 0.739302}
```

It looks like the iterates are converging. In order to chase down more iterates without having to look at them explicitly, we can combine the `Nest` and `NestList` commands by using the result of the former as the starting value to the latter. This way, as in the following example, we see only the results of iterations 100 to 110.

```
NestList[Cos, Nest[Cos, 1.5, 100], 10]
    {0.739085, 0.739085, 0.739085, 0.739085, 0.739085, 0.739085,
      0.739085, 0.739085, 0.739085, 0.739085, 0.739085}
```

The limiting value seems to be 0.739085. In fact, unformatting the output cell shows the raw form of the output: all but the first two values are the machine-precision number 0.7390851332151606428. Taking the cosine of this shows that it is the desired fixed point. As pointed out at the beginning of this chapter, it is important to avoid the buildup of long symbolic strings when using `Nest` or `NestList`.

There is a simple graphical interpretation of this procedure, illustrated in Figure 4.15. The successive points on the graph of the cosine function are the iterates with starting value 1.5. A natural question is whether convergence is affected by the choice of a starting value. One way to study this is to try random starting values between, say, −100 and 100. This can be done efficiently by using `Nest` to compute the value of the 100th iteration, `Random` to generate random starting values, and `Table` with iterator {20} to repeat 20 times.

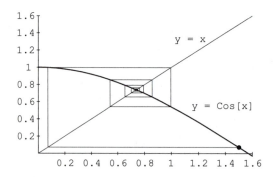

FIGURE 4.15 Graphical illustration of cosine iteration with starting value 1.5.

```
Table[Nest[Cos, Random[Real, {-100, 100}], 100], {20}]
{0.739085, 0.739085, 0.739085, 0.739085, 0.739085, 0.739085,
  0.739085, 0.739085, 0.739085, 0.739085, 0.739085, 0.739085,
  0.739085, 0.739085, 0.739085, 0.739085, 0.739085, 0.739085,
  0.739085, 0.739085}
```

The output gives the impression that this method always converges. In fact, it does. This can be proved with the help of the following theorem, whose proof is a simple manipulation using the Mean Value Theorem of calculus.

THEOREM. Suppose f is a differentiable function from $\mathbb{R}$ to $\mathbb{R}$, p is a fixed point of f, and K is a constant less than 1 such that $|f'(x)| < K$ in an interval around p. Then the orbit of any starting value in the interval converges, under iteration of f, to p. If $|f'(x)| > K$ in an interval about p where K is a constant greater than 1, then there is no value in the interval (excluding p itself) for which the orbit under f-iteration converges to p.

Another way to view the convergence is to plot the iterates of the cosine function, which can be done using the command that follows. The number of iterations can be increased or decreased. The plotting and interpretation of these iterates is left to the reader.

```
Plot[Nest[Cos, x, 4], {x, 0, 2 Pi}, PlotRange->{-.5, 1}]
```

In general, the behavior of the orbits of a point, by which is meant the sequence of iterates, is much more complex than the cosine example just discussed. There may be convergence for some starting values but not for others; there may be more than one fixed point; an orbit may get locked into a periodic loop; there may be periodic points that are repelling (that is, no point outside the cycle has an orbit that approaches the cycle, no matter how close the starting point is to the cycle); and so on. The fascination of the quadratic map f_r is that it displays all these complexities for differing values of r. We will not go into a lot of detail, referring the reader to the lucid discussion of the dynamics of this family in the book by R. Devaney [Dev1] (see also [CE, Dev2]); rather we will briefly show how *Mathematica* can be used to generate images related to the orbits of the quadratic map, or arbitrary functions.

First we will define a procedure, `Trajectory`, that accepts as input a function, a starting value, and several parameters and outputs the graph of the function together with a sequence of lines that illustrates what happens to the orbit of the starting value. `Trajectory` is a general-purpose function in that it produces a trace of the orbit for any function f, as shown in Figures 4.15 and 4.16. The method of attack is as follows. `Nest[f, x0, initial]` is used as the starting value to the displayed orbit. This allows the displayed orbit to be given a settling-down period of 100 or more iterations that are not shown; setting `initial` to 0 in the call to `Trajectory` will yield the entire orbit of the starting value `x0`. `NestList[f, start, orbitlength]` then generates the part of the orbit to be displayed.

Now, we wish to transform the orbit into a set of pairs such that the `Line` command will turn the pairs into the desired lines. Basically, we wish to transform a sequence of the form $\{a, b, c, d, e, f, \ldots\}$ (which is what `NestList` returns) into $\{a, b\}, \{b, b\}, \{b, c\}, \{c, c\}, \{c, d\}, \{d, d\}, \{d, e\}, \{e, e\}, \ldots$. We do this by using `Flatten[Transpose[{orbit, orbit}]]` to generate $\{a, a, b, b, c, c, d, d, e, \ldots\}$, and then using `Partition` to divide this list into pairs, dropping the pair $\{a, a\}$ (via `Rest`, which deletes the first element of a list). Of course, this could also be done in a more traditional manner with a `For` loop, but the program is both faster, shorter, and more transparent if we use built-in commands wherever possible. `DisplayFunction` is used to suppress the output when `plot` is defined, and to unsuppress the output in the `Show` command. Note the use of `N[start]`; if this were omitted, then a call with `start` equal to, say, 3 (as opposed to 3.) might produce a long string of symbolic values.

```
Trajectory::usage = "Trajectory[f, x0, initial, orbitlength,
 xrange:{0, 1}] returns a graphical trace of the iterations of f.
 Starting value is x0; orbit consists of orbitlength many
 iterations starting from the initial'th; the graph is displayed
 between values in xrange."

Trajectory[f_, x0_, initial_, orbitlength_, xrange_:{0, 1}] :=
    Block[{start, orbit, plot, lines, xmin, xmax},
        {xmin, xmax} = xrange;
        start = Nest[f, N[x0], initial];
```

```
orbit = NestList[f, start, orbitlength];
plot = Plot[f[x], {x, xmin, xmax},
                DisplayFunction->Identity];
lines = Line[Rest[Partition[
  Flatten[Transpose[{orbit, orbit}]], 2, 1]]];

Show[plot,
  Graphics[{{Thickness[.0001], PointSize[.02],
  lines,
  Point[{start, f[start]}],
  Line[{{xmin, xmin}, {xmax, xmax}}]}}],
        Axes->{xmin, xmin},
        DisplayFunction->$DisplayFunction,
        PlotRange->{xrange, xrange}]]
```

The diagram in Figure 4.15 (without the plot labels) was produced by Trajectory[Cos, 1.5, 0, 20, 0, 1.6]. The following commands yield Figure 4.16.

```
f[x_] := r x (1 - x)
r = 2
Trajectory[f, .1, 0, 10, 0, 1]

r = 3.45
Trajectory[f, .1, 0, 100, 0, .9]
Trajectory[f, .1, 300, 50, .3, .9]

r = 3.839
Trajectory[f, .1, 150, 50, 0, 1]

r = 4
Trajectory[f, .1, 200, 75, 0, 1]
Trajectory[f, .1, 1000, 50, 0, 1]
```

The interesting behavior of the quadratic map occurs for $r \geq 1$. (The orbit behavior for $r < 1$ is easily handled by the theorem about derivatives stated earlier.) For $1 < r < 4$ it is always the case that negative starting

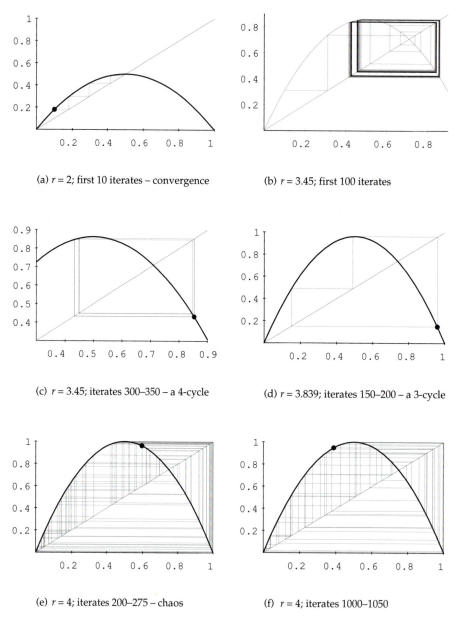

(a) $r = 2$; first 10 iterates – convergence

(b) $r = 3.45$; first 100 iterates

(c) $r = 3.45$; iterates 300–350 – a 4-cycle

(d) $r = 3.839$; iterates 150–200 – a 3-cycle

(e) $r = 4$; iterates 200–275 – chaos

(f) $r = 4$; iterates 1000–1050

FIGURE 4.16 These orbit graphs show some of the possibilities for orbits of the quadratic map.

values have orbits converging to negative infinity, as do starting values greater than 1. And a starting value of either 1 or 0 converges immediately to 0. Moreover, in the case $r > 4$ all starting values, except for a Cantor set, have orbits that converge to negative infinity (see [Dev1, §1.5]). Thus throughout this section we shall consider only values of r between 1 and 4 and starting values in the open unit interval. Note that the nonzero fixed point of f_r is simply $1 - 1/r$.

Some treatments of this subject (e.g., [CE]) use the function $1 - \mu x^2$ instead of f_r, with the parameter μ varying between 0 and 2; this version maps the interval $[-1, 1]$ into itself, whereas the function f_r maps the interval $[1 - r/4, r/4]$ into itself when r is between 2 and 4. Still another important quadratic family is given by $x^2 + c$, with c between -2 and $1/4$. This last family is the correct one to look at in order to relate the quadratic map to the quadratic map $z^2 + c$ in the complex plane, which underlies the definition of the Mandelbrot set (see Chapter 5). In any event, these three families are entirely equivalent as far as orbit behavior goes [Dev1, §1.7]; we will focus on f_r.

The values of r in the examples in Figure 4.16 yield functions with radically different orbit structure. For $r = 2$ there are two fixed points, 0 and $1/2$, and any starting value in (0, 1) converges to $1/2$; that is, points arbitarily close to 0 move away from 0, whence 0 is a repelling fixed point. For $r = 3.45$, the starting value 0.1 leads to a 4-cycle. Do all starting values lead to this 4-cycle? One quick way to check is by the following command, which shows that for 10 random starting values in the unit interval, the 400th iteration is very close to one of the four periodic points 0.445968, 0.852428, 0.433992, and 0.847468.

```
r = 3.45
Table[NestList[f, Nest[f, Random[Real, {0, 1}], 400], 3], {10}]
```

This might lead one to believe that all starting values in the open unit interval have orbits that are attracted to the 4-cycle. But this is not true! There are *infinitely* many points that fail to be attracted to the 4-cycle. For example, there is the nonzero fixed point of $f_{3.45}$, which is $1 - 1/r = {}^{49}/_{69} = 0.710144927\ldots$. This is a repelling fixed point because the absolute value of the derivative at the point is greater than 1. Therefore the orbit of any finite-digit approximation to ${}^{49}/_{69}$ will eventually drift away from ${}^{49}/_{69}$, and it is not hard to see that it will be sucked into the

4-cycle (see Figure 4.17). However, if the starting value is exactly equal to the rational fixed point, then the orbit will be simply $\{49/69\}$; one can see this by changing the parameter to be a true rational, as opposed to the floating-point real 3.45.

```
r = 345/100
f[49/69]
49
--
69
```

There are still more atypical points. The rational $^{20}/_{69}$ has the property that $f_{3.45}(^{20}/_{69}) = {}^{49}/_{69}$; the rational $^{20}/_{69}$ can be discovered by setting `r = 345/100` and invoking `FindRoot[f[x] == 49/69]`. We can keep working backwards in this way—there will be two inverse images of $^{20}/_{69}$—to come up with an infinite sequence of points whose orbits end up at $^{49}/_{69}$. This is related to the notion of the Julia set of a complex function, which will be discussed further in Chapter 5. Exercise: Find some more of the points in the inverse orbit of $^{49}/_{69}$ and generate a graph that illustrates them.

EXERCISE Prove that all starting values between 0 and 1, with the exception of the points in the inverse orbit of $^{49}/_{69}$, have orbits that converge to the 4-cycle, $\{0.445968, 0.852428, 0.433992, 0.847468\}$. Hint: Let f

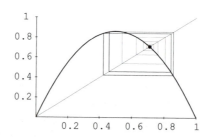

FIGURE 4.17 The graph generated by `Trajectory[f, 0.7101449, 0, 60, 0, 1]`. It may take a while, but the trajectory of any finite decimal approximation to the fixed point $^{49}/_{69}$ will escape from the region of the fixed point and converge to the 4-cycle.

denote $f_{3.45}$ and plot the two functions $h(x) = f(f(f(f(x))))$ and x; observe that the fourfold composition of f has six fixed points, four of which correspond to the four period-4 points of f. To examine the graph closely, it may be better to plot $h(x) - x$ on a small domain surrounding the fixed points. Now, convergence for any x can be proved by looking at the graph of $h(x)$ in sections and using the theorem on attracting fixed points stated earlier. Note: It is faster to plot iterates using `Plot[Nest[f, x, 4], .]` than to first evaluate the iterated function symbolically as a high-degree polynomial and then plot the polynomial.

The case of $r = 3.839$ seems to be similar to $r = 3.45$ in that there is an attracting 3-cycle. Here too there is a repelling fixed point, this time at $0.7395155\ldots$. But in fact this case is dramatically different from the preceding one. A consequence of a remarkable theorem due to A. N. Sarkovskii states that if a continuous function $f : \mathbb{R} \to \mathbb{R}$ has a periodic point whose period is three, then for each positive integer n, f has a periodic point of period n. The proof of this theorem is not too difficult and can be found, together with the general Sarkovskii theorem for other periods, in [Dev1]. So, $f_{3.839}$ has periodic points of all orders in the unit interval. Moreover, these points are all repelling ([Dev1, Cor. 11.10 and §1.13]).

EXERCISE Plot `Nest[f, x, 3]` and `x` (where `f` = $f_{3.839}$) to determine the approximate positions of the three repelling period-3 points. Then use `FindRoot[Nest[f, x, 3] == x, {x, {a,b}]` to locate them with more precision. Similarly, find a point of period 5 by plotting `Nest[f, x, 5]` and then using `FindRoot`.

The case $r = 4$ illustrated in Figures 4.16(e) and (f) has an even richer set of periodic points than the preceding cases: the set of periodic points is dense in the unit interval and there are period-n points for every n. But all these periodic points are repelling. (Exercise: Find some of these periodic points using the technique discussed in the preceding exercise.) Moreover, given any two intervals U and V, there is some positive integer k such that $f^k(U) \cap V = \varnothing$; in short, f is *topologically transitive*. This is illustrated by the all-over-the-place behavior of the orbit diagrams in Figure 4.16. Finally, the function depends sensitively on the starting value, as we can see from the following routine, which examines the effect of a perturbation of 10^{-10} in the starting value of an orbit. As is evident from the resulting graph in Figure 4.18, the first 25 values of the two orbits are indistinguishable, but from then on the orbits diverge. Proofs of all these assertions about f_4 can be found in [Dev1, §1.8].

```
r = 4; n = 80;
traj  = Transpose[{Range[0, n], NestList[f, 0.1, n]}]
traj1 = Transpose[{Range[0, n], NestList[f, 0.1 + 10^-10, n]}]

Show[ListPlot[traj, PlotJoined->True,
                       PlotStyle->Thickness[.0005]],
       ListPlot[traj1, PlotJoined->True,
                       PlotStyle->Thickness[.003]]]
```

Note the use of a decimal point in `0.1 + 10^-10`, which causes the sum to be an approximate real rather than a rational. The internal computations that generated Figure 4.18 are done in machine precision, which is 19 significant digits on a Macintosh. Executing `Precision[1.]` will yield the machine precision on other computers. If 10^{-10} were replaced by 10^{-30} in the example above, the computation would be incorrect, because *Mathematica* will reduce the number $0.1 + 10^{-30}$ to a 19-digit number. In order to use a much smaller perturbation, the computation must be forced into *Mathematica*'s high-precision arithmetic; this can be done by using `N[1/10 + 10^-30, 40]`, which will be a number whose

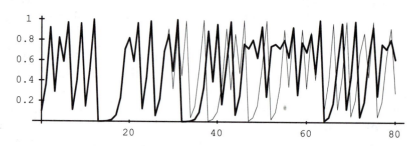

FIGURE 4.18 The first 80 values in the trajectories of 0.1 (thin lines) and 0.1000000001 (thick lines) under iteration by the chaotic function $4x(1 - x)$ stay together for a while, but then diverge. This illustrates how a seemingly negligible change in the initial condition of an iteration sequence can have large effects after only a few dozen iterations.

precision is 40 digits. The computation will then invoke high-precision routines that attempt to preserve this amount of precision. Note that `N[0.1 + 10^-30, 40]` is *not* a number having 40-digit precision. The approximate real 0.1 is interpreted as a machine real, that is, one with machine precision, and the sum of a low-precision number (precision 19) with a high-precision number (precision 40) is a low-precision number.

A function, such as f_4, is said to be *chaotic* if it has the three properties: a dense set of periodic points, sensitivity to small variations in the starting values, and topological transitivity. Part of the surge of interest in chaos and chaotic functions is due to the fact a function as seemingly simple as $4x - 4x^2$ (or $1 - 2x^2$) can exhibit the complexity of chaotic behavior (see [Gle]).

We now turn our attention to producing the now-famous diagram (Figure 4.19) that shows the entire orbit structure of the quadratic map as r varies from 2 to 4. The function `OrbitDiagram` takes `n + 1` parameter values uniformly spaced between `start` and `end` and for each parameter r generates the set $f_r^{init}(0.5), f_r^{init+1}(0.5), \ldots, f_r^{init+final}(0.5)$, where f^k denotes the k-fold composition of f with itself. (Starting values other than 0.5 yield essentially the same image so long as they don't coincide to infinite precision with one of the repelling periodic points, such as $49/69$, discussed earlier.) Then all these y values are displayed above the parameter value r. The main idea of the definition is to use `Nest` and `NestList` to generate the vertical coordinates for each r. Then the image is gathered together and displayed in the usual way via `Point` and `Map`. In this case we use a pure function to define f, rather than the familiar `f[x_] := r x (1 - x)`. Because `f` is called thousands of times, the speedup caused by feeding the pure function to `Nest` and `NestList` is substantial. (Exercise: Compare the time needed to run `OrbitDiagram` with a pure function to the time with an impure (i.e., variable-based) definition of f.)

A subtle point arises because of *Mathematica*'s use of machine precision. On a Macintosh, `4.0000000000000001 == 4` returns `True`, whereas `3.0000000000000001 == 3` returns `False`. This has to do with roundoff errors and the precision level used by `==`. Such "mistakes" can be avoided by using high-precision routines via `N[·, d]`, but that is slow. The problem arises in this program because of the Do loop that asks for the parameter to vary from, say, 2 to 4 in steps of $1/700$. The last value of the parameter will be slightly greater than 4 but will be interpreted as being equal to 4 and so will be included in the loop. This is disastrous, because orbits of f_r for $r > 4$ can diverge to infinity. We avoid the problem in this case by having the iterator in Table go backward.

```
OrbitDiagram::usage = "OrbitDiagram[start, end, n, init, final]
produces an orbit diagram of the quadratic map as r varies from
start to end in n steps. The number of initial iterations is
init; the number of displayed iterations is final."

f = r # (1-#) &

OrbitDiagram[start_, end_, n_, init_, final_] :=
Show[Graphics[{PointSize[.001], Table[
    Map[Point[{r, #}] &, NestList[f, Nest[f, .5, init], final]],
                          {r, end, start, (start - end)/n}]}],
    PlotRange->{0, 1}, Axes->{plotstart, 0}]
```

The image in Figure 4.19 ought to be generated by OrbitDiagram [2.9, 4, 600, 120, 150], but in fact that command would crash the Macintosh since it requires the storing of $600 \times 150 = 90{,}000$ points. One way to get such a large image is to generate it in pieces and then superimpose them after they have been generated (perhaps with the kernel turned off to save memory). In this instance that approach works especially well because on the left half of the domain—that is, for r in the interval [2.9, 3.45]—there is no need to generate 150 points for each r value; 4 points suffice. It is easy to modify OrbitDiagram to OrbitDiagram[start, end, plotstart, plotend, n, init, final] by adding two additional arguments, plotstart and plotend, which define the left and right sides of the viewing window; PlotRange is accordingly changed to {{plotstart, plotend}, {0, 1}}. Then Figure 4.19 can be generated by superimposing the output of the following two commands, which is done by unformatting the graphics cells, merging them, and then reformatting the merged cell.

```
OrbitDiagram[2.9,  3.45, 2.9, 4, 300, 120, 4];
OrbitDiagram[3.45, 4,    2.9, 4, 300, 120, 150];
```

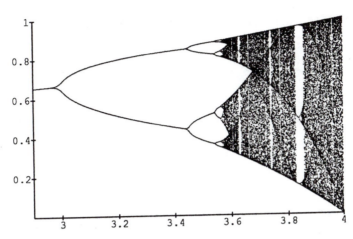

FIGURE 4.19 This diagram, which was generated by OrbitDiagram[2.9, 4, 600, 120, 150], summarizes the behavior of the 120th to the 270th iterations of f_r on starting value 0.5. Some of the many surprising features are the ever-smaller and ever-present windows of stability, and the regularity with which the bifurcations occur (see Figure 4.24).

Figure 4.19 shows several fascinating aspects of the orbits of the quadratic map. The examples of Figure 4.16 are visible in that $r = 3.45$ yields a 4-cycle, $r = 3.839$ yields a 3-cycle, and $r = 4$ shows chaotic behavior. The orbit diagram is intriguing in its complexity: There is a sequence of period doublings, or bifurcations, en route to the first chaotic value (3.56994...), and there seem to be several windows of stability, that is, intervals with no chaotic values. Indeed, there are still open questions about the character of the set of windows. But let's focus first on the bifurcation at $r = 3$. This is most easily understood by graphical analysis. The following command generates a 27-frame animation that shows the first two bifurcations in the orbit diagram; Figure 4.20 shows the frames corresponding to the r values 2.975, 3, 3.025, and 3.05.

```
Do[Trajectory[f, 0.5, 500, 5, 0, 1], {r, 2.9, 3.5, .025}]
```

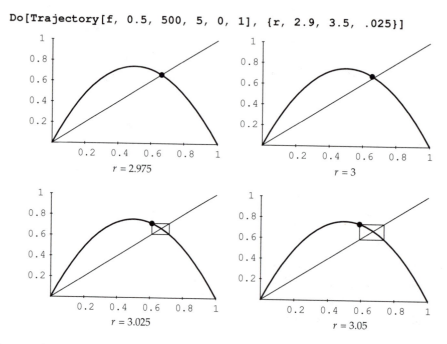

FIGURE 4.20 As r passes through 3, a single attracting fixed point becomes an attracting 2-cycle. When $r = 3$ there is a single attracting fixed point ($2/3$); the diagram is misleading because $2/3$ is a slowly attracting fixed point (derivative $= -1$) and the 500 initial iterations were not enough to get to it.

Another way of visualizing the bifurcation is to examine the function $g_r(x) = f_r(f_r(x))$. Studying iterations of g_r is quite similar to studying iterations of f_r; in particular, if a g_r orbit converges to a fixed point of g_r, then the corresponding f_r orbit converges to a 2-cycle (or possibly a fixed point). Consider the parameter value 3.2 (Figure 4.21). There are three nonzero fixed points of g_r; but the middle one is repelling because the derivative of g_r is greater than 1 there. The following commands show the g_r trajectories of six different starting values; their convergence to one of the two outside fixed points corresponds to the convergence of the f_r orbits to a 2-cycle.

```
f[f[x]]
```

$$r^2 (1 - x) x (1 - r (1 - x) x)$$

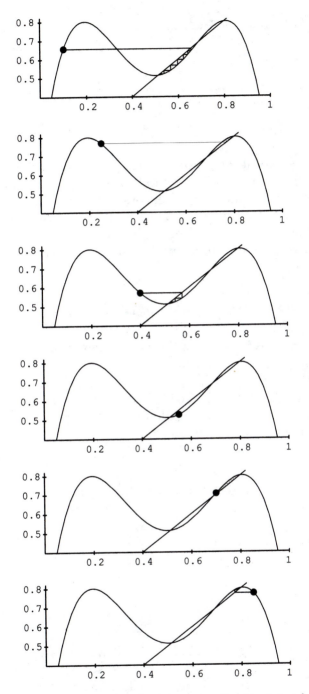

FIGURE 4.21 When $r = 3.2$, there are three nonzero fixed points of $f_r(f_r(x))$, but the middle one is repelling; the two outer fixed points correspond to an attracting 2-cycle for $f_r(x)$. The figures show the trajectories for six different starting values.

```
g[x_] := r^2*(1 - x)*x*(1 - r*(1 - x)*x)
r = 3.2;
Do[Trajectory[g, x0, 0, 10], {x0, .1, .9, .15}]
```

Now, let's look at the graph of $g_r(x)$ as the parameter passes through the bifurcation value $r = 3$. The following command (with some revisions to PlotRange and Ticks) generates Figure 4.22, which shows the bifurcation forming as the single fixed point is transformed to three fixed points, one of which is repelling. The sequence of images may be animated and, of course, a finer movie can be generated by reducing the step size on r.

```
r = .; Do[Trajectory[g, .1, 0, 10], {r, 2.9, 3.2, .05}]
```

Yet one more way to view the bifurcation is to use Plot3D to plot the graph of $g_r(x) = f_r(f_r(x))$ as a function of x and r. This surface is shown in Figure 4.23 (page 135), in which the dark regions correspond to fixed points of g_r. The two outside tines of the dark fork correspond to the bifurcation at $r = 3$. The middle tine is the repelling fixed point of g_r that is also illustrated in Figure 4.22.

```
g[r_, x_] := r^2*(1 - x)*x*(1 - r*(1 - x)*x)
Plot3D[{z = g[r,x], GrayLevel[If[Abs[z - x] <= .0028, 0, 1]]},
                        {r, 2.8, 3.2}, {x, 0, 1},
PlotRange->{0,.9}, Shading->False, Lighting->False,
AxesLabel->{"r", "x", None}, ViewPoint->{2, .8, 1.5}],
ClipFill->None, Boxed->False, PlotPoints->{30,90};
```

Even though the coloring function took on only the two values black and white, there are gray areas on the surface. This is because Plot3D averages the color values at the corners of each region. More precision is possible using ParametricPlot3D, in which case one could superimpose the relevant space curves onto the surface. (This is done for a different function at the beginning of Chapter 7.)

A most remarkable aspect of the orbit diagram in Figure 4.19 was discovered by Mitchell Feigenbaum in 1975 (and proved by O. Lanford, P. Collet, and J.-P. Eckmann; see [CE]). The visible sequence of bifurca-

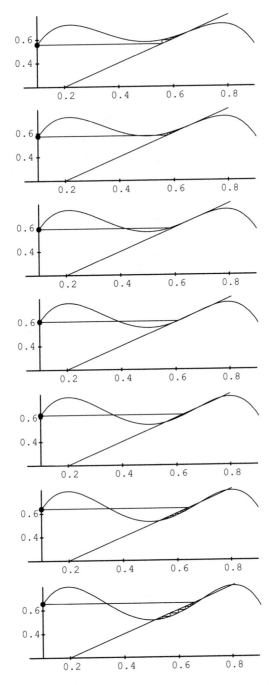

FIGURE 4.22 An attracting fixed point of g_r (first three figures, for which $r = 2.9$, 2.95, and 3) bifurcates into two attracting fixed points and a repelling fixed point (last four figures (see page 132), for which $r = 3.05$, 3.1, 3.15, and 3.2).

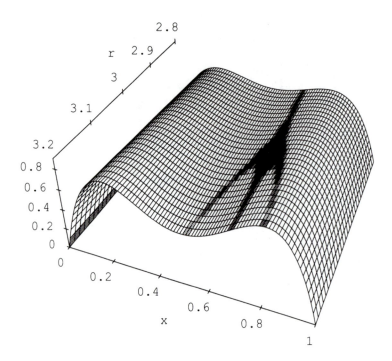

FIGURE 4.23 The dark areas are an approximation to the set of points for which $g_r(x) = x$ (see discussion on page 132). The trifurcation is really a bifurcation as far as trajectories are concerned, because only two of the three paths correspond to attracting fixed points of g_r.

tions from a fixed point to a 2-cycle to a 4-cycle to an 8-cycle to a 16-cycle continues through all the powers of 2, until the first chaotic r value, 3.569945..., is reached. The bifurcating values are at $r = 3$, 3.44949, 3.54409, 3.56441, 3.56876, 3.56969, 3.56989, 3.569934, 3.569943, 3.5699451, and 3.569945557. Moreover, these values increase at a uniform rate in that the distance between each bifurcating r value and the limiting value 3.569945... is approximately 1/4.669 times the distance between the preceding bifurcation value and the limit. And more surprising still, this speed of convergence occurs whenever iterates of a sufficiently smooth function exhibit period-doubling behavior! Because of this universal occurrence of 4.669..., the constant has come to be known as the *Feigenbaum number*. See the third chapter of [Gle] for more on the discovery of the complexity of the orbits of the quadratic map. The first chapter of [CE] contains a lucid survey of these ideas, and later chapters have rigorous proofs. Following [CE], we can generate a logarithmic view of the orbit diagram for r between 2.5 and 3.5699; such a view will show the uniformity of the bifurcations. The following code lets r run from 2.5 to $3.5699 - 10^{-3}$ and uses 200 logarithmically spaced r values; the output is shown in Figure 4.24, which is a modification of *Mathematica* output using *Adobe Illustrator*.

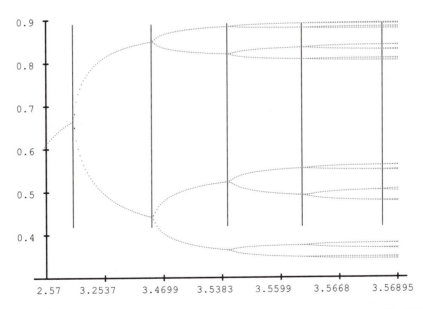

FIGURE 4.24 A logarithmic view of the first period-doubling sequence. The bifurcations occur at approximately equal intervals, having length $\log_{10} 4.669 = 0.669$. As Feigenbaum discovered and Lanford, Collet, and Eckmann proved, this distance between bifurcations is universal; that is, the constant 4.669201... governs the bifurcation rate for all sufficiently smooth functions.

```
f = r # (1-#) &; limitr = 3.569945557391440
Show[Graphics[{PointSize[.001],
    Table[(r = limitr - 10 ^ logr;
          Map[Point[{-logr, #}] &,
            NestList[f, Nest[f, .5, 150], 32]]),
      {logr, start = Log[10, limitr-2.5], -3, (-3-start)/200}]}],
    PlotRange->{0.3, .9}, Axes->{0, 0.3}];
```

EXERCISE Repeat the computations of this section with the function $r \sin \pi x$ replacing f_r. Use a logarithmic plot to check that the rate of period doubling obeys Feigenbaum's law. (You will have to find the first chaotic value of r; see Figure 4.25.)

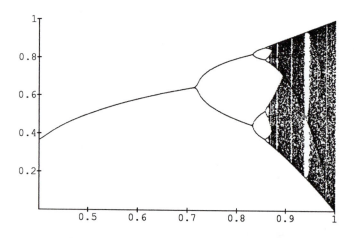

FIGURE 4.25 The orbit diagram of the function $r \sin \pi x$, which has much in common with the corresponding diagram for the quadratic map. For example, there is a sequence of bifurcations that approaches a limit (the first chaotic value of r) at the same asymptotic speed as for the quadratic map; that is, the distance between the first chaotic value and each bifurcation to its left is approximately $1/4.669$ times the distance to the preceding bifurcation.

We have barely scratched the surface of the dynamics of the quadratic map. There is a self-similarity in the orbit diagram of the quadratic map that leads to yet another universal constant. (Exercise: Use `OrbitDiagram` to examine various regions of Figure 4.19; good examples arise from the intervals [3.82, 3.86] and [3.8534, 3.8544], which show the period doubling to the right of the period-3 window at $r = 3.84$.) The orbit diagram also shows that windows of stability (regions where f_r has an attracting n-cycle) are intermixed with chaotic regions. This leads to the still unsolved problem of clarifying the nature of the set of chaotic parameters. It has been conjectured [CE, page 31] that each subinterval of [2, 4] contains a stable interval (that is, the nonchaotic parameters are dense in [2, 4]), but this has not been proved. On the other hand, the related conjecture that the set of chaotic parameters has positive Lebesgue measure has been proved (M. V. Jacobson, 1981). Finally, we mention that the orbit behavior of the quadratic map is related to iterations of quadratic maps in the complex plane and the Mandelbrot set (see [PS; Dev1, §3.8; Dev2, Chap. 8]).

The field of real and complex dynamical systems is very reliant on computation, both numerical and graphical. Some of those computations, especially those that generate high-resolution color images requiring lots of computation for each pixel, require a mainframe computer and a faster programming language than *Mathematica*. Yet *Mathematica*'s ease of programming and combination of numerical and graphics abilities make it a good tool for preliminary investigations.

4.5 Variations of Circular Motion

At the beginning of this chapter we described Peter Maurer's method of transforming familiar parametric plots to unusual images. In this section we describe an idea due to Norton Starr for transforming simple circular motion to complex and beautiful images. Starr's idea is to start with familiar circular motion $(r \cos t, r \sin t)$ and modify it so that the radius expands and contracts as t progresses from 0 to 2π and the angle varies in a nonmonotone fashion, travelling back and forth instead of just forth. The first variation is easy: If we wish, say, eight expansions and contractions of the radius, we need only have r vary according to $2 + (\sin 8t)/2$; this will cause the radius to shrink from 2 down to $1\frac{1}{2}$ and expand back up to $2\frac{1}{2}$. For the angular variation, suppose we wish 16 back-and-forth loops, each of a quarter of a radian. Then we need only have the argument to the trigonometric functions vary according to the function $t + (\sin 16t)/4$. We can incorporate these variations into a single parametric plotting command, with the options tweaked so as to obtain good resolution of all the loops.

```
ParametricPlot[
    (2 + Sin[8 t]/2) {Cos[tt = (t + Sin[16 t]/4)], Sin[tt]},
        {t, 0, 2 Pi},
    MaxBend->5, PlotPoints->50, PlotDivision->30, AspectRatio->1]
```

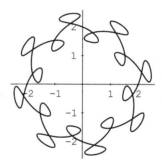

FIGURE 4.26 A circle modified by having the radius and the derivative of the angle shrink and expand.

We can turn this curve into a nice image by connecting the origin to points on the curve and by superimposing various shrunken images of the curve. With the parameters 8, 16, and 4 we get the image displayed in Figure 4.27(a). The code below achieves all this as follows: f defines the function; values stores the relevant values of f, computed efficiently by using Range; the appropriate Line command mapped onto values draws the lines; and values multiplied by the fifth root of a scaling factor s that varies from 0 to 1 in 20 steps gives the copies of the perimeter. The fifth root is used to vary the shrinking of the perimeter. In Figure 4.27(a),

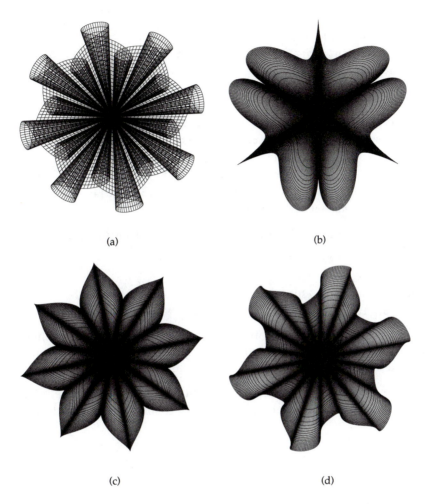

FIGURE 4.27 Some of the images generated by Norton Starr's variations on circular motion: (a) $a = 8$, $b = 16$, $c = 4$; (b) $a = 9$, $b = 6$, $c = 6$; (c) $a = 8$, $b = 16$, $c = 16$; (d) $a = 6$, $b = 18$, $c = 18$.

however, a simple linear scale was used; that is, r ^ 0.2 was replaced by just r. If your machine does not have enough memory to generate some of these images, try the writing-to-a-file trick discussed on page 149 (or increase the scaling increment, 0.05).

```
f[t_, a_, b_, c_] :=
        (2 + Sin[a t]/2) * {Cos[tt = (t + Sin[b t]/c)], Sin[tt]};
Attributes[f] = Listable;

Starr[a_, b_, c_, n_] :=
      (values = f[Range[0., 2 Pi, 2 Pi/n //N], a, b, c];
        Show[Graphics[{Thickness[.0005],
              Map[Line[{{0, 0}, #}] &, values],
              Table[Line[values r ^ 0.2 ], {r, 0., 1, .05}]}],
            PlotRange->{{-2.5, 2.5}, {-2.5, 2.5}},
            AspectRatio->1])
```

The following commands generate the images of Figure 4.27.

```
Starr[8, 16,  4, 720]
Starr[9,  6,  6, 720]
Starr[8, 16, 16, 720]
Starr[6, 18, 18, 720]
```

EXERCISE Find a condition on a, b, and c that determines whether or not the image loops back on itself as in Figure 4.27(a). What is it about the parameters that causes the asymmetry and cusps in Figure 4.27(b)?

These images look 3-dimensional, but are purely 2-dimensional objects. In Chapter 7 we'll turn one of them into a truly 3-dimensional object.

5 Iterative Complex Graphics

This chapter explores some examples of iterative graphics in the complex plane, starting with a discussion of complex Cantor sets and ending with a discussion of Julia sets for quadratic maps. The Chaos Game in the real plane is used to introduce the notion of an Iterated Function System, which forms the basis of one of the Julia set algorithms. The techniques are mostly the same as those used in the preceding chapter. Some of the images, such as the filled-in Julia sets shown overleaf, require a lot of pixel-by-pixel computation and so can take several hours to generate. On the other hand, *Mathematica*'s flexibility allows one to illustrate the mathematics underlying these images—in the case of Julia sets, trajectories of orbits in the complex plane—in a variety of ways, including animations.

About the illustration overleaf:

Shown overleaf are four examples of filled-in Julia sets, with attracting cycles superimposed in white on the upper images, while some orbits are superimposed on the lower pair. For a complex number c, the filled-in Julia set is the set of those points in $\mathbb{C}$ whose orbits under the function $z^2 + c$ do not approach infinity. The upper left image is the filled-in Julia set where $c = -0.123 + 0.745i$, known as Douady's Rabbit; in this case there is an attracting 3-cycle. The upper right image corresponds to $c = 0.32 + 0.043i$, which has an attracting 11-cycle. At the lower left is the case of $c = -0.390541 - 0.586788i$, an example of what is known as a Siegel disk; the orbits wander forever around circle-like curves. The image at the lower right is the Julia set for the quadratic map f_r studied in Chapter 4, where r is the bifurcating value 3. These images were generated by `FilledJuliaSet`, defined at the end of this chapter.

Many of *Mathematica*'s functions, such as the trigonometric, exponential, and logarithmic functions, work for complex numbers, that is, numbers of the form a + b I where a and b are reals (or rationals or integers) and I is the built-in constant $\sqrt{-1}$. Complex functions cannot be plotted directly, but have to be first transformed into objects in $\mathbb{R}^2$ or $\mathbb{R}^3$. Here we will explore a different, more elementary, aspect of complex graphics by plotting examples of interesting sets in the complex plane (denoted by $\mathbb{C}$). The basic tool for turning $\mathbb{C}$ into the real plane is the function that turns the complex number a + b I into the point {a, b} in $\mathbb{R}^2$. Because the real and imaginary parts are built in as Re[] and Im[], we can view any set S of complex numbers by using the usual 2-dimensional tools on the set of points obtained from Map[{Re[#], Im[#]}] &, S]. We begin with a generalization of the Cantor set to $\mathbb{C}$.

5.1 Complex Cantor Sets ▬▬▬▬▬▬▬

Every real number in [0, 1] has a base-2 representation, which can be viewed as $\sum_{i=0}^{\infty} a_i (1/2)^i$, where each a_i is either 0 or 1. Alternatively, this can be stated as

$$[0, 1] = \text{the set of sums} \sum \{(1/2)^i : i \in A\}$$

where A varies over all subsets of $\mathbb{N}^+$, the positive integers. What if other numbers are used in place of $1/2$? That is, what does $\mathcal{B}(x)$ look like, where $\mathcal{B}(x)$ denotes the set of all sums $\sum \{x^i : i \in A\}$? Recalling the characterization of the Cantor set in terms of base-3 expansions (Chapter 4), one sees that $\mathcal{B}(1/3)$ is $1/2\,C$ where C is the Cantor set. In fact, $\mathcal{B}(x)$ is a Cantor set (perfect, nowhere dense) for every x between 0 and $1/2$, while $\mathcal{B}(x)$ is an interval for x between $1/2$ and 1 (we assume $|x| < 1$, so that every set A leads to a convergent series). We may now wonder about the sets $\mathcal{B}(z)$ in the complex plane, where z is a complex number. In a sense, this is asking about a base-z number system for $\mathbb{C}$. This idea has been examined by several people (see [Gof] and the references therein; see also [Bar, Chap. 8]). It turns out that the sets $\mathcal{B}(z)$ take on a variety of interesting shapes as z varies among complex numbers in the unit disk.

Let's use b to denote the complex base. There are infinitely many points in $\mathcal{B}(b)$. A natural way of approximating these sets is to consider all points that arise in fewer than some fixed number m of digits, that is, all points of the form $\sum \{z^i\colon i \in A\}$, where A is a subset of $\{1,\ldots,m\}$. This set can be generated recursively by observing that the $(m+1)$-digit numbers consist of the m-digit numbers together with the translates of each m-digit number by z^m. If b denotes the base, then the complex numbers with successively more base-b digits are as follows:

.0 : 0

.1 : b

.01, .11 : $b^2 \quad b + b^2$

.001, .101, .011, .111 : $b^3 \quad b + b^3 \quad b^2 + b^3 \quad b + b^2 + b^3$

.0001, .1001, .0101, .1101, .0011,

.1011, .0111, .1111 : $b^4 \quad b + b^4 \quad b^2 + b^4 \quad b + b^2 + b^4 \quad b^3 + b^4$

$$b + b^3 + b^4 \quad b^2 + b^3 + b^4 \quad b + b^2 + b^3 + b^4$$

A natural way to program this is by introducing a function that transforms the list of numbers having at most i digits into the list having at most $i+1$ digits and then nesting this function on the set consisting of the single complex number 0. This function is simply `Join[set, set + b^i]`; in the code that follows, it is implemented as a pure function, and `i` is incremented each time it is called. The result of this nesting is a set of complex numbers. To plot them, we must transform them to points in the real plane and then to `Point` objects. This can be done by a mapping of the pure function `Point[{Re[#], Im[#]}]`.

```
ComplexBase[b_, m_] := Block[{i = 1},
    Show[Graphics[
            Map[Point[{Re[#], Im[#]}] &,
                Nest[Join[#, # + b ^ i++] &, {0}, m]]],
        PlotRange->All, Axes->Automatic, AspectRatio->1]]
```

The preceding code takes only a few seconds to produce the 10-digit image corresponding to `ComplexBase[.5 + .5I, 10]`. Of course, images with more digits take longer to produce, as the amount of work doubles with each new digit; the 15-digit, 33,000-point images in Figure 5.1 required seven minutes each on a Macintosh SE/30. Thus it is worth speeding up the program by working directly with pairs of reals rather than complex numbers. The crux of the code—the Join command—can be replaced by a version using the substitution operator /.. The restriction to patterns of the form {x_Real, y_Real} guarantees that the substitution will not work on lists of pairs, but only on lists of reals. The real and imaginary parts of the powers of the base are precomputed by direct use of the set $\{1, \ldots, m\}$ as an exponent.

```
ComplexBase[b_, m_] := Block[{i = 1,
         powers = Map[{Re[#], Im[#]} &, b ^ Range[m + 1]]},
   Show[Graphics[Map[Point,
     Nest[
       Join[#, # /. {x_Real, y_Real} -> {x, y} + powers[[i++]]] &,
       {powers[[1]]},
       m]]],
   PlotRange->All, Axes->Automatic, AspectRatio->1]]
```

This elimination of complex arithmetic reduces the time for a 10-digit set by about 30%. Several examples of the sets $\mathcal{B}(b)$ are illustrated in Figure 5.1 (these examples are discussed by D. Goffinet [Gof]). The images were generated by a slight variation of the preceding program (included in the Appendix), which allows the specification of a plot range and tick marks. Note the geometric variety Some are connected, some not; the set of b for which $\mathcal{B}(b)$ is connected is discussed in [Bar, Chap. 8]. In particular, it is shown there that $\mathcal{B}(b)$ is connected if $\sqrt{2}/2 < |b| < 1$ and totally disconnected (that is, the only nonempty connected subsets are singletons) if $|b| < 1/2$. Moreover, any disconnected $\mathcal{B}(b)$ is necessarily totally disconnected. The only disconnected example in Figure 5.1 is given by $b = 0.2 + 0.6i$ (see [Gof] for simple proofs of some of these facts; [Bar] contains a more detailed discussion, where the sets are treated as attractors of certain iterated function systems). Note that the figures can be misleading. For example, $\mathcal{B}(0.931i)$ is in fact a solid rectangle. (Exercise: Show that $\mathcal{B}(0.931i)$ is the rectangle consisting of complex numbers whose real part lies in [−3.48 . . . , 3.02 . . .] and whose imaginary part lies in [−3.24 . . . , 3.74 . . .].) The *Mathematica* output is an approximation; as pointed out by Goffinet, the closer the modulus of b is to 1, the less accurate a 15-digit approximation is.

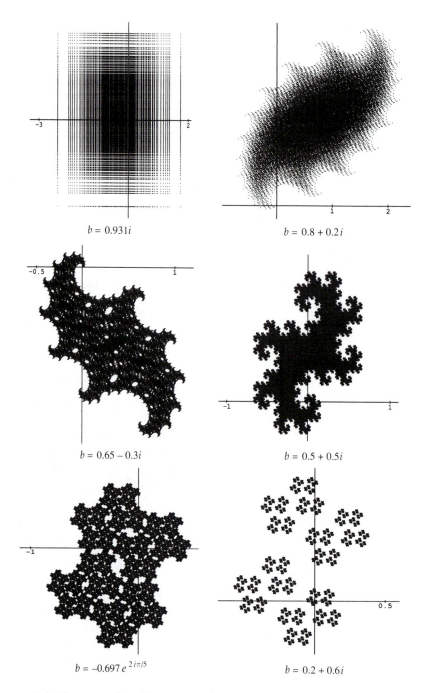

FIGURE 5.1 Six examples illustrating the geometric variety of the sets $\mathcal{B}(b)$. Of the six, only $b = 0.2 + 0.6i$ yields a disconnected set.

As often happens, there are other approaches to generating these images using *Mathematica*. It is usually the case that a program using more built-in functions will run faster. The built-in outer product command, `Outer`, is occasionally useful; this command takes as its arguments a function of n arguments and a sequence of n lists, and then it applies the function to all choices of n-sequences from the lists. As discussed in Chapter 0, the following use of `Outer` will produce all m-sequences of 0s and 1s.

```
m = 3
Flatten[Outer @@ Prepend[Table[{0, 1}, {m}], List],
            m - 1] //MatrixForm
```

```
0   0   0
0   0   1
0   1   0
0   1   1
1   0   0
1   0   1
1   1   0
1   1   1
```

We now form the matrix of real and imaginary parts of powers of b as follows. The powers of b are obtained by using a list as exponent, as was done previously. The entries of this complex vector can be transformed into real and imaginary parts by using `Map` on a pure function.

```
Map[{Re[#], Im[#]} &, b^Range[m]] //MatrixForm
```

```
Re[b]      Im[b]


     2          2
Re[b ]     Im[b ]


     3          3
Re[b ]     Im[b ]
```

The matrix product of the matrix of 0s and 1s with the matrix of real and imaginary parts is precisely the sought-after list of combinations of powers of b, already reduced to real and imaginary parts suitable for showing. As in the earlier approach via Nest and /., complex arithmetic has been kept to a minimum. Thus the following horrible-looking code does the trick, and it is a little bit faster than the first method.

```
FastComplexBase[b_, m_] := Show[Graphics[Point /@
  (Flatten[Outer @@ Prepend[Table[{0., 1.}, {m}], List], m - 1].
     Map[{Re[#], Im[#]} &, b^Range[m]])],
  PlotRange->All, Axes->Automatic, AspectRatio->1]
```

EXERCISE Replace {0., 1.} with {0, 1} and examine the resulting effect on speed.

Although faster programs are generally better, this is not so if the speed comes at the expense of efficient memory use. In fact, Fast-ComplexBase uses much more memory because of the need to store and multiply the large matrices that arise, and it will fail on digit sizes that ComplexBase can handle. One way to keep track of the memory consumption is via the MemoryInUse[] command. For example, one could insert it in the preceding code as follows (new code is italicized) to see how much memory was used at the heart of the computation, and one could similary modify ComplexBase.

```
FastComplexBase[z_, m_] := Show[Graphics[Point /@
 ((temp = -MemoryInUse[];
 Flatten[Outer @@ Prepend[Table[{0., 1.}, {m}], List], m - 1]).
 Map[{Re[#], Im[#]} &, z ^ Range[m]])],
    PlotRange->(Print[temp + MemoryInUse[]]; All),
    Axes->Automatic, AspectRatio->1]
```

For 8-digit sets the fast version uses 45,188 bytes whereas the slower program uses only 24,688 bytes. Thus it is not at all clear that the original approach is inferior. In fact, the code is easier to understand and to produce, and the program runs reasonably efficiently. But one should become familiar with how certain built-in functions are used. Outer is indispensable in certain sorts of computations, where it can save the user from having to program his or her own routine to generate various paths through sequences. The other point is that matrix operations are fast and can sometimes be used to advantage in situations that do not seem to be calling for them. Note one additional advantage of the first approach: It shows clearly the recursive nature of the construction, something that is masked by the second approach's use of built-in operations.

Another important point regarding memory conservation is that writing a large image directly to a file can save a lot of memory. One can open the file and view the image when the kernel is not running if that is necessary. A simple way to do this in the Macintosh environment is as follows, where the code writes the PostScript description of the image, in this case the upper right image in Figure 5.1, to the file **psfile**.

```
$Display = OpenWrite["psfile"]
ComplexBase[.8 + .2 I, 15, {{1, 2}, None},
     {{-.7, 2.5}, {-.2, 2.8}}];
Close["psfile"]
$Display = "stdout";
```

The commands before and after `ComplexBase[]` set the default display device to be the file *psfile*; after the image is produced, the file is closed and the default display is reset to the standard output device, for which *Mathematica*'s abbreviation is `"stdout"`. After execution, **psfile** can be opened, but only pages of PostScript will be visible. Select the cell, turn it into a PostScript cell via the Cell menu, and then format the cell (Graph menu), and the image will appear.

5.2 Iterated Function Systems

The book by Michael Barnsley [Bar] gives an extensive treatment of fractal images, both real and complex, using the *Iterated Function System* (IFS) point of view. As an introduction to the concept of an IFS, we'll study what has become known as the *Chaos Game*. Start with an equilateral triangle in the plane—let's use the triangle with vertices at (0, 0), (1, 0), and (0.5, $\sqrt{3}/2$)—and label the vertices 1, 2, and 3. Then pick an arbitrary point P_0 in the plane and define a sequence of points $\{P_n\}$ as follows: Start at P_0; then choose one of the triangle's vertices at random and let P_1 be the point halfway between P_0 and the chosen vertex; then again randomly choose one of the three vertices and let P_2 be the point halfway between P_1 and the chosen vertex. Continuing in this way yields an infinite sequence $\{P_n\}$. This process is called the Chaos Game because of the apparent patternless movement of the point, at least when one plots

10 or 20 points by hand. See Figure 5.2, where the points are connected by lines, and the point size is continually reduced so that the progression can be followed.

Note the difference between *Mathematica* and traditional programming languages, such as BASIC. If this process were programmed in BASIC, then each new point would appear on the screen as it was computed, which would give a nice feel for the apparently random movement of the point. *Mathematica* first generates the entire PostScript code and then displays it all, so one does not get to see the successive positions of the point. One can still illustrate the movement, at least in the case of small sets of points, by either an animation or by labelling the points in some way, as is done in Figure 5.2.

To program the Chaos Game, observe that the procedure defines P_{n+1} to be $(P_n + V)/2$ where V is a random vertex. This leads to the following code, which uses NestList to generate the first n points. The function being nested, f, is defined to be a random choice of functions, one for each vertex. Figure 5.3 shows two runs of 5000 points, and, somewhat surprisingly, a clear pattern emerges. It looks as if the sequence is attracted to the Sierpiński triangle, introduced in Chapter 4.

```
top = {.5, Sqrt[3.]/2}
f1[x_] := .5 x; f2[x_] := .5(x + {1,0}); f3[x_] := .5(x + top)
f[x_] := {f1,f2,f3}[[Random[Integer, {1,3}]]][x]

ChaosGame[start_, n_] :=
Show[Graphics[Map[Point, NestList[f, start, n]]],
    PlotRange->{{0, 1}, {0, .87}}, Axes->Automatic,
    AspectRatio->.87,
    Ticks->{{.25, .5, .75, 1}, {.25, .5, .75}}]

ChaosGame[{.1, .8}, 3^8]
ChaosGame[{.4, .3}, 3^8]
```

It is in fact the case that for any starting point, the sequence converges to the Sierpiński triangle. Well, not exactly. First one must ignore the first 10 or so points, whose positions do depend strongly on P_0. Second, this is a statement about probabilities. After all, if the same vertex is chosen repeatedly (not a true random choice), the points will all lie on a straight

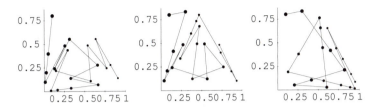

FIGURE 5.2 Three runs of the Chaos Game starting from the point (0.1, 0.8) and using the equilateral triangle with vertices at (0, 0), (1, 0), and (0.5, $\sqrt{3}/2$).

line. The correct statement is that the convergence occurs with probability 1. Finally, we must be sure to differentiate between the actual Sierpiński triangle and the approximations. In fact, none of the points will really lie on the Sierpiński triangle unless P_0 does. (Exercise: Prove this.) What we are seeing in Figure 5.3 are points that are indistinguishable from points on the Sierpiński triangle. Exercise: Modify `ChaosGame` so that it produces the images in Figure 5.2.

More insight can be gained by putting randomness aside and looking at *all* possible choices of vertices. That is, define a function f that acts on subsets of the plane as follows: $f(A) = f_1(A) \cup f_2(A) \cup f_3(A)$, where f_1, f_2, and f_3, correspond to the functions preceding the definition of

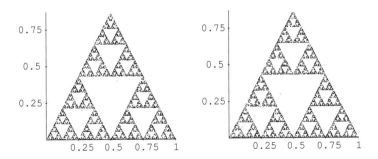

FIGURE 5.3 Two plays of the Chaos Game, one starting from (0.1, 0.8), the other from (0.3, 0.4), and each having length 3^8 (6,561). Surprisingly, this process, exclusive of the first 10 points, always yields the Sierpiński triangle.

ChaosGame. Now define a sequence of sets by choosing P_0 as before to be any point, letting A_0 be $\{P_0\}$, and setting A_{n+1} to be $f(A_n)$; this defines the sequence $\{A_n\}$. This is called the *deterministic algorithm* (as opposed to the *random algorithm* of ChaosGame) and can be coded as follows. We define f[A] to be the union of the three functions on A, using pure functions to speed things up and simplifying the first function to simply 0.5 A.

```
Clear[f];  f[A_] :=
0.5 Union[A, Map[# + {1,0} &, A], Map[# + {.5,Sqrt[3.]/2} &, A]]
```

```
ChaosGameDeterministic[start_, n_] := Show[Graphics[Map[Point,
    Nest[f, {start}, n]]],
    PlotRange->{{0,1}, {0,.87}}, Axes->Automatic,
    AspectRatio->.87, Ticks->{{.25,.5,.75,1}, {.25,.5,.75,1}}]
```

```
Do[ChaosGameDeterministic[{.1, .8}, i], {i, 0, 8}]
```

Figure 5.4 shows that the iterations of f converge to the same limit as does the random algorithm, but in a deterministic way. In fact, the convergence can be nicely illustrated by animating the images in Figure 5.4. The theoretical underpinnings of the deterministic method are given in Barnsley's book [Bar, §3.7, Thm. 1], where it is proved that whenever W is a set of finitely many contractions[1] of the plane and a function f on subsets of the plane is defined by setting $f(A)$ to be $\cup\{h(A) : h \in W\}$, then there is a unique *attractor* for f, meaning a unique closed and bounded set A such that $f(A) = A$. Moreover, starting with *any* closed and bounded set and iterating f on it yields a sequence of sets that converges[2] to the unique attractor. Often the contractions are *affine transformations*, that is, functions of the form $f(P) = LP + V$ where L is a 2×2 matrix and V is a vector.

---

[1]A *contraction* is a function f such that there is a constant $s < 1$ so that for any pair of distinct points P and Q, the distance between $f(P)$ and $f(Q)$ is at most s times the distance between P and Q. Note that a function f can always be viewed as a transformation of subsets of its domain via $f(A) = \{f(P) : P \in A\}$.

[2]Here convergence means convergence in the Hausdorff metric on compact sets; see [Bar].

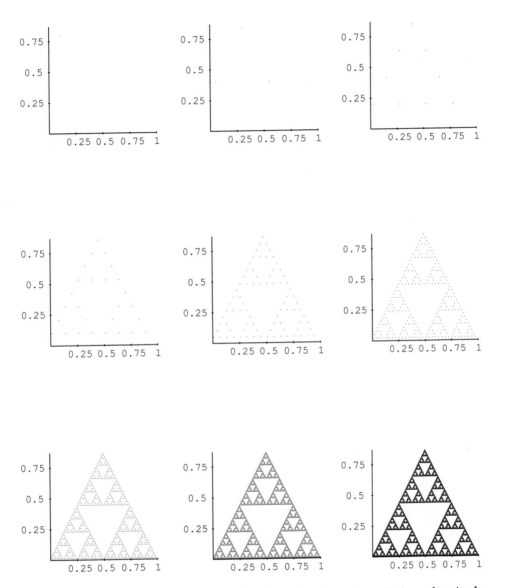

FIGURE 5.4 Repeatedly applying the function f to the set consisting of a single point yields a sequence of sets that converges to the Sierpiński triangle. The final image has $3^8 = 6,561$ points.

Why should the random approach yield a sequence that also converges to the attractor? Here's an explanation due to Gerald Goodman of the University of Florence. Note first that the three functions f_1, f_2, and f_3 are contractions with contractivity factor 0.5; that is, the distance between $f_i(P)$ and $f_i(Q)$ is at most one-half the distance between P and Q (in this case the distance is exactly halved). Now, let g be a random composition of 10 of the functions, say $g = f_1 \circ f_1 \circ f_2 \circ f_3 \circ f_3 \circ f_1 \circ f_3 \circ f_2 \circ f_2 \circ f_1$. It is easy to see that for any points P and Q, the distance between $g(P)$ and $g(Q)$ is 2^{-10} of the distance between P and Q. In particular, if P and Q both lie in the unit square, then $g(P)$ and $g(Q)$ are within $\sqrt{2}\ 2^{-10}$, or approximately $1/724$, of each other; as far as pixels on a computer screen go, this means that the same pixel will be hit by $g(P)$, *for any point P in the unit square*. This, in turn, means that to hit all the correct pixels of the limiting set, one need only consider all 3^{10} possibilities for a string of 10 functions. This is essentially what would be accomplished by running the deterministic version to 10 iterations (59,049 points).

But consider the random sequence of 5,000 compositions used in the random approach of `ChaosGame`. If it has the form $\cdots \circ f_1 \circ f_1 \circ f_2 \circ f_1 \circ f_3 \circ f_1 \circ f_2 \circ f_2 \circ f_1 \circ f_3 \circ f_3 \circ f_2 \circ f_3 \circ f_1$, then the tenth point will be a correct pixel, the one corresponding to $f_3 \circ f_1 \circ f_2 \circ f_2 \circ f_1 \circ f_3 \circ f_3 \circ f_2 \circ f_3 \circ f_1(P_0)$; and the eleventh point, which is $f_1 \circ f_3 \circ f_1 \circ f_2 \circ f_2 \circ f_1 \circ f_3 \circ f_3 \circ f_2 \circ f_3(f_1(P_0))$ will also be a correct pixel, the one corresponding to the 10-string $f_1 \circ f_3 \circ f_1 \circ f_2 \circ f_2 \circ f_1 \circ f_3 \circ f_3 \circ f_2 \circ f_3$; and so on. In other words, in any long string of functions, only the last 10 (i.e., leftmost 10) matter as far as accuracy to the nearest pixel is concerned. Therefore, except for the first 10 points, the rest will all yield correct pixels. Again, we point out that unless the starting point happens to lie on the attractor, none of the ideal, full-precision versions of these points actually belongs to the limiting set. But to the accuracy of the computer screen, they do! A random string of 5,000 functions chosen from $\{f_1, f_2, f_3\}$ will generate 4,991 consecutive substrings of length 10. If all these 10-strings were different, this would yield 4,991 correct pixels of the limit object. Although there is almost surely some repetition among these 10-strings, a long enough random string will contain all possible 10-strings among its consecutive substrings and so will hit all the correct pixels. Exercise: Use the following routine to generate a table that gives the number of distinct 10-strings in an

n-string of random 0s, 1s, and 2s. What happens to the ratio of distinct 10-strings to total number of 10-strings as the length of the random string increases?

```
distinctsubstrings[n_] := Length[Union[Partition[
  Table[Random[Integer, {1, 3}], {n}], 10, 1]]]
```

In the case of simple attractors where the contractivity constants are not too close to 1, such as the Chaos Game example, both the deterministic and random approaches work reasonably well in generating the attractor. As pointed out earlier, there are important differences between *Mathematica* and the traditional microcomputer programming environment. In the traditional environment, each point is drawn on the screen as it is generated, and so there is no need to store all the points in memory. Thus the random method for generating an image having 10,000 or more points requires very little memory. The deterministic approach must keep track of the entire current level of the tree, which requires a lot of memory. But *Mathematica* generates the complete PostScript description of an image before drawing it on the screen. This means that in *Mathematica*, a 10,000-point image will require a lot of memory independent of the means used to generate it. But there are many virtues in having a PostScript image: (1) it can be resized; (2) certain primitives, such as the point size, can be changed without having to rerun the graphics-generating program; (3) the PostScript code yields high-resolution images on printers ranging from a desktop laser printer to a commercial typesetting machine. Nevertheless, the random approach is much better for generating attractors in general, as will be discussed in the next section.

EXERCISE (Gerald Goodman): Play the Chaos Game with 3^8 points, but instead of making random choices, make quasi-random choices, which guarantee that *all possible 8-substrings* occur. This can be done by the use of *universal sequences*. Such a sequence can be generated very quickly by a simple linear recurrence. In the case at hand, the following rule will generate 3^8 0s, 1s, and 2s in such a way that there are no duplications among the consecutive substrings of length 8. Start with the sequence $(s_0, \ldots, s_8) = (0, 0, 0, 0, 0, 0, 0, 0, 1)$, and apply the recurrence $s_{n+8} \equiv s_n + 2s_{n+5} \pmod 3$, for $n = 1, 2, \ldots, 3^8 - 2$. More information on such universal recurrences, including tables for parameters other than 3 and 8, can be found in [LN, Chaps. 8, 10, App. F]. The resulting image (Figure 5.5; the generating program is in the Appendix) will have fewer duplications than when the standard algorithm is used.

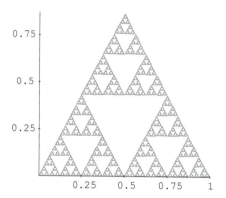

FIGURE 5.5 Using $3^8(= 6{,}561)$ quasi-random choices forces the appearance of all 8-strings of 0s, 1s, and 2s. The resulting Sierpiński triangle is more highly resolved than in the traditional approach as there are fewer duplications among the pixels that are hit.

5.3 Biasing the Chaos Game: Barnsley's Fern ▪

In the preceding section we pointed out that from the point of view of memory requirements, the deterministic and the random methods of generating an attractor for an IFS are comparable. There are, nevertheless, important advantages to the random approach. In particular, we can assign nonuniform probabilities to the different choices at each step. For example, if in the Chaos Game the choice of vertex (that is, the choice of one of f_1, f_2, or f_3) is biased so that f_3 is chosen with probability $8/10$ while the other two are chosen with probability $1/10$ each, then, although there is no change in the final image after infinitely many points—it will still be the Sierpiński triangle—there is an important change in how this image is approached. If A denotes the full Sierpiński triangle, then points will be more likely to lie in $f_3(A)$ than in $f_1(A)$ or $f_2(A)$ [recall that $A = f_1(A) \cup f_2(A) \cup f_3(A)$]. Moreover, points will be more likely to lie in $f_3 f_1(A)$ than in $f_1 f_1(A)$ or $f_2 f_1(A)$. And this occurs at each level: every small triangle A_0 in A will receive points in a way that is biased toward its upper part, that is, toward $f_3(A_0)$. See Figures 5.6(a), (b), and (c), which were generated by variations on the following code, using 10,000 points and starting at (0, 0). A random integer and the Which command are used to generate the probabilities.

```
Clear[f];  top = {.5, Sqrt[3.]/2}
f1[x_] := .5x
f2[x_] := .5(x + {1,0})
f3[x_] := .5(x + top)
f[x_] := Which[(r = Random[Integer,{1,4}]) <= 2, f3[x],
                r == 3, f1[x], r == 4, f2[x]]


BiasedChaosGame[start_, n_] :=
    Show[Graphics[Map[Point, NestList[f, start, n]],
    PlotRange->{{0, 1}, {0, .87}}, AspectRatio->.87]]
```

The use of nonuniform probabilities causes the attractor to be formed in a way that visits some regions to a deep level of the corresponding tree, whereas others are visited only shallowly. (Exercise: Generate close-ups similar to those in Figures 5.6 (b) and (c), but near the origin rather than the top of the triangle.) This can be extremely useful when an IFS converges slowly toward its attractor. We give one example, Barnsley's famous fern (Figure 5.7), which is the attractor of the following set of four affine transformations, which we call the *fern functions*.

$$f_1(x, y) = \begin{pmatrix} 0.85 & 0.04 \\ -0.04 & 0.85 \end{pmatrix} \begin{pmatrix} x \\ y \end{pmatrix} + \begin{pmatrix} 0 \\ 1.6 \end{pmatrix}$$

$$f_2(x, y) = \begin{pmatrix} -0.15 & 0.28 \\ 0.26 & 0.24 \end{pmatrix} \begin{pmatrix} x \\ y \end{pmatrix} + \begin{pmatrix} 0 \\ 0.44 \end{pmatrix}$$

$$f_3(x, y) = \begin{pmatrix} 0.2 & -0.26 \\ 0.23 & 0.22 \end{pmatrix} \begin{pmatrix} x \\ y \end{pmatrix} + \begin{pmatrix} 0 \\ 1.6 \end{pmatrix}$$

$$f_4(x, y) = \begin{pmatrix} 0 & 0 \\ 0 & 0.16 \end{pmatrix} \begin{pmatrix} x \\ y \end{pmatrix}$$

It is not immediately evident that these four affine functions are contractions. Let's use the notation $||v||$ for the usual norm in the plane; $||v||$ is simply the Euclidean length of the vector v, and $||v - w||$ is the distance between the endpoints of the vectors v and w. The *norm of a linear transformation* T is defined to be the maximum value of $||T(v)||/||v||$ over all nonzero vectors v. Equivalently, the norm of T is the maximum of

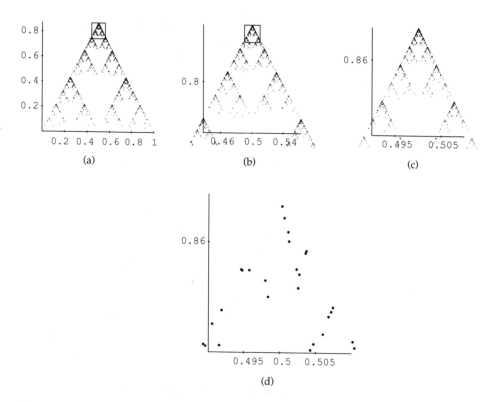

FIGURE 5.6 An eightfold bias of the choices in the Chaos Game toward the top yields an image (a) for which the bias makes itself felt in every small triangle. The close-up views in (b) and (c) show that at least toward the top, this biasing causes the point to visit deeper levels of the attractor; there are at least ten inverted triangles visible as one proceeds upward. In the hundredfold magnification of 10,000 points of the unbiased Chaos Game (d), no triangles are visible.

$||T(u)||$ where u is a unit vector. We will use $||T||$ to denote the norm of T. Now, a general property of norms is that $||T(v)|| \leq ||T||||v||$; this means that $||T(v) - T(w)|| = ||T(v - w)|| \leq ||T||||v - w||$. It follows that a linear transformation is a contraction if and only if its norm is less than 1; moreover, the smallest s for which the transformation contracts by a factor of s is the norm of the transformation. The additional translation in an affine transformation does not affect the contractivity factor. Therefore,

FIGURE 5.7 The random iteration algorithm on the IFS $\{f_1, f_2, f_3, f_4\}$, with nonuniform probabilities underlying the choices of the four functions at each step, yields a good approximation to the fern-like attractor.

we can show that the four fern functions are contractions by determining the norms of the matrices of their linear parts. A result of linear algebra states that the norm of a square matrix A is simply the square root of the largest eigenvalue of the symmetric matrix $A^T A$; this matrix, being symmetric and positive definite, has only positive real eigenvalues (see [Str, §§6.2, 7.2]). Thus the following routine computes matrix norms.

```
MatrixNorm[A_] := Max[Sqrt[Eigenvalues[Transpose[A] . A]]]
```

Now, we can show that the fern functions are contractions by computing the norms of their linear parts. Moreover, this approach will give the smallest possible value of the contractivity factor.

```
{A1, A2, A3, A4} = {   {{.85,    .04}, {-.04, .85}},
                       {{-.15,   .28}, { .26, .24}},
                       {{0.2,   -.26}, { .23, .22}},
                       {{0,       0 }, { 0,   .16}} };


Map[MatrixNorm, {A1, A2, A3, A4}]
   {0.850941, 0.379152, 0.340712, 0.16}
```

An affine contraction taking v to $Lv + b$ must have a unique fixed point, because the matrix $L - I$ is nonsingular; moreover, iterating the transformation on any starting value yields a sequence that converges to the fixed point. We can easily find the fixed points in the case of the fern functions as follows. Of course, f_4 is especially simple: it maps any point (x, y) to the point $(0, 0.16y)$ on the y-axis and has the origin as its fixed point.

```
{fixed1, fixed2, fixed3, fixed4} = {
          Inverse[A1 - IdentityMatrix[2]] . {0, -1.6 },
          Inverse[A2 - IdentityMatrix[2]] . {0,  -.44},
          Inverse[A3 - IdentityMatrix[2]] . {0, -1.6 },
          Inverse[A4 - IdentityMatrix[2]] . {0,   0 }  }
{{2.6556, 9.95851}, {0.153769, 0.631553}, {-0.608365, 1.87189},
    {0, 0}}
```

Before discussing the fern functions at greater length, we present their attractor, using code that is similar to the code for the biased Chaos Game. One difference that speeds things up is that the function being nested is defined as a pure function within the scope of NestList. The probabilities for the four functions are 0.85, 0.7, 0.7, and 0.01, which were found by Barnsley to yield an attractive image, one that, in fact, looks very much like a black spleenwort fern. The order of the functions is chosen so that Which will, 85% of the time, find the true statement in its first argument. The 38,000-point image in Figure 5.7 uses more points than my Macintosh could deal with at one time; it was formed by combining two runs of the program by merging the PostScript output. First the graphics cells must be unformatted (Cell menu); then the PostScript code must be merged (Edit menu) and reformatted.

```
BarnsleyFern[n_] :=
  Show[Graphics[Map[Point, NestList[
   Which[
    (r = Random[Integer, {1,100}]) <= 85,  A1.# + {0, 1.6},
                          r <= 92,  A2.# + {0, .44},
                          r <= 99,  A3.# + {0, 1.6},
                          r == 100, A4.# ] &,
      {0,0}, n]],      PlotRange->All]]
```

```
BarnsleyFern[28000]
BarnsleyFern[10000]
```

The tip of the fern is the fixed point of f_1, which is therefore a function that attracts toward the tip. The tips of the lowest two branches are the images of the main tip under f_2 and f_3. We can illustrate the action of these transformations by nesting them on certain regions. For example, Figure 5.8(a) shows the result of 10 iterations of f_1 on the quadrilateral formed by the main tip, the tips of the lowermost two branches, and the origin. The slowness of convergence is evident, as 11 copies of the region are clearly visible. (Exercise: Generate a similar sequence for one of the three functions of the Chaos Game.) It is this slowness of attraction of f_1—recall that its contractivity factor was 0.851—that makes either the deterministic or unbiased random methods poor generators of the attractor. The nonuniform approach forces the appearance of many f_1's in the strings that generate the points; this yields points at high levels of the tree toward the tip, that is, points in h(fern) where h is the composition of 10 or more f_1's. For example, 20% of the points (0.85^{10}) occur in the 10th iterate of f_1 on the fern, that is, outside of the bottom 20 side branches. The action of f_2 on a quadrilateral and on the main stem is illustrated in Figure 5.8(b). As with the Chaos Game, this bias is felt in every region, and therefore the entire fern and the various copies of the fern on the branches all have lots of branches. Exercise: Compare Figure 5.7 with an unbiased version of this attractor using 10,000 or more points.

The following code generated Figure 5.8. The If-clause (via /;) in the first line of each function definition guarantees that the first case will not apply to arguments that are lists of points. The argument specification in the second line of each definition, set:{_List..}, covers the case where the function is to apply to a set of points. The double dot refers to possible repetitions; thus the pattern being matched is that of a list consisting of one or more lists.

```
Clear[f1, f2, f3, f4]
f1[{x_, y_}]        := A1.{x,y} + {0, 1.6} /; Length[x] != 2
f1[set:{_List..}] := Map[f1, set]

f2[{x_,y_}]         := A2.{x,y} + {0, .44} /; Length[x] != 2
f2[set:{_List..}] := Map[f2, set]
```

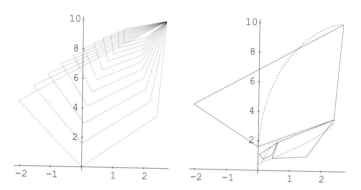

FIGURE 5.8 (a) The contraction f_1 attracts points at a relatively slow rate. It maps the entire fern in Figure 5.7 onto the fern with the lowest two branches and the lowest part of the stem removed. (b) The contraction f_2 transforms the entire fern to the branch on the lower right; it shrinks, narrows, and flips.

```
f3[{x_,y_}]        := A3.{x,y} + {0, 1.6}/;  Length[x] != 2
f3[set:{_List..}]  := Map[f3, set]


f4[{x_,y_}]        := A4.{x,y}/; Length[x] != 2
f4[set:{_List..}]  := Map[f4, set]


region = {fixed1, f2[fixed1], {0,0}, f3[fixed1], fixed1}
Show[Graphics[Map[Line, NestList[f1, region, 10]]],
AspectRatio->1, Axes->Automatic];


region1 = {fixed1, f2[fixed1], f4[fixed1], f3[fixed1], fixed1}
spine = NestList[f1, {0,0}, 35]
Show[Graphics[{
    Thickness[.001], Map[Line, NestList[f2, region1, 2]],
    Dashing[{.01}], Map[Line, NestList[f2,  spine,2]]}],
AspectRatio->1, Axes->Automatic]
```

The generation of a fern from such little information—the functions and probabilities require only 28 real numbers to specify them exactly—is perhaps not that surprising, since a fern has evident self-similarity. But Barnsley and his associates have carried this idea much farther, to the point where color photographs that show no evident self-similarity can be coded as the attractor of an IFS consisting of one or two hundred affine transformations. Their procedures are capable of compressing images that would ordinarily require, say, a million bytes of storage into 2,000 bytes—a development that has important application in the electronic storage and transmission of photographs. For some striking examples of color photographs coded as IFS attractors, as well as more theoretical details about IFS attractors, see [Bar].

EXERCISE Show that for a fixed complex number b of absolute value less than 1, the two transformations of $\mathbb{C}$ given by the functions bz and $b(z + 1)$ are contractions. Show that the attractor of these two functions is just the set $\mathcal{B}(b)$ defined in the first section of this chapter. Generate some of the sets of Figure 5.1 using the methods, unbiased and biased, of this section.

5.4 Julia Sets

A very active area of current mathematical research, one that uses computations both as a means of discovery and an aid to proof, is the area of complex dynamical systems, or iteration of complex functions. The section on the quadratic map in Chapter 4 presented a glimpse into the area of iteration of real functions. Here we look at analogous ideas for complex functions. Recall from Chapter 4 that for the real quadratic function $f_r(x) = rx(1 - x)$, the possible orbit behaviors of a starting value are: (1) the orbit could converge to a fixed point or a periodic cycle; (2) the orbit could diverge to infinity; (3) the orbit could remain bounded without convergence (in these cases the quadratic function is chaotic).

In this section we'll consider the complex function $Q_c(z) = z^2 + c$ where c is a fixed complex parameter. The family of real maps $\{Q_c(x) : c \in \mathbb{R}\}$ has the same dynamics (that is, orbit behavior) as the family $\{f_r : r \in \mathbb{R}\}$ studied in Chapter 4. As some experimentation will show, orbits of complex starting values can show the same three types of behavior as the real quadratic map. In fact, we can plot orbits in a way similar to the use of `Trajectory` in Chapter 4. `ComplexTrajectory` displays n iterates of Q_c with starting value `z` and starting iterate number `init` (default for `init` is 0). The `If` statement involving `Precision`

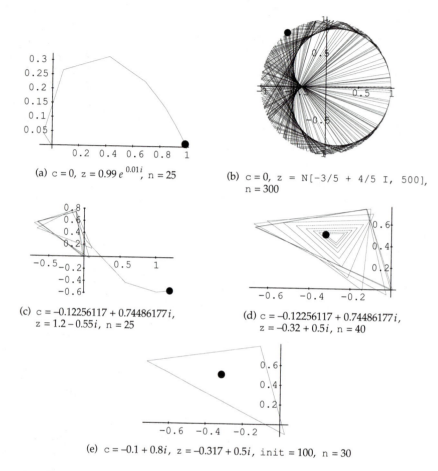

(a) $c = 0$, $z = 0.99\, e^{0.01i}$, n = 25

(b) $c = 0$, z = N[−3/5 + 4/5 I, 500], n = 300

(c) $c = -0.12256117 + 0.74486177i$, $z = 1.2 - 0.55i$, n = 25

(d) $c = -0.12256117 + 0.74486177i$, $z = -0.32 + 0.5i$, n = 40

(e) $c = -0.1 + 0.8i$, $z = -0.317 + 0.5i$, init = 100, n = 30

FIGURE 5.9 Some samples of bounded orbits of Q_c. Illustrated are: (a) rapid convergence to a fixed point at the origin; (b) infinite wandering around the unit circle; (c)–(e) convergence to a 3-cycle; (f)–(h) convergence to an 11-cycle; (i)–(j) behavior similar to the wandering about a curve illustrated in (b), but in this case the wandering is retained arbitrarily close to the fixed point inside the curve, an example of what is known as a *Siegel disk*.

serves two purposes: (1) If **z** is entered as a symbolic value, such as 2 + 3**I**, then the corresponding floating-point value is fed to Nest. (2) If **z**

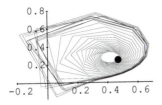

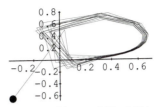

(f) $c = 0.32 + 0.043i$, $z = 0.47 + 0.25i$, $n = 300$ (g) $c = 0.32 + 0.043i$, $z = -0.36 - 0.64i$, $n = 150$

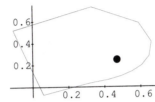

(h) $c = 0.32 + 0.043i$, $z = 0.47 + 0.25i$, $\text{init} = 800$, $n = 25$

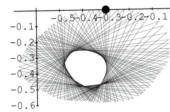

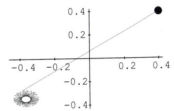

(i) $c = -0.390541 - 0.586788i$, $z = -0.3$, $n = 100$ (j) $c = -0.4 - 0.4i$, $z = -0.2 + 0.15i$, $n = 30$

FIGURE 5.9 (cont.)

is entered as a high-precision complex number (which will be necessary for some of the examples that follow), then that precision is retained.

```
ComplexTrajectory[z_, c_, init_:0, n_] :=
Show[Graphics[{PointSize[.025],
    Point[{Re[z],Im[z]}], Thickness[.0001],
    Line[Map[{Re[#],Im[#]} &,
    NestList[#^2 + c &,
            Nest[#^2+c &,
                If[Precision[z] < Infinity, z, N[z]], init],
            n]]]}],
    PlotRange->All, Axes->Automatic]
```

Figure 5.9 shows several examples of the sorts of bounded orbits that can occur, all of which are generated by `ComplexTrajectory[z, c, n]`, with an argument for the optional `init` in cases (e) and (h). Note the use of a high-precision argument (500 digits) in Figure 5.9(b), which causes the entire computation to be done using 500-digit accuracy. Exercise: What happens in (b) if `z` is set to be simply `-0.6 + .8 I`?

EXERCISE Experiment further with the c values used in Figure 5.9. In particular, try the Siegel disk example (Figure 5.9(i) and (j)) with a large value of `init`. Use `Solve` to find the fixed points in this example and try starting values near the fixed point.

EXERCISE Note the cardioid that apparently occurs as an envelope of the lines in Figure 5.9(b). This arises because the envelope of the set of lines connecting $e^{i\theta}$ and $e^{i2\theta}$ as θ varies from 0 to $\pi/2$ is the cardioid given in the form of a parametric curve in $\mathbb{R}^2$ by $(-1/3, 0) + 2/3(1 - \cos t)(-\cos t, \sin t)$. Prove this.

A more global understanding of these orbits arises from the notion of a Julia set. Let $\text{Orbit}_c(z)$ denote the orbit of z under Q_c, that is, the set $\{Q_c(z), Q_c(Q_c(z)), Q_c(Q_c(Q_c(z))), \ldots\}$. Note that there are always values of z such that $\text{Orbit}_c(z)$ diverges to infinity; just let the starting value be much greater than c. The *Julia set* of Q_c (named after Gaston Julia) is defined to be the boundary of the set of z such that $\text{Orbit}_c(z)$ diverges to infinity. It turns out that this set is the same as the boundary of the set of z such that $\text{Orbit}_c(z)$ is bounded. Thus the Julia set separates the region of infinite dynamics from the region of bounded dynamics. This leads to the *filled-in Julia set*, which consists of all points z such that $\text{Orbit}_c(z)$ is bounded. The boundary of the filled-in Julia set is the Julia set. For more details on these definitions and the entire theory of Julia sets and of the Mandelbrot set, which serves as a catalog of all the Julia sets of Q_c, see [Dev1, Dev2, DK]. The simplest example is when $c = 0$. In this case, as can be easily verified, $\text{Orbit}(z)$ converges to 0 if $|z| < 1$ and diverges to infinity if $|z| > 1$. If $|z| = 1$, that is, if z lies on the unit circle, then $\text{Orbit}(z)$ is entirely contained within the unit circle (and, in fact, the behavior of Q_c on the unit circle is chaotic). Thus the Julia set is just the unit circle and the filled-in Julia set is the unit disk. Figure 5.10 shows the filled-in Julia set in gray, with a sampling of orbits superimposed on it; starting values inside the disk (white) have orbits that converge to the origin, whereas orbits that start outside the disk (black) diverge to infinity.

EXERCISE Use *Mathematica* to generate Figure 5.10.

The changing trajectories in the $c = 0$ case can be illustrated by an animation in which the starting values move. For example, one can move the starting value from $-0.5 + 0.8i$ to $-0.7 + 0.8i$ in steps of 0.01 (or

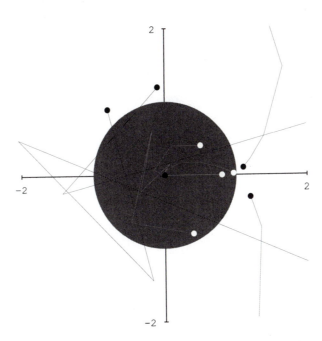

FIGURE 5.10 The Julia set of the function z^2 is just the unit circle. Points inside the circle have orbits (white) that converge to the fixed point 0; points outside the circle have orbits (black) that diverge to infinity. The behavior of the orbits on the circle is chaotic. There is a fixed point ($z = 1$) and periodic orbits (e.g., $z = \pm i$), but these are repelling and most orbits are nonconvergent, as shown in Figure 5.9(b).

smaller). The division between converging and diverging orbits occurs at $-0.5 + 0.6i$, which is the case illustrated in Figure 5.9(b).

EXERCISE Generate such an animation, treating the point on the unit circle as a special case for which 50 or 100 line segments are drawn. The optimal number of orbit segments to display depends on how close the absolute value of the starting value is to 1. Generate similar animations for other values of c.

For nonzero values of c the Julia set can be exceedingly complicated. There is a straightforward algorithm to generate the filled-in Julia set for Q_c, but such images are very time consuming to generate, so we postpone that discussion. We will first show how to generate the (unfilled) Julia sets; this can be done relatively quickly and yields a rough idea of what the set looks like and where it lies in the complex plane. The simplest algorithm relies on the fact that the Julia set for Q_c is an attractor of an iterated function system (see [Bar, §7.1] for a proof). That is, we consider the IFS consisting of the two functions $\sqrt{z - c}$ and $-\sqrt{z - c}$, which are just the functions inverse to Q_c, and generate the attractor using techniques discussed earlier in this chapter. The choice of a starting value is immaterial except for one case: if $c = 0$, the starting value 0 will not generate the Julia set. In general, we may choose any starting value and use either the deterministic algorithm or the random algorithm, both of which are discussed in the section on the Chaos Game earlier in this chapter.

We will focus on the random algorithm, where a random choice of the two square roots is made at each step. This method for generating Julia sets is called the *Inverse Iteration Method (IIM)*. It is implemented in the code that follows, which takes advantage of the fact that a complex number z lies in a Julia set of Q_c if and only if $-z$ does, by having Map produce two points rather than just one. Because it takes a dozen or so iterations before the points lie sufficiently close to the Julia set, we discard the first 50 iterations via Drop. The default range for Random is {0, 1}.

```
JuliaIIM[c_, n_] := Show[Graphics[
  Map[{Point[{Re[#], Im[#]}], Point[-{Re[#], Im[#]}]} &,
    Drop[NestList[If[Random[Integer] == 1, 1, -1] Sqrt[# - c] &,
      0.2, n + 50], 50]]]]
```

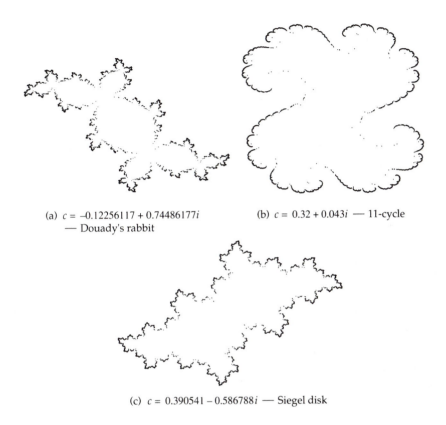

(a) $c = -0.12256117 + 0.74486177i$
— Douady's rabbit

(b) $c = 0.32 + 0.043i$ — 11-cycle

(c) $c = 0.390541 - 0.586788i$ — Siegel disk

FIGURE 5.11 Three 28,000-point Julia sets generated by `JuliaIIM[c, 14000]`. Fine detail is missing, but the variety and beauty of Julia sets are apparent.

Figure 5.11 shows several 28,000-point Julia sets obtained by the Inverse Iteration Method, all generated by `JuliaIIM[c, 14000]`. Figure 5.11(a) is the Julia set, known as Douady's rabbit, for the function with an attracting 3-cycle shown in Figure 5.9; in fact, this is an example of a superattracting cycle (see [DK, pp. 61, 78]). Figure 5.11(b) is the Julia set for the function with an attracting 11-cycle shown in Figure 5.9. And Figure 5.11(c) is an example of a Julia set having a Siegel disk structure, by which is meant a fixed point such that nearby orbits wander forever on a curve surrounding the fixed point (Figure 5.9(i) and (j)). As with Barnsley's fern, certain areas of the Julia sets are visited very seldom by the IIM algorithm. Thus the images in Figure 5.11 have some gaps and are missing fine detail (compare with Figure 5.15, which shows fine images of filled-in Julia sets).

Mathematica's 3-dimensional capabilities can be used to generate a histogram that shows how often certain pixels are visited. First we need a way to get at the pixels. One approach is to truncate each point to the nearest $1/600$, which corresponds roughly to rounding to the nearest pixel. This is done by the following function, which works on both complex and real numbers.

```
chop[z_] := (Round[600 Re[z]] + I Round[600 Im[z]]) / 600.
Attributes[chop] = Listable

chop[.75024652465 + .15146426I]
0.75 + 0.151667 I
```

A function that counts the numbers of occurrences of a number in a set is built in as `Count[set, x]`, and so we can move directly to the histogram-generating program. The idea is to round all the points in the Julia set generated by the IIM method to the nearest $1/600$ and then erect a line above each point; the line's length is the number of times that the point is generated. This can be done by using `Count` and `chop` as follows.

```
JuliaIIMHistogram[c_, n_] := Show[Graphics3D[Map[
    Line[{{Re[#], Im[#], 1}, {Re[#], Im[#], Count[temp, #]}}] &,
    Union[temp = chop@Drop[NestList[
      If[Random[Integer] == 1, 1, -1]  Sqrt[# - c] &, .2, n+40],
                          40]]]],
    Boxed->False, BoxRatios->{1,1,1/3}, PlotRange->All]

JuliaIIMHistogram[-0.1 + 0.8 I, 10000];
```

EXERCISE Modify `JuliaIIMHistogram` so that it prints out the number of distinct points generated and the maximum frequency.

EXERCISE Generate histograms for other values of c.

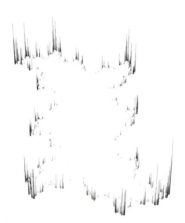

FIGURE 5.12 A histogram based on 10,000 points, with each real and imaginary part rounded to the nearest $\frac{1}{600}$, shows the tendency of the Inverse Iteration Method to bunch up in certain regions of the Julia set and avoid other regions. The 10,000 iterations yielded only 4,218 different points; the largest number of times a point occurred was 37. One way to get a more detailed view of a Julia set is to generate the filled-in Julia set (see Figure 5.15).

We can now return to the real quadratic map studied in Chapter 4 and examine some of the corresponding Julia sets. To fit things in with the system used in Chapter 4, that is with $rx(1-x)$ rather than $x^2 + c$, we must rewrite JuliaIIM slightly, using the appropriate inverse functions $\frac{1}{2} \pm \sqrt{\frac{1}{4} - z/r}$.

```
JuliaIIMf[r_, n_] := Show[Graphics[
    Map[{Point[{Re[#],   Im[#]}], Point[{Re[#],   -Im[#]}],
         Point[{1-Re[#], Im[#]}], Point[{1-Re[#], -Im[#]}]} &,
      Drop[NestList[.5 + If[Random[Integer]==1, 1, -1] *
                    Sqrt[.25 - #/r] &,  0.2, n + 50], 50]]],
    Axes->Automatic, Ticks->{{0,1}, Automatic}]
```

Before examining some images, we return to the theory briefly. The Julia set of a polynomial transformation of $\mathbb{C}$ is the closure of the set of repelling periodic points [Dev1, §3.2]. Now, recall the bifurcation in the orbit behavior of f_r that takes place near $r = 3$. An attracting fixed point becomes a repelling fixed point and gives birth to two attracting period-2 points (see Figures 4.19, 4.22, and 4.23). In terms of the Julia set (and using the fact that it is the closure of the set of repelling periodic points), the attracting fixed point will move from the interior of the Julia set to a position on the Julia set itself as the parameter passes through the bifurcating value. This can be seen by examining the Julia sets for f_3 and nearby values of r. Figure 5.13 shows the IIM's version of the Julia set of f_3.

```
JuliaIIMf[3, 5000];
```

With this method it is difficult to get enough detail near the real axis, where the Julia set has infinitely many cusp-like points; see the filled-in Julia set in Figure 5.15(d). In particular, the Julia set is cusp-like near the attracting fixed point at $2/3$. Arbitarily close to this fixed point (and to all the other real points on the Julia set, such as $1/3$) are nonreal, repelling periodic points. (Exercise: Use `NRoots[Nest[f, z, n] == z, z]` to find the nonreal points of period n.) For smaller values of the parameter r, the fixed point $1-1/r$ is not a limit of repelling periodic points and thus lies in the interior of the filled-in Julia set. As r increases, an attracting 2-cycle is introduced, with the period-2 points moving left and right from the cusp as r increases. The cusp itself remains, though it moves to the right, because the fixed point becomes a repelling fixed point as r increases (see Figure 4.23) and so is on the Julia set.

There are various modifications to the IIM that one can make with a view to resolving the gaps in the images generated by the basic method

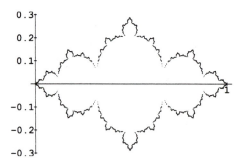

FIGURE 5.13 The Julia set of $3z(1-z)$. The cusp-like behavior near $x = 2/3$ is related to the bifurcation in the real quadratic map f_r as the parameter passes through 3.

(see [Dev2; PS, Chap. 4]). One approach is to generate the filled-in Julia set by a method we will discuss in a moment. Another possibility, suggested by M. Barnsley, is to bias the random choices of ±1, as was done with the fern attractor earlier in this chapter, to force the wandering point to visit certain regions of the Julia set. We leave the exploration of this idea to the reader. For example, choosing –1 90% of the time, rather than 50% of the time as is done by the IIM, yields a version of Figure 5.13 that shows more detail near the cusps (Figure 5.14).

> EXERCISE Examine the Julia sets of f_r for some other values of r. For example, the case of $f_{3.839}$ is interesting. This is an example (see Chapter 4) that has an attracting period-3 cycle of real numbers, and therefore, by Sarkovskii's theorem, real cycles of all periods. These other cycles are all repelling and so lie on the Julia set.

The fundamental algorithm for the computation of a filled-in Julia set, called the *Escape Time Algorithm*, is a straightforward application of the definition. The region of interest (perhaps determined by a quick IIM computation) is divided into a fine grid and for each grid point a decision is made whether that point has an orbit that diverges to infinity. If not, the point is colored black; *Mathematica* does this by placing a small point over the grid value. The decision is made by simply iterating Q_c a certain number of times, say 30. For values of the parameter that satisfy $|c| \leq 2$, if any member of an orbit has absolute value greater than 2, then the orbit is definitely attracted to infinity (the proof is easy; see [Dev2, §6.1]); if the

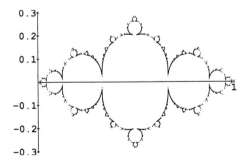

FIGURE 5.14 The Julia set of $3z(1 - z)$ generated by biasing the choices of ±1 heavily toward –1.

value fails to escape this region, that is, the origin-centered disk of radius 2, after the specified number of iterations, then the point is deemed not to be attracted to infinity. Some errors may creep in because of points that approach infinity very slowly, but this problem can be dealt with as it arises by increasing the number of iterations per point. If this method is used on f_r rather than Q_c, then an orbit will approach infinity if some iterate has absolute value greater than $1 + 1/|r|$ [Dev2, p. 95].

The function `FilledJuliaSet`, whose definition follows, implements this algorithm. A subroutine, `orbitcheck`, performs `iters` iterations; after each iteration it checks for escape from the region and thus avoids unnecessary computations when escape occurs early. The `While` statement is very concise, as the counter is preincremented via `++i` and Q_c is iterated at the same time as the size of the current value is checked. For a nonescaping orbit, the last `While` check will compare `++i` with `iters`; when the check fails, it will do so with `i` being `iters + 1`. This last condition is then checked, and if it fails, that is, if the orbit has escaped, `{}` is returned; otherwise the points $\pm z$ are returned in a form suitable for plotting. As the reader can confirm by experiment, using Map via `{Re[z], Im[z]}*# & /@ {1,-1}` is slightly faster than `{{Re[z], Im[z]}, {-Re[z], -Im[z]}}`. The main routine accepts bounds on x and y where the user is assumed to know that symmetry will be used; thus these bounds should define two adjacent quadrants in the complex plane, that is, one of `x0` and `y0` should be 0; this explains why the aspect ratio is defined in terms of the largest absolute values among the bounds. `PlotRange` is specified in case one wants to superimpose other lines or points on the Julia set without recomputing it; this can be done by generating the lines or points separately with the same plot range and superimposing the two graphics cells.

Arguments to `FilledJuliaSet` also include the fineness of the grid in each direction. One new trick is the use of `Outer` to generate the points of the grid and check their orbits. First, note that if `s1` and `s2` are sets of real numbers, then `Outer[#1 + #2 I &, s1, s2]` will form the set consisting of all complex numbers having their real part in `s1` and imaginary part in `s2`. Wrapping `orbitcheck` around `#1 + #2 I`, and passing the parameters `c` and `iters` as well, collects the values returned by the subroutine on all these complex numbers. The many empty sets that the subroutine returns are all deleted by the `Flatten[·, 2]` operation, which returns exactly the set of points in the real plane corresponding to the filled-in Julia set.

```
orbitcheck[z_, c_, iters_] := (s = z; i = 0;
    While[++i <= iters && Abs[s = s^2 + c] < 2];
    If[i == iters+1, {Re[z], Im[z]}*#& /@ {1,-1}, {}])


(* One of x0, y0 should be 0 *)
FilledJuliaSet[c_, meshx_Integer, meshy_Integer,
                x0_, x1_, y0_, y1_, iters_:20] :=

Show[Graphics[{PointSize[.002], Point /@ Flatten[

Outer[orbitcheck[#1 + I #2, N[c], iters]&,
    Range[x0, x1, (x1-x0)/meshx], Range[y0, y1, (y1-y0)/meshy]],
                                    2]}],
AspectRatio->(ymax=Max[Abs[{y0,y1}]])/(xmax=Max[Abs[{x0,x1}]]),
PlotRange->{{-xmax,xmax}, {-ymax,ymax}}]
```

The following commands generated the four filled Julia sets shown in Figure 5.15. The superimposed points or lines that illustrate the attracting cycles were generated separately by merging PostScript cells.

```
c = -.12256117 + .74486177 I (* rabbit *)
FilledJuliaSet[c, 230, 195, -1.31, .52, 0, 1.11, 30]


c =.32 + .043 I (* 11-cycle dragon *)
FilledJuliaSet[c, 160, 210, -.85, .80, 0, 1.12, 80]


c = -0.390541 - 0.586788*I   (* Siegel disk *)
FilledJuliaSet[c, 230, 165, -.77, 1.42, 0, 1.03, 30]


FilledJuliaSetReal[3, 140, 84, .5, .3, 60];
```

The last command uses a slightly different version of FilledJuliaSet appropriate for f_r, where the symmetry of the Julia set about 0 becomes symmetry about $1/2$. Moreover, if r is real (or if c is real in the case of Q_c), the Julia set is invariant under complex conjugation (proof left as exercise). Using these two symmetries yields four times as many points as

(a) (b)

(c) (d)

FIGURE 5.15 Some filled-in Julia sets. Examples (a)–(c) correspond to the examples of Figure 5.11; example (d) is the example of Figure 5.14. In (a) the attracting 3-cycle is shown as three white dots. In (b) the attracting 11-cycle is shown using white lines. In (c) two bounded orbits are shown, each of which wanders forever about a circle-like curve; there is no attracting cycle. Figure (d) shows the Julia set for the real quadratic map f_3; the attracting fixed point is at $2/3$, the rightmost point of the central blob, and 200 points of an orbit are shown; note the slow rate of convergence.

runs of `orbitcheck`. A version of `FilledJuliaSet` called `FilledJuliaSetReal` that is appropriate for the f_r case is given in the Appendix. Note the slow convergence in Figure 5.15(d), where 200 points of an orbit are shown. It appears that the points are perhaps converging to a 2-cycle, when in fact they are converging to the fixed point $2/3$. However, $r = 3$ is a bifurcation value and for slightly larger values of r there is indeed an attracting cycle of two period-2 points.

Warning: These images take several hours to produce, as opposed to the few minutes that the IIM takes for the unfilled Julia sets. If one wishes to see many Julia sets on the screen without printing them, then a special-purpose program is much more efficient than *Mathematica*. For example, the program, *The Game of Fractal Images, Part I,* by Marc Parmet (marketed by Springer-Verlag, New York), is quite fast, and has several nice features including options for using a variety of algorithms and for examining orbits by simply clicking the mouse on the starting value.

The images in Figure 5.15 require a prodigious amount of memory as well, as the final image consists of thousands of small points. One way around the memory problem is to use a pixel-by-pixel approach to compute the Julia set, as opposed to the filled Julia set, by an algorithm called the Boundary Scanning Method. It will produce very accurate unfilled Julia set pictures, using much less memory than the filled Julia sets, but it takes as much time—several hours for a fine image—as does the Escape Time Algorithm for filled sets. We leave the implementation of this method as an exercise. The details of the Boundary Scanning Method are as follows (see [Dev2, §7.5]). As with the Escape Time Algorithm, consider all points in some grid in the region of interest. Color a point black only if: (1) the orbit of that point does not escape in the specified number of iterations and (2) the orbit of at least one of the four adjacent points in the real and imaginary directions does escape. Thus the black points correspond to points on the boundary of the set of points attracted to infinity. Naturally, symmetry about the origin should be used.

EXERCISE Generate other Julia sets, perhaps using the Inverse Iteration Method first, both to find appropriate values for the bounding frame and to decide which filled-in Julia sets to generate, as the latter take a lot of time to produce.

EXERCISE Use `FilledJuliaSet` to generate some blowups of the Julia sets shown in Figure 5.15. This can be done simply by changing the arguments; however, the value of `iters` may have to be increased because the finer the work gets, the more iterations may be necessary for an accurate rendition. When deciding on a blowup it can be useful to select points using the cursor. On a Macintosh this is possible by holding down the ⌘ key while placing the cursor on a graphics image. The coordinates then appear at the bottom of the window and can be stored in the clipboard via ⌘-C.

EXERCISE When a program takes a lot of time, it is a good idea to introduce a `Print` statement so that its progress can be monitored. Revise `FilledJuliaSet` and `orbitcheck` so that every time the real part of the point being scanned changes it is printed on the screen.

The Mandelbrot set, pictures of which can be seen in [Dev1, Dev2, DK], is the collection of parameters $c \in \mathbb{C}$ such that the Julia set of Q_c is connected; loosely speaking, it serves as a dictionary of all the Julia sets of Q_c. A comprehensive exposition of the subject, in particular, the connection between Julia sets and the Mandelbrot set, may be found in the expository article by Bodil Branner included in [DK]. She points out that all computations support the conjecture, called the hyperbolicity conjecture, that c values in the interior of the Mandelbrot set correspond to functions Q_c for which there is an attracting cycle. Such cycles do not always exist, as shown by the Siegel disk example [Figures 5.9(i) and (j), 5.15(c)]. The c value for the Siegel disk lies on the boundary of the Mandelbrot set.

6 The Turtle Road to Recursion

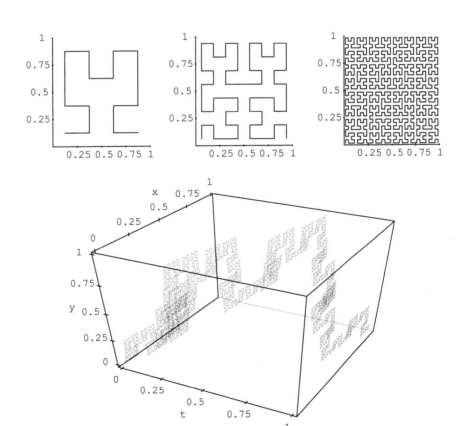

T his chapter continues the discussion of iterative graphics by simulating a turtle in two and in three dimensions and using it on various recursive problems, from trees (mathematical and botanical) to Peano space-filling curves.

About the illustration overleaf:

A Peano space-filling curve is a continuous function $P(t)$ from the unit interval onto the square. An example is illustrated overleaf. The upper diagrams show approximations to the image of P in the square; further approximations would yield a fully black square. The 3-dimensional diagram shows the true graph of the curve, which is the subset of $\mathbb{R}^3$ given by $\{(t, x, y) : P(t) = (x, y)\}$.

After examining a few approximations, it will be clear that the limiting object gets arbitrarily close to every point in the square. What is mind boggling is that the limiting object, which is indeed a continuous curve, *is* the square. This chapter contains a general program for iteratively rewriting strings and having them interpreted by a turtle (in two or three dimensions). Using the abbreviations for forward ("F"), left ("+"), right ("-"), and flipping ("i"), the planar images overleaf can be generated by the following command, which causes n rewrites of the string "X" according to the specified rule. A more complicated rewriting rule generates a Peano curve in a cube.

```
RecursiveTurtle[{"X" -> "+iXiF-XFX-FiXi+"}, "X", n, 90]
```

6.1 Introducing the Turtle ▬▬▬▬▬▬

A turtle, which will be familiar to readers who have experience with the LOGO language, is an abstract object that wanders about in the plane; it occupies a point and is oriented in a specific direction from that point. The turtle can move forward or back a specified distance and can turn left or right through any angle. We will simulate a turtle in *Mathematica* and then use it to generate a variety of images in a uniform way.[1] As has happened before, we will begin with a straightforward approach and then modify it for speed and power—and then slow it down again by adding enhancements!

A straightforward simulation defines five commands, `initialize`, `left`, `right`, `forward`, and `back`. The `forward` and `back` commands move the turtle to a new point and add the point to a list being maintained. The direction-changing commands (which accept their arguments in degrees) do not affect the list, but affect subsequent movement commands. The `Turtle` package shows how to amply document a package and wrap it inside its own *context* so that its variables become local variables. However, the `BeginPackage` and `Begin` commands *must be executed before the rest of the package* (store them in a separate cell). The use of contexts is subtle and is explained in more detail in the section on Linear Diophantine Equations in Chapter 8.

```
BeginPackage["Turtle`"];


(* This package provides four functions for controlling the
movement and orientation of a turtle graphics device. It
maintains a list of the points visited by the turtle in "path",
which can then be manipulated and displayed as a Graphics object.
The calling routine must begin by invoking initialize[]; it can
end by either showturtlepath, or by its own
Show[Graphics[Line[path]], options] command. *)
```

---

[1] I am indebted to Eric Halsey of the University of Washington for pointing out the value of a turtle and the ease with which it could be implemented in *Mathematica*.

```
initialize::usage = "initialize[p:{0, 0}] places the turtle at p
(default is {0, 0}), points it in the direction {1, 0}, and sets
path to {p}."

showturtlepath::usage = "showturtlepath displays the turtle's
path"

right::usage = "right[a] turns the turtle a degrees to the
right."

left::usage = "left[a] turns the turtle a degrees to the left."

forward::usage = "forward[s] moves the turtle forward s units,
and appends the coordinates of the new position to path."

back::usage = "back[s] moves the turtle back s units, and appends
the coordinates of the new position to path."

Begin["Turtle`Private`"];

initialize[start_:{0,0}] := (X = start; U = {1, 0}; path = {X})

right[a_] :=
 U = {{Cos[aa = a Degree//N], Sin[aa]}, {-Sin[aa], Cos[aa]}} . U

left[a_] :=
 U = {{Cos[aa = a Degree//N], -Sin[aa]}, {Sin[aa], Cos[aa]}} . U

forward[s_] := AppendTo[path, X += s U]

back[s_]    := AppendTo[path, X -= s U]

showturtlepath := Show[Graphics[Line[path]],
                             PlotRange->All, AspectRatio->1]

End; EndPackage[];
```

The operative code of the Turtle package is very short. Note the use of AppendTo[path, X += s U]; the location is first incremented by the appropriate multiple of the direction, and because an assignment returns the assigned value, the resulting point is appended to the path. A calling routine must begin with initialize[], which sets up the list path and assigns a starting location and direction. Here are some simple examples that use a turtle. The first just generates a regular polygon; the second generates a random walk along a hexagonal grid, with dots marking the start and finish points. Because `Random[Integer, 2]` returns a value in $\{0, 1, 2\}$ and $120 \cdot 2 - 60 = 180$, the walk can go directly backward.

```
polygon[n_] := ( initialize[];
                 Do[left[360/n]; forward[1], {n}];
                 showturtlepath)
polygon[6]


randomwalk[n_] :=
     (initialize[];
      Do[left[120 Random[Integer, 2] - 60]; forward[1], {n}];
      Show[Graphics[{PointSize[.03], Point[{0,0}], Line[path],
                  PointSize[.02], Point[Last[path]]}],
          PlotRange->All, Axes->Automatic])
randomwalk[200]
```

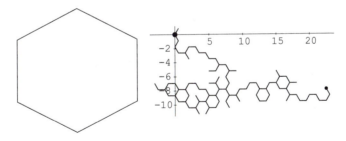

FIGURE 6.1 The output of the two simple turtle routines polygon and randomwalk.

EXERCISE Write a turtle routine that defines a function `Tree[depth, length, angle, ratio]` that draws a binary tree as shown in Figure 6.2, where the branching depth is given by `depth`, the length of the lowest branch is `length`, half the angle between the branches is given by `angle`, and the factor by which the length shrinks from one

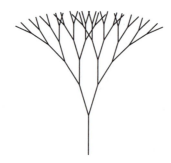

FIGURE 6.2 A turtle-generated tree.

level to the next is `ratio`. Thus the tree in Figure 6.2 is the result of `Tree[5, 1, 22.5, 0.8]`. (The actual angle between branches in the illustration is not the specified 45° because the aspect ratio of `show-turtlepath` was used.) One such program, together with some instructions that generate some amusing animations, is given in the Appendix.

Some experimentation will convince you that the `AppendTo` and `PrependTo` commands are slow when compared with the alternative approach of predefining an array and then modifying its elements. So if we can predefine `path` to be, say, a list of 1,000 `Null`s (`Null` is a symbol that represents the absence of anything else), then it will be faster to have each turtle move invoke `path[[i]] = ...` instead of an `AppendTo` instruction. (Exercise: Compare `ByteCount[{Null}]` with `ByteCount[{0}]` and `ByteCount[{0.}]`.) The following code implements this idea; the user is given the option of inserting a maximum path size larger than 1,000. A counter, `count`, which is preincremented whenever a step is taken, keeps track of the length of the path, and `finished` cuts the path down to its true size. By using `finished` in this way, `path` can be displayed by the calling routine with its own set of display options. A further simplification is that `back` and `left` are defined in terms of `forward` and `right`.

```
(* Faster turtle. Calling routine must begin with initialize[]
and end with either finished or showturtlepath *)


Clear[initialize]
initialize[start_List:{0., 0.}, dim_Integer:1000] :=
```

```
              (path = Table[Null, {dim}];
               X = start//N; U = {1., 0.}; path[[1]] = X; count = 1)

  right[a_]    :=
    U = {{t1 = Cos[aa = a Degree//N], t2 = Sin[aa]}, {-t2, t1}} . U
  left[a_]     := right[-a]
  forward[s_]  := path[[++count]] = (X += s U)
  back[s_]     := forward[-s]
  finished     := path = Take[path, count]


showturtlepath := (finished;
   Show[Graphics[Line[path]], PlotRange->All, AspectRatio->1];)
```

As an example of how a turtle can be used recursively, we'll construct the Koch snowflake. This classic example of a fractal starts with a line segment and breaks it into four straight pieces by adding a bump as shown in Figure 6.3. The length of each piece is one-fourth the length of the original segment. Then this process is repeated on each of the 4 segments, and then on each of the 16 segments, and so on. One usually starts with an equilateral triangle rather than a single segment, as in Figure 6.3. The limiting curve is called the Koch snowflake, or if one is thinking of the enclosed region, the Koch island. The latter

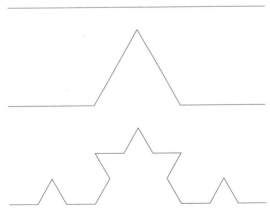

FIGURE 6.3 The first two fractalizations in the development of the Koch curve.

terminology derives from its use to illustrate the difficulty of coastline measurement (see [Man]). The following routine uses a recursive procedure, `flakeside`, that simply moves forward if its second argument (`depth`) is 0. Otherwise, it puts off moving forward and just calls itself four times with `depth` lowered by 1 and the step length scaled down by a factor of 3; the calls are separated by appropriate direction changes. For example, `flakeside[1., 1]` generates the sequence: {`forward[0.333333]`, `left[60]`, `forward[0.333333]`, `right [120]`, `forward[0.333333]`, `left[60]`, `forward[0.333333]`}. The `Do` loop fractalizes each side of the triangle in turn. The result of several iterations, up to `KochSnowflake[6]`, is shown in Figure 6.4.

```
flakeside[length_, 0] := forward[length]
flakeside[length_, depth_] := (
        flakeside[length/3, depth - 1];
        left[60];
        flakeside[length/3, depth - 1];
        right[120];
        flakeside[length/3, depth - 1];
        left[60];
        flakeside[length/3, depth - 1])


KochSnowflake[n_] := ( initialize[];
                    Do[flakeside[1., n]; right[120], {3}]
                    showturtlepath )
```

An important aspect of the snowflake curve is its infinite wiggliness. Before discussing this further, we must pause to point out exactly what the limiting curve is. Let $S_n(t)$ denote the function from [0, 1] to the plane that gives the nth approximation to the Koch curve, illustrated in Figure 6.3. An abstract way to see that the limiting curve exists is to observe that for any t in [0, 1], the sequence $S_n(t)$ satisfies the Cauchy condition and therefore has a limit. A more concrete approach is first to define the limiting curve on numbers whose base-2 expansion terminates after n steps. These points correspond to the bends in the curves in Figure 6.3; for example, the first iteration locates $S(0)$, $S(1/4)$, $S(1/2)$, $S(3/4)$, and $S(1)$ at the endpoints of the straight segments. Then one can extend continuously by defining $S(t)$ to be the limit of the $S(t_n)$ where t_n is

FIGURE 6.4 The first six iterations in the development of the snowflake curve.

the sequence of numbers formed by looking at longer and longer initial segments of the base-2 expansion of t. To do this, we must know that the sequence $S(t_n)$ has a limit, and again the Cauchy condition can be used. To a human eye the limiting curve does not look different from the final iteration in Figure 6.3. It is instructive to consider an example where the limiting object is perhaps not what one might expect. Consider a sequence of "sawteeth," as shown in Figure 6.5. Each iterate has length exactly 2 and is nondifferentiable. Yet the limiting object is a straight line having length $\sqrt{2}$. Exercise: Write a *Mathematica* routine to generate Figure 6.5.

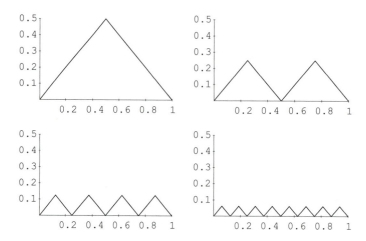

FIGURE 6.5 The sawtooth function shows that care is needed when taking limits of curves. Each sawtooth is jagged and has length $\sqrt{2}$, yet the limiting curve is a straight line having length 1.

Now, we can turn to the snowflake curve and ask about its length and the area it encloses. It is not hard to see that if the side length of the initial triangle is s, then the length of the nth iterate is $(4/3)^n s$ (which approaches infinity as n increases) and if the initial area is A, then the limiting area is $8/5 A$. Recalling the coastline analogy, one sees that a measurement of the coastline of the Koch island will depend on the resolution of the measuring stick. The shorter the measuring stick, the larger will be the measurement, and the measurement can grow without bound. This was experimentally observed for real-world coastlines and borders (see [Man]).

The Koch snowflake also serves to illustrate the notion of similarity dimension, which is a finer notion than the intuitive topological dimension by which a line is 1-dimensional, a square 2-dimensional, and so on. Suppose a closed and bounded subset X of $\mathbb{R}^n$ has the property that there is a finite set of contracting similarities (that is, transformations of the form $x \mapsto sL(x) + v$ where L is an orthogonal linear transformation and s is a positive constant less than 1)$\sigma_1, \ldots, \sigma_n$ with scaling factors s_i and such that $X = \sigma_1(X) \cup \sigma_2(X) \cup \cdots \cup \sigma_n(X)$. Then the *similarity dimension* of X is defined to be the unique real number d for which $(\sum s_i^d) = 1$. It often happens that the contraction factor is the same number s for each of the similarities, in which case the definition of d reduces to simply $\log n/\log(1/s)$. In the case of the Koch curve (here it is simpler to consider the Koch curve growing from a line rather than the full snowflake growing from a triangle) there are four transformations, each of which scales by $1/3$. It follows that the similarity dimension of the Koch curve is $\log 4/\log 3 = 1.26186\ldots$.

Let's take a moment to relate the similarity dimension to more familiar concepts. Two other closely related concepts of dimension are fractal dimension and Hausdorff dimension. The reader is referred to Chapter 5 of [Bar] for the definitions and theory regarding these notions. A major point is that for any subset of $\mathbb{R}^n$ the values of these two dimensions are no greater than n. The similarity dimension, however, can exceed the topological dimension. Consider a tree such that each branch divides into two branches and the length of the branches shrinks by a factor of 0.8 at each level. Its similarity dimension is $\log 2/\log 0.8$, which is greater than 3! The problem is that, unlike the snowflake curve, the tree will intersect itself as it grows. If we eliminate this possibility by insisting that the similarities with respect to which the set is invariant satisfy the *open set condition*, then the similarity dimension, fractal dimension, and Hausdorff dimension all coincide (and in such cases the common value is often called the fractal dimension). The open set condition simply asks for a nonempty bounded open set U such that $\cup \sigma_i(U) \subseteq U$ and the sets $\sigma_i(U)$ are pairwise disjoint. Exercise: Find an open set that shows that the four contractions involved in the Koch curve satisfy the open set condition.

Now, the fact that the snowflake curve has fractal dimension $1.26\ldots$ means that in one sense, it is richer than a purely 1-dimensional object, but not so rich as a 2-dimensional object. (Exercise: Show that the Cantor set is invariant under similarities satisfying the open condition and that the fractal dimension of the Cantor set is $0.63093\ldots$.) The original definition of a fractal was a set whose similarity dimension exceeds its topological dimension; however, the term is currently used for a wider range of self-similar sets. In any event, for both the Koch snowflake and the Cantor set, the similarity dimension is greater than the topological dimension (The Cantor set's topological dimension is 0, since its only connected subsets are singletons.) The Sierpiński triangle, discussed in Chapters 4 and 5 and later in this chapter, is another example; its similarity dimension is $\log 4/\log 3 = 1.58496\ldots$.

A proof of the coincidence of fractal and similarity dimension can be found in [Bar, §5.2]. A proof of equality of Hausdorff and similarity dimension, as well as a deep discussion of Hausdorff dimension and Hausdorff measure, can be found in [Fal, §8.3]. Part of the importance of Hausdorff dimension is that for sets of Hausdorff dimension d, the Hausdorff d-dimensional measure can be used to compare the "size" of the sets.

6.2 Recursion via String Rewriting ▬▬▬▬

The formation of the snowflake curve (from a line segment rather than a triangle) can be summarized in terms of a rewriting rule on a certain alphabet. Let's abbreviate a forward move by F, backward by B, left by +, and right by −. Then we can summarize the Koch fractalization by the string rewriting system that begins with the single character F (the axiom) and repeatedly applies the rule that replaces each F by the string F+F−−F+F. To see the result after a few substitutions, we can use the substitution operator to define a pure function that is iterated by `NestList` as follows.

```
NestList[
 Flatten[# /. "F" -> {"F", "+", "F", "-", "-", "F", "+", "F"}] &,
 {"F"}, 2] //TableForm
{F}
{F, +, F, -, -, F, +, F}
{F, +, F, -, -, F, +, F, +, F, +, F, -, -, F, +, F, -, -, F, +,
    F, -, -, F, +, F, +, F, +, F, -, -, F, +, F}
```

Thus after two substitutions the initial string is turned into a sequence of rules that upon interpretation by a turtle, will yield the bottom figure in Figure 6.3.

The use of a string rewriting system, also known as a Lindenmayer system, or L-system, to drive a turtle is a much more compact method than the direct approach used earlier to draw the snowflake. Although a more explicit turtle program such as the fast turtle allows finer control of the lengths of lines and the turning angles, a Lindenmayer system is more suited to initial explorations of patterns. Because many mathematical and botanical objects can be generated by the use of a rewriting system, it is worth writing a general purpose routine that requires only the initial string (or "axiom") and the rewrite rule(s). For more information on rewriting systems see [Sau, PH]. These references are invaluable in part for the examples they contain: it is not always easy to discover the rules that one suspects exist for a given object.

There are two main points in the `RecursiveTurtle` routine that follows: (1) how to allow single characters such as F and + to be interpreted as turtle moves and (2) how to implement the substitution. For the first problem we have the turtle work internally just as before, with the symbols `forward`, `back`, and so on, and we translate characters to these symbols[2] by use of a symbol table. For example, if the axiom is, say, `"F+F"`, then `Characters[axiom]` returns `{F, +, F}`. Using the symbol table via `... /. symboltable` then returns `{forward, left, forward}`. The translation of the rule or rules in `recursion` is more complicated and is accomplished by the `replacerules` line, whose function we now illustrate.

```
symboltable =
        {"F" -> forward, "B" -> back, "-" -> right, "+" -> left};
Map[
   First[Characters[#[[1]]]] -> Characters[#[[2]]] &,
      {"F" -> "F-" , "-" -> "F-B+"}] /. symboltable
{forward -> {forward, right}, right -> {forward, right,
                                        back, left}}
```

The preceding command does not work on a rewrite rule of the form `"F+B" -> "F+B-F+F+B"`, but only on sets of rules where each rule rewrites a single character at a time.

The problem of repeatedly invoking the rewrite rule and then having it interpreted by the turtle is solved in one line. The following command produces a (possibly very long) list of turtle commands that can simply be passed to `turtle`. Note that `turtle` is made to be a listable function so that it can act on a nested list as if the nesting were absent.

---

[2]We could have asked the turtle to work directly with the characters, but that would have used significantly more memory because of the very long strings that would be generated. Exercise: Compare `ByteCount[{"a"}]` with `ByteCount[{a}]`.

```
Nest[# /. {forward -> {forward, forward}} &, (Characters["+F"] /.
    symboltable), 3]
{left, {{{forward, forward}, {forward, forward}},
        {{forward, forward}, {forward, forward}}}}
```

With these preliminaries, the definition of the RecursiveTurtle program should be simple to decipher. Note the use of defaults, which are separated from arguments by a colon. Using types with the arguments means that, for example, if startposn and startdir are omitted but a value for dim is included, the latter will be interpreted properly. However, one cannot omit startposn and expect that the next argument, if it is a list of two numbers, will be interpreted as startdir; the first list among the optional arguments will be interpreted as startposn.

```
BeginPackage["RecursiveTurtle`"];

RecursiveTurtle::usage = "RecursiveTurtle[recursion, axiom,
depth, angle, steplength, startposn:{0.,0.}, startdir:{1.,0.},
dim:1000] returns the image obtained by applying a turtle to the
sequence of movements generated in depth many rewritings of the
axiom. Characters are F, B, -, +. If the path is expected to
visit more than 1000 points, a larger value of dim should be
used. The rewrite rules in recursion should each transform a
single character."

path::usage = "path contains the turtle's coordinates and
may be accessed externally";

Begin["RecursiveTurtle`Private`"];

RecursiveTurtle[recursion_List, axiom_String, depth_Integer,
  angle_, steplength_, startposn_List:{0,0},
  startdir_List:{1,0}, dim_:1000] := (

symboltable = {"F"->forward, "B"->back, "-"->right, "+"->left};

X = startposn//N; U = startdir//N;
count = 1;
c = Cos[angle Degree //N]; s = Sin[angle Degree //N];
```

```
Attributes[turtle] = Listable;
    turtle[forward]  := path[[++count]] = (X += steplength U);
    turtle[back]     := path[[++count]] = (X -= steplength U);
    turtle[left]     := U = rotateleft . U;
    turtle[right]    := U = rotateright . U;

replacerules =
  Map[First[Characters[#[[1]]]] -> Characters[#[[2]]] &,
      recursion] /. symboltable;

path = Table[Null, {dim}]; path[[1]] = X;
rotateleft = {{c,-s},{s,c}}; rotateright = Transpose[rotateleft];
turtle[Nest[# /. replacerules &,
        Characters[axiom]/.symboltable, depth]];
path = Take[path, count];
Show[Graphics[Line[path]], AspectRatio->1, Axes->None,
        PlotRange->All])

End[]; EndPackage[];
```

With `RecursiveTurtle` loaded, we can generate the snowflake curve by the single invocation that follows. There is no automatic matching of step length to the depth, and so the correct step length must be given as an argument.

```
KochSnowflake[n_] :=
    RecursiveTurtle[{"F" -> "F+F--F+F"}, "+F--F--F",
                    n, 60, 3.^-n]
```

The use of rewriting is significantly faster than our first method of generating the snowflake. For example, the time for generating `KochSnowflake[3]` is reduced by 30%. We can also use this approach to generate an *exterior snowflake*, which is of theoretical interest since the limiting Koch snowflake lies between the approximations to the snowflake and the exterior snowflake (see Figure 6.6); this provides an alternative approach to the rigorous definition of the Koch snowflake as it can be defined as the region inside all the exterior snowflake approximations and outside all the standard Koch snowflake approximations. The exterior snowflake can be generated by the following rewriting rule and axiom.

```
RecursiveTurtle[{"F" -> "F-F++F-F"}, "F-F-F-F-F-F", 0, 60, 1.]
```

EXERCISE What happens if the same rewriting rule used to generate the standard Koch snowflake is applied to the axiom "F++F++F"?

EXERCISE Try to predict what sort of image will be produced by the rule "B" -> "+FB--FB+B" applied to the axiom "FB". (A more efficient approach to this object will be discussed in the section on stacks later in this chapter.)

It is easy to see that the single rule "F" -> "F-F+F+F-F" applied to the axiom "F-F-F" yields the Sierpiński triangle (see Chapter 4) when the angle is set to 120°. However this approach causes a lot of rewriting. (Why?) For a more efficient method imagine a temporary variable Y whose job it is to affix an upside-down equilateral triangle to the midpoint of a line segment. Now, suppose the two rules "F" -> "FF" and "Y" -> "F-Y+Y+Y-F" are applied to the axiom "Y", where the fundamental angle is still 120° and the step size is assumed to be 1. The first two iterations yield F-Y+Y+Y-F and FF-F-Y+Y+Y-F+F-Y+Y+Y-F+F-Y+Y+Y-F-FF. When interpreted by the turtle, this last string yields simply FF-

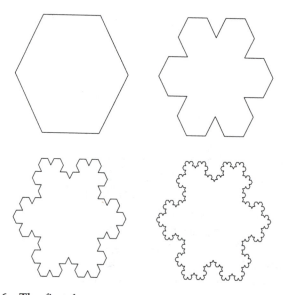

FIGURE 6.6 The first few approximations to the exterior snowflake.

FF+FF+FF–FF, since none of the Ys cause any turtle action and lots of directions cancel. Thus each Y in the third-from-the-end step will cause the turtle to affix an equilateral triangle of side length 2 to a line. Now, a Y at the fourth-from-the-end step will generate some Ys and two Fs; the Fs will be quadrupled by the end, and so such a Y will yield an equilateral triangle of side length 4 on a segment, where each side of the triangle has a side-length-2 triangle at its midpoint (see Figure 6.7). Thus the rewriting rule recursively affixes an equilateral triangle to a segment; this is exactly what it takes to generate the Sierpiński triangle. Adding two more Fs at the start yields the additional two sides of the triangle.

```
depth = 4
RecursiveTurtle[{"F"->"FF", Y -> "F-Y+Y+Y-F"}, "Y-F-F", depth,
      120, 2^(-depth), {0,0}, {.5, Sqrt[.75]}, 1 + 2 * 3 ^ depth]
```

Because rewriting rules can lead to very long strings, and hence to very long lists of points in path, it may be necessary to have some idea of how long the strings are getting. In the case of the Sierpiński triangle, it is easy to see that each application of the rule triples the number of Fs. Thus the length of path will be 1 greater than 2*3^depth. When the relationship is this simple, we may as well insert the function as the value of the dim argument; this will speed things up when fewer than 1,000 points are needed and will allocate exactly the right amount of memory when 1,000 is insufficient. Usually it is not too difficult to compute the

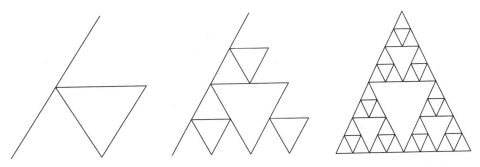

FIGURE 6.7 The first two curves are obtained by rewriting the axiom "Y" two and three times, respectively, via the rules "F" -> "FF" and "Y" -> "F-Y+Y+Y-F". The rightmost is a depth-four rewriting from the axiom "Y-F-F".

exact growth rate. For confirmation, it can be useful to generate some data from small values of depth, and this can be easily done by replacing the last two lines of RecursiveTurtle by Print[count]. (Exercise: Insert the correct path size in the rewriting routine that generates the snowflake and the exterior snowflake.)

6.3 A Space-Filling Curve

Consider Figure 6.9, which shows some approximations to a space-filling curve. Such curves are usually called Peano curves, in honor of Giuseppe Peano who in 1890 discovered the amazing fact, revolutionary for its time, that one could map an interval continuously onto a square. The example illustrated here is a variation of Peano's original idea due to David Hilbert in 1891. Let's stop for a moment and ponder the limiting curve, which we shall denote by H but refer to as a Peano curve. It is easy to look at the approximations and agree that the limit gets arbitrarily close to every point in the square, that is, that the limiting curve is dense in the square. But the amazing thing is that the limiting curve is not merely dense, it is the square.

As with the snowflake curve, one must prove the limiting curve exists. Let's use base-4 expansions to define the Peano curve $H(t)$ as a function from [0, 1] to the square as follows. First divide the square into four equal squares and label them with the base-4 numbers 0, 0.1, 0.2, and 0.3 as in Figure 6.8(a). Then subdivide each of these and label them slightly differently, as indicated in Figure 6.8(b). Continue in this way [the labelling rules can be determined by superimposing the curves in Figure 6.9 over the appropriate grid, as in Figure 6.8(b)] to obtain finer and finer grids and labellings. Now, if $t \in [0, 1]$, then there is a nested sequence of squares corresponding to the initial segments of t's base-4 representation. These squares intersect in a unique point, which is taken as the definition of $H(t)$. The function H is continuous because if two numbers are close enough to have the same first m digits in base-4, then they lie in the same square at the mth subdivision, and so they are taken by H to points no farther apart than $\sqrt{2}/2^m$. Thus H defines a curve in the plane. However, H is not a one-to-one function. Exercise: Write each of $1/2$, $1/6$, and $5/6$ in base 4, and conclude that H maps each of them to the center of the square; note also that 0.21_4 and 0.13_4 are mapped to the same point. In fact, it is easy to see that there can be no continuous, one-to-one function from an interval onto a square: The interval has the property that it can be disconnected by a point and the square does not have that property; such a property would be preserved by a continuous one-to-one function.

It is noteworthy that an object as abstract as a space-filling curve has found application: It can be used to provide an important heuristic solution to the Travelling Salesman Problem (TSP). The TSP seeks, given a collection of points in the plane, a path of minimum length that passes through all these points. Here "heuristic" means a method that runs quickly and finds a path that is not too much longer than the theoretically shortest path through for the given points, which may be impossible to discover in reasonable time. J. J. Bartholdi and L. K. Platzman have used space-filling curves to develop a system by which, *without having to use a computer*, a delivery organization can generate a reasonable route that visits a collection of houses in a city. The idea is simply to visit the houses in the order in which a certain space-filling curve would visit them. In their words, a space-filling curve may be thought of as "the route of an obsessive salesman who visits every point in the unit square" [BP]. See [BP, BPCW, PB] for more details of the TSP application as well as other applications of space fillers (e.g., assigning numbers to bins in a warehouse) and a comparison of the space-filling heuristic with other heuristics for the TSP.

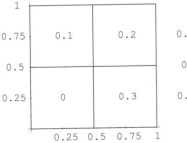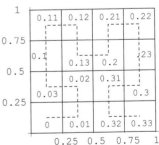

FIGURE 6.8 The labelling of subsquares of the unit square with terminating base-4 numbers; the continuation of this subdividing and labelling process defines a space-filling curve.

EXERCISE Using any of the space-filling curves discussed in this section, write a *Mathematica* program that implements the space-filling heuristic for the TSP. The key step is defining a function that is a one-way inverse to a space-filling curve $P(t)$, that is, a function f from the square to the line such that $f(P(t)) = t$ for each t in $[0, 1]$.

With the rigorous definition behind us, we can see that the sequence of piecewise linear curves shown in Figure 6.9 is an approximating sequence to a Peano curve in the following sense. The nth approximation can be viewed as the curve $H_n(t)$ that maps numbers whose base-4 representation terminates after n digits to the center of the corresponding square in the nth subdivision and then is extended linearly to other values. It follows that for each $t \in [0, 1], H(t) = \lim_{n \to \infty} H_n(t)$.

We can now turn to the problem of generating the approximations via our recursive turtle. We do this with two auxiliary variables X and Y. The idea is that X gets interpreted by the turtle as "draw a U loop to my right," while Y draws a loop on the left. At the end of the substitution the Xs and Ys are ignored and the direction and movement commands (which become "-F+F+F-" and "+F-F-F+") show that the penultimate Xs and Ys are interpreted properly. This intermingling of left and right U loops generates the Peano curve.

```
Hilbert[n_] := Show[
    RecursiveTurtle[{"X" -> "-YF+XFX+FY-", Y -> "+XF-YFY-FX+"},
                    "Y", n, 90, 2. ^ -n, 4 ^ n],
AspectRatio->1, PlotRange->{{0, 1}, {0,1}},
Axes->{0,0}, AxesStyle->GrayLevel[1],
Ticks->{{.25, .5, .75, 1}, {.25, .5, .75, 1}}]
```

Keep in mind that a Peano curve is just that, a curve. It is wrong to identify the limit of the approximations in Figure 6.9 as simply being the square. Rather, the limit is a function from the unit interval to the square. The graph of such a function is a space curve in $\mathbb{R}^3$, using a (t, x, y) coordinate system. Because Hilbert[n] leaves a list of points in path, we can easily generate this curve and look at it in 3-space. A virtue of this approach is that further approximations yield visually finer depictions; further approximations along the lines of Figure 6.9 yield only blackness.

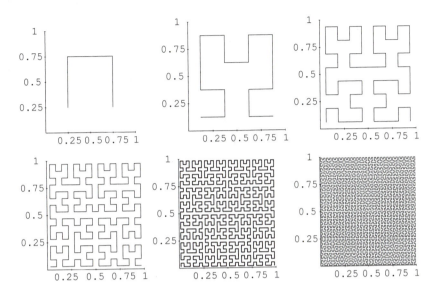

FIGURE 6.9 The first six iterations of Hilbert's version of a Peano space-filling curve. It is evident that the limiting object gets arbitrarily close to every point in the square. What is mind boggling is that the limiting object, which is indeed a continuous curve, *is* the square.

As a warmup, which will have an unexpected dividend, let's view the Peano curve $H(t)$ as $(x(t), y(t))$ and plot $x(t)$ against t. The following command uses First@Transpose to produce a list of the x-coordinates of points in path. To speed up this procedure and the following 3-dimensional routine as well, modify the RecursiveTurtle routine by deleting the Show command. The use of Range and Transpose to generate a list of points was discussed near the end of Chapter 1.

```
n = 6
RecursiveTurtle[{"X" -> "-YF+XFX+FY-", Y -> "+XF-YFY-FX+"},
            "Y", n, 90, 2. ^ -n,   4 ^ n]
Show[Graphics[Line @ Transpose @
     {Range[0., 1 - 4^-n, 4^-n], First@Transpose[path]}],
     Axes->Automatic, AxesLabel->{"t", "x(t)"}]
```

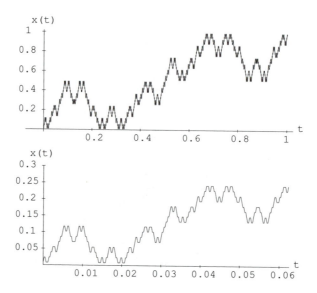

FIGURE 6.10 The graph of the x-coordinate of the Peano curve $H(t)$ as a function of t, along with a 16-fold magnification, which is theoretically identical to the unmagnified function; this illustrates its self-similarity. Here the upper image is a level-6 rendering, whence the magnification looks like a level-4 rendering. This one-variable function is an example of a function that is nondifferentiable at every point of its domain, even though it is everywhere continuous. The upper image is, on the scale shown, essentially identical to the true, infinitely deep function.

EXERCISE Generate approximations to the function in Figure 6.10 directly, using a `RecursiveTurtle` call with a small angle. (In order to match the scale of Figure 6.10 exactly, the angle will have to be a function of the depth.)

Before constructing the 3-dimensional graph of $H(t)$, we consider yet another way to visualize a Peano curve. The approximating curves shown in Figure 6.9 are incorrect for all specific t-values. By this is meant that for each n and each specific t-value, $H_n(t) \neq H(t)$; of course, in the limit this incorrectness disappears, as we have seen. But why not generate a sequence of approximations $K_n(t)$ as follows? First compute the exact positions of $H(0)$, $H(\frac{1}{2})$, and $H(1)$ and then connect them to form the curve $K_0(t)$. Of course the first and third of these points are $(0, 0)$ and $(1, 0)$, respectively, and we have already seen that $H(\frac{1}{2})$ is $(\frac{1}{2}, \frac{1}{2})$. Thus, K_0 is simply an inverted V. Define K_1 to be the curve connecting the exact images under H of the nine multiples of $\frac{1}{8}$ (it is convenient, though not essential, to have the denominators grow by a factor of 4 rather than 2). Continuing in this way yields a family of curves that converges to Hilbert's curve in a nice way; namely, each approximating curve provides the exact location for an ever-increasing number of points. The function K_n locates correctly all points whose base-2 expansion terminates after the first $2n + 1$ digits. This is analogous to the way in which the snowflake approximations converge to a limit. The images of K_0 to K_5 are shown in Figure 6.11. To summarize, Hilbert's curve is the limit of both the sequence of K curves and the sequence of H curves, but the K curves contain more information as they show the exact limiting value at each 90° bend. (We assume that all these parametrizations are in terms of arc length; that is, the traversal of K_n is at uniform speed.) In particular,

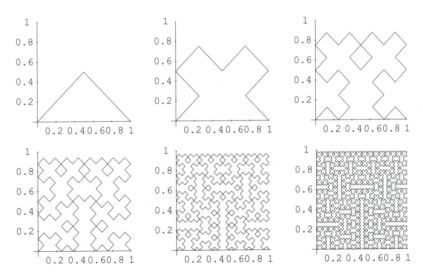

FIGURE 6.11 The sequence of approximations K_0 to K_5 to Hilbert's Peano curve. These approximations have the advantage that all the points at the bends agree exactly with the value of the limiting curve; for example, $H(\frac{1}{2}) = K_0(\frac{1}{2}) = (\frac{1}{2}, \frac{1}{2})$.

K_2 shows that the Hilbert curve maps the points $^{14}/_{32}$ and $^{18}/_{32}$ to the same point of the square. We leave the formal verification that the curves in Figure 6.11 really represent the Ks as an exercise. The generation of Figure 6.11 will be discussed later.

We now return to the issue of generating the true graph of $H(t)$ as a subset of $\mathbb{R}^3$. The point of this is to emphasize that a square-filling curve is not simply the filled-in square, but is *a way of traversing the filled-in square*. We proceed just as in the generation of Figure 6.10 and first construct a list that introduces t-coordinates. Here the list's elements have the form $\{t, \{x, y\}\}$; mapping `Flatten` onto this list yields the desired list of triples. The 3-dimensional `Line` command is entirely analogous to the 2-dimensional version. Then `Graphics3D` (as opposed to ordinary `Graphics`) produces the object to be shown. Of course, setting `View-Point` to, say, `{20, 0, 0}` will yield a projection identical to an image in Figure 6.9. The following commands generate the graphs of H_6 (4,096 points) and K_5 (2,049 points) shown in Figure 6.12.

```
n = 6
RecursiveTurtle[{"X" -> "-YF+XFX+FY-", Y -> "+XF-YFY-FX+"},
                "Y", n, 90, 2. ^ -n,   4 ^ n]
Show[Graphics3D[Line  [Flatten /@ Transpose @
                            {Range[0,  1 - 4^-n, 4^-n], path}]],
      Axes->Automatic, AxesLabel->{"t", "x", "y"}]


n = 5  (*requires that HilbertVariation[5] (p. 205) be executed*)
len = 1 + 2 4^n
Show[Graphics3D[Line  [Flatten /@ Transpose @
                     {Range[0., 1 - 1/len, 1/len], path[[1]] }]],
      Axes->Automatic, AxesLabel->{"t", "x", "y"}]
```

EXERCISE What is the similarity dimension of the Hilbert space-filling curve viewed as a subset of $\mathbb{R}^3$?

We can enhance the recursive turtle (as well as the ordinary, more general turtle) in several ways. One feature that might be worth adding is the ability to raise the pen up and put it down somewhere else. This would require closing off the path variable and starting a new path at the position where the pen goes down. We leave the implementation as an exercise, one that should seem straightforward after a study of the stack

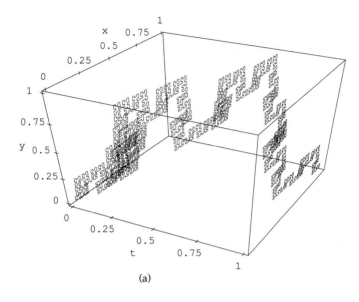

(a)

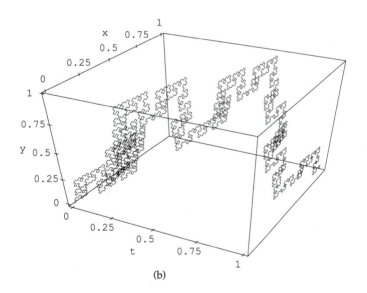

(b)

FIGURE 6.12 (a) The true graph of the traditional level-6 approximation to the Hilbert curve, which illustrates the actual motion in the square. Part (b) shows the graph of the approximation K_5 rather than H_6; these space curves look roughly the same, because they share a common limit, namely Hilbert's curve H.

enhancement of the turtle presented at the end of this chapter. Another enhancement is to give our turtle the ability to flip over and walk on its back. This allows certain types of turtle programs to be programmed more simply; indeed, it allows a simplification in the generation of the Peano curve *H*. Using "i" to denote a flip, we can make the necessary modifications to RecursiveTurtle as follows:

1. Add "i" -> flip to symboltable.

2. Add flip to the variable list of Block.

3. Add turtle[flip] :=
   {rotateleft, rotateright} = {rotateright, rotateleft};
   to the list of turtle instructions.

Now, the Peano curve *H* can be generated with only one auxiliary variable rather than two. In the command below, X is to be interpreted as "draw a U loop to my right"; in other words, X is equivalent to an F, except that the straight path that an F would cause is replaced by a three-sided loop. To see that this is indeed the effect of X, note that each penultimate X yields +iiF-F-Fii+, which is the same as +F-F-F+. The presence of the inversion causes left loops to become right loops and vice versa as the levels deepen; this is what was accomplished by the use of X and Y in the previous implementation.

```
RecursiveTurtle[
    {"X" -> "+iXiF-XFX-FiXi+"}, "X", n, 90, 2. ^ -n, 4 ^ n]
```

EXERCISE Which is faster, the generation of Hilbert[n] by two rewriting rules using RecursiveTurtle or by one rule using a flipping turtle?

There is no end to the enhancements one might make to the rewriting system introduced here. A useful feature is the ability to perform a terminating substitution. Given an object that one suspects will be produced by a rewriting system, it can be very difficult to discover the correct rules and axiom. The use of a terminating substitution can ease the task. Suppose we use only some free characters, say X and Y, and some direction changes in the rules and axioms. Several substitutions will yield a string with no forward or back moves, and upon receiving such a string, the turtle will spin its wheels without going anywhere. But, after all the rewriting is done, we may wish to substitute a specific string of moves for the Xs and Ys. The following code shows the necessary modifications: (1) an extra, optional list argument, terminal, which takes the empty list as default, is introduced; (2) replacerules is turned into a function, because it will have to act on the main rewriting rules and on the terminal rule(s); and (3) the terminal rule is applied to the turtle's argument just before the turtle gets it.

```
RecursiveTurtle[recursion_List, axiom_String, terminal_List:{},
    depth_Integer, angle_, steplength_, startposn_List:{0.,0.},
    startdir_List:{1.,0.}, dim_:1000] :=
  . . .
replacerules[r_List] :=
  Map[First[Characters[#[[1]]]] -> Characters[#[[2]]] &, r] /.
    symboltable;
  . . .
turtle[Nest[  # /. replacerules[recursion] &,
              Characters[axiom] /. symboltable,
              depth] /. replacerules[terminal]];
```

The Appendix contains a version of RecursiveTurtle called UltraTurtle that supports both flipping and the use of a terminal substitution.

The use of a terminal string made it much easier to discover some rules to generate the *K* curves in Figure 6.11. To understand the rules that follow, ignore the direction changes momentarily and observe that each L becomes RLLR and each R becomes LRRL. This is a natural way of looking at the recursion, where L means draw a V on the left and R draws a V on the right. The direction changes paste the Vs together properly, and the terminal substitution interprets the final Ls and Rs correctly.

```
HilbertVariation[n_] := Show[UltraTurtle[
    {"R" -> "L+R-R+++L--", "L" -> "R-L+L---R++"},
    "+L",
    {"R" -> "F++F-", "L" -> "F--F+"},
    n, 45, 2^-(n+.5), 1 + 2.^(2n+1)],
  PlotRange->{{0,1}, {0,1}}, Axes->Automatic]
```

One could also use the flipping turtle and the single rewriting rule L -> iL+iL+Li+++Li++ applied to the axiom +L, with the terminal rule L -> F--F+. Exercise: Examine the output of the following command and verify that it gives the approximations to the Hilbert curve obtained by precisely locating the multiples of ¼, then the multiples of ¹⁄₁₆, then of ¹⁄₆₄, and so on. Placing these approximations in between the approximations in Figure 6.11 will yield a more detailed sequence of approximations to the Hilbert curve.

```
UltraTurtle[{"L" -> "+iLi--L+LiLi-"}, "L",
            {"L" -> "+F-FF-F"}, n, 90, 2^-(n+1), 4^(n+1) + 1, 1]
```

As mentioned, [PH] is an excellent source for more information about and examples of rewriting systems. Two noteworthy examples are:

Axiom: F+XF+F+XF

Rule: X -> XF-F+F-XF+F+XF-F+F-X

Angle: 90°

and

Axiom: X

Rules: X -> XFYFX+F+YFXFY-F-XFYFX and
         Y -> YFXFY-F-XFYFX+F+YFXFY

Angle: 90°

The first yields a variation on the closed Sierpiński space-filling curve (Figure 6.13); this is interesting because even though, in the limit, the approximations fill up the square, the area enclosed by each approximation converges to ½. (Exercise: Prove this by finding an expression for the number of squares in the nth approximation.) The second example above yields Peano's original space filler. The code to generate these curves so that the dimensions and positioning are correct is given in the Appendix. A good exercise is to find alternative approximations that approach these curves in such a way that each approximation is correct at each bend, as was done for the Hilbert curve, and then to discover rewriting schemes to generate these alternative approximations. A further exercise is to generate the x-coordinate graphs and the true graphs in $\mathbb{R}^3$ for the Sierpiński and Peano curves.

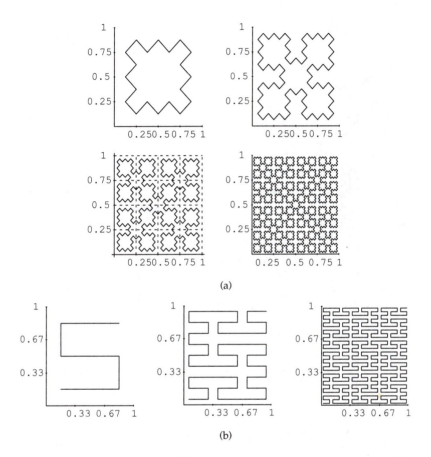

FIGURE 6.13 (a) Iterations 1 to 4 of the Sierpiński curve; comparing it with a grid similar to that used for the Hilbert curve allows one to see that the approximations have a limit. (b) Iterations 1, 2, and 3 of Peano's original space-filling curve; it can be analyzed using base-3 notation (that is, a $3^{-n} \times 3^{-n}$ grid) in a similar way to the base-4 analysis of Hilbert's curve.

When they were discovered, space-filling curves were controversial objects, but no more controversial than the 1872 discovery by Georg Cantor of a one-to-one function from the unit interval onto the unit square. Cantor's function showed that an interval has the same number of points as a square, though it fell short of being continuous. Here is an example that is not one-to-one, but does map the interval onto the square and thus shows that the interval has at least as many points as the square.

Define f, a mapping of the closed unit interval onto the closed unit square, as follows. Given $t \in [0, 1]$, write t in base-2 notation in such a way that it does not end in a tail of 1s; then concatenate the digits in odd positions to form a new binary number r and in even positions to form s. Define $f(t)$ to be (r, s). For example, $f(\frac{7}{8}) = (\frac{3}{4}, \frac{1}{2})$ because $\frac{7}{8}$ is 0.111000... in base 2, and the odd positions yield .11000, or $\frac{3}{4}$, whereas the even positions yield .1000... , or $\frac{1}{2}$; $f(1)$ is taken to be $(0, 1)$. The function f maps $[0, 1]$ onto the square, though it is not one-to-one. We may view this function in a manner similar to that used for the other curves in this section. Figure 6.14 shows some piecewise linear approximations to the image of f based on locating the terminating binary numbers and connecting the dots. [Exercise: Generate these images in *Mathematica* (solution in Appendix).] The images seem, at first glance, to be similar to some of the space-filling approximations, but a closer

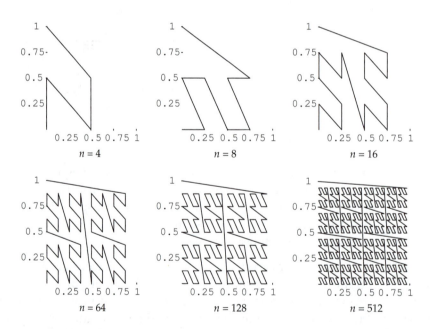

FIGURE 6.14 Several approximations to a (discontinuous) function f mapping the unit interval onto the unit square. The images are obtained by joining $f(0)$, $f(2^{-n})$, $f(2 \cdot 2^{-n})$, $f(3 \cdot 2^{-n})$, ... , $f((2^n - 1)2^{-n})$, $f(1)$, with n as indicated.

examination makes the discontinuity evident. Exercise: Use the definition of f to explain why it is not a continuous function.

6.4 Flying a Space Turtle along a Peano Curve

Our 2-dimensional turtle can be generalized to three dimensions, though the situation in three dimensions is a bit more complicated. Imagine an airplane instead of a turtle and note that there are three ways to change orientation: an airplane can pitch, roll, or yaw. Yaw is the basic left-right motion that is similar to the way a car (or a turtle) steers; pitch is a tipping forward (down) or back (up); and roll is a rotation around the fuselage. Alternatively, shaking the head is a yawing motion, nodding the head down or up is a pitching motion, and inclining the head to either side is a rolling motion. We wish to implement each direction change by matrix multiplication. To that end, the state of the airplane is given by its location and a 3×3 matrix V that starts out being the identity matrix. The first column of V gives the traditional direction or heading (the initial heading is along the x-axis), the second column gives the direction that corresponds to left (initially, along the y-axis), and the third column is the normal vector to the plane in which the airplane lies (assuming a thin airplane with initial normal along the z-axis). Then the effect of a leftward yaw on the the default starting orientation is just a rotation of each of the three direction vectors around the z-axis. For other sets V of direction vectors the effect of a yaw left will be a rotation around the third column of V. This can be effected (view it as a change of basis) by multiplying V on the *right* by the first of the three matrices displayed below (c and s refer to the cosine and sine of the appropriate angle). The other two matrices correspond to pitching down and rolling left.

$$\begin{pmatrix} c & s & 0 \\ -s & c & 0 \\ 0 & 0 & 1 \end{pmatrix} \quad \begin{pmatrix} c & 0 & s \\ 0 & 1 & 0 \\ -s & 0 & c \end{pmatrix} \quad \begin{pmatrix} 1 & 0 & 0 \\ 0 & c & s \\ 0 & -s & c \end{pmatrix}$$

For a straightforward extension of the fast turtle program to three dimensions, one would use `pitch[]`, `roll[]`, and `yaw[]`. However, we wish to generalize the string-rewriting turtle, which worked with a prespecified angle. Thus we can use `pitch`, `roll`, and `yaw` without arguments, just as `left` and `right` were used in `RecursiveTurtle`. However, we must allow for backward direction changes, so we use the six turtle commands `pitch`, `pitchback`, `rollleft`, `rollright`, `yawleft`, and `yawright`. The implementation of `RecursiveTurtle3D` is relegated to the Appendix and should be straightforward to understand or modify once the basics of 3-dimensional direction changes are grasped.

To use the program, one need only know the abbreviations for the direction changes. We will use the same notation as in the discussion of a 3-dimensional turtle in [PH], namely, F = forward, B = back, & = pitch, ^ = pitch back, \ = roll left, / = roll right, + = yaw left, − = yaw right. A small problem is that *Mathematica* reserves the backslash character as a way of introducing troublesome characters; for example, "\"" would be the way to define a character that was a quotation mark. This, of course, makes the backslash itself into a troublesome character, and so it is entered as "\\". This is a little inconvenient. On the other hand, the use of the slashes for rolling are quite appropriate, so we will simply put up with the extra characters. The program in the Appendix could be easily modified so that some other character defines `rollright`. Finally, the angles, in degrees, are to be inserted as a list of three angles, in the order pitch angle, roll angle, and yaw angle.

As an introductory example,[3] we consider the problem of using our 3-dimensional turtle to trace out the edges of a cube or a dodecahedron in a tree-like manner. That is, we start along one edge, then branch to the left and to the right; if we do this in a recursive manner, that is, find the correct string-rewriting rule, the branches will all eventually close up to form the cube. When the turtle is tracing an edge, we wish to have the normal to the plane containing it be an external bisector of the interior right angle of the cube. This means that at the start, a 45° roll is required. There will also be 45° yawing, but all pitches will be through 90°. Recall the example, given as an exercise earlier in this chapter, of a string-rewriting system that yields a tree: "B" -> "+FB--FB+B" was applied to the axiom "FB". Modifying that example to our cube yields the rule "B" -> "^+/FB\\--\\FB/+&B" applied to the axiom "\\FB"; the 2-dimensional turns become combinations of

---

[3]These 3-dimensional examples, including the rule generating the Hilbert curve in $\mathbb{R}^3$, were provided by Eric Halsey.

pitching, yawing, and rolling. Grab a handy cube-like object—a book will do—and fly a turtle (or substitute) along it using the strings that arise as the first and second iterations of the rewrite rule, and the procedure should become clear.

The following command, for various values of k and with the default thickness and Boxed values in the main program changed, yields the images in Figure 6.15, which show different levels of this tree construction. Of course, there are simpler ways to generate these polyhedra; these examples are given only to illustrate the use of a 3-dimensional turtle.

```
RecursiveTurtle3D[
    {"B" -> "^+/FB\\--\\FB/+&B"}, "\\FB", k, {90, 45, 45}, 1]
```

Applying the same rewriting rule to the angles {58.28°, 31.72°, 54°} yields a tree path along the edges of a regular dodecahedron.

The construction of a cube-filling Peano curve is entirely similar to the case of the square, if harder to visualize, with base-8 notation replacing

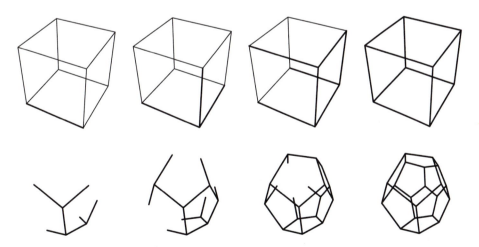

FIGURE 6.15 Flying a turtle around a tree embedded on a cube or dodecahedron eventually yields all the edges of the polyhedron. Shown are levels 0 to 3 for the cube, and levels 2 to 5 for the dodecahedron.

base-4 notation. The rewriting rule that follows is a generalization of the implementation of the Peano curve $H(t)$ via the flip turtle; consecutive 90° rolls play the role of flipping.

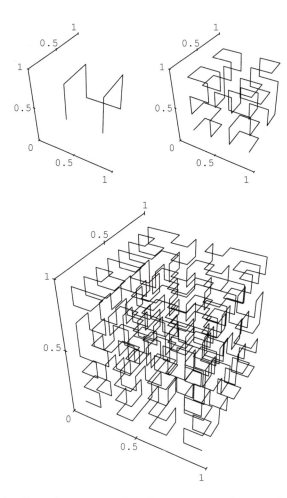

FIGURE 6.16 The first three approximations to a continuous function from the unit interval *onto* the unit cube, that is, a Peano cube-filling curve. Curves such as this show that a naive idea of the meaning of *dimension*, which would imply that it is impossible to map a 1-dimensional line segment continuously onto a 3-dimensional cube, can be misleading.

```
Hilbert3D[n_] := Show[RecursiveTurtle3D[
                {"X" -> "^\\XF^\\XFX-F^//XFX&F+//XFX-F/X-/"}, "X",
                n, {90, 90, 90}, 2^-n, {2.,2.,2.}^(-n-1)],
    Axes->Automatic, PlotRange->{{0,1}, {0,1}, {0,1}}]
```

It is worth doing an animation of one of these approximations from different viewpoints in order to get a better feeling for how the turnings work. The following code generates a sequence of 20 images whose animation spins the 3-dimensional curve; it is assumed that the level-3 curve illustrated in Figure 6.16 has been stored in `path`.

```
Do[Show[Graphics3D[Line[path],
        ViewPoint->{11 + 12 Cos[-Pi/2 + t Pi/20],
                    -8 + 12 Sin[-Pi/2 + t Pi/20],
                    16 - t}]], {t, 20}]
```

6.5 Trees, Mathematical and Botanical ▬▬▬▬

We close this chapter with one final enhancement of our 2-dimensional recursive turtle. We wish to add a stack to the turtle with which it can remember its state at a certain moment and return to it later. Using standard stack terminology, we'll let `push` be the turtle command that pushes the current state onto the top of a stack and `pop` be the command that allows the turtle magically to materialize at the state currently atop the stack (and deletes this state from the stack). The corresponding characters will simply be [for push and] for pop.

The implementation uses `paths`, a list of paths. Each time the turtle pops, a new path in `paths` is started. An extra complication is that two dimensions must be considered: the maximum length of a path in `paths` (`dim1`) and the number of paths in `path` (`dim2`). The defaults are taken to be 10 and 200, respectively. But of course it is a good idea to figure out exactly what the memory requirements will be in a specific instance where you wish to compute a very fine image. The stack is initialized with the initial state of the turtle, and then the axiom is modified to begin with a pop. This is the most complex program we have looked at so far, but it is worth pondering what it would take to implement it in a traditional programming language. An implementation of a stack turtle is included in [PH] and takes over 14 pages of code in the C lan-

guage (it does include a context-sensitivity feature, however). The routine
`UltraTurtle` in the Appendix supports stack operations as well.

```
StackTurtle[recursion_List, axiom_, depth_Integer, angle_,
    steplength_, startposn_List:{0., 0.},
    startdir_List:{1., 0.}, dim1_:10, dim2_:200] := Block[

    {X, U, turtle, rotateleft, rotateright,
     symboltable = {"F" -> forward, "B" -> back,
                    "-" -> right, "+" -> left,
                    "[" -> push, "]" -> pop},
    start, replacerules, i = 0,
    stack = {{startposn//N, startdir//N}},
    c = Cos[angle Degree]//N, s = Sin[angle Degree]//N,
    count = Table[1, {dim2}]},

start = Prepend[Characters[axiom] /. symboltable, pop];
replacerules = Map[
  Characters[First@#][[1]] -> Characters[#[[2]]] &, recursion] /.
    symboltable;

turtle[left]    :=   U = rotateleft . U;
turtle[right]   :=   U = rotateright . U;
turtle[forward] :=
                paths[[i, ++count[[i]]]] = (X += steplength U);
turtle[back]    :=
                paths[[i, ++count[[i]]]] = (X -= steplength U);
turtle[push]    :=   PrependTo[stack, {X, U}];
turtle[pop]     :=   ({X, U} = First[stack]; paths[[++i, 1]] = X;
                      stack = Rest[stack]);
Attributes[turtle] = Listable;

paths = Table[Null, {dim2}, {dim1}];
rotateleft = {{c, -s}, {s, c}}; rotateright = {{c, s}, {-s, c}};
turtle[Nest[# /. replacerules &, start, depth]];
paths = Map[Take[paths[[#]], count[[#]]]&, Range[i]];
Show[Graphics[Line /@ paths], AspectRatio->1, Axes->None,
        PlotRange->All, AspectRatio->1]]
```

A simple example of the usefulness of stacks is in the generation of a binary tree. The following code generates a sequence of paths that form a tree without any unnecessary backtracking. Recall that the straightforward rewriting scheme for a tree discussed earlier in this chapter had a lot of inefficient backtracking. The implementation of the stacking turtle does not include a way to change the size of the steps, but it could be modified to have the step length decrease according to the stack depth. A more interesting, but quite straightforward, modification would be the introduction of new characters that would allow the step size to be scaled down or up; the turtle command would simply be, for example, steplength *= scalefactor, where scalefactor was an argument to StackTurtle.

```
n = 4;
StackTurtle[{"F" -> "F[+F][-F]"}, "FB", n, 180/7,
                        1., {0,0}, {0,1}, 3, 3^n]
```

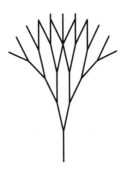

FIGURE 6.17   A tree generated by the stack rewriting rule F -> F[+F][-F].

The books by P. Prusinkiewicz and J. Hanan [PH] and by P. Prusinkiewicz and A. Lindenmayer [PL] contain several examples of incredibly lifelike plant images produced by systems of rewriting rules. The book discusses various enhancements to rewriting systems, such as context-sensitive substitutions, randomization, size changes, and rules that generate surfaces. Figure 6.18 contains two striking examples from [PH] that make use of the stack turtle. In the generating code that follows, the exact memory requirements are given as arguments. These can be estimated, or computed exactly, by examining Length[paths] and Union[Map[Length, paths] after the generation of images for n = 1, 2, and 3.

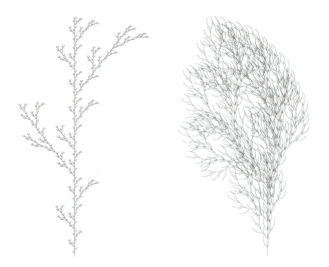

FIGURE 6.18 Two examples that give a feeling for the potential of rewriting rules to generate images similar to those found in the botanical world.

```
n = 5
StackTurtle[{"F" -> "F[+F]F[-F]F"}, "F", n, 180/7, 1.,
          {0, 0}, {0, 1}, 4, (5^n + 1)/2 ]

n = 4
StackTurtle[{"F" -> "FF+[+F-F-F]-[-F+F+F]"}, "F", n, 180./8, 1.,
          {0, 0}, {0, 1}, 6, (16 8^n + 5)/7]
```

The book by Prusinkiewicz and Hanan [PH] also shows how mathematical tilings can be generated by rewriting rules. Here is one example, the execution of which we leave for the reader. (Start with small values of n.)

```
StackTurtle[{"A" -> "X+X+X+X+X+X+",
            "Y" -> "[F+F+F+F[---Y]+++++F+++++++++F-F-F-F]",
            "X" -> "[F+F+F+F[---X-Y]+++++F+++++++++F-F-F-F]"},
           "AAAA", n, 15, 1., 13, 289]
```

For a theoretical discussion of *L*-systems in the context of free group endomorphisms, see [Dek].

7 Advanced Three-Dimensional Graphics

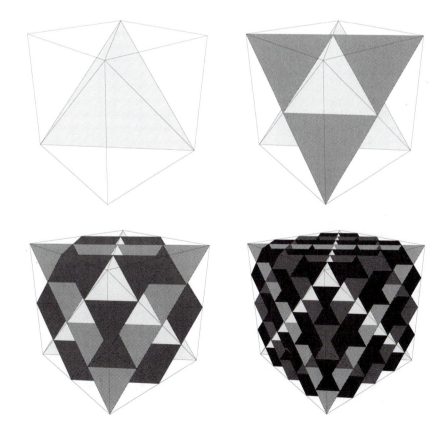

This chapter continues the discussion of 3-dimensional graphics begun in Chapter 3. Here we focus on more advanced points such as combining surfaces with space curves, using polar coordinates to display certain surfaces that are awkward in rectangular coordinates and to generate views of a torus or Möbius strip, and using graphics primitives to generate polygons in 3-space that make up polyhedra.

About the illustration overleaf:

If the Koch island construction is extended to three dimensions by starting with a regular tetrahedron, erecting a half-size tetrahedron in the middle of each face, erecting a half-again-size tetrahedron on all the faces that result, and so on, the limit object is surprising in its simplicity: It's just a cube. The figure overleaf shows the first three iterations. The first iteration yields a polyhedron considered by Kepler, called the *Stella Octangula*. The images were generated by KochPlanet3D[{1, 2, 3, 4}], which is defined near the end of this chapter.

7.1 Optimizing a Root Cellar ▬▬▬▬▬

An extremely useful package that comes with *Mathematica* is **Parametric-Plot3D.m**. It has several functions; two of the most useful are `ParametricPlot3D` and `SpaceCurve`. The latter is a straightforward generalization of `ParametricPlot`, which draws parametric curves in the plane. `ParametricPlot3D` generates parametric surfaces in 3-space and thus allows us to construct a much wider variety of surfaces than is possible using `Plot3D`. We begin with a discussion of the root-cellar problem, whose solution is a nice exercise in differential equations (see [Ber] for details). The problem is to determine the ideal depth for a root cellar, given that the temperature at a certain depth varies throughout the year in partial, but not total, synchronicity with the surface temperature. We want a root cellar to be cool in summer and warm in winter, so the ideal depth is one at which the temperature function is exactly 6 months out of phase with the surface temperature.

The analysis in [Ber] shows that the following function gives the temperature at a depth x (in feet) at time t (in years, with $t = 0$ being the time of the yearly temperature maximum): $f(x, t) = \cos(2\pi t - cx)e^{-cx}$, where $c = \sqrt{\pi/(24 \cdot 365 \cdot 0.008)} = \sqrt{\pi/70.08}$. This function is based on a normalized temperature scale, with the maximum and minimum surface temperatures being +1 and −1, respectively. Before going further, let's take a look at this function, using just the default settings in `Plot3D`.

```
c = 0.211728
f[x_, t_] := Cos[2 Pi t - c x] Exp[-c x]
Plot3D[f[x, t], {x, 0, 30}, {t, 0, 2}]
```

Because the time scale stretches over 2 years, we can see the seasonal rise and fall at the surface. And at 30 feet below the surface the temperature is unaffected by the seasonal changes, as shown by the constancy of the $f(30, t)$ cross-section. What is only suggested by the rough graph in Figure 7.1 is the salient fact for a root-cellar builder, namely that the extremes at intermediate depths do not occur at the same t-values as the surface extremes, but are phased forward in time according to the laws of physics governing heat transfer through a solid material, in this case soil. The details are lucidly presented by G. C. Berresford [Ber]. In Figure 7.1 this is suggested by the fact that the ridge lines descending from a hot

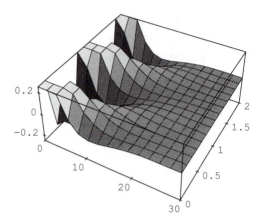

FIGURE 7.1 A rough image of the temperature-at-depth function $f(x, t)$. This image uses all the default settings of `Plot3D` and so does not have as much detail as one would like. On the other hand, it took only a few seconds to generate.

time on the surface do not descend in a straight constant-time line, but veer to the left (future). In fact, this veering is on a straight line, whose explicit form, as we shall now discover, will yield the desired optimal depth.

```
f[x, t]
Cos[2 Pi t - 0.211728 x]
-----------------------
        0.211728 x
    E


D[f[x, t], t]
-2 Pi Sin[2 Pi t - 0.211728 x]
------------------------------
        0.211728 x
    E
```

The preceding partial derivative vanishes on infinitely many lines, and the built-in solver will find only one of these lines. Let's try it anyway, specifying x as the underlying variable because we are interested in how

t, the time of a maximum (or minimum), varies with the depth. We use N[] so that the solver does not have to think symbolically.

```
Solve[N[%] == 0, t]
Solve::ifun:
    Warning: inverse functions are being used by Solve, so some
    solutions may not be found.
{{t -> 0.0336976 x}}
```

The warning message lets us know that not all roots have been found. The solution given, $t = 0.0336976x$, is the one corresponding to the fundamental branch of the arcsine function; other solutions will have the form $0.0336976x + n\pi$, with odd n giving minima and even n giving maxima. The optimal depth of a root cellar is simply the depth at which the time of the first maximum is 6 months, or 0.5; because of the linear function giving the time of the first maximum at a given depth, the optimal depth is 0.5/0.0336976, or 14.838 feet, which we'll approximate by 15 feet in the discussion that follows.

The preceding can all be nicely illustrated by superimposing the space curve $C(t) = \{x, 0.0336976x, f(x,t))$ on the surface that is the graph of f. This is done in Figure 7.2, in which three space curves show the future-trending ridge lines and the half-year phase shift at a depth of 15 feet (located with the help of the vertical lines over the axes at $t = 0.5$ and $x = 15$).

The code that generates Figure 7.2 follows (see Color Plate 2 for a color version). As usual, it is optimized for the amount of memory on my machine. If you have less memory (or time) available, then a less fine image should be generated by increasing the values 0.75 and 1/12.

```
<<:Graphics:ParametricPlot3D.m;      (* use separate cell *)

Show[

    ParametricPlot3D[{x, t, f[x, t]},
    {x, 0, 30, 0.75}, {t, 0., 40/12, 1/12}],

    SpaceCurve[{15, t, f[15, t] + .01}, {t, 0, 40/12, 1./12}],

    Release[Table[SpaceCurve[
        {x, 0.0336 x + n, f[x, 0.0336 x + n]}, {x, 0, 30, 1}],
            {n, 0, 1}]],
```

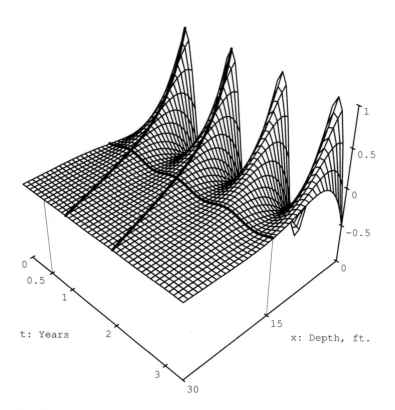

FIGURE 7.2 The graph shows the temperature variation over time at soil depths down to 30 feet. The ridges (and valleys) trend toward the future; this means that the annual variation below the surface is out of phase with the surface extrema. At a depth of 15 feet the phase shift is exactly a half-year; thus 15 feet is the optimal depth for a root cellar.

```
Graphics3D[{Thickness[.0005],
    Line[{{30, .5, -1}, {30, .5, 0}}],
    Line[{{15, 40/12, -1}, {15, 40/12, f[15, 40/12]}}]}],

PlotRange->{{0, 30}, {0, 40/12}, {-1, 1}},
BoxRatios->{1, 1, .8}, Boxed->False,
Axes->Automatic, AxesEdge->{{1, -1}, Automatic, Automatic},
```

```
Ticks->{{0, 15, 30}, {0, .5 , 1, 2, 3}, {-.5, 0, .5, 1}},
AxesLabel->{"x: Depth, ft.", "t: Years", None},
ViewPoint->{2, 2, 2}]
```

The sequence of commands begins with the loading of the requisite package. Then four `Graphics3D` images are shown together: the surface, the single space curve, the two ridge lines, and the two vertical pointer lines.

`ParametricPlot3D` generates a shaded image; the simplest way to get rid of the shading is to toggle off the Show Filled Areas item in the Graph menu. Alternatively, one could use a variation to `ParametricPlot3D` that allows the specification of a coloring function. Such a package can be found in [Mae]; it will be built into the next version of *Mathematica*. On the other hand, the defaults and toggle allow greater flexibility, as one can then decide after the image is generated whether shading is or is not desirable. The use of `ParametricPlot3D[{x, y, f[x,y]} ...]` is basically the same as the built-in `Plot3D[f[x, y] ...]`. However, the latter is not a `Graphics3D` object and so cannot be combined with other objects without further massage. In fact, this can be done via `Graphics3D[Plot3D[f[x, y] ...]]`, which produces the appropriate list of 3-dimensional faces. If an image is being generated specifically for the purpose of combining it with other images, however, it makes more sense to use `ParametricPlot3D`, which produces a `Graphics3D` object directly. The step sizes in `ParametricPlot3D` are governed by the fourth entry in the lists giving the ranges of x and t; $1/12$ is chosen so that the time grid corresponds to months.

The first `SpaceCurve` command generates the temperature curve 15 feet down. The z-coordinate has been raised by 0.01 to avoid the problem that parts of the curve may be hidden underneath the surface because of approximation error inherent in the grid. The other two space curves have been generated via `Release[Table[]]`. The advantage over listing the curves individually is that simply changing the range of n to, say, `{n, 0, 2, 0.5}` will superimpose additional space curves on the surface. The use of `Release` to plot a list of functions is dicussed in Chapter 3 (page 86). Exercise: Modify the code using `$DisplayFunction` (see the commands used to generate Figure 1.8) to suppress the display of all the intermediate images.

It is evident from the graph that the temperature variation 15 feet down is much less than the variation at the surface. Exercise: Use the function $f(x, t)$ to show that the variation at a depth of 15 feet is 4.35% of the surface temperature variation. Thus if the surface temperature varies from –5 to 95°F, then the temperature in the optimal root cellar ranges from 42.8 to 47.2°.

7.2 A Parametric Trochoid

The preceding example used `ParametricPlot3D` in a routine way; the image it produced differed only technically from that produced by `Plot3D`. The power of parametric surface plotting is that it allows us to look at not only graphs of functions from $\mathbb{R}^2$ to $\mathbb{R}$, but also the surfaces that arise as the image of a function from $\mathbb{R}^2$ to $\mathbb{R}^2$, that is, a function of the form $f(x,y) = (u(x,y),\ v(x,y))$. As a first example, consider the various cycloidal curves discussed in Chapter 2. Recall that the locus of the center of a rolling wheel of unit radius is a horizontal line, whereas a point on the circumference generates a cycloid and a point on a spoke extending past the circumference generates a trochoid with loops. The parametric representation of the locus is $(t - a\sin t, 1 - a\cos t)$, where a is the distance of the generating point from the center. We can paste all these curves together into a single parametric surface as follows.

```
ParametricPlot3D[{a, t - a Sin[t], 1 - a Cos[t]},
    {a, 0, 2, .1}, {t, 0., 5 Pi, Pi/16},
    BoxRatios->{4, 5 Pi, 3}, Boxed->False,
    ViewPoint->{1.8, 0, 1.7}]
```

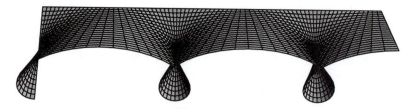

FIGURE 7.3 A family of trochoids pasted together into a single surface. Imagine a rod extending downward from the center of a wheel at a 45° angle. This surface is the one swept out by the rod as the wheel rolls.

7.3 The Polar View ▬▬▬▬▬▬▬

Even an ordinary function—that is, $f(x, y)$ mapping $\mathbb{R}^2$ to $\mathbb{R}$—can benefit from being plotted as a parametric surface. In particular, polar coordinates are often a useful way of looking at a function; the graph of $f(x, y)$ may be viewed in polar coordinates via

```
ParametricPlot3D[
        {r Cos[theta], r Sin[theta], f[r Cos[theta], r Sin[theta]]},
                      {theta, 0, 2 Pi}, {r, 0, rmax}]
```

This will show the same surface as would be shown by plotting f using Plot3D, but the domain will be a circle of radius rmax and the radial lines on the surface will bring out quite different features than those shown by the usual rectangular grid.

Consider the following standard function from multivariable calculus, which is undefined at the origin.

```
Clear[f]; f[x_, y_] := x y / (x^2 + y^2)
```

The function has a discontinuity at the origin, and so the standard rectangular approach to plotting via

```
Plot3D[f[x, y], {x, -2, 2}, {y, -2, 2},
 BoxRatios->{1.5, 1, 1.5}, ViewPoint->{-1.5, -2.8, 2.8},
 AxesEdge->{{-1, -1}, {-1, -1}, Automatic},
 AxesLabel->{"x", "y", None}]
```

does not yield a very satisfactory image [Figure 7.4(a)]. The problem is that this function is constant on straight lines from the origin; this causes the rectangular grid lines to make some large jumps. Refining the grid would improve things, but the nonuniformity of the grid would always yield a less-than-satisfactory image. The polar coordinate version using the same number of surface patches is much clearer [Figure 7.4(b)]. To generate it, we first simplify the polar form of the function.

```
f[r Cos[theta], r Sin[theta]]

    2
   r  Cos[theta] Sin[theta]
------------------------------
    2           2    2           2
   r  Cos[theta]  + r  Sin[theta]
```

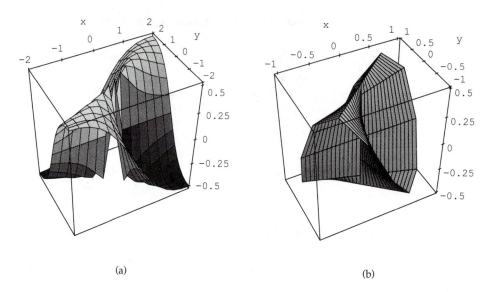

(a)   (b)

FIGURE 7.4 Two views of a discontinuous function using rectangular coordinates (a) and polar coordinates (b). The polar view more clearly reveals the ribbon-like structure of the surface.

```
Simplify[% /. Cos[x_]^2 -> 1 - Sin[x]^2]
Cos[theta] Sin[theta]
```

This last form is independent of r; this explains why the function is constant on straight lines through the origin. Moreover, the function is easily recognized as being simply `Sin[2 theta]/2`. The following command now generates Figure 7.4(b).

```
ParametricPlot3D[{r Cos[theta], r Sin[theta], Sin[2 theta]/2},
                 {r, 0, 1}, {theta, 0, 2 Pi},
    BoxRatios->{1.5, 1, 1.5}, ViewPoint->{-1.5, -2.8, 2.8},
    AxesLabel->{"x", "y", None}, Axes->Automatic,
    AxesEdge->{{-1, -1}, {-1, -1}, Automatic}]
```

Another advantage of the polar form is that we can excise the discontinuity by avoiding small values of r. The output of the following command, where the grid has been refined to 9 radial and 60 angular steps, is shown in Figure 7.5, which also contains a refined image of the unexcised ribbon.

```
ParametricPlot3D[{r Cos[theta], r Sin[theta], Sin[2 theta]/2},
                {r, 0, 1, .1}, {theta, 0, 2 Pi, Pi/30},
      Boxed->False, BoxRatios->{1.5, 1, 1.5},
      ViewPoint->{-1.5, -2.8, 2.8}]
```

Another example enhanced by a polar view is B. Calvert and M. K. Vamanamurthy's fifth-degree counterexample to the only-critical-point-in-town test mentioned in Chapter 3. Recall that $x^2(1+y)^3 + y^2$ has a local minimum at the origin that is not an absolute minimum, but has no other critical points. A polar view brings out the behavior more clearly than a rectangular view. The critical point is just visible in the center, as is the long valley caused by the fact that the function is the constant 1 on the line $y = -1$. The view in Figure 7.6 has been enhanced by increasing the coefficient of y^2 to 7. The usual circular polar domain has been turned into an elliptical one by scaling x by 4. And the graph has been clipped to the interval $[-20, 20]$ by using Min and Max in the z-coordinate. When

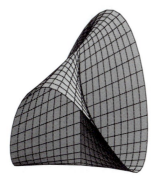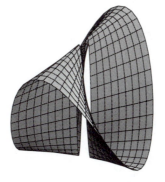

FIGURE 7.5 Two views of a discontinuous function using polar coordinates. Because the function is not defined at the origin, it is more honest to excise a narrow cylinder about the origin, which is easily done when polar coordinates are used.

Plot3D is used, clipping can be handled automatically by the ClipFill option. Shading was eliminated via the switch in the Graph menu. The image in Figure 7.6 was generated by the following code.

```
g[x_,y_] := x^2 (1+y)^3 + 7 y^2
ParametricPlot3D[{x = 4 r Cos[theta], y = r Sin[theta],
                                  Max[-20, Min[20, g[x, y]]]},
     {r, 0, 3, .07}, {theta, 0, 2 Pi, Pi/25},
PlotRange-> {{-12, 12}, {-3, 3}, {-20, 20}},
Axes->Automatic, BoxRatios->{1, 1, .6}, Boxed->False,
ViewPoint->{-1.1, -.4, .7}, AxesLabel->{"x", "y", "z"},
AxesEdge->{Automatic, Automatic, {-1, +1}},
AmbientLight->GrayLevel[.1]]
```

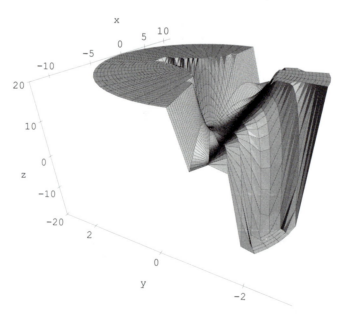

FIGURE 7.6 The graph of $x^2(1+y)^3 + 7y^2$, which is a minimal-degree polynomial counterexample to the only-critical-point-in-town test. The origin is the only critical point and it is a minimum, but not an absolute minimum.

7.4 Rotating Circles to Produce a Torus or Möbius Strip

Some surfaces are very easy to generate by using parametric representations. For example, a torus can be obtained just by rotating one circle about another circle. First we define the rotation matrix that rotates about the z-axis, then we define the circle to be rotated (it sits in the x-z plane), and finally we multiply the two to get the general position of a point on the circle.

```
rotate[t_] := {{Cos[t], -Sin[t], 0},
                {Sin[t],  Cos[t], 0},
                {  0,        0,    1}};
circle[t_] := {4, 0, 0} + {Cos[t], 0, Sin[t]};
rotate[theta] . circle[phi]
{(4 + Cos[phi]) Cos[theta], (4 + Cos[phi]) Sin[theta], Sin[phi]}
```

We can now insert the preceding output into the plotting command. We could have simply used rotate[theta].circle[phi] as the function to be plotted, but it's faster to use the multiplied-out version. Figure 7.7(a) shows the torus that the following command produces.

```
ParametricPlot3D[
        {(4 + Cos[phi]) Cos[theta],
         (4 + Cos[phi]) Sin[theta],
         Sin[phi]},
    {phi, 0, 2 Pi, Pi/12}, {theta, 0, 2 Pi, Pi/12}, Boxed->False]
```

The version of ParametricPlot3D included with Version 1.2 does not support user-defined coloring; future releases will correct this. Meanwhile, a modification that does allow for such coloring can be found in [Mae, p. 223], and its use as follows will yield the shaded torus in Figure 7.7(b).

```
ModifiedParametricPlot3D[
     {(4 + Cos[phi])*Cos[theta],
      (4+Cos[phi])*Sin[theta], Sin[phi],
      GrayLevel[Abs@Sin[theta/2]]},
    {phi, 0, 2 Pi, Pi/12}, {theta, 0, 2 Pi, Pi/12},
    Boxed->False, Lighting->False]
```

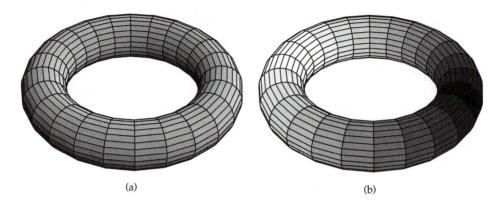

(a)   (b)

FIGURE 7.7 Two views of a torus. The left one uses the default illumination; the right is shaded according to the position with respect to a horizontal circle.

We will return to the topic of torus-coloring later in this chapter, when we consider a map on the torus that requires seven colors.

A Möbius strip can be generated in an entirely analogous way. First imagine the torus-generating circle itself rotating about its center at half the speed that it is being rotated about the origin. Then its diameter will undergo a half-twist; this produces a Möbius strip. We get at the diameter by introducing a multiplier, s, that will take on only the values ± 1.

```
circle[t_] := {4, 0, 0} + s {Cos[t], 0, Sin[t]}
ParametricPlot3D[rotate[theta] . circle[theta/2],
     {s, -1, 1, 2}, {theta, 0, 2 Pi, Pi/30},
     Boxed->False, ViewPoint->{2.7, -1.7, 2.3}]
```

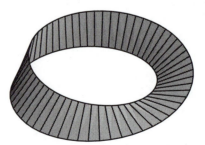

FIGURE 7.8 A Möbius strip is generated by rotating a rotating line segment about a circle.

EXERCISE What surface will be generated by plotting the dot product of `rotate[theta]` and `circle[phi]`, where `circle[t_]` is simply `{Cos[t], 0, Sin[t]}`?

As pointed out earlier, 3-dimensional graphics objects can be combined in a way that properly hides the parts that are hidden from view. As an example, consider Figure 7.9, which is a diagram used to illustrate cylindrical coordinates [TF]. First the cylinder is generated and then three planes and three axis lines; finally the two images are shown together with the desired options. Some ambient light is included so that the dark side of the plane is not totally black.

```
ParametricPlot3D[{Cos[theta], Sin[theta], z},
                  {theta, 0, 2 Pi, Pi/16}, {z, 0, 2, 2}]


Show[Graphics3D[{GrayLevel[0],
Polygon[{{1.1,1.1,.5}, {1.1,-1.1,.5}, {-1.1,-1.1,.5},
                                      {-1.1,1.1,.5}}],

GrayLevel[.5],
Polygon[{{1.1,1.1,0}, {-1.1,-1.1,0}, {-1.1,-1.1,2}, {1.1,1.1,2}}],
```

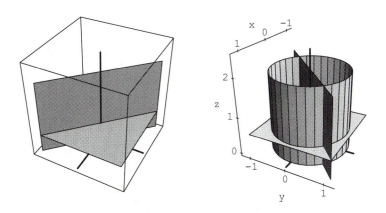

FIGURE 7.9 Combining a cylinder ($r = 1$) with the two planes ($\theta = \pi/4$ and $z = 1/2$) illustrates the use of cylindrical coordinates. The thick lines are the axes through the origin. The point in the foreground where the cylinder meets the two planes has the cylindrical coordinates $(1, \pi/4, 1/2)$. The image on the left is an intermediate image, generated with all the default settings.

```
    GrayLevel[0], Line[{{0,0,0}, {0,0,2.5}}],
    Line[{{0,-1.2,0}, {0,1.2,0}}], Line[{{1.2,0,0}, {-1.2,0,0}}]}]]

    Show[%, %%, Boxed->False, BoxRatios->{1, 1, 1},
        ViewPoint->{2.4, 1.3, 1.3},
        Axes->Automatic, AxesLabel->{"x", "y", "z"},
        AmbientLight->GrayLevel[.15]]
```

Mathematica comes with a package, **Shapes.m**, that includes routines for generating the three surfaces considered here, as well as a cone, sphere, and helix. But more control and understanding comes from developing such routines oneself.

7.5 Map Coloring on a Torus

The celebrated four-color theorem, which was long conjectured but proved only in 1976, implies that any map on a plane or the surface of a sphere can be colored with four colors so that countries that share a border in common are colored differently. By "border in common" we mean that two countries share at least an arc of a border curve; countries sharing only a point or a disconnected set of points are not considered to be adjacent.

It is a curious fact that maps on a torus or an n-holed torus are easier to color than maps on a sphere or plane. Well, really they are harder to color because more colors are generally required, but the exact determination of the maximum possible number of colors is easier. In 1890 P. Heawood discovered the formula

$$\chi(n) = \left\lfloor \frac{7 + \sqrt{48n + 1}}{2} \right\rfloor$$

and proved that the number of colors required to color a map on an n-holed torus ($n \geq 1$) is at most $\chi(n)$. In 1968 G. Ringel and J. W. T. Youngs [Rin] succeeded in showing that for every $n \geq 1$, there is a configuration of $\chi(n)$ countries on an n-holed torus such that each country shares a border with each of the $\chi(n) - 1$ other countries; this shows that $\chi(n)$ colors may be necessary. This completed the proof that Heawood's formula is indeed the correct chromatic number function for the n-holed torus.

Note that $\chi(1)$ is 7, whence seven colors are sufficient and sometimes necessary to color maps on the torus. This case was proved by Heawood, who was the first to describe a seven-country toroidal map such that each country is adjacent to all six other countries. In this section we will use the techniques discussed earlier in this chapter to produce an image of such a map on the torus.

Heawood's formula is in fact valid for $n = 0$, in which case it states that a map on the sphere (the zero-holed torus) requires at most four colors. That is precisely the four-color theorem, but the proof of this last case required completely different methods, including a vast amount of computer verification, than the case $n \geq 1$.

Coloring questions on surfaces are usually discussed in terms of graphs on the surface, with each country represented by a vertex and adjacent vertices corresponding to countries that share a border. Here we will focus on countries and maps rather than graphs, since our goal is to present an actual map on the torus. In graph theory terms we are simply embedding K_7, the complete graph on seven vertices, on the torus. For more on topological graph theory see [Gro, Whi].

It is topologically equivalent but conceptually much easier to consider the torus as a rectangle in the plane with opposite sides identified. Doing this makes the problem of embedding K_7 on a torus an easy 2-dimensional exercise, and makes the generation of the corresponding map on the toroidal surface much easier as well.

Consider the 12×12 rectangle shown in dashed lines in Figure 7.10; this rectangle can be viewed as a torus if its opposite sides are identified. Alternatively, the whole plane is viewed as a torus with identifications modulo the rectangle, that is, two points of the form (x, y) and $(x, y) + (12, 12)$ are identified. The dashed grid corresponds to a grid on the torus similar to the one illustrated in Figure 7.6, except that that image was based on a 24×24 grid. Superimposed over the standard dashed grid is a grid of parallellograms, arranged so that the point $(11, 11)$ is taken to $(12, 12)$ and the point $(12, 0)$ is taken to a point that coincides, toroidally speaking, with the point that $(0, 1)$ is taken to [and similarly for $(0, 12)$ and $(1, 0)$]. The result is a uniform spiral grid, spiralling 12 times in each direction. Exercise: Write a program that generates Figure 7.10(b), with curves that spiral n times in one direction and m in the other.

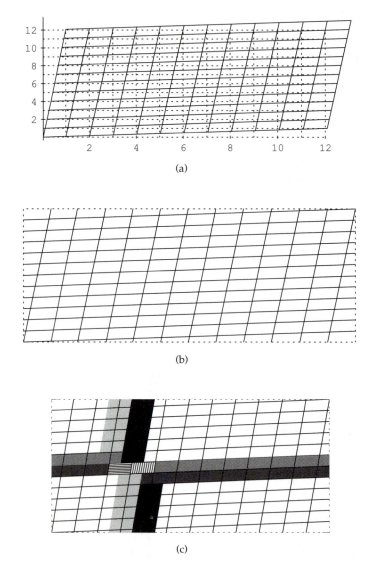

(a)

(b)

(c)

FIGURE 7.10 The appropriate linear transformation of the rectangular grid on a rectangle yields a spiral grid on a torus, where the identification of opposite sides turns a rectangle topologically into a torus. The bottom diagram shows seven mutually adjacent countries embedded on a torus.

In order to get the linear transformation that generates the spiral grid, simply observe that T satisfies: $T(11, 11) = (12, 12)$, $T(12, 0) = T(0, 1) + (12, 0)$, and $T(0, 12) = T(1, 0) + (12, 0)$. Since T is given by a 2×2 matrix, it can be determined by hand, but we may as well let *Mathematica* do the work.

```
T = {{a, b}, {c, d}}
Solve[T . {11, 11} == {12, 12} &&
      T . {12, 0}  == T . {0, 1} + {12, 0} &&
      T . {0, 12}  == T . {1, 0} + {0, 12}, {a, b, c, d}]
         144           12          12          144
{{a -> ---, b -> ---, c -> ---, d -> ---}}
         143          143         143         143
```

This gives us the correct matrix.

EXERCISE Generate the spiral-like grids that would be obtained by using either of the two matrices

$$\begin{pmatrix} 1 & 1/12 \\ 1/12 & 1 \end{pmatrix} \qquad \begin{pmatrix} 1 & 1/12 \\ 0 & 1 \end{pmatrix} \begin{pmatrix} 1 & 0 \\ 1/12 & 1 \end{pmatrix}$$

and explain how they differ from the grid shown in Figure 7.10.

The matrix just obtained has determinant $144/143$; this means that the area of each small parallellogram in Figure 7.10(a) has area $144/143$ and therefore that only 143 parallellograms from Figure 7.10(a) are used to translate the grid to the original rectangle as shown in Figure 7.10(b). This is because the upper rightmost parallellogram in (a) is not used in (b). Another way of looking at the small discrepancy is by observing that two cycles on the torus, one cycling m times in one direction and the other cycling n times in the orthogonal direction, divide the torus into $mn - 1$ regions (provided each of m and n is greater than 1).

Figure 7.10(c) shows seven mutually adjacent countries on a torus. It was not essential to use the spiral as one could, with a fine enough rectangular grid, define seven mutually adjacent countries so that each country consists of small rectangles. The advantage of using parallellograms is that each country can be taken to be a parallellogram on the torus. We may now move directly to the rendering of this map on a toroidal surface (Figure 7.11) by modifying the approach in the preceding section

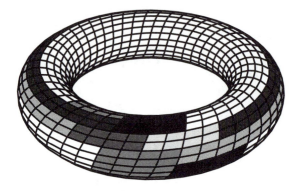

FIGURE 7.11 A map on the torus with seven countries, each of which is adjacent to the other six.

so as to take the linear transformation into account. Because we want a shaded surface, we will have to use `ModifiedParametricPlot3D`, which as mentioned earlier, may be found in [Mae] and will be included in a future release of *Mathematica*.

The definition of `spiral` below generates only the grid parallelograms corresponding to a single country and colors them according to `color`. The 12×12 grid has been replaced by a `theta-phi` coordinate system based on a 48×24 subdivision of a square of side length 2π; the range on `phi` in `spiral` was chosen to center the map on the torus. The `DisplayFunction` settings are included so that the display of each partial surface is suppressed. The turning off of `RenderAll` means that the final image will not contain the PostScript code for any hidden patches of the surface; this saves memory in those cases where the viewpoint will not be changed. For increased speed, change the step sizes for `theta` and `phi` in `spiral` to `Pi/12` and `Pi/6`, respectively.

```
spiral[start_, end_, color_] := ModifiedParametricPlot3D[
Append[
  rotate[(144theta + 12phi)/143].circle[(12theta + 144phi)/143],
  GrayLevel[color]],
{theta, start, end, Pi/24}, {phi, -2 Pi/6, -Pi/6, Pi/12},
    DisplayFunction->Identity]
```

```
white1 = spiral[10 Pi +   Pi/12,  21 Pi,              1]
white2 = spiral[ 8 Pi +   Pi/12,  10 Pi - 3 Pi/12,    1]
white3 = spiral[ 2 Pi + 3 Pi/12,   4 Pi -   Pi/12,    1]
white4 = spiral[ 2 Pi - 4 Pi/12,   2 Pi -   Pi/12,    1]
white5 = spiral[       - 3 Pi/12,        -   Pi/12,    1]
white6 = spiral[         3 Pi/12,          7 Pi/12,    1]
green1 = spiral[10 Pi - 3 Pi/12,  10 Pi -   Pi/12,   .5]
green2 = spiral[ 4 Pi -   Pi/12,   4 Pi +   Pi/12,   .5]
green3 = spiral[ 2 Pi -   Pi/12,   2 Pi +   Pi/12,   .5]
green4 = spiral[       -   Pi/12,            Pi/12,   .5]
green5 = spiral[12 Pi - 3 Pi/12,  12 Pi -   Pi/12,   .5]
brown1 = spiral[10 Pi -   Pi/12,  10 Pi +   Pi/12,    0]
brown2 = spiral[ 8 Pi -   Pi/12,   8 Pi +   Pi/12,    0]
brown3 = spiral[ 2 Pi +   Pi/12,   2 Pi + 3 Pi/12,    0]
brown4 = spiral[         Pi/12,          3 Pi/12,    0]
yellow = spiral[ 6 Pi -   Pi/6,    6 Pi,             .3]
red    = spiral[ 4 Pi +   Pi/12,   6 Pi -   Pi/6,    .7]
blue   = spiral[ 6 Pi +   Pi/6,    8 Pi -   Pi/12,   .1]
purple = spiral[ 6 Pi,             6 Pi +   Pi/6,    .9]


Show[white1, white2, white3, white4, white5, white6, brown1,
     brown2, brown3, brown4, green1, green2, green3, green4,
     green5, yellow, red, purple, blue,
   Lighting->False, ViewPoint->{2, 0.2, 1.2},
   Boxed->False, RenderAll->False,
   PlotRange->{{-5, 5}, {-5, 5}, {-1, 1}},
   DisplayFunction->$DisplayFunction]
```

Users with a color monitor may wish to generate a color version of Figure 7.11. This is easily done by substituting RGBColor[r, g, b] for GrayLevel[color] in the definition of spiral. The following red-green-blue values yield a pleasing map: white = (0.7, 1, 1); green = (0.25, 1, 0.25); brown = (1, 0.4, 0); yellow = (1, 1, 0); red = (1, 0, 0.1); blue = (0.2, 0.2, 1); purple = (1, 0, 1). The result can be seen in Color Plate 3.

7.6 A Fractalized Tetrahedron Is a Cube ▬▬

The essence of each iteration of the Koch island construction discussed in Chapter 5 is that a segment is broken into thirds and the central third is made into the base of an equilateral triangle. The new triangle may be thought of as being obtained by folding the two end thirds toward each other until they meet. This can be generalized to a 3-dimensional *Koch planet* construction where the starting solid is a regular tetrahedron. Each face of the tetrahedron can be divided into four congruent half-size triangles by joining the bisectors of the segments bounding the face. Then a regular tetrahedron is erected on the central half-size triangle. As in the plane, the erected object can be obtained by folding the three noncentral triangles upward toward the center. This first iteration yields a polyhedron with 24 faces, each of which is an equilateral triangle; thus the process can be repeated on each face, to yield a polyhedron with $6 \cdot 24 = 144$ triangular faces. Endless repetition leads to a limiting object that one might expect would be highly irregular, as is the Koch fractal in the plane. But, remarkably, it turns out that the limiting object is simply a cube (a discovery of B. Mandelbrot; see [Mor]). Some 3-dimensional images can surely help us understand what is going on here.

We first consider the simpler problem of starting with a triangle, erecting a tetrahedron on its middle, and so on (see Figure 7.12). To be precise, let's start with the equilateral triangle with vertices $(\sqrt{3}/3, 0, 0)$, $(-\sqrt{3}/6, 1/2, 0)$, and $(-\sqrt{3}/6, -1/2, 0)$; these vertices are chosen so that the

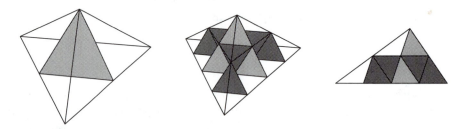

FIGURE 7.12 The first two steps in the 3-dimensional fractalization of a triangle, along with a cross-sectional view of the second step. The limit object fills the nonregular tetrahedron.

triangle's side has length 1. The iterative step is implemented by frac-
talize[], which transforms a triangle into the six half-sized triangles
that result from the fractalization process. This function also takes a gray
level as input and leaves it alone if the returned triangle is contained
in the input triangle and changes it to newgray if the new triangle is
not in the plane of the input triangle. By incrementing newgray at each
fractalization, the faces will be shaded in the order of their appearance,
except that subfaces of old faces are not considered to be new. The function is preceded by a definition of unitnormal, which implements the
usual cross-product formula via a symbolic determinant (see [TF, §13.5])
to obtain a unit vector perpendicular to two given vectors. The geometrical ideas underlying the fractalization process are (1) the centroid of an
equilateral triangle with vertices at **P**, **Q**, and **R** is $1/3$ (**P** + **Q** + **R**) and
(2) the altitude of the erected tetrahedron is $1/\sqrt{6}$ times the side of the
large triangle (an easy consequence of Pythagoras's Theorem and the fact
that the centroid of a triangle divides each median in a 2:1 ratio). The
main routine is Koch3D[n], which shows n steps of this fractalization
process together with the tetrahedron obtained by connecting the original
three vertices to the top of the first new tetrahedron. The iteration is accomplished by nesting a pure function that is a substitution, where each
{GrayLevel, Polygon} pair is replaced by its fractalization, which
consists of six {GrayLevel, Polygon} pairs in two groups of three.
The braces that build up are of no consequence as the substitution operator and Graphics3D see through all braces. The nested function also
decrements newgray; this changes the gray level of the new faces.

```
norm[v_] := Sqrt[v . v]
unitnormal[v1_List, v2_List] :=
    (cross = Det[{IdentityMatrix[3], v1, v2}]) / norm[cross]


fractalize[{gray_, {p_, q_, r_}}] := Block[

{pq = (p+q)/2, qr = (r+q)/2, pr = (p+r)/2,
  new = (p+q+r)/3 + unitnormal[q-p, r-p]*norm[p-q]/Sqrt[6.]},

{Map[{gray, Polygon[#]} &, {{p,pq,pr}, {pq,q,qr}, {pr,qr,r}}],
  Map[{GrayLevel[newgray],
      Polygon[#]} &, {{pr,pq,new}, {pq,qr,new}, {qr,pr,new}}]}]
```

```
Koch3D[n_] := (newgray = 1.;
vertices =
   {{Sqrt[3]/3,0,0}, {-Sqrt[3]/6,.5,0}, {-Sqrt[3]/6,-.5,0}}//N;
triangle = {GrayLevel[newgray], Polygon[vertices]};
tetrahedron = {Thickness[.0001],
                 Line[{{0, 0, 1/Sqrt[6.]}, #}] & /@ vertices};
Show[Graphics3D[{tetrahedron,
    Nest[(newgray -= .3;
      # /. {gray_, Polygon[v_]} -> fractalize[{gray, v}]) &,
        triangle, n]}],
  Lighting->False, Boxed->False,
  BoxRatios->{Sqrt[3]/2, 1, 1/Sqrt[6]},
  ViewPoint->({2, .3, 1.3}),
  PlotRange ->
      {{-Sqrt[3]/6, Sqrt[3]/3}, {-1/2, 1/2}, {0, Sqrt[2/3]/2}}])
```

Note that the figure stays within the large tetrahedron and the smaller tetrahedra never crash. In fact, they just touch, as can be seen in the cross-sectional view in Figure 7.12, which was obtained by using the viewpoint (0, 200, 0). We leave the rigorous verification of these geometrical observations as an exercise. The volume computation of the limiting object is straightforward if one recalls that the volume of a tetrahedron is one third the product of the height and the area of the base, which yields $s^3\sqrt{2}/12$ as the volume of a regular tetrahedron over an equilateral triangle having side length s. The first new tetrahedron therefore has volume $\sqrt{2}/96$, and this is multiplied by $^6\!/_8$ at each fractalization; summing the resulting geometric series yields a volume of $\sqrt{2}/24$, which is exactly the volume of the enclosing tetrahedron, since its height is half that of the regular tetrahedron over the large triangle.

We can now see how a fractalized tetrahedron yields a cube. The diagonals of the faces of a cube form a regular tetrahedron that, when subtracted from the cube, leaves four nonregular tetrahedra similar to the enclosing tetrahedron used in Figure 7.12. Since fractalizing each triangular face fills up these nonregular tetrahedra, combining all the pieces yields a limiting object that fills the cube (Figure 7.13). The limiting figure is not exactly the entire cube, as a certain collection of regions on the large cube and on each of countably many subcubes will be omitted;

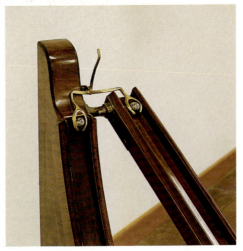

Color Plate 1 A cycloid made in 1775 by Francesco Spighi, using sandalwood, olive wood, and violet ebony, can be seen at the Museum of the History of Science in Florence, Italy. The straight arm is attached for a demonstration that a straight line does not yield the fastest path between two points. When the arm is raised so that its lower end lies on the cycloid, then a ball released on the cycloid will reach the end of the arm sooner than a ball released on the straight piece, even though the cycloidal route takes the ball below its destination. Note the brass mechanism (inset) that ensures a simultaneous release. Similar experiments, with many variations, can be performed by combining *Mathematica*'s computational and animation abilities (see Chapter 2).

(Photos by Franca Principe, Istituto e Museo di Storia della Scienza, Florence, Italy)

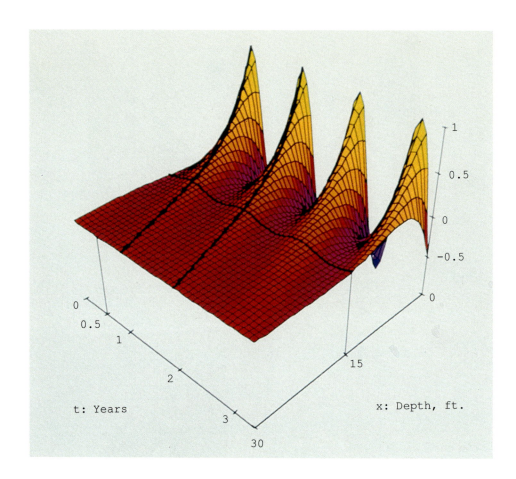

Color Plate 2   A graph that shows how the temperature down to 30 feet below
the surface of the earth varies over a period of three and a half years. Because
changes at the surface take time to have an effect on soil, there is a phase shift
in the date of yearly highs and lows the deeper one goes underground; this
shift is shown both by the slanting of the superimposed black lines and by
the colors (yellow = hot, purple = cold). The shift is exactly six months at a
depth of about 15 feet, indicating that 15 feet is an appropriate depth for a root
cellar, which should be warmest in winter and coolest in summer. This function is discussed at the beginning of Chapter 7.

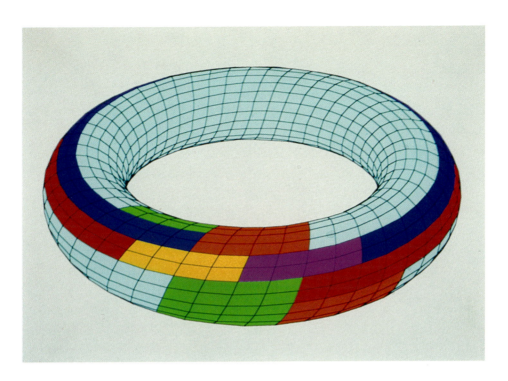

Color Plate 3 The four-color theorem states that any map on the surface of a sphere requires no more than four colors if adjacent countries are to be colored differently. A much older result of Heawood (1890) states that seven colors are necessary and sufficient for maps on the torus. The torus illustrated has seven countries arranged so that each country shares a border with each of the six other countries, thus explaining why seven colors are necessary. Further discussion of this example may be found in Chapter 7.

Color Plate 4 A 3-dimensional extension of an idea used by Norton Starr to generate some interesting 2-dimensional graphics. The underlying idea is quite simple: Imagine a point rotating around a circle in the plane; then suppose that the radius shrinks and expands as the point rotates; then let the progression around the circle have backward motion alternating with the forward motion; finally, raise or lower the point outside of the plane in direct proportion to the amount the radius differs from the average radius. *Mathematica*'s default illumination scheme was used to color the surface. This surface is discussed in the section titled "A Pretty Example" in Chapter 7.

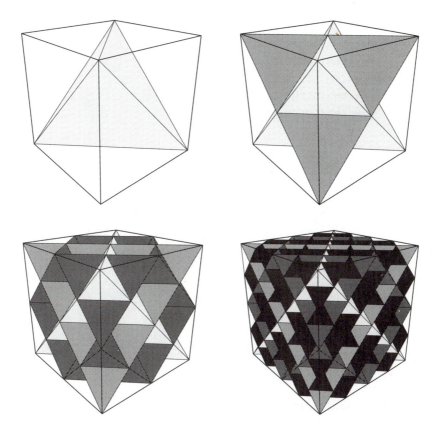

FIGURE 7.13 These first four iterations in the fractalization of a tetrahedron were generated by KochPlanet[{0, 1, 2, 3}]. The first iteration yields two intertwined tetrahedra, a polyhedron that Kepler christened the *stella octangula*. The limiting object is, up to a set of measure zero, a cube.

but the total 3-dimensional volume of the omitted set is zero. Note that as the fractalization progresses octahedral holes develop in the interior, but they will eventually be filled in, at least up to a set of measure zero.

```
cube = {Thickness[.0001], Line /@ Join[
    Transpose[{
        Flatten[Outer[List, {-1,1}, {-1,1}, {-1}], 2],
        Flatten[Outer[List, {-1,1}, {-1,1}, { 1}], 2]}],
```

```
Transpose[{
    Flatten[Outer[List, {-1,1}, {-1}, {-1,1}], 2],
    Flatten[Outer[List, {-1,1}, {+1}, {-1,1}], 2]}],
Transpose[{
    Flatten[Outer[List, {-1}, {-1,1}, {-1,1}], 2],
    Flatten[Outer[List, {1}, {-1,1}, {-1,1}], 2]}]] //N}

KochPlanet[n_] := (newgray = .95;
    tetrahedron = Map[{GrayLevel[newgray], Polygon[#]} &, {
        {{-1,-1,-1}, {1,-1,1}, {-1,1,1}},
        {{-1,-1,-1}, {1,1,-1}, {1,-1,1}},
        {{1,-1,1},   {1,1,-1}, {-1,1,1}},
        {{-1,-1,-1}, {-1,1,1}, {1,1,-1}} } //N];

    Show[Graphics3D[{cube,
        Nest[(newgray -= .3;
            # /. {gray_, Polygon[v_]} -> fractalize[{gray, v}]) &,
            tetrahedron, n]}],
    Lighting->False, Boxed->False,
    ViewPoint->{-1.65, 1.4, .9},
    BoxRatios->{1, 1, 1}])

Attributes[KochPlanet] = Listable
```

7.7 A Pretty Example

We conclude our chapter on 3-dimensional plotting with a pretty example of a parametric surface that is a variation on Norton Starr's 2-dimensional examples illustrated in Figure 4.27. Those images, which were simple variations on circular motion, have a 3-dimensional feel to them. Using ParametricPlot3D, we can turn those objects into true 3-dimensional surfaces. We present one example, using the parameters 8, 16, and 4 for a, b, and c, respectively, and shading the surface according to the value of the radius (r in the code that follows). The view in Figure 7.14 is from a point on the z-axis; the surface travels in front of and behind the x-y

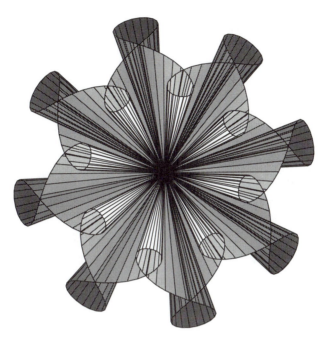

FIGURE 7.14 By introducing a z-value that is essentially the difference between the radius and 2, the planar image of Figure 4.27(a) can be transformed to a parametric surface in 3-space.

plane because the z-coordinate is set to be 2 - r/5 (multiplied by the mesh factor). The following code uses ModifiedParametricPlot3D to accomplish the shading, which is based on a normalized value of r. Because the computation uses a lot of memory, the PostScript form of the image is written to a file (named **psfile**) by the method discussed in Chapter 4 (where it is explained how to display the image in the file). One slight change in the definition of r is that the multiplier of Sin[8 phi] is increased from 0.5 to 0.7. As usual, the code will run faster if values less than 360 are used for n. See Color Plate 4 for a color version of Figure 7.14.

```
$Display = OpenWrite["psfile"]
n = 360
ModifiedParametricPlot3D[
   {mesh (r = 2+Sin[8 phi]*.7) Cos[theta = phi + Sin[16 phi]/4],
    mesh r Sin[theta],
    mesh * (2 - r/5),
    GrayLevel[(3.3 - r)/2]},
      {phi, 0, 2 Pi, 2 Pi / n}, {mesh, 0, 1, 1},
          Boxed->False,
          Lighting->False,
          BoxRatios->{1, 1, 1},
          ViewPoint->{0, 0, 6}]

Close["psfile"]; $Display = "stdout";
```

8 Some Algorithms of Number Theory

```
170361669146983324854254847 —— 3
                          2
               3 —— 2
                  2
              11 —— 2
                  2
               5 —— 2
                  2
              43 —— 3
                  2
               3 —— 2
                  2
               7 —— 3
                  2
                   3 —— 2
                      2
             521 —— 3
                  2
               5 —— 2
                  2
              13 —— 2
                  2
                   3 —— 2
                      2
            4909 —— 6
                  2
               3 —— 2
                  2
             409 —— 21
                  2
                   3 —— 2
                      2
                  17 —— 3
                      2
```

```
5458336229704571 —— 6
              2
       5 —— 2
          2
  545833622970457 —— 10
              2
       3 —— 2
          2
     107 —— 2
          2
      53 —— 2
          2
      13 —— 2
          2
           3 —— 2
              2
  212552033867 —— 2
              2
     36857 —— 3
              2
      17 —— 3
          2
     271 —— 6
          2
           3 —— 2
              2
           5 —— 2
              2
  2883469 —— 10
              2
       3 —— 2
          2
       7 —— 3
          2
           3 —— 2
              2
     34327 —— 5
              2
       3 —— 2
          2
    1907 —— 2
              2
     953 —— 3
          2
       7 —— 3
          2
           3 —— 2
              2
      17 —— 3
          2
```

T his chapter uses the high precision of *Mathematica* to illustrate several fundamental algorithms of number theory, including the ancient and venerable Euclidean algorithm for finding greatest common divisors and a modern nondeterministic method for certifying primality. The advantage of using very large numbers in algorithms such as these is that they bring out clearly the difference between efficient and inefficient algorithms. For example, an algorithm that requires $\sqrt{p}$ operations to determine that p is a prime number will work well on numbers near one million, since only about 1,000 operations will be required. But on a number near 10^{100}, the same algorithm will fail miserably, as 10^{50} operations will overwhelm even a supercomputer.

About the illustration overleaf:

The prime numbers lie in the complexity class **NP**; that is, any prime number can be proved to be prime by a proof or *certificate* that is relatively short (its length is bounded by a polynomial in the length of the given prime). The data overleaf form a Pratt certificate that certifies the primality of the 28-digit integer 1,703,616,691,469,833,244,854,254,847; it was generated using the PrattCertify function discussed in this chapter. Note that proving primality of this number by trial division would require at least a trillion divisions. Verifying the certificate overleaf requires only a few dozen multiplications.

To read the certificate, note first that it is split into two parts, but it should be read as one long column. Below every leftmost entry lies a list of the primes dividing that entry minus 1. For example, near the end of the tree can be found the assertion that the prime divisors of $7 - 1$ are 2 and 3 and that the prime divisors of 952 are 2, 7, and 17; the entire tree states that the prime divisors of the given 28-digit number are 2, 3, 11, 43, 521, 4909, and 5458336229704571. The numbers to the right of the dashes are primality witnesses that satisfy conditions explained in this chapter.

8.1 The Ancient and Modern Euclidean Algorithm

The greatest common divisor (gcd) of two integers is the largest integer that divides each of the given integers. The Euclidean algorithm for computing the gcd is arguably the best algorithm in all mathematics. According to Knuth [Knu, §4.5.2], it is the oldest nontrivial algorithm that has survived to the present day. It is very fast and very important; two uses are (1) writing a rational number in lowest terms and (2) finding the mod-a inverse of b when a and b are relatively prime ($\gcd(a, b) = 1$). It is the algorithm used by *Mathematica*'s built-in GCD function. The following example shows that this algorithm can determine the greatest common divisor of 500-digit numbers in a few seconds. This is quite an achievement considering that the most obvious way of computing $\gcd(m, n)$ is to first find the prime factorizations of m and n; the fastest known factoring algorithm would require hundreds of years to factor a 500-digit number.

```
GCD[10^500 + 134270000, 10^500 + 12466625460000000]//Timing
{4.28333 Second, 10000}
```

How is such speed attained? The idea is very simple and goes back to the ancient Greek method of finding the largest length that can be used to "measure" two given lengths. That method would, given two lengths a and b with $b < a$, place as many copies as possible of the smaller length side by side in the larger until a remainder r that is less than b is left. Then the same procedure would be applied to b and r, and reapplied continually until the process terminated, that is, one length evenly divided the other. At that point the last remainder would be the largest length such that each of the two originally given lengths was a multiple of it. One problem is that this method may not terminate! If applied to the diagonal and side of a square, the process goes on indefinitely—a consequence of the fact, discovered in 500 B.C., that these two lengths are incommensurable or in modern terms, that $\sqrt{2}$ is an irrational number. However, if one starts with two integers, then the process does indeed terminate in finitely many steps. It is easy to program this recursively, since the remainder is given by Mod[a, b]. To summarize, the following algorithm works because: (1) $\gcd(a, b)$ coincides with $\gcd(b, r)$ where r is the remainder upon division of a by b and (2) the recursion eventually falls into the gcd[·, 0] case because Mod[a, b] is less than b and so the remainders form a decreasing sequence of nonnegative integers.

```
gcd[a_, b_] := gcd[b, Mod[a, b]]
gcd[a_, 0]  := a
```

```
gcd[55492163484645888, 33787461185758215936]
1307674368
```

Of course, gcd will not be as fast as the built-in GCD. But it is useful as it can be modified to yield more information. For example, suppose we wish to see the remainders and quotients at each step. Then the following modification of the preceding recursive routine will show them.

```
FullGCD[a_, b_] := FullGCD[a, b, {a}, {}]
FullGCD[a_, b_, r_, q_] :=
    FullGCD[b, Mod[a, b], Append[r, b], Append[q, Floor[a/b]]]
FullGCD[a_, 0, r_, q_]  := {r, q}
```

```
FullGCD[33787461185715936, 92163484645888]
{{33787461185715936, 92163484645888, 55625805320928,
    36537679324960, 19088125995968, 17449553328992, 1638572666976,
    1063826659232, 574746007744, 489080651488, 85665356256,
    60753870208, 24911486048, 10930898112, 3049689824, 1781828640,
    1267861184, 513967456, 239926272, 34114912, 1121888, 458272,
    205344, 47584, 15008, 2560, 2208, 352, 96, 64, 32},
  {366, 1, 1, 1, 1, 10, 1, 1, 1, 5, 1, 2, 2, 3, 1, 1, 2, 2, 7, 30,
    2, 2, 4, 3, 5, 1, 6, 3, 1, 2}}
```

In this example we see that the remainders decrease at a regular rate until the final value of 32 is reached; we can easily look at the number of digits in each remainder.

```
Map[Length[Digits[#]] &, First[%]]
{17, 14, 14, 14, 14, 14, 13, 13, 12, 12, 11, 11, 11, 11, 10, 10,
  10, 9, 9, 8, 7, 6, 6, 5, 5, 4, 4, 3, 2, 2, 2}
```

In fact, this is true in general. The number of steps (that is, divisions, including the final division even if it is just division by 1) in the Euclidean algorithm applied to two numbers less than N is never more than $4.785 \log_{10} N + 1.6723$. This is a consequence of a theorem of G.

Lamé (1845) that the worst case occurs when the Euclidean algorithm is applied to two consecutive Fibonacci numbers: applied to F_{n+2} and F_{n+1}, the Euclidean algorithm takes n steps. Exercise: Prove that the Euclidean algorithm applied to F_{n+2} and F_{n+1} requires n steps. (Hint: Find the pattern in the remainders and quotients in several cases and prove that the pattern is true for all pairs of consecutive Fibonacci numbers).

We will prove Lamé's theorem in the next section. It often happens in complexity theory that worst-case behavior is too pessimistic and that an algorithm performs much better on average. The average-case behavior of the Euclidean algorithm has been extensively studied, and although it is a little better, it is not significantly better than the worst-case behavior. It has been proved by H. Heilbronn (see [Knu, §4.5.3, Exs. 33, 34]) that T_n is approximately $1.94 \log_{10} n$, where T_n is the average number of steps in the Euclidean algorithm for all pairs (n, b), with $b < n$. Exercise: Use *Mathematica* to generate a table of values of T_n.

Note that in the output of the FullGCD example many of the quotients are small. Indeed, on average it is true that 1 is the most common quotient, followed by 2, then 3, and so on. (Exercise: Write a routine that applies the Euclidean algorithm to random large integers and computes the percentage of the quotients that are each of 1, 2, and 3.) The book by Knuth [Knu] contains a detailed discussion of the distribution of quotients; it turns out that a 1 occurs 41.5% of the time, a 2 occurs 17% of the time, a 3 occurs 9.3% of the time, and so on. The fact that the quotients are so often small has led to various variations on the Euclidean algorithm that avoid the use of Mod, with its inherent division, and use only repeated subtractions. For very large numbers, subtraction is much faster than division.

EXERCISE Compare the times needed for a – b and Mod[a, b] where a and b are 500-digit numbers. Note that Mod[a, b] is significantly faster than the full-precision division b/a.

EXERCISE Investigate some of the variations to the Euclidean algorithm given in [Knu].

A variation to the traditional Euclidean algorithm that will be important when we pursue complex gcds in Chapter 9 arises by allowing the quotient to be the nearest integer to a/b rather than Floor(a/b). Recall that the essential point guaranteeing termination of the Euclidean algorithm is that the remainder Mod[a, b] is less than b. There is no need to keep the remainders positive, however, so long as the absolute values of the remainders decrease. This leads to the idea of allowing a negative remainder if its absolute value is less than the usual positive remainder. In other words, given a and b, let q be the nearest integer to a/b and let the remainder be $a - qb$. As is the case for the traditional algorithm, the subtraction of multiples of b does not change the gcd, and so this is a valid gcd algorithm that should take fewer steps because each remainder will, in absolute value, be less than one-half the preceding remainder. Let's try it.

One way is to simply replace Mod[a, b] by a - Round[a/b]*b in the recursive step. But this will involve an explicit high-precision division, which is much slower than a call to Mod. A better approach is to realize that when the nearest integer is used, the remainder is whichever of Mod[a, b] and Mod[a, b] - b is smaller in absolute value. In fact, we may as well simplify by considering the positive quantity b - Mod[a, b], for then the central relationship becomes either $a = qb + r$ or $a = (q + 1)b - r$, where q and b are as in the traditional method. Because this simplification yields a value of r that is positive and less than b, the algorithm halts. Here is a modification of one of the preceding routines that implements these ideas.

```
FullGCDRound[a_, b_] := FullGCDRound[a, b, {a}, {}]
FullGCDRound[a_, b_, r_, q_] :=
    FullGCDRound[b, Min[Mod[a,b], b-Mod[a,b]],
                 Append[r, b], Append[q, Round[a/b]]]
FullGCDRound[a_, 0, r_, q_]  := {r, q}


FullGCDRound[33787461185715936, 92163484645888]
{{33787461185715936, 92163484645888, 36537679324960,
   17449553328992, 1638572666976, 574746007744, 85665356256,
   24911486048, 10930898112, 3049689824, 1267861184, 513967456,
   239926272, 34114912, 1121888, 458272, 205344, 47584, 15008,
   2560, 352, 96, 32},
 {367, 3, 2, 11, 3, 7, 3, 2, 4, 2, 2, 2, 7, 30, 2, 2, 4, 3, 6, 7,
   4, 3}}
```

Only 21 division steps occur, versus 29 for the traditional method. In this variation, the remainder is always at most one-half the preceding remainder; in fact, it can be shown that in the worst case this method takes about $2.6 \log_{10} N$ steps for starting values less than N (A. Dupré, 1846; see [Knu, §4.5.3, Exs. 30, 31]), almost half the number of steps in the traditional method. On the other hand, each step involves an extra comparison.

A curious property of relatively prime pairs is that they occur with probability $6/\pi^2 = 0.6079\ldots$. Consider Table 8.1, which shows some of these probabilities.

> EXERCISE Use GCD and Count to generate some of the values of Table 8.1. (Count[S, 1] returns the number of 1s in S; if S is nested, then Count[S, 1, n] returns the number of 1s in any of the first n levels of S.)

Instead of counting with GCD, it is better to use EulerPhi, a built-in function that computes $\phi(n)$, the number of integers in $\{1,\ldots,n\}$ that are relatively prime to n. The computation of ϕ requires the prime factorization of n and so is in general an intractable computation. However, it is a useful function for moderate-sized numbers: EulerPhi[1000000], say, is very much faster than computing 1,000,000 individual gcds. The following code generated Table 8.1. Recall that @@ is used to Apply a function and /@ abbreviates Map. EulerPhi is not listable, but it could be made so by SetAttributes[EulerPhi, Listable]; then EulerPhi[Range[k]] could be computed without using Map. The denominator k + Binomial[k, 2] is used because that is how many pairs there are from $\{1,\ldots,k\}$ including pairs of the form (i,i).

```
Table[(Plus @@ EulerPhi /@ Range[200 n]) /
      (200 n + Binomial[200 n, 2]),              {n, 10}]//N
```

200	400	600	800	1000	1200	1400	1600	1800	2000
0.6086	0.6070	0.6073	0.6078	0.60778	0.60753	0.60782	0.60761	0.60772	0.60799

TABLE 8.1 The probabilities that a pair from $\{1, 200\}$, $\{1, 400\}$,..., $\{1, 2000\}$ is relatively prime. The limit of these probabilities is $6/\pi^2$.

The fact that the probabilities converge to $6/\pi^2$ is a consequence of the fact that the infinite series $1 + 1/4 + 1/9 + 1/16 + 1/25 + \ldots$ converges to the sum $\pi^2/6$ (see [Knu] or [KW, §24] for details).

8.2 The Extended Euclidean Algorithm ▬▬

An important property of the gcd is that if $d = \gcd(a, b)$, then there are two integers s and t such that $d = sa + tb$. This is especially useful in the case that a and b are relatively prime, for then the equation $sa + tb = 1$ implies that $tb \equiv 1 \pmod{a}$; in other words, t is the mod-a inverse of b. *Mathematica* displays values of s and t when ExtendedGCD is used.

```
ExtendedGCD[Prime[1000], 1000000]
{1, {17679, -140}}
```

This shows that $17,679 \cdot 7,919 - 140 \cdot 1,000,000 = 1$ and therefore that the inverse of the 1,000th prime (7,919) modulo 1,000,000 is 17,679. (The mod-a inverse of b can also be obtained via PowerMod[b, -1, a].) The values of s and t are most easily obtained by keeping track of two additional sequences as the various quotients and remainders are computed. Let the s-sequence start with $\{1, 0\}$ and let the t-sequence start with $\{0, 1\}$ (i.e., let $s_0 = 1, s_1 = 0, t_0 = 0, \ldots$). Then if $q_1, q_2, \ldots$ are the quotients, with $q_1 = \text{Floor}(a/b)$, additional s and t values are computed according to the rules $s_k = s_{k-2} - q_{k-1}s_{k-1}$ and $t_k = t_{k-2} - q_{k-1}t_{k-1}$. The following exercise shows that the last terms of the s- and t-sequences satisfy $d = sa + tb$. Exercise: Let $r_0 = a, r_1 = b, r_2, r_3, \ldots, r_n = \gcd(a, b)$ be the sequence of remainders in the Euclidean algorithm. Show that at each stage k, $s_ka + t_kb = r_k$.

Because FullGCD returns the complete sequence of quotients, we can easily get the s- and t-sequences as follows. The Scan[*function, list*] command executes *function* for each element of the *list*. It is used below to define new values of s and t for each quotient. Note also the use of t[[-2] for the next-to-last member of the list t.

```
FullExtendedGCD[a_, b_] := FullExtendedGCD[a, b, {a}, {}]
FullExtendedGCD[a_, b_, r_, q_] := FullExtendedGCD[
     b, Mod[a,b], Append[r, b], Append[q, Floor[a/b]]]
```

```
FullExtendedGCD[a_, 0, r_, q_]  :=
    Block[{s = {1, 0}, t = {0, 1}},
      Scan[(AppendTo[t, t[[-2]] - t[[-1]] #];
            AppendTo[s, s[[-2]] - s[[-1]] #]) &, q];
      {r, q, s, t}]
```

```
FullExtendedGCD[1000000, 7919]
{{1000000, 7919, 2206, 1301, 905, 396, 113, 57, 56, 1},
 {126, 3, 1, 1, 2, 3, 1, 1, 56},
 {1, 0, 1, -3, 4, -7, 18, -61, 79, -140, 7919},
 {0, 1, -126, 379, -505, 884, -2273, 7703, -9976, 17679,
   -1000000}}
```

Because the quotient list includes the quotient of the next-to-last remainder and 1 (the last remainder), the s and t lists each contain one extra term. It is not completely obvious why the extra terms, at least in the case of relatively prime a and b, are $\pm b$ and $\pm a$. This will be explained shortly.

We can verify that the s and t lists, when multiplied by a and b, yield the remainder sequence (see earlier exercise).

```
%[[3]]*1000000 + %[[4]]*7919
{1000000, 7919, 2206, 1301, 905, 396, 113, 57, 56, 1, 0}
```

An application of ExtendedGCD will be given in the next section. And FullExtendedGCD will be used in the discussion of the sum-of-two-squares algorithm in Chapter 9, where we shall explain the following interesting phenomenon. Note that the extended Euclidean algorithm applied to the pair 73 and 27 yields a t-sequence that except for minus signs, is identical to the sequence of remainders. What is it about 73 and 27 that causes this? Can you find other pairs with this property? In such cases, what is the mod-a inverse of b?

```
FullExtendedGCD[73, 27]//TableForm
{73, 27, 19, 8, 3, 2, 1}
{2, 1, 2, 2, 1, 2}
{1, 0, 1, -1, 3, -7, 10, -27}
{0, 1, -2, 3, -8, 19, -27, 73}
```

If $\gcd(a, b) = 1$, it is fairly clear that from the sequence of quotients $\{q_1, \ldots, q_n\}$ one can reconstruct the entire list of remainders in the Euclidean algorithm applied to a and b. For q_n is just r_{n-1}, and the equation $r_{n-2} = r_{n-1}q_{n-1} + r_n$ yields r_{n-2} in terms of q_{n-1} and q_n; we can continue in this way all the way back to a and b. Consider the function Q that turns a list of quotients into a remainder; it satisfies the following two conditions, where the second condition is a translation of the central relationship $r_{k-2} = r_{k-1}q_{k-1} + r_k$. We are still assuming that $r_n = \gcd(a, b) = 1$.

$$Q[\{q_1\}] = q_1$$
$$Q[\{q_1, \ldots, q_k\}] = q_1 Q[\{q_2, \ldots, q_k\}] + Q[\{q_3, \ldots, q_k\}]$$

In order for the latter equation to be valid, we must also set $Q[\{\}]$ to be 1. Let's define the Q function in *Mathematica* and try it out on the two `FullExtendedGCD` examples.

```
Q[{}] := 1
Q[{q_}] := q
Q[qlist_] := First[qlist] Q[Rest[qlist]] + Q[Drop[qlist,2]] /;
                                        Length[qlist] > 1

Q[{2,1,2,2,1,2}]
73

Q[{126, 3, 1, 1, 2, 3, 1, 1, 56}]
1000000
```

We can also check that Q, as it works its way up the list of quotients, yields the list of remainders.

```
Table[Q[Drop[{126, 3, 1, 1, 2, 3, 1, 1, 56}, n]],{n, 9, 0, -1}]
{1, 56, 57, 113, 396, 905, 1301, 2206, 7919, 1000000}
```

EXERCISE If $\gcd(a, b) = d - 1$, then the remainders are recoverable as a certain function of the quotients together with d. Find the appropriate function.

We can gain a better understanding of the Q function by trying it on abstract variables as follows.

```
Expand[Q[{a,b,c,d,e}]]
a + c + a b c + e + a b e + a d e + c d e + a b c d e
```

If longer sequences are tried, the pattern that emerges is that $Q(q_1, \ldots, q_n)$ consists of the sum of all possible products of the q_n with pairs of neighboring elements excised. That is, excising no pairs from $\{a, b, c, d, e\}$ leaves $abcde$, excising one pair leaves abc or abe or ade, and excising two pairs leaves a or c or e. (Exercise: Use the definition of Q to prove, by induction on the number of arguments, that Q does in fact coincide with this sum of products.) The Q functions are called *continuants*, and their properties were known to Euler. The Euclidean algorithm for the pair a, b is closely related to the continued fraction expansion of the rational number a/b; see the section on continued fractions later in this chapter. The alternative characterization of Q in terms of a sum of products has a surprising consequence, namely, that $Q(q_1, \ldots, q_n) = Q(q_n, \ldots, q_1)$. This can help us better understand the s- and t-sequences.

Let's focus on just the t-sequence. First observe that for any starting values a and b to the Euclidean algorithm, the t-sequence alternates its sign and is, in absolute value, strictly increasing. Moreover, because the signs of t_{k-2} and t_{k-1} differ, the defining equation $t_k = t_{k-2} - q_{k-1}t_{k-1}$ becomes $|t_k| = |t_{k-2}| + q_{k-1}|t_{k-1}|$; and since $|t_{k-2}| \leq |t_{k-1}|$, this means that q_{k-1} and $|t_{k-2}|$ are the quotient and remainder, respectively, when $|t_k|$ is divided by $|t_{k-1}|$. In short, $|t_{n+1}|, |t_n|, |t_{n-1}|, \ldots, 1$ is itself a Euclidean algorithm remainder sequence with quotients $q_n, \ldots, q_1$, that is, the reverse of the quotient sequence from a and b. This means that $|t_n| = Q(q_n, \ldots, q_1)$ which as we have just seen, is identical to $Q(q_1, \ldots, q_n) = a$. This explains why the absolute value of the last term of the t-sequence (that is, t_{n+1}) is just a. A similar argument shows that s_{n+1} is $\pm b$. We will use these facts about the t-sequence in the next chapter's discussion of the sum-of-two-squares algorithm.

As another application of continuants we can quite easily prove Lamé's theorem: If a is the least integer for which there is a smaller integer b such that a and b generate a Euclidean algorithm remainder sequence having n steps, then a is the Fibonacci number F_{n+2}. For a must equal $Q(q_1, \ldots, q_n)$ and the smallest possible value of this function occurs when the last quotient q_n is 2 (the last quotient cannot be 1) and each q_i, $i < n$, is 1. But it is a straightforward induction directly from the definition of Q that $Q(2) = 2$, $Q(1, 2) = 3$, $Q(1, 1, 2) = 5$, and so on, as claimed.

Now, Binet's formula for the Fibonacci numbers states that $F_n = [\phi^n - (1/\phi)^n]/\sqrt{5}$, where ϕ is the golden ratio $(1 + \sqrt{5})/2$. We can prove it by observing its correctness for $n = 0$ and $n = 1$ and showing that the formula satisfies the same recurrence as the one that generates the Fibonacci numbers. *Mathematica* can help.

```
Binet[n_] := (GoldenRatio^n - (-1/GoldenRatio)^n)/Sqrt[5]
Attributes[Binet] = Listable
Binet[Range[0, 10]]//N
{1., 1., 2., 3., 5., 8., 13., 21., 34., 55.}
```

We must now teach *Mathematica* about the quadratic relationship that the golden ratio satisfies. This is a rule for `Power`, rather than for `Golden-Ratio`, so it is `Power` whose protection must be removed.

```
Unprotect[Power]
GoldenRatio^2 = 1 + GoldenRatio
Protect[Power]


Simplify[Binet[n]+ Binet[n+1] - Binet[n+2]]
0
```

This shows that the claimed recurrence is valid. It is a good idea to check complicated uses of `Simplify`, perhaps by trying numerical values in the symbolic argument and seeing that the output agrees numerically with the symbolic result. In any event, this result is correct and verifies the induction step of the proof of Binet's formula. Because $[\phi^n - (1/\phi)^n]/\sqrt{5}$ is asymptotic to $\phi^n/\sqrt{5}$, the fact that the Fibonacci numbers are the worst inputs to the Euclidean algorithm means that the algorithm never takes more than approximately $\log_\phi(\sqrt{5}N)$ steps for inputs less than N.

8.3 Linear Diophantine Equations: The Problem of Shielding Variable Names ▬▬▬

One application of the extended Euclidean algorithm is to find all integer solutions (x, y) to linear equations of the form $ax + by = c$. Equations for which only integer solutions are considered are called *Diophantine equations*. It is easy to prove that an integer solution to $ax + by = c$

exists if and only if c is divisible by $d = \gcd(a, b)$. Necessity is clear, and sufficiency follows from the following explicit solution: $(x_0, y_0) = (cs/d, ct/d)$ where s and t are the coefficients from the extended Euclidean algorithm applied to the pair (a, b). When a solution exists, the complete set of solutions is the set of pairs of the form $(x_0 + mb/d, y_0 - ma/d)$ for $m \in \mathbb{Z}$. (Exercise: Fill in the details of the preceding proof sketch.) Now, we can easily write a routine that returns the complete solution set to a linear Diophantine equation in two variables. However, some important programming subtleties arise. We must first decide whether we wish the routine to return the specific solution or the general set of solutions. Consider the equation $28x + 91y = 147$, for which $x = -63$, $y = 21$ is one solution, obtained as follows:

```
ExtendedGCD[28,91][[2]] 147 / GCD[28,91]
{-63, 21}
```

The general solution consists of all pairs of the form $(-63, 21) + m(13, -4)$; this can be checked as follows. We follow *Mathematica*'s lead in representing a solution to an equation as a substitution rule.

```
Simplify[ 28 x + 91 y /. {x -> -63 + 13 m , y -> 21 - 4 m}]
147
```

Although it seems as if all we have done is plugged values into the rule for the solution set, we have in fact done something more. We have chosen a new variable m that has not yet occurred in the problem and used it to parametrize the solution set. *Mathematica* does have the ability to do this; for example, Unique["x"] generates a symbol whose name is x1 unless x1 has been used, in which case it is x2 unless x2 has been used too, and so on. But let's put this problem aside because we have a much more serious problem to deal with first, as will be seen shortly. Let's be content now with simply generating the particular solution, in the form of a substitution rule for the two variables, together with the pair $\{b/d, -a/d\}$ that generates the general solution when added to the particular solution. This would seem straightforward enough via the following approach.

```
LinearDiophantine[a_ x_ + b_ y_ == c_] := Block[{s, t, d},
     {d, {s, t}} = ExtendedGCD[a,b];
     If[Mod[c, d] == 0,
```

```
{ {x -> c s / d, y -> c t / d}, {b/d, -a/d} },
{}]]
```

LinearDiophantine[28 x + 91 y == 147]
{{x -> -63, y -> 21}, {13, -4}}

So far so good; the reader can check that this routine works in the case of no solutions as well. But suppose someone else for whom this routine is written tries it on the equation $28t + 91u = 47$.

LinearDiophantine[28 t + 91 u == 147]
{{1 -> -63, u -> 21}, {13, -4}}

Disaster! Although the variable t in the routine has been blocked from interfering with other ts that might be around, the use of t in the input equation destroys its protection (as it must), and when t is returned (because the pattern x_ is really t), it is returned with the value 1 that it picked up within the routine as opposed to retaining its status as an unassigned symbol. There is a way around this that requires some familiarity with the notion of a *context*. *Mathematica* sets up different contexts in which variables occur. A context is a string that ends in the character " ` ". Up to this point in this book we have been working in the default context, "Global`"; all variable names have had a hidden prefix of the form Global` to distinguish them from variables of the same name that might be used in another context. For example, the integration package might use the variable n. That variable would be in another context, that is, it would have a different hidden prefix than the variable of the same name that we might use, and so a clash is averted.

We must set up a context for LinearDiophantine so that its variables are outside of the Global context. The problem now is that if the function LinearDiophantine itself is given a hidden prefix, then it will not be accessible from Global`. What we need is a semiprivate context and a private context: the first should hold the function name and make it accessible; the second should be truly private but assign new private names *only* to those variables not in the semiprivate context (otherwise it would create a new version of the function name that was hidden from the global context). And between the invocation of the semiprivate and private packages, the function name must be used, so that it gets defined in the semiprivate context. This is best done by inserting a usage statement at the right point in the sequence. This is all quite complicated, and we must stop with this brief introduction to the topic. The best place to learn more about contexts is from a Wolfram Research pamphlet[1] on contexts and packages that discusses the objects `Context[]`, `$Context`, and `$ContextPath`, which can help you keep track of what's going on.

But we must discuss yet one more complication. The `BeginPackage` command, the mandatory usage statement, and the `Begin` command must each be executed *in separate cells* before the main body of the function definition.[2] So, the following is the proper way to define a package. You should reboot *Mathematica* at this point, because of the possibility of a clash if you defined `LinearDiophantine` as it was given at the beginning of this section. Alternatively, execute `Remove[LinearDiophantine]`.

```
BeginPackage["LinearDiophantine`"];

LinearDiophantine::usage =
    "LinearDiophantine[(a x + b y) == c] returns a solution to
the equation in integers, together with a pair such that the
sum of the particular solution with all integer multiples of
the pair yield the general solution. If no solution exists, {}
is returned.";

Begin["LinearDiophantine`Private`"];
```

In the preceding preamble cells the last command could be abbreviated to `Begin[" `Private`"]`. At this stage, executing `Context["LinearDiophantine"]` will show the full name of this symbol, which includes the semiprivate context in which it lies. Now, any variable names encountered will be put into a superprivate context, except for variable names that are already in the semiprivate context. So we can now execute the function definition, secure in the knowledge that `LinearDiophantine` will not be hidden away, but that all other variables, `t`, `s`, and `d`, will be.

---

[1]This pamphlet, WRI Technical Report No. 3, was distributed with some versions of *Mathematica* and may be obtained directly from WRI, P.O. Box 6059, Champaign, IL 61826-6059, USA.

[2]This assumes that the package will be read in by opening it and executing the cells in the usual way. Packages that are instead loaded via <<*package* do not require this use of separate cells.

```
LinearDiophantine[a_ x_ + b_ y_ == c_] := Block[{s, t, d},
    {d, {s, t}} = ExtendedGCD[a,b];
    If[Mod[c, d] == 0,
        { {x -> c s / d, y -> c t / d}, {b/d, -a/d} },
        {}]]
End[];
EndPackage[];
```

The preceding modifications now yield the correct answer on our troublesome example.

```
LinearDiophantine[28 t + 91 u == 147]
{{t -> -63, u -> 21}, {13, -4}}
```

One final point: precede any editing of the definition of the function by executing the cell containing Begin["LinearDiophantine`Private`"], so that the variables in the revised function are placed in their proper context. Frequent use of the information functions ?? and Context["*vblename*"] should help keep things straight. For example, executing ??LinearDiophantine when back in the global context will return a lengthy transcription of the function definition with all variable prefixes shown.

EXERCISE Find a linear Diophantine equation that has only negative solutions. Revise LinearDiophantine so that it returns the least solution to the linear equation in positive integers, if such a solution exists.

8.4 The Chinese Remainder Theorem ▬▬▬

The Chinese Remainder Theorem states that certain systems of linear congruences can always be solved. Moreover, there is a constructive proof that yields a fast algorithm for the solution. Like the Euclidean algorithm, the CRT has several applications. It will be used in the next chapter in a routine to find square roots modulo an integer. Another noteworthy application of the CRT is to yield the so-called modular notation for integers; this notation can be used to speed up high-precision computations (see [Knu, Ros]); indeed, it was used in one of the recent record-breaking computations of millions of digits of π [Bai].

We are here considering systems of congruences of the form

$$x \equiv a_1 \ (\text{mod} \ m_1)$$

$$x \equiv a_2 \ (\text{mod} \ m_2)$$

$$\vdots$$

$$x \equiv a_n \ (\text{mod} \ m_n)$$

The CRT states that if the m_i are relatively prime in pairs, then there is a solution x_0 to the system of congruences. Moreover, if $m = m_1 m_2 \cdots m_n$, then the set $\{1, 2, 3, \ldots, m\}$ contains exactly one solution. The constructive proof is simple. First let b_i be the mod-m_i inverse of m/m_i, which exists because m_i and m/m_i are relatively prime. Then $(m/m_i)b_i a_i$ is congruent to a_i modulo m_i and to 0 modulo m_k when $k \neq i$. It follows that if x_0 is the following sum, reduced modulo m, then x_0 solves the given system.

$$\sum_{i=1}^{n} \frac{m}{m_i} a_i b_i$$

EXERCISE Prove that the hypothesis of the CRT implies the uniqueness of a solution modulo m.

EXERCISE Find the least positive integer that is congruent to 3 modulo 7 and 5 modulo 16.

EXERCISE Define a function `PairwiseCoprime[mlist_List]` that uses GCD to test a sequence of numbers to see if they are relatively prime in pairs. Hint: One can avoid a loop by using `Outer`; a solution is in the Appendix.

To implement the CRT solution in *Mathematica* we will use `PowerMod` `[·, -1, ·]` to take inverses. Since we wish to take inverses of a set, it would be convenient if `PowerMod` were a listable function. Its built-in attributes do not include `Listable`, but this is easily fixed. While we're at it, there is currently a small bug in `PowerMod` in that, for example, `PowerMod[17, 1, 3]` returns 17 when it ought to return 2. We can take care of both points as follows.

```
SetAttributes[PowerMod, Listable];
Unprotect[PowerMod];
PowerMod[a_, 1, n_] := Mod[a, n]; Protect[PowerMod];
```

The preceding code can now be inserted into the **init.m** file so that it will be executed whenever *Mathematica* is started. This same technique can be used for other minor repairs or modifications. Now, the following function accepts two lists, the a values and m values, and returns the unique CRT solution modulo m, the product of the m values.

```
CRT[alist_, mlist_] := Block[{m = Times @@ mlist, mm},
    mm = m/mlist;
    Mod[Apply[Plus, alist*mm*PowerMod[mm, -1, mlist]], m]]
```

Here's an example, where we seek a number that is congruent to 0 modulo 4, 1 modulo 9, 2 modulo 25, and 3 modulo 49.

```
CRT[{0,1,2,3}, {4,9,25,49}]
14752
```

We can check our answer easily, since Mod is listable.

```
Mod[14752, {4,9,25,49}]
{0, 1, 2, 3}
```

The preceding example is a special case of the following problem: Show that there are arbitrarily long sequences of consecutive integers, each one divisible by a square. Equivalently, this is asking for arbitrarily long strings of 0s in the sequence of values of the Möbius function, $\mu(n)$, defined in Chapter 1. (Exercise: Show that the result of applying the CRT to the a-list $\{0, -1, -2, -3, -4, -5, \ldots\}$ and the m-list $\{22, 32, 52, 72, 112, 132, \ldots\}$ yields the first integer in a string of consecutive integers each of which is divisible by a square.) The generation of such sequences can be automated as follows.

```
n = 5
CRT[Range[0, -n + 1, -1], Prime[Range[1, n]]^2]
1308248
```

Therefore each of 1308248, 1308249, 1308250, 1308251, and 1308252 is divisible by a square.

EXERCISE Write a routine that uses the built-in `MoebiusMu` function to find a much smaller string of five consecutive integers, each of which is divisible by a square. Your routine should avoid computing any values of `MoebiusMu[r]` more than once. The `RotateLeft` function for lists can be useful here.

EXERCISE Modify CRT so that it returns a `BAD INPUT` message if the moduli are not pairwise relatively prime. Note, however, that this does *not* mean that the system has no solution (see the following exercise).

EXERCISE Show that the following extension of the CRT is valid. If for each pair of distinct i and j, $a_i - a_j$ is divisible by $\gcd(m_i, m_j)$, then the system of congruences $\{x \equiv a_i \pmod{m_i}\}$ has a solution; moreover, the solution is unique in the set $\{1, 2, \ldots, \text{lcm}(m_1, m_2, \ldots, m_n)\}$, where lcm denotes the least common multiple of a set of integers. See [Ros, §3.3, Exs. 11–14]. Write a *Mathematica* routine that implements this extension.

8.5 Continued Fractions

A real number can be decomposed into a single, infinitely continuing fraction as follows. Let's use π as an example. The equation $\pi = 3 + 1/7$ is not exactly true; to make it true 7 would have to be replaced by a larger number, whose value we can find as follows.

```
Solve[3 + 1/x == Pi]
          1
{{x -> -(------)}}
        3 - Pi

%//N
{{x -> 7.06251}}
```

However, we wish to generate integers in our continued fraction, so let's write 7.06251... as $7 + 1/x$ where x is obtained from $1/(\pi - 3)$ in the same way that 7.06251 was obtained from π. Then continue, replacing x by Floor(x), and so on. In this case one would obtain, to 12 terms, the following expression for π:

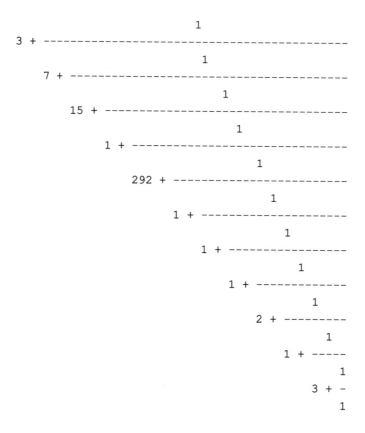

A fraction of the preceding form, possibly continuing through in-finitely many terms, is called a *simple continued fraction (SCF)*; the more general term *continued fraction* applies to the case where the numerators are not all restricted to be 1. A simpler notation for SCFs is to simply list the quotients as $[q_1, q_2, q_3, q_4, \ldots]$, where the square brackets indicate that this is to be viewed as an SCF; there may be infinitely many or only finitely many terms in this list. Thus the SCF generated by π becomes $[3, 7, 15, 1, 292, \ldots]$. The terms q_i are called the *partial quotients* of the SCF because of the connection to the quotients in the Euclidean algorithm, which will be discussed shortly. There are several theoretical points that must be dealt with: How exactly does an SCF represent a real number? Does every SCF converge to a real number? If we start with a real number and form the SCF as above, does the SCF converge to the real that gen-

erated it? We summarize, without proofs, the answers to these questions
and more in the following definitions and theorems. For more details see
[Knu, Ros].

DEFINITION. The sequence of *convergents* of an SCF are the rational numbers obtained by simplifying each of $[q_1]$, $[q_1, q_2]$, $[q_1, q_2, q_3]$, ... for
example, the SCF for π yields the convergents $3, {}^{22}/_{7}, {}^{333}/_{106}, {}^{355}/_{113}$,
${}^{103,993}/_{33,102}, \ldots$. If the sequence of convergents of an SCF converges
to a real number, then we say that the SCF *converges* to that real number. An SCF is called *finite* if it has only finitely many partial quotients;
note that an infinite SCF in which one of the partial quotients is zero
is effectively the same as a finite SCF.

THEOREM.

a. Every SCF with nonnegative terms is convergent.

b. The SCF obtained from a real number by using the procedure illustrated in the example of π converges to the real number.

c. Every SCF with infinitely many positive partial quotients converges
   to an irrational real number; every irrational number yields an infinite SCF with positive terms.

d. A rational number yields an SCF with finitely many terms and an
   SCF with finitely many terms yields a rational.

e. The SCF obtained from an irrational is the only SCF that converges
   to that irrational. However, there are always exactly two SCFs that
   converge to a given rational: $[q_1, q_2, \ldots, q_{n-1}, q_n] = [q_1, q_2, \ldots, q_{n-1}, q_n - 1, 1]$.

f. The SCF corresponding to an irrational real number that is the root of
   a quadratic equation with integer coefficients is eventually periodic;
   conversely, every SCF that is eventually periodic converges to such
   a real.

Mathematica comes with a package that evaluates the SCF of a real
number in floating-point form. Load the package, perhaps having a look
at it first to see what's in it. Recall that loading via <<*package* is not
the same as simply executing the cell containing the package; see the
discussion of contexts earlier in this chapter.

```
<<:NumberTheory:ContinuedFractions.m        (* use separate cell *)
ContinuedFraction[N[Pi,50], 12]
ContinuedFractionForm[{3, 7, 15, 1, 292, 1, 1, 1, 2, 1, 3, 1}]
```

The output is not just the sequence forming the SCF, but the sequence prefixed by `ContinuedFractionForm`. This serves to identify the sequence that follows, so that we recognize it, but also so that the built-in function `Normal`, which can be used on a variety of special forms, will know how to convert the SCF to a real number.

```
Normal[%]
5419351
-------
1725033
```

Note that when using floating-point approximations, one must be sure that there are enough digits given so that the continued fraction is correct to the number of terms sought. One way to get a handle on this error is to change the final partial quotient by 1 and use `N[Normal[]]` to see what effect this change has on the resulting floating-point number. In the case of the 12-term SCF for π, the effect is roughly 10^{-12}, so the 50-digit accuracy that we used for `Pi` was overly conservative. We can take a quick look at the SCFs for some other familiar numbers.

```
ContinuedFraction[N[Sqrt[2], 50], 12]
ContinuedFractionForm[{1, 2, 2, 2, 2, 2, 2, 2, 2, 2, 2, 2}]
ContinuedFraction[N[GoldenRatio, 50], 12]
ContinuedFractionForm[{1, 1, 1, 1, 1, 1, 1, 1, 1, 1, 1, 1}]
ContinuedFraction[N[E, 50], 12]
ContinuedFractionForm[{2, 1, 2, 1, 1, 4, 1, 1, 6, 1, 1, 8}]
```

If we want to see the SCF as a properly formatted fraction, we can outwit `Normal` by replacing the last term of the sequence by the corresponding string. Because *Mathematica* cannot add `1 + "1"`, it leaves it in symbolic form, which gets carried through the entire operation of `Normal`. Thus the following command yields the formatted 12-term continued fraction for π displayed on page 264.

```
Normal[ContinuedFractionForm[{3,7,15,1,292,1,1,1,2,1,3,"1"}]]
```

The continued fraction package works on floating-point reals and does not deal with infinitely precise rational numbers; but we can modify it so it does. As can be easily proved, the partial quotients of the SCF for a rational number a/b are simply the quotients in the Euclidean algorithm. So we can modify the FullGCD routine discussed earlier in this chapter to yield the SCF for a rational. We conform to *Mathematica*'s notation by wrapping it inside ContinuedFractionForm. We use the same name for this function, ContinuedFraction, as is used in the package because we are dealing with rational, as opposed to real, arguments. In effect, we are extending the ContinuedFraction function of the package; by adding this extension to the package (along with a revision to the usage statement), we increase the package's usefulness. We also define a function that implements the trick mentioned earlier to force Normal to return a formatted continued fraction.

```
quotients[a_, b_] := (AppendTo[qlist, Floor[a/b]];
                              quotients[b, Mod[a, b]])
quotients[a_, 0] := 0

ContinuedFraction[r_Rational] := (qlist = {};
    quotients[Numerator[r], Denominator[r]];
    ContinuedFractionForm[qlist])

CFFormatted[r_Rational] :=
    Block[{qlist = ContinuedFraction[r][[1]]},
        Normal@ContinuedFractionForm[
            Rest[Append[qlist, ToString[Last[qlist]]]]]]

CFFormatted[x_Real, n_Integer?Positive] :=
    Block[{qlist = ContinuedFraction[x, n][[1]]},
        Normal[ContinuedFractionForm[
            Rest[Append[qlist, ToString[Last[qlist]]]]]]]

ContinuedFraction[43/99]
ContinuedFractionForm[{0, 2, 3, 3, 4}]
```

```
CFFormatted[43/99]
          1
    -------------
           1
  2 + ---------
             1
      3 + -----
               1
          3 + -
               4
```

```
ContinuedFraction[1000000/7919]
ContinuedFractionForm[{126, 3, 1, 1, 2, 3, 1, 1, 56}]
```

```
Normal[%]
1000000
-------
 7919
```

We can use `Normal` on the initial segments of the partial quotients to generate the convergents. The following definition does the trick.

```
convergents[q_Rational] :=
    Block[{qlist = ContinuedFraction[q][[1]]},
    Map[Normal[ContinuedFractionForm[Take[qlist, #]]] &,
             Range[Length[qlist]]]]
```

```
convergents[1000000/7919]
        379  505  884  2273  7703  9976  17679  1000000
{126,   ---, ---, ---, ----, ----, ----, -----, -------}
         3    4    7    18    61    79    140     7919
```

It turns out that this routine is really redundant, as we have in essence already programmed this function. Compare the preceding output with the output of `FullExtendedGCD[1000000, 7919]` earlier in this chapter. This indicates that the convergents are nothing but the quotients of the s- and t-sequences, in absolute value. That is in fact always true; we leave the proof as an exercise (see [Ros]). However, `convergents` can be extended to real arguments as follows.

```
convergents[r_Real, n_Integer] :=
    Block[{qlist = ContinuedFraction[r, n][[1]]},
    Map[Normal[ContinuedFractionForm[Take[qlist, #]]] &,
            Range[Length[qlist]]]]
```

Convergents of an SCF for a real x yield very good rational approximations to x. The following output shows that many of the historically well-known rational approximations to π occur as convergents to its SCF.

```
convergents[N[Pi,100], 10]
     22   333   355   103993   104348   208341   312689   833719   1146408
{3,  --,  ---,  ---,  ------,  ------,  ------,  ------,  ------,  -------}
     7    106   113   33102    33215    66317    99532    265381   364913
```

Finally, we show that an eventually periodic SCF is the root of a quadratic equation with integer coefficients. Consider first a purely periodic SCF $[b_1, b_2, \ldots, b_m, b_1, b_2, \ldots, b_m, b_1, \ldots]$. It satisfies the equation $x = [b_1, b_2, \ldots, b_m, x]$, which simplifies to a quadratic equation. Now if any nonperiodic partial quotients precede the periodic part, they can be easily incorporated by another application of `Normal[ContinuedFrac-tionForm[a]]`, as is done in the following routine, which returns the quadratic irrational corresponding to an eventually periodic SCF. Since we wish to simplify the result, we introduce a routine to conjugate quadratic irrationals. Then the raw form of the quadratic irrational returned by `Normal` is simplified by multiplying the numerator and denominator by the quadratic conjugate of the denominator. It takes some experimentation to find a sequence of `Together`, `Expand`, and `Simplify` that at least in most cases, produces the simplest form. The routine also contains an `If` statement to set `persoln` equal to the positive root of the quadratic equation satisfied by the periodic part.

```
PeriodicCF::usage = "PeriodicCF[initial:{}, periodic] returns
the quadratic irrational represented by an eventually periodic
simple continued fraction; the default is the case of no
nonperiodic part"

QuadConjugate[a_Integer] = a
QuadConjugate[a_:0 + b_:1 * Sqrt[c_Integer]] := a - b Sqrt[c]
```

```
PeriodicCF[initial_List:{}, periodic_List] :=
    Block[{raw, persoln},
    persoln = Solve[x ==
            Normal[ContinuedFractionForm[Append[periodic,x]]]];
    persoln = If[N[persoln[[1,1,2]]] < 0, persoln[[2,1,2]],
                                           persoln[[1,1,2]]]];
    raw = Together[
        Normal[ContinuedFractionForm[Append[initial, persoln]]]];
  Simplify[
        Expand[Numerator[raw]   QuadConjugate[Denominator[raw]]]/
        Expand[Denominator[raw] QuadConjugate[Denominator[raw]]] ]]
```

PeriodicCF[{1}]

    1 + Sqrt[5]

         2

PeriodicCF[{2}]

    1 + Sqrt[2]

PeriodicCF[{1},{2,3}]

    -1 + Sqrt[15]

          2

PeriodicCF[{1,2,3,4}]

    135 + 30 Sqrt[39]

          225

PeriodicCF[{2,2},{1}]

    -(-14 + 2 Sqrt[5])

          4

PeriodicCF[{10},{100,1000}]

    -490 + Sqrt[250010]

The preceding examples show that the symbolic manipulations have not been completely successful, as some further cancellation is possible in some of the outputs. The interested reader can attempt to modify the code, perhaps adding Cancel and Together to the returned value. As usual, a check is called for.

```
ContinuedFraction[N[(135 + 30 Sqrt[39])/225, 50], 12]
ContinuedFractionForm[{1, 2, 3, 4, 1, 2, 3, 4, 1, 2, 3, 4}]
```

EXERCISE Examine the SCF for numbers of the form $\sqrt{d^2 - 1}$. Can you identify a pattern? Prove it. Similarly, identify the pattern for SCF of numbers of the form $\sqrt{d^2 - d}$.

EXERCISE Modify `PeriodicCF` so that it returns the quadratic equation satisfied by an eventually periodic SCF.

EXERCISE Which positive integers d have the property that the SCF for $\sqrt{d}$ has the form $[a, b, b, b, \ldots]$?

8.6 Egyptian Fractions

The ancient Egyptians had an unusual and original way of dealing with arithmetic involving fractions, a system that differs markedly from those used by other civilizations. The Egyptians had special symbols for the *unit fractions*, that is, the reciprocals of the integers: $1/2, 1/3, 1/4, 1/5$, and so on. But they did not have symbols for fractions with numerators larger than 1 (with the single exception of $2/3$), and they represented such fractions as sums of unit fractions. Of course, this can be done in the obvious way by writing $4/23$, for example, as a sum of four summands, each equal to $1/23$, but there are generally shorter representations. One way of finding a representation with no repetition of summands is by the so-called greedy algorithm, which repeatedly chooses the largest unit fraction that will fit. More precisely, given a fraction a/b, where a and b are positive integers, choose a sequence of unit fractions $1/c, 1/d, 1/e$, and so on by letting c be the least integer such that $1/c \leq a/b$, letting d be the least integer different from c such that $1/d \leq a/b - 1/c$, and so on; for example, this technique applied to $4/23$ yields $1/6 + 1/138$. The adjective "greedy" is used because at each step we choose the unit fraction that eats up as much of the given fraction as possible. The Egyptians were apparently aware of this method, although in practice they used a combination of the greedy method and other ad-hoc techniques, perhaps because, as we shall see, the greedy method sometimes yields ridiculously long denominators. Exercise: Use *Mathematica* to find the greedy representation of $5/121$ as an Egyptian fraction.

A proof that the greedy algorithm always terminates in finitely many steps was provided by Fibonacci in 1202 AD. Before addressing that issue, let's implement the algorithm in *Mathematica*. The main ingredient is the observation that given a/b, the denominator of the largest unit fraction that is less than or equal to a/b is simply the first integer past b/a, that is, Ceiling(b/a). A recursive program is appropriate here, for once a unit fraction is found, the algorithm repeats its main step on the part of the given fraction that remains after the unit fraction is subtracted. This leads to the following code, which works only because we know (thanks to Fibonacci) that the method will eventually leave a 0 remainder. (Exercise: Show that the greedy algorithm always yields *distinct* unit fractions.) As with all functions whose arguments are numbers, as opposed to lists, it is useful to make the function listable so that it can be applied to sets of numbers.

```
EgyptianFraction[0]  := {}
EgyptianFraction[q_] := Prepend[
        EgyptianFraction[q - 1/Ceiling[1/q]], Ceiling[1/q]]
Attributes[EgyptianFraction] = Listable
```

```
EgyptianFraction[4/23]
{6, 138}
```

Results should be checked whenever possible. In this case a check is very fast, as `Plus @@ (1/%)` will add up the reciprocals of the integers in the set forming the preceding output (recall that `@@` abbreviates `Apply`). We can see the representations of all the multiples of $1/23$ as follows. Note how some quite large numbers occur as denominators.

```
EgyptianFraction[Range[0,1,1/23]]
{}                              {2, 46}
{23}                            {2, 16, 368}
{12, 276}                       {2, 10, 115}
{8, 184}                        {2, 7, 108, 17388}
{6, 138}                        {2, 6, 35, 2415}
{5, 58, 6670}                   {2, 5, 26, 1495}
{4, 92}                         {2, 4, 31, 2852}
{4, 19, 583, 1019084}           {2, 4, 14, 215, 138460}
{3, 69}                         {2, 3, 28, 1932}
{3, 18, 414}                    {2, 3, 13, 359, 644046}
{3, 10, 690}                    {2, 3, 9, 83, 34362}
{3, 7, 483}                     {1}
```

The proof that the greedy algorithm terminates is quite straightforward once one sees a certain pattern in the remainders at each step. A simple modification to `EgyptianFraction` yields the list of remainders instead.

```
Remainders[0]  := {}
Remainders[q_] := Prepend[
        Remainders[q - 1/Ceiling[1/q]], q - 1/Ceiling[1/q]]

Remainders[19/23]
  15   7    3       1
{--, --, ---, ------, 0}
  46  92  644  138460
```

Note that the numerators of the remainders form a decreasing sequence. In fact, as additional examples will confirm, this is always the case. Exercise: Prove that when the greedy algorithm is used, the numerators in the remainders form a strictly decreasing sequence of nonnegative integers. Because such a sequence cannot go on forever, the algorithm must reach a remainder of 0 eventually.

Some explorations based on `EgyptianFraction` will quickly lead to some interesting decompositions. One example comes from $65/131$:

$$\frac{65}{131} = \frac{1}{3} + \frac{1}{7} + \frac{1}{51} + \frac{1}{2599} + \frac{1}{8103163} + \frac{1}{82076555152549} +$$

$$\frac{1}{898208120761247499099310653} +$$

$$\frac{1}{1210166742302177655931328288012543297686621335726600189 61} +$$

$$\frac{1}{29290070883485305257170727916346131549433432526041820570286255057924204445456330131039739635641147751253099020081}$$

EXERCISE What is the greedy representation of $31/311$? (There are 10 terms, the last of which has a denominator with over 500 digits!)

There are much shorter representations of $65/131$ as an Egyptian fraction. For example, one can combine the representations of, say, $30/131$ and $35/131$; this yields the representation as a sum of $1/3$, $1/7$, $1/99$, $1/102$, $1/12,969$, and $1/93,534$. Exercise: Find a shorter and smaller representation of $65/131$ by checking all decompositions such as $65 = 20 + 35$ using the following command:

```
Table[EgyptianFraction[{n/131, (65 - n)/131}], {n, 1, 32}]
```

The greedy representation of $^{31}/_{311}$ yields inordinately long denominators; the reader may enjoy trying to find a shorter representation of that fraction, either by using the decomposition idea just given or by other ad-hoc methods, perhaps including the splitting algorithm, discussed shortly. By way of illustration of some possible techniques, consider $^5/_{121}$, for which the greedy algorithm yields

$$^1/_{25} + {}^1/_{757} + {}^1/_{763,309} + {}^1/_{873,960,180,913} + {}^1/_{1,527,612,795,642,093,418,846,225}.$$

If one first applies the greedy algorithm to $^5/_{11}$ and then multiplies each denominator by 11, one gets the succinct representation $^5/_{121} = {}^1/_{33} + {}^1/_{99} + {}^1/_{1,089}$.

Examining the output of the greedy algorithm leads to the conclusion that the denominators grow quickly; that is, the more unit fractions in a fraction's representation, the larger—much larger—the denominators are. In fact, it is always true that the denominators grow at an exponential rate. We leave the proof of the following as an exercise (use induction on k): If for a positive rational $a/b < 1$ the greedy algorithm outputs, in order, the reciprocals of the integers $m_1, m_2, \ldots, m_k$, and if $d = m_1^2 - m_1$, then $m_2 > d$, $m_3 > d^2$, $m_4 > d^4$, $\ldots$, $m_k > d^{(2^{k-2})}$.

There are several other algorithms for generating Egyptian fractions and the interested reader might enjoy programming some of them in *Mathematica* and comparing the performance of different algorithms in terms of a representation's length or its largest denominator. A paper by M. N. Bleicher [Ble], in which he presents a method based on continued fractions, is a good place to start. His algorithm guarantees a representation of a/b in which each denominator is at most b^2. Among the handful of theoretical results in this area is a theorem of P. Erdős, who showed that $(b-1)/b$ requires at least Floor($\ln \ln b$) terms in any representation as a sum of distinct unit fractions. Programming the algorithm called the *splitting method* is an excellent exercise, even though this method yields very long lists of fractions. The method begins by writing a/b as $1/b + 1/b + \cdots + 1/b$ and then using the identity $1/n = 1/(n + 1) + 1/n(n + 1)$ to eliminate all but the first of the $1/b$s. Then the new list is taken, and for each term that appears more than once, all but the first occurrence is eliminated by another use of the identity. The identity is used repeatedly until no repetitions remain. Here's an example that terminates quickly:

$$3/7 = 1/7 + 1/7 + 1/7 = 1/7 + 1/8 + 1/56 + 1/8 + 1/56$$

$$= 1/7 + 1/8 + 1/56 + 1/9 + 1/72 + 1/57 + 1/3,192.$$

The fact that the splitting method always terminates was proved by R. L. Graham and R. I. Jewett (late 1960s); a proof can be found in [Bee]. A program that implements the splitting algorithm is given in the Appendix.

It is amusing to use *Mathematica* to check the greedy algorithm's output on numbers of the form $9/10, 99/100, 999/1,000$, and so on. Table 8.2 shows the size of the largest denominator in the representations of such numbers. Exercise: Use a `Table` command to generate the first few terms of Table 8.2 (a solution is in the Appendix). The 12th term takes quite a while as it involves arithmetic on numbers having over 27,000 digits. (There are 18 terms in the representation.)

n	1	2	3	4	5	6	7	8	9	10	11	12	13
Number of digits in largest denominator	2	9	10	14	14	220	865	855	241	1,726	879	27,803	1,693

TABLE 8.2 The number of digits in the largest denominator in greedy representations of $(10^n - 1)/10^n$ as a sum of distinct unit fractions. Note that the representation of 1 minus a trillionth ($n = 12$ in the table) involves a number having more than 27,000 digits!

An intriguing variation of the greedy algorithm arises from the consideration of the parity of denominators. It is an easy exercise to see that any fraction can be expressed as a sum of distinct unit fractions with even denominators. But clearly only fractions that, when reduced, have odd denominators can be a sum of unit fractions with odd denominators. It is a true, but by no means obvious, result that such a representation of a fraction with an odd denominator always exists (R. Breusch and B. M. Stewart [Bre]). Of course, one can try to find such representations using a greedy algorithm. Here is some code to do this. It is a modification of the earlier recursive program, but with two complications. First, the denominator at each stage must be odd; this explains the `While[EvenQ[]]`

loop. Second, an additional check must be inserted to make sure the new unit fraction differs from preceding ones. Consider $4/5$, for example: the first output of the odd greedy algorithm is $1/3$, with a remainder of $7/15$; but the largest odd unit fraction under $7/15$ is again $1/3$. In the following code this problem is handled by carrying along the largest denominator obtained at each stage and making sure, via the `Max[]` statement, that the next denominator is larger.

```
EgyptianFractionOdd[0, old_]    := {}
EgyptianFractionOdd[q_, old_:1] :=
     Block[{m = Max[old + 1, Ceiling[1/q]]},
           Prepend[While[EvenQ[m], m++];
           EgyptianFractionOdd[q - 1/m, m], m]]
Attributes[EgyptianFractionOdd] = Listable
```

```
EgyptianFractionOdd[Range[1,4]/5]
{{5}, {3, 15}, {3, 5, 15}, {3, 5, 7, 9, 79, 24885}}
```

The preceding output shows that the odd greedy algorithm does indeed halt on each of $\{1/5, 2/5, 3/5, 4/5\}$. However, it has never been proved that the odd greedy algorithm *always* halts (see [KW]). Further experimentation confirms the conjecture that the algorithm terminates, although the denominators get large very quickly. For example, the following shows that the odd greedy representation of $4/13$ has a denominator with 210 digits.

```
Ceiling[Log[10, EgyptianFractionOdd[4/13]//N]]
{1, 2, 2, 4, 7, 14, 27, 53, 105, 210}
```

As we did for the standard greedy algorithm, we can examine the remainders of the odd greedy algorithm. We leave the coding of `RemaindersOdd` as an exercise. Unfortunately, the remainders show no obvious pattern, as they did in the unrestricted greedy algorithm.

```
Map[Numerator, RemaindersOdd[999/1001]]
{1996, 6977, 4832, 9491, 5396, 1931, 646, 229, 38, 1, 0}
```

The halting of the odd greedy algorithm is even unproved for the seemingly simple case of $2/b, b$ odd. Perhaps some data generated by *Mathematica* can point the way to a solution in at least this one case.

EXERCISE Use the routines of this section to find an example of a fraction with an odd denominator such that the greedy algorithm to represent it as a sum of odd unit fractions yields fewer terms than does the ordinary greedy algorithm.

8.7 Prime Certificates

The Euclidean algorithm is an example of an algorithm that works in polynomial time. This means that the number of basic bit operations (the "time" the algorithm uses) is a polynomial function of the number of bits in the input. In the case of the Euclidean algorithm, this time-complexity function is bounded by a cubic,[3] for if the two inputs have at most n binary digits, then the larger input is less than 2^n and the number of steps in the algorithm is bounded by $K \log_{10}(2^n)$, or $K_0 n$. But each step involves a division, which, if one uses the naive long-division method, involves about n^2 bit operations for two inputs having fewer than n digits. In short, there is a constant K such that the time complexity is bounded by $K n^3$. Algorithms that run in polynomial time [that is, halt on all inputs and, for some fixed positive integers K and d, take a number of steps that is bounded by $K(\text{length of input})^d$] are said to lie in the class **P**.

A different type of complexity, called *nondeterministic*, has become important in computer science. It concerns problems that, although they may not be solvable in polynomial time, at least have the property that a solution can be recognized quickly if it miraculously drops into your computer's IN box. A good example is the problem of recognizing composite numbers. It is not easy to determine if an integer having, say, 1,000 digits is composite. But if a number theory genie gives you (or your computer) two integers and claims that they multiply to the given large number, then this claim can be verified relatively quickly (in time that is a polynomial function of the lengths of the given integer and the purported factors). We can say that the two factors form a *certificate* of the number's compositeness. This notion is related to the class **NP** of al-

---

[3]Using the fact that the sizes of the numbers decrease rapidly, it can be shown that the time complexity of the Euclidean algorithm is in fact bounded by a quadratic function of the length of the inputs (see [BS, Chap. 4]).

gorithms that run in nondeterministic polynomial time; loosely speaking, an algorithm is in **NP** if it solves a problem in polynomial time under the assumption that a certain certificate has been given. For more precise details of the definition of **NP** and related complexity classes, see [GJ, Wil]. It might seem that this is not a fruitful notion, because certificates do not materialize out of thin air. Nevertheless, no one has been able to show that **NP** and **P** do not coincide, and the **P** = **NP** question is the most important problem in theoretical computer science.

Returning to the question of composites, we saw that short certificates do exist. What about primes? It is by no means clear that short certificates for primality exist. The most naive approach would certify the primality of p by providing a list of all the numbers less than $\sqrt{p}$. The certifying program could then check that p is divisible by none of the numbers in this list. The problem is that such a certificate would not have its length bounded by a polynomial function of the length of p. (Exercise: Show that $\sqrt{p}$ is not bounded by any polynomial function of $\log p$.) In 1975 V. Pratt discovered that a recursive view of a classical number theory result yields a proof that short certificates of primality do exist; in this section we present his proof and some examples of *Pratt certificates*.

Recall that Fermat's Little Theorem (see Chapter 1) tells us that if n is prime and $\gcd(x, n) = 1$, then $x^{n-1} \equiv 1 \pmod{n}$. But the converse is false and so cannot be used as a primality test; the smallest counterexample is the composite number 341, because $2^{340} \equiv 1 \pmod{340}$. However, the following theorem, a modification by D. H. Lehmer of an 1878 result of E. Lucas, proves an assertion that although weaker than the strict converse of Fermat's Little Theorem, has the advantage of being true! The proof uses only basic facts about congruences, such as $a \equiv b \pmod{n}$ implies $a \equiv b \pmod{d}$ whenever d divides n.

THEOREM. Suppose n is a positive integer and $\{p_i\}$ is the set of prime factors of $n-1$. Suppose further that there exists an integer x, called a *witness*, such that $x^{n-1} \equiv 1 \pmod{n}$, but $x^e \not\equiv 1 \pmod{n}$ whenever e is one of the numbers $(n-1)/p_i$. Then n is prime.

PROOF. First observe that $\gcd(x, n) = 1$, for if d divides x and n, then the congruence $1 \equiv x^{n-1} \pmod{n}$ implies that $1 \equiv x^{n-1} \equiv 0 \pmod{d}$; this is true only when $d = 1$. Now, reduce the powers $1, x, x^2, \ldots, x^{n-2}$ modulo n. The resulting integers in $\{1, \ldots, n-1\}$ are all relatively prime to n. We claim that these $n-1$ integers are all distinct; this will conclude the proof, for it implies that the number of positive integers less than n that are relatively prime to n is $n-1$, a fact that is true only of prime numbers n. To prove the claim, observe first that if the reduced powers are not distinct, say, $x^{i+s} \equiv x^i \pmod{n}$, then, using the fact that x is relatively prime to n and therefore invertible modulo n, $x^s \equiv 1 \pmod{n}$, where $1 < s < n-1$. Now let t be the least positive integer such that $x^t \equiv 1 \pmod{n}$. If t fails to divide $n-1$, then $n-1 = qt + r$, where $1 < r < t$. Raising x to both sides modulo n yields that $x^r \equiv 1 \pmod{n}$; this contradicts t's minimality. Therefore t is a proper divisor of $n-1$. But we can now let p_i be any prime divisor of $(n-1)/t$; then t divides $e = (n-1)/p_i$, whence $x^e \equiv 1 \pmod{n}$, contradicting the hypothesis.

The preceding theorem implies that the following two objects form a certificate for the primality of p:

1. A list $\{p_i\}$ of the prime divisors of $p-1$

2. A positive integer x such that $x^{n-1} \equiv 1 \pmod{n}$ and $x^e \not\equiv 1 \pmod{n}$ whenever e is one of the numbers $(n-1)/p_i$

This is not yet a valid certificate in that it cannot be checked in polynomial time. Where is the bottleneck? The number of primes in (1) is at most $\log p$, so that list is adequately short. And it can be quickly verified that $\{p_i\}$ consists of all prime divisors of $p-1$: just repeatedly divide $p-1$ by each p_i in turn as long as p_i divides evenly; the remainder should be 1. And the exponentiations in (2) can be checked by using the fast method of doing exponentiation modulo a base. (This method is used by `PowerMod` and was mentioned briefly in Chapter 1.) The problem is: How do we check that the purported primes in (1) are in fact prime? We think recursively: we simply add some information to the data in (1) by attaching to each of the primes p_i a certificate of its primality. The prime 2 is taken to be self-certifiable; in other words, we take as given that 2 is prime. Now, we leave it as an exercise to show that the number of steps needed to check that all the conditions are satisfied by a set of data of the form just described, that is, (1) with certificates of each p_i added and (2), is bounded by a constant times $\log p$ (see [Wil, §4.10]). Such primality certificates are called *Pratt certificates*.

An example should help clarify the meaning of a certificate. Consider the thousandth prime, 7919, for which two views of a Pratt certificate are given in Figure 8.1, one in hard-to-read straight-line form and the other in the form of a tree. The tree is easier to understand: the primes in (1) appear vertically and the witnesses in (2) appear horizontally. That is, 7 is the witness for 7919 and the prime divisors of 7918 are 2, 37, and 107. The first 2 is self-certified; the witness for 37 is 2 and 36's prime divisors are 2 and 3; the witness for 107 is also 2 and $106 = 2 \cdot 53$; the witness for 53 is 2, and so on. The straight-line version of this certificate is the raw form of the certificate as a nested list of witnesses followed by pairs consisting of primes and their certificates.

EXERCISE Check that the witnesses in Figure 8.1 are valid, that is, that 7 is a witness for 7919 [meaning: $7^{7918} \equiv 1 \pmod{7919}$ while $7^{7918/2}$, $7^{7918/37}$, and $7^{7918/107}$ are not congruent to 1 (mod 7919)], that 2 is a witness for 37, and so on. Write a *Mathematica* routine that accepts x, p, and L (the list of primes that divide $p-1$) and returns the set of powers x^e modulo p where e runs through the set $\{(p-1)/q : q \in L \cup \{1\}\}$.

```
{7919, 7, {2, {37, 2, {2, {3, 2, {2}}}},
        {107, 2, {2, {53, 2, {2, {13, 2, {2, {3, 2, {2}}}}}}}}}}
```

```
              7919 ——— 7
               2
              37 ——— 2
               2
               3 ——— 2
               2
       107 ——— 2
        2
       53 ——— 2
        2
       13 ——— 2
        2
        3 ——— 2
        2
```

FIGURE 8.1 Two views of a Pratt certificate attesting to the primality of 7919. The straight-line certificate is generated by PrattCertify[7919] and the tree by PrattTree[7919]. Finding such certificates for large primes p can be difficult, but the verification that a certificate does indeed prove p's primality can be carried out quickly. These certificates show that the set of primes lies in the class **NP**.

Finally, we can turn to *Mathematica* for some help. Before we can attempt to verify that a certificate proves the primality of a number, we must have that certificate. Such certificates will not be easy to find in general, because the information in (1) requires a factorization of $p - 1$, which is not feasible for large numbers. However, for numbers of modest size and for some easily factorable large numbers, we can obtain the primes in (1); then we can search for a witness x (just by trying 2, 3, 4, and so on until a proper witness is found) and further certificates for the primes p_i, and so on until the tree dies out in a series of 2s. The code on page 282 is due to I. Vardi and returns the straight-line certificate illustrated in Figure 8.1. Note that the routine factors p - 1; this may take inordinately long for large inputs. Some other points to note in the definition of `PrattCertify` are:

- `Transpose` is used to place the primes in the output of `Factor-Integer` into `primes`.

- The `While` condition checks only the second of the two conditions required of a witness. Because it is assumed (more on this assumption shortly) that the input is prime and because all the intermediate values in `primes` are definitely prime, the first condition $x^{p-1} \equiv 1 \pmod{p}$ will always hold by Fermat's Little Theorem. The second condition is checked using a disjunction formed by applying `Or` to the set of conditions, which in turn is formed by using `Map` (via `/@`) on a pure function.

- Because `PrattCertify` is set to be listable, the recursive step can simply return the triple consisting of p, the witness x, and the certificates for each member of `primes`.

Finally, we point out that the program can run forever if p is not prime. The code could be modified to avoid such an infinite loop, but we may as well not bother, for the following reason. Certificates are generally sought in cases where one has a number p that has passed various pseudoprime tests for primality and so is almost certainly prime. The certificate provides the definitive proof. For example, suppose one wants to know the first prime beyond 10^{30}. One can run the built-in `PrimeQ`, as we did in Chapter 1, to eliminate several dozen composites. The first integer for which `PrimeQ` yields `True` is $10^{30} + 57$. To be absolutely sure that this number is prime, one needs a certificate, that is, an ironclad proof. Then one moves to a slower procedure than `PrimeQ` in the hope of finding the desired certificate and eliminating any doubt about the number's primality. There are more modern certification techniques based on the theory of elliptic curves; they do not require the factoring of large integers and work fairly rapidly on primes of up to 100 or 200 digits. One of these methods has been programmed in *Mathematica* by I. Vardi, and it may be included in a future release.

```
PrattCertify::usage = "PrattCertify[p] returns a Pratt
certificate of p's primality. If p is not a prime number the
program does not halt."


SetAttributes[PrattCertify, Listable]


PrattCertify[2] := 2


PrattCertify[p_Integer] := Block[{x = 2, primes},
    primes = First[Transpose[FactorInteger[p - 1]]];
    While[
     Apply[Or, PowerMod[x, (p-1)/#, p] == 1 & /@ primes], x++];
    Return[{p, x, PrattCertify[primes]}]] /; p > 2
```

EXERCISE Is the performance of `PrattCertify` improved by caching the certificates as they are found? See the end of Chapter 1 for more information on caching and its use in recursion.

The perceptive reader will notice that we have not estimated the number of steps that might be needed to find x in the `While` loop, nor, in fact, have we proved that, given a prime p a witness x exists. These matters are related to the notion of primitive roots for a prime, as x is nothing but a primitive root of p. The set of integers $\{1, \ldots, p-1\}$ together with the operation of multiplication mod p form a multiplicative group that is cyclic. Any generator of this group is called a *primitive root* of p and satisfies the conditions defining a witness. Moreover, the number of primitive roots of p is $\phi(p-1)$, where ϕ is Euler's phi function, discussed earlier in this chapter (see [Ros, Chap. 8] for the basic results about primitive roots). Therefore the primitive roots are fairly numerous and a brute force search for one starting from 2 works pretty well. However, it is not known that the first primitive root of p always lies below a fixed power of $\log p$, and therefore this is a theoretical weakness in the algorithm. Of course, the practical weakness of having to factor $p-1$ is much more important here. Exercise: Use *Mathematica* to generate a table of the two smallest primitive roots for the first hundred or so primes.

We can modify the definition of `PrattCertify` so that the output is in the form of a tree, as in Figure 8.1. The idea is to print out the data, using a number of spaces that is a function of the depth of the recursion. We do this by keeping track of the depth in `level`. It would not do to set `level` to 0 at the beginning, as it would then get reset in every recursive call. Rather we give it a default value of 0 and use larger values at each call. With `level` at hand, we can insert a check that $x^{p-1} \equiv 1 \pmod{p}$ in the level-0 case, to provide a partial guard against the possibility of a nonprime input at the very beginning; but because the converse to Fermat's Little Theorem can fail, a composite number can slip by this test and cause the program to run forever in search of a witness.

```
PrattTree::usage = "PrattTree[p] returns a Pratt certificate
of p's primality in the form of a tree. If p is not a prime
number, the program will probably halt with a NOT PRIME
message."

Attributes[PrattTree] = Listable

space[n_] := StringJoin @@ Table["   ", {n}];

PrattTree[2, level_] := Print[space[level], 2];

PrattTree[p_Integer, level_:0] := Block[
     {x = 2, primes = First[Transpose[FactorInteger[p-1]]]},
     While[Apply[Or, PowerMod[x, (p-1)/#, p] == 1 & /@ primes],
                                                  x++];
     If[level == 0 && PowerMod[x, p-1, p] != 1,
          Return["NOT PRIME"],
               Print[space[level], p, "  --------- ", x];
               PrattTree[primes, level+1];]]   /; p > 2
```

As we have pointed out, these methods will not always work on large integers because of the factorization problem. But sometimes we can be lucky. The tree shown on the cover of this chapter was generated by `PrattTree[1703616691469833244854254847]` and so establishes without a doubt that this 28-digit number is prime. The naive method of proving primality by checking all possible divisors less than the square root of the number would require about 10^{12} divisions. The certificate on the cover proves primality with the need for only a few dozen multiplications and exponentiations. Note the plethora of 2s in these certificates. That is because 2 always divides $p-1$ for any odd prime p, and also because 2 is the first number tried in the search for witnesses. When we try to certify the primality of $10^{30}+57$ luck is again on our side, and the following certificate, reformatted into a partial tree, is returned by `PrattCertify[10^30 + 57]` in a few minutes.

```
{1000000000000000000000000000057, 5,
    {2,
    {3, 2, {2}},
    {79043, 2,
        {2,
        {39521, 3,
            {2,
            {5, 2, {2}},
            {13, 2, {2, {3, 2, {2}}}}},
        {19, 2, {2, {3, 2, {2}}}}}}}},
    {3998741, 2,
        {2,
        {5, 2, {2}},
        {17, 3, {2}},
        {19, 2, {2, {3, 2, {2}}}},
        {619, 2,
            {2,
            {3, 2, {2}},
            {103, 5,
                {2,
                {3, 2, {2}},
                {17, 3, {2}}}}}}}},
    {290240017, 10,
        {2,
```

```
     {3, 2, {2}},
     {11, 2, {2, {5, 2, {2}}}},
     {181, 2, {2, {3, 2, {2}}, {5, 2, {2}}}},
     {3037, 2,
          {2,
          {3, 2, {2}},
          {11, 2, {2, {5, 2, {2}}}},
          {23, 5, {2, {11, 2, {2, {5, 2, {2}}}}}}}},
{454197539, 2,
     {2,
     {331, 3,
          {2,
          {3, 2, {2}},
          {5, 2, {2}},
          {11, 2, {2, {5, 2, {2}}}}}},
     {686099, 2,
          {2,
          {7, 3, {2, {3, 2, {2}}}},
          {7001, 3,
               {2,
               {5, 2, {2}},
               {7, 3, {2, {3, 2, {2}}}}}}}}}}}}
```

In order to illustrate the fact that a certificate can be checked quickly, we should write a program that takes a certificate in the straight-line form and checks that the sets of primes exhaust the various numbers of the form $p-1$ and that the powers of the witnesses behave as claimed. Such checking would be superfluous in the cases considered above, since the procedure that generated the certificates verified along the way that the certificates were valid, that is, that the witnesses had the correct properties and that the primes in primes were all the prime divisors of each $p-1$ (of course they were: we factored $p-1$ to get them). Thus we leave the following as an exercise in recursive programming: Write a routine that accepts a straight-line certificate, verifies that it really is a Pratt certificate, and outputs all the intermediate values of $x^{(p-1)/p_i}$ modulo p that occur.

9 Imaginary Primes and Prime Imaginaries

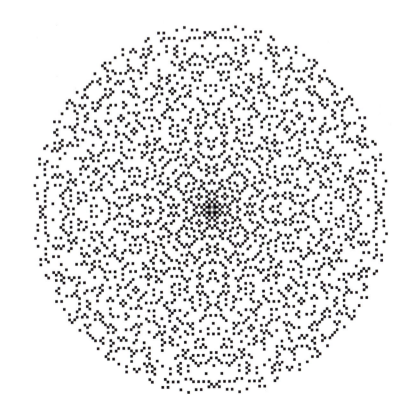

This chapter explores some deeper aspects of number theory from an algorithmic viewpoint. The title refers to the following two closely related ideas.

1. In the complex numbers some ordinary integers remain prime and others do not. For example, 2 factors as $(1 + i)(1 - i)$ and 5 factors as $(2 + i)(2 - i)$, so 2 and 5 are not complex primes; on the other hand, 3 is a complex prime. We will completely characterize the set of complex primes of the form $a + bi$, where a and b are in $\mathbb{Z}$—called *Gaussian primes*—and discuss the factorization of complex numbers into Gaussian primes.

2. For an ordinary prime p, the notion of an imaginary number in the integers modulo p, that is, in $\{0, 1, 2, \ldots, p-1\}$, may not be imaginary at all. For example, in the integers modulo 5 one can say that $\sqrt{-1}$ exists as either 2 or 3, because $2^2 \equiv 4 \equiv -1 \pmod 5$ and $3^2 \equiv 9 \equiv -1 \pmod 5$; in the integers modulo 3, however, there is no number whose square is -1 (i.e., 2) modulo 3. This distinction will be studied in detail; it turns out that except for 2, the primes that admit a solution to $x^2 \equiv -1 \pmod p$ are precisely the primes that do not remain prime in the complex numbers.

The main goal of the chapter is to use *Mathematica* to list all the representations of an integer as a sum of two squares, a task that will use the two preceding concepts. The final routine for doing so will be by far the most complex program considered in this book. We will see how attacking a large problem in bits and pieces, debugging and refining the pieces as we go, yields reliable and easy-to-revise code.

About the illustration overleaf:

The black squares correspond to complex numbers that are primes, the white squares to composites. The image shows all Gaussian primes having norm less than 5,000, and was generated by GaussianPrimes[70], which is defined in this chapter.

9.1 The Complex Euclidean Algorithm ▬▬▬

A central idea in number theory is to extend the notion of ordinary integers to larger sets of integer-like objects. Knowledge about these extensions can yield deep results about the ordinary integers. The classic example is the set of *Gaussian integers*, by which is meant the set consisting of all complex numbers having the form $a + bi$ where a and b are integers. This set is denoted by either $\mathbb{Z}[i]$ or simply $\mathbb{G}$. Other types of extensions arise by replacing i by, say, $\sqrt{-n}$ where n is a positive integer. The arithmetic of Gaussian integers is much like the arithmetic of ordinary integers: the sum, difference, and product of elements of $\mathbb{G}$ are also in $\mathbb{G}$, but the quotient of two Gaussian integers may or may not lie in $\mathbb{G}$. The divisibility relation is defined in the same way as for $\mathbb{Z}$: β divides α if there is a Gaussian integer γ such that $\beta\gamma = \alpha$. Note that every Gaussian integer is divisible by ± 1 *and* $\pm i$. These four numbers are called *units* and if $\alpha = \beta\gamma$ where γ is a unit, then α and β are called *associates* of each other; this is just a generalization of the familiar facts that 1 and –1 divide every ordinary integer and that from the point of view of divisibility properties an integer is equivalent to its negative.

A Gaussian integer is *prime* if it is not a unit and whenever it factors into two Gaussian integers, one of them is a unit. Already this yields some surprises. For example, in the Gaussian integers –1 is a square, and so $1 + 1 = 2$ becomes $1 - (-1) = 2$, a representation of 2 as a difference of two squares; hence $2 = (1 + i)(1 - i)$ and 2 is not a prime Gaussian integer. Later in this chapter we'll turn to the problem of characterizing the prime Gaussian integers (called *Gaussian primes*). For more details of the proofs of the basic facts about divisibility in $\mathbb{G}$ see [Fla, §2.4].

A crucial distinction between the complex and real numbers is that unlike $\mathbb{R}$, $\mathbb{C}$ does not form an ordered field: there is no natural way of linearly ordering the complex numbers according to size. So, for example, it is by no means clear that the notion of greatest common divisor of two Gaussian integers makes sense. How would we choose the "greatest" among all common divisors? The way around this is to define gcd in $\mathbb{G}$ as follows: γ is the gcd of α and β if γ divides α, γ divides β, and any other Gaussian integer that divides α and β also divides γ. It turns out that under this definition each pair of Gaussian integers does admit a unique gcd (up to an associate factor). This, in turn, can be used to show that as for ordinary integers, prime factorization of Gaussian integers is unique (up to associates). This is not true in all extensions of the integers. For example, if $\mathbb{Z}[\sqrt{-5}]$ denotes the collection of all complex numbers of the form $a + b\sqrt{-5}$, where a and b are in $\mathbb{Z}$, then gcds cannot be defined uniquely and, in fact, unique factorization into primes is false. We leave it as an exercise for the reader to prove that 6 admits the two factorizations $2 \cdot 3$ and $(1 + \sqrt{-5})(1 - \sqrt{-5})$, where the four factors are all prime numbers in $\mathbb{Z}[\sqrt{-5}]$ (use a generalization of the norm function, defined in the next paragraph).

A very important function in $\mathbb{G}$ is the *norm*, defined by $N(a + bi) = a^2 + b^2$; $N(\alpha) = |\alpha|^2$ where $|\cdot|$ denotes the usual absolute value of a complex number. Facts N1 to N9 below are all easily proved and will be used throughout this chapter.

> EXERCISE Prove the following assertions about the norm function and the divisibility relation in $\mathbb{G}$. (Recall that the conjugate of a complex number $a + bi$ is $a - bi$; in *Mathematica* this is built in as `Conjugate[z]`. The usual notation for the conjugate of z is $\overline{z}$.)

N1. $\alpha\overline{\alpha} = N(\alpha)$.

N2. $N(\alpha) = N(\overline{\alpha})$.

N3. $N(\alpha\beta) = N(\alpha)N(\beta)$.

N4. If β divides α in $\mathbb{G}$, then $N(\beta)$ divides $N(\alpha)$ in $\mathbb{Z}$.

N5. The units are the only Gaussian integers that are invertible in $\mathbb{G}$ (i.e., have reciprocals in $\mathbb{G}$).

N6. If α divides β and β divides α, then α and β are associates.

N7. If a and b are integers and a divides b in $\mathbb{G}$, then a divides b in $\mathbb{Z}$.

N8. If β divides α, then $\overline{\beta}$ divides $\overline{\alpha}$.

N9. If β divides α and β is neither a unit nor an associate of α, then $1 < N(\beta) < N(\alpha)$.

We can now state the fundamental facts about greatest common divisors and unique factorization in the Gaussian integers.

THEOREM 1.

a. If α and β are Gaussian integers with $\beta \neq 0$, then there exist Gaussian integers q and r such that $\alpha = q\beta + r$ and $N(r) < N(\beta)$.

b. Every pair of Gaussian integers not both 0 has a greatest common divisor, which is unique up to associates.

c. Every nonzero Gaussian integer may be written in a unique way (up to order and associates) as a product of Gaussian primes.

PROOF.

a. Suppose the true quotient α/β in $\mathbb{C}$ equals $u + vi$. Let $\mathbb{G}$ be the nearest integer to u and let n be the nearest integer to v. Then q may be taken to be $m + ni$, and we leave it as an exercise to show that $r = \alpha - q\beta$ is such that $N(r) < N(\beta)$.

b. This follows from (a) as for the ordinary integers. Namely, one uses a division algorithm based on part (a) to form a sequence of remainders whose norms are a decreasing sequence of nonnegative integers. The sequence must therefore terminate with a remainder having norm 0, that is, a zero remainder. We leave the details of proving that the final nonzero remainder is a gcd of α and β under the $\mathbb{G}$-definition of gcd as an exercise. Uniqueness follows from N6 and the fact that two gcds would divide each other.

c. This also is similar to the proof of the same result in $\mathbb{Z}$ (see [Fla]).

Note the similarity of part (a) to the variation on the Euclidean algorithm given in Chapter 8 (page 250). In both cases the nearest-integer function is used as a way of getting a smaller remainder (that is, smaller in absolute value for $\mathbb{Z}$, smaller in norm for $\mathbb{G}$). The theorem leads immediately to a Euclidean algorithm for $\mathbb{G}$ that starts with two Gaussian integers and produces their gcd, the last nonzero remainder in the sequence of remainders. We can use recursion in a way almost identical to the ordinary Euclidean algorithm discussed in Chapter 8. A Print statement is included so that we can see the sequence of remainders; it can be deleted if one desires only the gcd.

```
ComplexGCD[z_, u_] := Block[{q = z/u}, Print[z];
         ComplexGCD[u, z - u (Round[Re[q]] + I Round[Im[q]])]]
ComplexGCD[z_, 0_] := z

ComplexGCD[73, 27+I]
73

27 + I

-8 - 3 I
```

The preceding shows that the ordinary prime 73 is divisible by $8 + 3i$ and so is not prime in $\mathbb{G}$. Note also that $N(-8 - 3i) = 73$, which implies that $73 = 8^2 + 3^2$; we will shortly discuss the special property of 27 that yields such a result. As with the ordinary Euclidean algorithm, an important virtue of `ComplexGCD` is that it works quickly on fairly large inputs. In the second example that follows (in which the `Print` statement has been deleted) the gcd of two very large numbers is computed in only a few seconds.

```
ComplexGCD[-1350180 + 3266646 I, -4416 + 1040 I]
-1350180 + 3266646 I
-4416 + 1040 I
780 - 1882 I
128 + 718 I
-400 - 190 I
-82 + 128 I
-16 + 56 I
6 + 32 I

4 - 14 I


ComplexGCD[Product[a + b I, {a, 1, 8},    {b, 1,  7}],
         Product[a + b I, {a, 12, 16}, {b, 12, 15}]]
270015132441600000 + 4044308486400000 I
```

EXERCISE Prove that if γ is the gcd of α and β in $\mathbb{G}$, then there are δ and η in $\mathbb{G}$ such that $\delta\alpha + \eta\beta = 1$. Write a *Mathematica* routine that produces δ and η.

9.2 Quadratic Residues

For prime p, let $\mathbb{Z}_p$ denote the integers modulo p, that is, the set $\{0, 1, 2, \ldots, p-1\}$ with addition and multiplication taken to be modulo p; we often use -1 (or $-r$) instead of $p-1$ (or $p-r$). Some of these integers are squares in the mod-p sense, while others are not. In fact, for odd p exactly half of the nonzero integers in $\mathbb{Z}_p$ are squares. The reason can be easily seen by examining the pattern in the following output, which shows that each square has the two square roots $\pm r$. Recall that the following command will work only after `PowerMod`'s attributes have been amended to include `Listable`; see the discussion of `PowerMod` in the section on the Chinese Remainder Theorem on page 262.

```
PowerMod[Range[1, 18], 2, 19]
{1, 4, 9, 16, 6, 17, 11, 7, 5, 5, 7, 11, 17, 6, 16, 9, 4, 1}
```

An integer a is called a *quadratic residue* mod p if the congruence $x^2 \equiv n \pmod p$ has a solution, in which case x and $-x$ are called *mod-p square roots* of a. If the congruence has no solution, then n is said to be a *quadratic nonresidue mod p*. We will often suppress "quadratic." The Legendre symbol is useful: given an odd prime p and any integer a, the Legendre symbol $\left(\frac{a}{p}\right)$ is defined to be +1 if a is a quadratic residue mod p and −1 otherwise. There are two basic ways of determining the quadratic character of n mod p. First, there is Euler's criterion, which states that for an odd prime p and any positive integer a that is not a multiple of p,

$$a^{\frac{p-1}{2}} \equiv \left(\frac{a}{p}\right) \pmod p$$

For proofs of Euler's criterion and other facts about quadratic residues, see [Ros, Chap. 9]. Euler's criterion can be used for computation because `PowerMod` is fast, but it is even faster to use an algorithm based on the law of quadratic reciprocity. This algorithm is essentially built into *Mathematica* under the name `JacobiSymbol`. The Jacobi symbol is an extension of the Legendre symbol that need not concern us here; the important point is that for odd primes p, `JacobiSymbol[a, p]` coincides with the Legendre symbol $\left(\frac{a}{p}\right)$. It is convenient to first make `JacobiSymbol` listable.

```
SetAttributes[JacobiSymbol, Listable]
JacobiSymbol[Range[18], 19]
{1, -1, -1, 1, 1, 1, 1, -1, 1, -1, 1, -1, -1, -1, -1, 1, 1, -1}
```

The +1s occur in the positions corresponding to squares, as can be seen by comparing the output of the following command with the list of squares generated earlier by `PowerMod`.

```
Flatten[Position[%, 1]]
{1, 4, 5, 6, 7, 9, 11, 16, 17}
```

A special case of the residue-nonresidue dichotomy that will be especially important to us is the case $a = -1$. Sometimes -1 is a quadratic residue mod p (e.g., $p = 5$) and sometimes it is not (e.g., $p = 3$). The following command returns the set of odd primes among the first 50 primes for which -1 is a quadratic residue mod p. Recall that `Prime[n]` returns the nth prime.

```
Select[Prime[Range[2, 50]], JacobiSymbol[-1, #] == 1 &]
{5, 13, 17, 29, 37, 41, 53, 61, 73, 89, 97, 101, 109, 113, 137,
   149, 157, 173, 181, 193, 197, 229}
```

As can be seen by comparing the output with that of `Select[Prime[Range[2,50]], Mod[#, 4] == 1 &]`, the primes for which -1 is a square—the primes for which $\sqrt{-1}$ exists in $\mathbb{Z}_p$—are precisely the primes that are congruent to 1 modulo 4. This is not hard to prove directly, with the help of Wilson's theorem (see Chapter 1); but it also follows immediately from Euler's criterion, since if $p = 4k + 1$, then

$$\left(\frac{-1}{p}\right) \equiv (-1)^{\frac{p-1}{2}} = (-1)^{2k} = +1$$

It is not difficult to find a square root of -1 in the cases that such exist. Suppose $p = 4k + 1$ and c is a nonresidue mod p. Then Euler's criterion implies that $c^{2k} \equiv -1 \pmod{p}$, whence c^k is one of the two square roots of -1. So all that remains is to find a single nonresidue mod p (recall that half of the integers in $\mathbb{Z}_p$ are nonresidues). The least nonresidue must be a prime (this is a consequence of the identity $\left(\frac{a}{p}\right)\left(\frac{b}{p}\right) = \left(\frac{ab}{p}\right)$, which follows from Euler's criterion), and therefore a simple trial-and-error search for a nonresidue starting at 2 may be programmed as follows.

```
Nonresidue[p_?OddQ] := Block[{n = 0},
    While[JacobiSymbol[Prime[++n], p] == 1]; Prime[n]]
Attributes[Nonresidue] = Listable

Nonresidue[Prime[Range[100000, 100030]]]
{2, 7, 5, 2, 11, 2, 5, 2, 2, 3, 19, 2, 2, 2, 5, 2, 2, 3, 2, 3, 2,
   2, 2, 2, 13, 2, 3, 3, 3, 5, 7}
```

The preceding output shows that the search for a nonresidue often stops at 2 or 3. One search went as far as 19. We can check this case as follows (19 is the eighth prime, so the following sequence of ±1s confirms the preceding computation).

```
JacobiSymbol[Prime[Range[10]], Prime[100010]]
{1, 1, 1, 1, 1, 1, 1, -1, -1, -1}
```

EXERCISE Use Euler's criterion and `PowerMod` to check the results of the preceding computation, that is, to determine which of the first 10 primes are residues modulo the 100,010th prime.

EXERCISE Find the smallest prime for which the least nonresidue is 11. Repeat with 13, 17, 19, and larger values. Use `PrimeQ` and `JacobiSymbol` to investigate the size of the least nonresidue for some large primes. For example, how many of the first 100 primes past 10^{15} have their least nonresidue outside of $\{2, 3, 5, 7\}$? (Remember, though, that `PrimeQ` is not known to be an absolute certifier of primality; see Chapter 1.)

The trial-and-error method of finding a nonresidue works quite well in practice, but its theoretical underpinnings are slightly shaky. It is conceivable that for some primes p the distribution of residues and nonresidues is badly skewed, and a very large initial segment of the integers consists entirely of residues. However, it is a consequence of a certain deep hypothesis of number theory known as the Extended Riemann Hypothesis[1] that the first nonresidue mod p is less than $2(\log p)^2$ (E. Bach [Bac]). Thus if `Nonresidue` ever fails to find a nonresidue less than $2(\log p)^2$, the Extended Riemann Hypothesis will be thereby refuted! In fact, computations indicate that the situation is even better than indicated by ERH; for example, for primes under 36,000,000 the least nonresidue is always less than 60.

We can now solve the problem of determining the square root of -1 modulo those primes for which it exists. Later in this chapter we will address the general problem of finding a complete solution to the congruence $x^2 \equiv a \pmod{n}$ for any integers a and n.

---

[1] We have met the Riemann Hypothesis and the Extended Riemann Hypothesis already in Chapter 1. The former is closely connected with the theory of the distribution of the primes; the latter implies that the primality of a number can be definitively tested in polynomial time.

```
SqrtNegOne[p_] :=
        PowerMod[Nonresidue[p], (p-1)/4, p]  /; Mod[p, 4] == 1
SqrtNegOne[2] := 1


SqrtNegOne[73]
27
```

We can check this routine on those of the first 100 primes that are congruent to 1 modulo 4 as follows.

```
primes = Select[Prime[Range[100]], Mod[#, 4] == 1 &]
PowerMod[SqrtNegOne /@ primes, 2, primes] - primes
{-1, -1, -1, -1, -1, -1, -1, -1, -1, -1, -1, -1, -1, -1, -1, -1,
  -1, -1, -1, -1, -1, -1, -1, -1, -1, -1, -1, -1, -1, -1, -1, -1,
  -1, -1, -1, -1, -1, -1, -1, -1, -1, -1, -1, -1, -1, -1, -1}
```

EXERCISE Modify SqrtNegOne so that it returns the set of both square roots of –1 in $\mathbb{Z}_p$, in increasing order.

EXERCISE Show by an example, perhaps aided by a search using *Mathematica*, that for composite n there may be more than two noncongruent mod-n square roots of –1.

9.3 Sums of Two Squares via Complex GCDs ▪

We can now combine the results on unique factorization in the Gaussian integers with the preceding results about primes for which –1 is a square to obtain a proof of the classical result that primes congruent to 1 modulo 4 are representable as a sum of two squares.

THEOREM 2. A prime p is a sum of two squares if and only if $p = 2$ or $p \equiv 1 \pmod 4$.

PROOF. The easy direction is the result that a prime (or any integer) that is congruent to 3 (mod 4) is not a sum of two squares. Because a square is congruent to 0 or 1 (mod 4), a sum of two squares is necessarily congruent to 0, 1, or 2 (mod 4).

   For the other direction, there is an integer x whose square modulo p is –1. This means that p divides $x^2 + 1$. Therefore, in the Gaussian integers, p divides $(x + i)(x - i)$. But p fails to divide either of these two factors because p fails to divide the imaginary parts, $\pm i$. Therefore p is not prime in $\mathbb{G}$, and so $p = \alpha\beta$, where $\alpha = \gcd(p, x + i)$ and $\beta = \gcd(p, x - i)$ and each of α and β has norm greater than 1. But then, by N3, $p^2 = N(\alpha)N(\beta)$. This is an equation in $\mathbb{Z}$, whence p's primality implies that $N(\alpha) = N(\beta) = p$. If $\alpha = u + vi$, then $p = u^2 + v^2$, as desired.

The preceding proof yields a nifty algorithm for representing a prime as a sum of two squares: first find x, a square root of -1 modulo p, and then find the complex gcd of p and $x + i$. The result will be $a + bi$ where $a^2 + b^2 = p$. The following implementation assumes that p is prime; since we plan to use this as a subroutine later where the input will be known to be prime, it would be redundant to put in a prime-checking clause, as that takes several seconds for large values. The congruence-mod-4 check, on the other hand, takes only a small fraction of a second and guarantees that the routine will never run on a prime input that is not a sum of two squares. As with all functions whose arguments are integers, it is convenient to define the function to be listable.

```
Sum2SquaresViaComplexGCD[p_] :=
    Block[{g = ComplexGCD[p, SqrtNegOne[p] + I]},
    Abs[{Re[g], Im[g]}]]                /; Mod[p, 4] == 1 || p == 2
Attributes[Sum2SquaresViaComplexGCD] = Listable
```

```
Sum2SquaresViaComplexGCD[73]
{8, 3}
```

```
Sum2SquaresViaComplexGCD[848654483879497562821]
{28440994650, 6305894639}
```

This last computation took only a few seconds, and the routine can be used efficiently on even larger values. However, an even faster method for solving this problem will be discussed later in this chapter.

EXERCISE Verify that Sum2SquaresViaComplexGCD works as claimed by writing a routine that checks it on several dozen primes that are congruent to 1 modulo 4.

The representation of a prime as a sum of two squares is essentially unique (a proof follows Theorem 4). Later in this chapter we will develop a routine that finds all the representations of an arbitrary integer as a sum of two squares. Let's use the term *bisquare* for an integer that is a sum of two squares. Note that a product of bisquares is again a bisquare. This is most easily seen using complex numbers, since an integer is a bisquare if and only if it has the form $N(\alpha)$ for some $\alpha \in \mathbb{G}$. Now, if $m = N(\alpha)$ and $n = N(\beta)$, then $mn = N(\alpha\beta)$. More concretely, the product of $a^2 + b^2$ and $c^2 + d^2$ has the form $(ac - bd)^2 + (ad + bc)^2$. This leads to the following characterization of the bisquares.

THEOREM 3. A positive integer n is a bisquare if and only if the prime factorization of n has the form

$$2^t \prod p_i^{r_i} q_j^{s_j}$$

where the p_i are congruent to 1 modulo 4, the q_j are congruent to 3 modulo 4, and each s_j is even.

PROOF. Any number with a factorization as in the theorem is a product of the bisquares 2, $\{p_i\}$, and $\{q_j^2\}$, and so is a bisquare. Conversely, suppose that n is a bisquare, say $n = a^2 + b^2$; q is a prime congruent to 3 modulo 4; and s is the highest power of q that divides n. Let q^s be the highest power of q that divides both a and b; suppose q^{s+1} does not divide b. Then q^{2s} divides n, and it remains to show only that q^{2s+1} does not divide n. Let $A = a/q^s$, $B = b/q^s$, and $N = n/q^{2s}$. Then $A^2 + B^2 = N$ and q does not divide B. Now, if q^{2s+1} did divide n, then $A^2 + B^2 = N \equiv 0 \pmod{q}$ and, because B is invertible modulo q, $(AB^{-1})^2 \equiv -1 \pmod{q}$. This is a contradiction because $q \equiv 3 \pmod{4}$, and so square roots of -1 modulo q do not exist.

9.4 Gaussian Primes

We have seen that 2 and the primes congruent to 1 modulo 4 are not Gaussian primes. We now turn to the problem of completely characterizing the Gaussian primes.

THEOREM 4. A Gaussian integer α is a Gaussian prime if and only if either:

a. α is an ordinary prime congruent to 3 modulo 4.

b. $N(\alpha)$ is a prime integer.

PROOF. Part (b) of the reverse direction is easy, for if α is not a $\mathbb{G}$-prime, then by N9 some Gaussian integer β divides α, where $1 < N(\beta) < N(\alpha)$. Then N4 implies that $N(\beta)$ divides $N(\alpha)$; this contradicts the primality of $N(\alpha)$. For part (a), suppose p is prime, $p \equiv 3 \pmod 4$, and p fails to be a Gaussian prime. Then $p = \alpha\beta$ where α and β are not units. This implies that $p^2 = N(\alpha)N(\beta)$, and this in turn implies that $p = N(\alpha)$ and is therefore a sum of two squares, in contradiction to Theorem 2.

For the forward direction, suppose α is a $\mathbb{G}$-prime. If $\alpha \in \mathbb{Z}$ then α must be a prime integer. It cannot be 2 or a prime congruent to 1 modulo 4 because, by Theorem 2, it would then have the form $a^2 + b^2$ and so be divisible by $a + bi$. If α is not an integer, then $\alpha\overline{\alpha} = N(\alpha) \in \mathbb{Z}$ and α, being a divisor of a product of ordinary primes, must, by unique factorization in $\mathbb{G}$, divide one of the ordinary primes. But if α is a proper divisor of an ordinary prime p, then $N(\alpha)$ divides $N(p)$, which is p^2; therefore $N(\alpha) = p$, as desired.

One consequence of Theorem 4 is that the solution to $p = a^2 + b^2$, when it exists, is unique, up to order and sign. For suppose p has the two representations $p = a^2 + b^2 = c^2 + d^2$. Then $N(a \pm bi)$ and $N(c \pm di)$ are all equal to p, whence by Theorem 4, these four Gaussian integers are prime. But then $p = (a+bi)(a-bi)$ is the prime factorization of p, and so by unique factorization, the $\mathbb{G}$-prime $c + di$ must equal one of $a + bi, a - bi$, or their associates. Therefore the pair $\{c, d\}$ is one of $\{a, b\}$, $\{a, -b\}$, $\{-a, b\}$, $\{-a, -b\}$, $\{-b, a\}$, $\{b, a\}$, $\{b, -a\}$, or $\{-b, -a\}$.

The characterization of the Gaussian primes provided by Theorem 4 can be used to generate a two-dimensional image of them. Actually, it is more efficient to use the proof, rather than the theorem. The proof shows that a Gaussian prime is either an ordinary prime (equal to 2 or congruent to 3 modulo 4) or of the form $a + bi$ where $p = a^2 + b^2$. We have already shown that such decompositions into a sum of two squares are essentially unique. Thus we can generate the Gaussian primes by first listing the ordinary primes that are $\mathbb{G}$-primes and then, for the other ordinary primes, finding representations as a sum of two squares. The following code uses the listable function Sum2SquaresViaComplexGCD (which in turn requires SqrtNegOne, Nonresidue, and ComplexGCD) to deal with the 1-modulo-4 case. The symmetries of the Gaussian primes are most apparent if the image is restricted to a disk in $\mathbb{C}$; this explains why one of the Range functions has n as its upper bound whereas the other goes to n^2. The units are neither prime nor composite, and so they are given a gray shade.

```
boxes[q_] := Map[Rectangle[#, #+1] &,
              { q, Reverse[q],   q*{1,-1}, Reverse[q*{1,-1}],
               -q, Reverse[-q], -q*{1,-1}, Reverse[-q*{1,-1}]}]

units = {GrayLevel[.5], boxes[{1,0}]}

GaussianPrimes[n_] := Show[Graphics[{units,
 Map[boxes,
   {{1,1}} ~Join~
   Map[{#,0} &, Select[Range[3, n, 4], PrimeQ]] ~Join~
   Sum2SquaresViaComplexGCD[Select[Range[5,n^2,4], PrimeQ]]]}],
AspectRatio->1]
```

The result of GaussianPrimes[20] is shown in Figure 9.1.

The pattern of the $\mathbb{G}$-primes is visually quite pleasing and it can be used effectively as a model for tiling a wall. The chapter cover shows more of the pattern. A noteworthy unsolved problem is whether one can walk from $1 + i$ to infinity stepping only on the $\mathbb{G}$-primes and taking steps of bounded length. Such a prime walk in the ordinary integers does not exist, as there are arbitrarily long sequences of composites. For

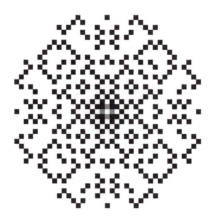

FIGURE 9.1 The Gaussian primes having norm at most 400.

a more visual interpretation of the problem, imagine the white space in the picture of the $\mathbb{G}$-primes to be water, and the black, land. Then the question is: Are there arbitrarily wide moats around the central castle? A moat of width 2 is visible in Figure 9.1; it goes from 12 to $12 + 5i$ to $9 + 5i$ to $9 + 9i$, and so on around; the width 2 arises from the distance between $11 + 4i$ and $11 + 6i$, which are on opposite sides of the moat. The best result known is due to J. H. Jordan and J. R. Rabung [JR], who by examining larger plots of the Gaussian primes, found a moat of width 4 starting at 868. A moat of width $2\sqrt{2}$ can be found in the image forming the chapter cover. Exercise: Find a moat having width greater than 3.

We can also attack the more general problem of finding the complete factorization of a Gaussian integer into Gaussian primes. An algorithm for doing so is based on the fact that if β is a Gaussian prime factor of α then $N(\beta)$ is a prime divisor of $N(\alpha)$.

1. Factor the integer $N(\alpha)$.

2. If $N(\alpha)$ is even, place the appropriate power of $1 + i$ into the final list of factors [recall that 2 is an associate of $(1 + i)^2$].

3. For each prime divisor p of $N(\alpha)$ that is congruent to 3 modulo 4, place the appropriate power of p [half of its exponent in $N(\alpha)$] in the factor list.

4. For each prime divisor p of $N(\alpha)$ that is congruent to 1 modulo 4, let $p = a^2 + b^2$ and let r be the power of p that divides $N(\alpha)$. Then determine s, the exact power of $a + bi$ that divides α, and adjoin the pair $\{a+bi, s\}$ to the factor list if $s > 0$, as well as the pair $\{a-bi, r-s\}$, if $s < r$.

The following is a straightforward implementation of this algorithm, using a subroutine for the divisibility relation in $\mathbb{G}$ and using Scan to proceed through the prime factors of norm(z). Scan[*expr*, list] goes through list, performing *expr* for each element in the list. The output of GaussianFactors is a list similar in form to the list produced by FactorInteger. Note that the factorization is correct only up to a unit; that is, the factors, when multiplied out, might yield any of $\pm z$ and $\pm iz$.

```
(* Uses Sum2SquaresViaComplexGCD, SqrtNegOne, Nonresidue, and
   ComplexGCD; built into Version 2.0 -- see Preface *)

divides[u_, z_] := IntegerQ[Re[z/u]] && IntegerQ[Im[z/u]]

GaussianFactors[z_] := Block[
    {norm = Abs[z]^2, plist, factors = {}, w, s, a, b},
    plist = FactorInteger[norm];
    If[EvenQ[norm], AppendTo[factors, {1 + I, plist[[1,2]]}];
    plist = Rest[plist]];
    Scan[
      If[Mod[#[[1]], 4] == 3, AppendTo[factors, {#[[1]], #[[2]]/2}],
      {a, b} = Sum2SquaresViaComplexGCD[#[[1]]];
      w =  a + b I;
      s = 0;
      While[divides[w, z], s++; w *= a + b I];
      If[s > 0, AppendTo[factors, {a + b I, s}]];
      If[s < #[[2]], AppendTo[factors, {a - b I, #[[2]] - s}]]] &,
     plist];
    factors]

GaussianFactors[1488311206705990 + 8526860574095268 I]
{{1 + I, 2}, {6 + I, 11}, {6 - I, 3}, {40 + 17 I, 1},
  {994 - 335 I, 1}}

GaussianFactors[21!]
{{1 + I, 36}, {3, 9}, {2 + I, 4}, {2 - I, 4}, {7, 3}, {11, 1},
  {3 + 2 I, 1}, {3 - 2 I, 1}, {4 + I, 1}, {4 - I, 1}, {19, 1}}

GaussianFactors[270015132441600000 + 4044308486400000 I]
{{1 + I, 22}, {3, 4}, {2 + I, 5}, {2 - I, 5}, {7, 1},
  {3 + 2 I, 2}, {3 - 2 I, 1}, {4 + I, 1}, {4 - I, 2}, {6 + I, 1},
  {4 + 5 I, 1}, {4 - 5 I, 1}, {8 + 3 I, 1}, {8 + 7 I, 1}}
```

This last example is related to the last example in first section of this chapter.

EXERCISE Write a routine that takes a list of pairs of Gaussian primes and exponents and computes the product of the primes raised to the exponents. A one-line solution is possible. Use the routine to check the preceding outputs of `GaussianFactors`.

EXERCISE Modify `GaussianFactors` so that the output is perfectly correct, not just correct up to multiplication by a unit.

The main bottleneck in `GaussianFactors` is the call to `FactorInteger`, which may take inordinately long for inputs whose norm is difficult to factor. However, once the factorization is done, the rest of the routine runs efficiently, even for very large Gaussian integers.

9.5 Sums of Two Squares via Real GCDs

We now present a method for writing a prime as a sum of two squares that is faster than the algorithm using complex gcds. This extremely concise and fast algorithm was discovered by G. Cornacchia in 1908 ([Cor]; see [Wag]), although the ideas go back even earlier to Hermite and Serret, who had a similar approach using continued fractions.

THEOREM 5. If p is a prime congruent to 1 modulo 4, let $x \in \mathbb{Z}_p$ be a solution to $x^2 \equiv -1 \pmod{p}$ in $\mathbb{Z}_p$ and let a be the first remainder that is smaller than $\sqrt{p}$ when the Euclidean algorithm is applied to the pair p and x. Then $\sqrt{p - a^2}$ is an integer; that is, a is one member of a pair (a, b) that satisfies $p = a^2 + b^2$.

Because a square root of -1 can be obtained in short order via `SqrtNegOne` and because the Euclidean algorithm is fast, the algorithm implicit in Theorem 5 is very efficient. Before implementing the algorithm, we prove the theorem, which also serves as an alternative proof of Theorem 2. The proof is elementary, if a bit intricate.

PROOF OF THEOREM 5. Because the two square roots of -1 in $\mathbb{Z}_p$ have the form x and $p - x$, we may assume that x is the smaller square root. Now, recall the sequence $\{t_i\}$ that was produced by `FullExtendedGCD` introduced in Chapter 8; its main property is that $t_i x \equiv r_i \pmod{p}$ where $\{p, x, r_2, \ldots, r_n\}$ is the sequence of remainders, with $r_n = 1$. Moreover, as was shown in Chapter 8, the t-sequence alternates in sign, $t_{n+1} = \pm p$, and the absolute values of the t_i themselves form a Euclidean algorithm remainder sequence in reverse, with quotients the reverse of the main sequence of quotients $\{q_i\}$. It may be helpful to have an example in mind—indeed, it was the examination of several examples with the help of *Mathematica* that led the author to the proof given here—so recall an example from the preceding chapter: If $p = 73$, then $x = 27$ and the sequences are as in the table that follows. We shall prove that several of the patterns evident in the table hold whenever x is the smallest positive mod-p square root of -1.

r	q	t
73 ($p = r_0$)		0 (t_0)
27 ($x = r_1$)	2 (q_1)	1
19	1	-2
8	2	3
3	2	-8
2	1	19
1 (r_6)	2 (q_6)	-27 (t_6)
		73

The proof leans heavily on the continuant functions Q, which give each remainder as a function of the quotients that follow it; these functions were introduced in Chapter 8. Now, let r_m be the first remainder that is less than $\sqrt{p}$. Then

$$p = Q(q_1, \ldots, q_n), \quad r_{m-1} = Q(q_m, \ldots, q_n),$$
$$|t_m| = Q(q_{m-1}, \ldots, q_1) = Q(q_1, \ldots, q_{m-1}) \tag{*}$$

The first two equations hold because p and r_m each begin a Euclidean algorithm remainder sequence; the third equality holds because the absolute values of the t_i are a remainder sequence with the same quotients and, as shown on page 255, Q is invariant under reversal of its arguments. Now, the sum-of-products characterization of Q given in Chapter 8 implies that

$$Q(q_1, \ldots, q_n) \geq Q(q_1, \ldots, q_{m-1})Q(q_m, \ldots, q_n)$$

since each product occurring as a summand in the expanded right-hand side also occurs in the left-hand side. This last inequality combines with (*) to yield $p \geq r_{m-1}|t_m|$, and because $r_{m-1} > \sqrt{p}$, t_m must be less than $\sqrt{p}$.

Now, to conclude the proof, simply observe that $t_m x \equiv r_m \pmod{p}$, so p divides $t_m^2 x^2 - r_m^2$. But $t_m^2 x^2 \equiv -t_m^2$. Thus $r_m^2 + t_m^2$ is divisible by p. Each of r_m and t_m is less than $\sqrt{p}$, so $r_m^2 + t_m^2 < 2p$. The only positive integer less than $2p$ that is divisible by p is p itself, whence $r_m^2 + t_m^2 = p$.

EXERCISE Show that, in the notation of the preceding proof: (1) $t_n = -x$ (Hint: First show that t_n equals one of $-x$ and $p - x$; the latter is impossible for it would imply that the t-sequence (excluding t_0) is longer than the r-sequence); (2) the t-sequence is, in absolute value, exactly the reverse of the r-sequence; (3) n is even; (4) the sequence of quotients is symmetric about its center; (5) $m = n/2$; and (6) $|t_m| = r_{m+1}$. Thus one can rephrase Theorem 6 to state that the first two remainders under $\sqrt{p}$ yield the desired representation.

Theorem 5 can be implemented directly to solve the equation $p = a^2 + b^2$ for primes p congruent to 1 modulo 4. We first modify the Euclidean algorithm gcd from the beginning of Chapter 8 to a function, MiddleRemainder[p, x], that returns the first remainder in the Euclidean algorithm sequence for p and x that is less than the square root of p. Because the first argument must be carried along, Middle-Remainder has three arguments, with a special case to transform the initial call to a three-argument call. Then it takes only one line to define Sum2Squares[p], which returns one of a or b. This routine is somewhat faster than Sum2SquaresViaComplexGCD, which solves the same problem.

```
(* Uses SqrtNegOne and Nonresidue *)

Attributes[MiddleRemainder] = Listable
Attributes[Sum2Squares] = Listable
MiddleRemainder[p_, m_, x_] := x /; x^2 < p
MiddleRemainder[p_, m_, x_] :=
            MiddleRemainder[p, x, Mod[m, x]] /; x^2 >= p
MiddleRemainder[p_, x_]      := MiddleRemainder[p, p, x]


Sum2Squares[p_] :=
      MiddleRemainder[p, SqrtNegOne[p]] /; Mod[p, 4] == 1


Sum2Squares[848654483879497562821]
28440994650
```

EXERCISE Use `Prime[n]` to generate several large primes congruent to 1 modulo 4 and use them to compare the performance of `Sum2Squares` with that of `Sum2SquaresViaComplexGCD`.

EXERCISE Revise `GaussianFactors` by replacing `Sum2SquaresVia-ComplexGCD` with `Sum2Squares` and do some timing experiments to estimate the resulting speedup.

EXERCISE Verify that the primality of p was never used in the proof of Theorem 5. That is, prove that for any positive integer n, if $x^2 \equiv -1 \pmod{n}$, then the first remainder in the Euclidean algorithm sequence applied to n and x that is smaller than $\sqrt{n}$ yields a solution to $n = a^2 + b^2$. Note, however, that for composite n the solution may not be unique. (What's the smallest example?) A method of generating all solutions will be discussed later in this chapter.

9.6 Square Roots Modulo an Integer

It turns out that the method of the preceding section is much more general and can be modified so that starting from the collection of all square roots of –1 modulo n, it produces all representations of n as a sum of two squares. In this section we set the stage by presenting an algorithm that takes any pair of integers n and a as input and returns the set (possibly empty) of all mod-n square roots of a. There are several difficulties to overcome. First, we must find all square roots modulo a prime that is congruent to 3 modulo 4; second, the method used in `SqrtNegOne` for finding $\sqrt{-1}$ modulo a prime congruent to 1 modulo 4 must be extended to find square roots of any integer; and third, the techniques must be extended to composite moduli. Putting all this together will yield quite a long *Mathematica* routine; in such cases it is important to approach the problem in modules and carefully check, debug, and refine each of the component parts. Of the three problems facing us, the second is the most difficult. For the first problem there is quite a quick method based on Euler's criterion. And the third problem can be dealt with by an elementary technique based on the Chinese Remainder Theorem that obtains all square roots modulo an integer from the square roots modulo the prime factors of the integer.

One important point has not yet been mentioned; namely, if p is an odd prime, then $\mathbb{Z}_p$ contains at most two mod-p square roots of any integer. Proof: If x and y are both square roots of a modulo p, then p divides $y^2 - x^2$, whence p divides one of $y \pm x$, so y is congruent to one of $\pm x$ modulo p.

Let's begin with some trivial cases. The main routine, called SqrtModPrime, will begin with the following three cases.

```
SqrtModPrime[a_, 2]  := Mod[a, 2]
SqrtModPrime[a_, p_] := {}  /;  JacobiSymbol[a, p] == -1
SqrtModPrime[a_, p_] := 0   /;  Mod[a, p] == 0
```

Because the rules for SqrtModPrime[a_, p_] will be invoked in the order in which they are loaded, the presence of the no-square-root case in the middle of these first three cases means that in all following cases it can be assumed that a square root exists. Moreover, it will be assumed throughout that p is prime, because this routine will be used in other routines that send it only primes. Such an assumption should be explicitly stated in the usage statement, which follows. As usual, we also make the function listable for ease of use on sets.

```
SqrtModPrime::usage = "SqrtModPrime[a, p] assumes p is prime
and returns the least nonnegative square root of a mod p if
such exists, {} otherwise."
Attributes[SqrtModPrime] = Listable
```

Now, let's deal with the $p \equiv 3 \pmod 4$ case, say $p = 4k - 1$. By Euler's criterion and the assumption that a square root exists, $a^{(p-1)/2} \equiv 1 \pmod p$. Multiplication by a yields $a^{(p+1)/2} \equiv a \pmod p$; this implies that $a^{2k} \equiv a \pmod p$. It follows that a^k gives the required square root. This case is therefore easily handled, with a Min statement added to select the smaller of the two nonnegative square roots.

```
SqrtModPrime[a_, p_] :=
  Min[PowerMod[a, (p+1)/4, p]*{-1,1} + {p,0}] /; Mod[p, 4] == 3
```

To complete the treatment of the case of prime modulus, we present an algorithm that goes back to A. Tonelli in 1891. The idea of the case just discussed generalizes to the following: If k is an odd integer, say $k = 2m + 1$, and $a^k \equiv 1 \pmod p$, then a square root of a is given by a^{m+1}. In fact, if a nonresidue h is at hand, we can also deal with the case $a^k \equiv -1 \pmod p$, for then by Euler's criterion, $a^k h^{(p-1)/2} \equiv 1 \pmod p$

and a desired square root of a is $a^{m+1}h^{(p-1)/4}$. This leads to the following idea: Form two exponents e_1 and e_2, which start off as $\frac{1}{2}(p-1)$ and $p-1$, respectively. Then e_1 will be repeatedly halved until it yields the odd integer k. After each halving, e_2 will be modified so that it remains an even integer and so that the following congruence holds:

$$a^{e_1}h^{e_2} \equiv 1 \ (\text{mod } p) \qquad (**)$$

Note that (**) holds for the initial values of the exponents. When k is reached, (**) will hold and so the desired square root is available as $a^{m+1}h^{e_2/2}$. Now, at each step e_2 is modifed as follows. First it is halved, and then the new value is inserted into (**), which must yield either ±1, since those are the only two square roots of $+1$. If (**) yields $+1$, do nothing more; otherwise, add $\frac{1}{2}(p-1)$ to e_2. This will have the effect of turning the left-hand side of (**) into the desired $+1$. Because k has not yet been reached, e_2 remains even. Note that at the last stage, when k is odd, e_2 must go through the modification process a final time.

Here's an example where we seek a solution to $x^2 \equiv 49 \ (\text{mod } 3329)$. Nonresidue[3329] returns 3, so that is the value of h. The factorization of 3329 is $1 + 13 \cdot 256$, and so e_1 will take on the successive values $13 \cdot 128$, $13 \cdot 64, \ldots, 13$. The corresponding sequence of mod-3329 powers that will be needed is $49^{128 \cdot 13}$, $49^{64 \cdot 13}$, $49^{32 \cdot 13}$, $49^{16 \cdot 13}$, $49^{8 \cdot 13}$, $49^{4 \cdot 13}$, $49^{2 \cdot 13}$, 49^{13}, which an application of PowerMod shows to be: $\{1, 3328, 1729, 2580, 2642, 2267, 2447\}$. The initial 1 corresponds to 49 being a quadratic residue. Now, e_2 starts as 3328 and changes at the first stage by being halved to 1664. Because 1*PowerMod[3, 1664, 3329] returns 3328, or -1, 1664 must be added to e_2; this yields 3328. Now, at the next stage e_2 is again halved to 1664, but this time Mod[3328*PowerMod[3, 1664, 3329], 3329] returns $+1$, and so we proceed directly to the third stage. The entire sequence of transformations of e_2 ends up being:

$$3328 \to 1664, 3328 \to 1664 \to 832, 2496 \to 1248 \to 624,$$

$$2288 \to 1144, 2808 \to 1404.$$

The final value satisfies (**) where e_1 is now the odd value 13 and so, taking $m = \frac{1}{2}(13 + 1) = 7$ and halving e_2 once more yields the desired square root.

```
Mod[PowerMod[49, 7, 3329]*PowerMod[3, 702, 3329], 3329]
3322
```

In this case, a value of –7 was returned, and a use of Min as in the $p \equiv 3$ (mod 4) case will yield 7.

For efficiency, our implementation proceeds a little differently. We begin by computing k in a While loop and then NestList is used to form a list that has all the mod-p powers of k that will be needed; this avoids repeated use of PowerMod and also avoids the need for maintaining e_1. Then we go back to the top and call on the elements of this list as needed, using Scan[*expr*, Reverse[*list*]]. The routine Nonresidue must be loaded for the following to work.

```
SqrtModPrime[a_, p_] := (k = (p - 1)/4; s = 0;
  h = Nonresidue[p];
  While[EvenQ[k], k /= 2; s++];
  e2 = p-1;
  Scan[(e2 /= 2;
      If[Mod[# * PowerMod[h, e2, p], p] != 1, e2 += (p-1)/2]) &,
      Reverse[NestList[Mod[# #, p]&, PowerMod[a, k, p], s]]];
  Min[Mod[PowerMod[a, (k+1)/2, p]*PowerMod[h, e2/2, p], p] *
      {-1,1} + {p,0}])                    /; Mod[p, 4] == 1
```

As a check, we compute $\sqrt{49}$ modulo the first 20 primes beyond 10,000, half of which turn out to be congruent to 1 modulo 4.

```
testprimes = Prime[Range[10000, 10020]]
SqrtModPrime[49, testprimes]
{7, 7, 7, 7, 7, 7, 7, 7, 7, 7, 7, 7, 7, 7, 7, 7, 7, 7, 7, 7, 7}
```

Of course, a nonsquare such as 48 will be a residue for some primes and a nonresidue for others.

```
SqrtModPrime[48, testprimes]
{{}, {}, 30153, 10443, 36940, {}, {}, {}, {}, {}, 43550, {}, {},
    10977, 28462, 561, {}, 7126, {}, {}, 39920}
```

We can check the preceding output by squaring.

```
Mod[%^2, testprimes]
{{}, {}, 48, 48, 48, {}, {}, {}, {}, {}, 48, {}, {}, 48, 48, 48,
    {}, 48, {}, {}, 48}
```

We should test the routine somewhat more extensively, but it is correct, and so we now have a way of extracting square roots of an arbitrary integer modulo an arbitrary prime.

The method used in `SqrtModPrime` can be described as a top-down approach because we proceed down through the powers of a, changing e_2 as we go. A variation on this algorithm that is more of a bottom-up approach is due to D. Shanks and has come to be known as Shanks's algorithm. It runs substantially faster than the method just presented, and an implementation is given in the Appendix; for an explanation of Shanks's algorithm see [Knu, §4.6.2, Ex. 15 and solution] or [Sha].

The general modular square root problem can be reduced to the case of solving the congruence $x^2 \equiv a \pmod{p^r}$ where p is prime. And that case breaks into subcases according as p is 2 or not and according as a is divisible by p or not. We summarize the rules in the following theorem, whose proof we omit (see [Fla, §3.2]). The theorem translates in a straightforward way to an algorithm for solving the square root problem modulo a prime power.

THEOREM 6. **Case 1: p is an odd prime and $\gcd(p, a) = 1$.** In this case $x^2 \equiv a \pmod{p^r}$ has a solution if and only if $x^2 \equiv a \pmod{p}$ does, and there are precisely two solutions modulo p^r. The two solutions are given by induction on r: If x is a solution modulo p^{r-1}, then $x - (2x)^{-1}(x^2 - a)$ is a square root of a modulo p^r where the inverse is the mod-p inverse. (An aside: this formula is identical to Newton's method for finding square roots.)

Case 2: $p = 2$, $\gcd(a, 2) = 1$.
   Subcase (i): $r = 2$. Because a is odd in this case, the congruence $x^2 \equiv a \pmod 4$ has a solution if and only if $a \equiv 1 \pmod 4$, and the solutions are 1 and 3.
   Subcase (ii): $r \geq 3$. In this case $x^2 \equiv a \pmod{2^r}$ has a solution if and only if $x^2 \equiv a \pmod 8$ has a solution [which occurs iff $a \equiv 1 \pmod 8$]. If solutions exist, there are four of them: if x is one of them, the other three are $-x$, $x + 2^{r-1}$, and $-x + 2^{r-1}$. A particular solution may be built up from 1, the mod-8 solution, by using the following rule: If $x^2 \equiv a \pmod{2^{r-1}}$, then $[\frac{1}{2}(x^3 + (2 - a)x)]^2 \equiv a \pmod{2^r}$.

Case 3: p any prime, $\gcd(a, p) \neq 1$. Let s be the exact power of p that divides a. If $s = r$, then the set of roots is simply $\{0, p^{\lceil r/2 \rceil},$

$2p^{\lceil r/2 \rceil}, \ldots, p^r - p^{\lceil r/2 \rceil}\}$. Otherwise, if s is odd, there are no solutions and if s is even, a solution exists if and only if there is a solution to $x^2 \equiv a/p^s \pmod{p^{r-s}}$; the solution set is then obtained by taking, for each solution y to $x^2 \equiv a/p^s \pmod{p^{r-s}}$, the set $\{p^{r/2}(y + jp^{n-r}) : a = 0$ $1, \ldots, p^{r/2-1}\}$.

In the following implementation of the algorithm given in Theorem 6, square roots modulo primes are obtained via Shanks's algorithm (in Appendix), since that is faster than SqrtModPrime defined earlier.

```
SqrtModPrimePower::usage = "SqrtModPrimePower[a, p, r] returns
the set of all mod-p^r square roots of a, in increasing order;
it uses SqrtModPrimeShanks, which in turn uses Nonresidue."

Attributes[SqrtModPrimePower] = Listable

(* Exponent = 1 case reduces to previous routine *)
SqrtModPrimePower[a_, p_, 1] :=
    Block[{root = SqrtModPrimeShanks[a, p]},
        If[!NumberQ[root], {}, Union[Mod[{p,0}+{-1,1} root,p]]]]

(* Non-coprime case, any prime, reduces to coprime case *)
SqrtModPrimePower[a_, p_, r_] := Block[{s = 1, j},
 If[Mod[a, p^r] == 0, Return[Range[0, p^r-1, p^Ceiling[r/2]]]];
 While[Mod[a, p^s] == 0, s++]; s--;
 If[OddQ[s], {},
    Flatten@Table[
    (SqrtModPrimePower[a/p^s, p, r-s] + (j-1) p^(r-s)) p^(s/2),
                {j, p^(s/2)}]]]          /; Mod[a, p] == 0 && r > 1

(* Coprime case, odd prime *)
SqrtModPrimePower[a_, p_, r_] :=
 Block[{j, root = SqrtModPrimeShanks[a, p]},
 If[!NumberQ[root], Return[{}]],
 Do[root = Mod[root - PowerMod[2 root, -1, p]*(root^2-a), p^j],
                                {j, 2, r}];
 Return[Sort[{-1,1}*root + {p^r, 0}]]]] /;
                    p != 2 && Mod[a, p] != 0 && r > 1
```

```
(* Coprime case, prime is 2, no solution *)
SqrtModPrimePower[a_, 2, r_] := {}   /;
  (r==2 && Mod[a, 4] == 3) || (3<=r && OddQ[a] && Mod[a, 8] != 1)

(* Coprime case modulo 4 *)
SqrtModPrimePower[a_, 2, 2] := {1, 3}  /; Mod[a, 4] == 1

(* Coprime case, prime is 2, exponent is at least 3, solutions
   exist *)
SqrtModPrimePower[a_, 2, r_] :=
 Block[{root = Nest[Mod[(#^3 + (2-a)#)/2, 2^r]&, 1, r-3]},
 Union[
    {root, 2^r-root}, Mod[{root, 2^r-root} + 2^(r-1), 2^r]]] /;
                                          OddQ[a] && 3 <= r
```

A routine as complicated as the preceding should be tested extensively. In this case this can be done by writing a short routine that evaluates a square root by a brute-force search and then comparing the results
of such searches with the output of SqrtModPrimePower.

```
bruteforce[a_, n_] := Select[Range[0, n-1],
                            Mod[#^2, n] == Mod[a, n] &]
Attributes[bruteforce] = Listable
```

Now, we can test the modulus 32 as follows.

```
a = 16; p = 2; r = 5
{SqrtModPrimePower[a, p, r], bruteforce[a, p^r]}
{{4, 12, 20, 28}, {4, 12, 20, 28}}
```

Because the functions have all been defined to be listable, we can check
many cases at once.

```
a = Range[32]; p = 2; r = 5
SqrtModPrimePower[a, p, r] == bruteforce[a, p^r]
True
```

EXERCISE Perform much more extensive testing on SqrtModPrime-
Power; try all possible cases that can arise.

The final step of the square-root problem is quite easy compared
with the intricacies of the prime and prime-power steps. For any positive
integer n and any integer a, a mod-n square root of a exists if and only if

a mod-q square root exists for each of the prime powers q that divide n. Moreover, if for each prime power q dividing n, x_q is one of the mod-q square roots of a, then the unique element y of $\mathbb{Z}_n$ that is congruent to x_q modulo q, for each q, is a mod-n square root of a, and all roots $\mathbb{Z}_n$ are obtained by such choices of the x_q. For example, the two square roots of 1 modulo each of 3, 5, and 7 are $\{1,2\}$, $\{1,4\}$, and $\{1,6\}$. These numbers can be combined in eight ways via the Chinese Remainder Theorem to yield the eight numbers 1, 29, 34, 41, 64, 71, 76, and 104 modulo $3 \cdot 5 \cdot 7 = 105$ (for example, 29 is congruent to 2, 4, and 1 modulo 3, 5, and 7, respectively). These eight numbers form the complete set of square roots of 1 modulo 105. The proof of the general result is straightforward and is left as an exercise.

We have already implemented the Chinese Remainder Theorem in Chapter 8 as CRT; thus the complete set of mod-n square roots of an integer is easily obtained. The implementation of these ideas on page 314 first places the roots modulo the prime powers dividing n into a list of lists called rootlist. Then an Outer construction is used to proceed through all possible choices from each of these root sets and apply the Chinese Remainder Theorem to each choice. This idea is implemented by prepending a function to rootlist and then applying Outer. The prepended function is a function of an unspecified number of variables (the number of primes dividing n) and the symbol ## is *Mathematica*'s way of referring to such an argument sequence; more precisely, CRT[List[##], moduli]& is a pure function that applies the Chinese Remainder Theorem to a sequence of numbers with respect to a fixed sequence, moduli, of moduli.

Because the input must be fully factored, SqrtMod will fail on large integers that are difficult for the built-in factoring routine to factor. Note also that large integers that have many prime factors will also be troublesome; in such a case the number of choices of square roots modulo the prime powers, being an exponential function of the number of distinct primes, will be excessively large and cause both memory and time problems.

The square root project has led us to quite an involved *Mathematica* procedure, with many and varied subroutines. Piecemeal development is essential, both to the debugging and to the understanding of such a program.

```
SqrtMod::usage = "SqrtMod[a, n] returns the set of all mod-n
square roots of a, in increasing order; it uses CRT,
SqrtModPrimePower, SqrtModPrimeShanks, and Nonresidue.";
Attributes[SqrtMod] = Listable

SqrtMod[a_, n_] := Block[{factors = Transpose@FactorInteger[n]},
   rootlist = SqrtModPrimePower[a, factors[[1]], factors[[2]]];
   If[MemberQ[rootlist, {}], Return[{}]];
   PrependTo[rootlist,
     CRT[List[##], factors[[1]]^factors[[2]]] &];
   Union@Flatten[Outer @@ rootlist, Length[rootlist] - 2]]
```

As usual, the routine should be thoroughly tested. A few examples follow.

```
{{SqrtMod[1, 3*5*7], bruteforce[1, 3*5*7]}
{{1, 29, 34, 41, 64, 71, 76, 104}, {1, 29, 34, 41, 64, 71, 76,
   104}}
```

```
SqrtMod[4, 234535662466]
{2, 20429237894, 24102849916, 30319719362, 38739333488,
  44532087808, 50748957254, 55983196106, 59168571380,
  74851807172, 76412433998, 83271421298, 95281045064,
  100515283916, 103700659190, 113591140658, 120944521808,
  130835003276, 134020378550, 139254617402, 151264241168,
  158123228468, 159683855294, 175367091086, 178552466360,
  183786705212, 190003574658, 195796328978, 204215943104,
  210432812550, 214106424572, 234535662464}
```

```
Mod[%^2, 234535662466]
{4, 4, 4, 4, 4, 4, 4, 4, 4, 4, 4, 4, 4, 4, 4, 4, 4, 4, 4, 4, 4,
  4, 4, 4, 4, 4, 4, 4, 4, 4, 4, 4}
```

This last example took only a few seconds. The modulus is a product of six distinct primes, one of which is 2; there are two square roots of 4 for each of the odd primes, and one square root modulo 2. Thus there are $1 \cdot 2 \cdot 2 \cdot 2 \cdot 2 = 32$ square roots in all. Exercise: Perform more rigorous testing of SqrtMod.

9.7 A General Solution to the Sum-of-Two-Squares Problem ▰▰▰▰▰▰

Theorem 3 gave a characterization of the bisquares, that is, the integers that are sums of two squares. The Euclidean algorithm method of representing a prime bisquare as a sum of two squares given in Theorem 5 did not use the primality of p. Thus that method can be used to find a representation of any bisquare as a sum of two squares. In fact, the method can be used to find a complete set of representations. Call a representation of a bisquare as $a^2 + b^2$ *primitive* if $\gcd(a, b) = 1$.

THEOREM 7.

a. Suppose n is a bisquare and $n > 1$. Then there is a one-to-one correspondence between the set of all pairs $\{x, n - x\}$ where x is a mod-n square root of –1 and the set of all pairs $\{a, b\}$ of relatively prime positive integers such that $n = a^2 + b^2$.

b. A positive integer n is a bisquare iff $x^2 \equiv -1 \pmod{n}$ has a solution.

PROOF.

a. The one-to-one correspondence is simply the one given by the Euclidean algorithm method used in Theorem 5. That is, given a pair $\{x, n - x\}$, the method produces a pair $\{a, b\}$ such that $n = a^2 + b^2$; and $\gcd(a, b) = 1$ because otherwise n and a would have a factor in common; this would contradict $\gcd(n, a) = \gcd(n, x) = 1$. Moreover, the proof of Theorem 5 shows that $bx \equiv a \pmod{n}$, so $x \equiv ab^{-1} \pmod{n}$. It follows that different choices of pairs $\{x, n - x\}$ yield distinct primitive solutions.

Now, suppose $a^2 + b^2$ is any primitive representation of n. Then, as just shown, ab^{-1} is congruent to a mod-n square root of –1; call it y. Interchanging a and b if necessary allows us to assume that $y < n - y$. Applying the Euclidean algorithm method to y yields a primitive solution $\{c, d\}$ such that $cd^{-1} \equiv y \pmod{n}$. Therefore $ab^{-1} \equiv y \equiv cd^{-1} \pmod{n}$, so $ad \equiv bc \pmod{n}$. But, each of a, b, c, and d is less than $\sqrt{n}$, so ad and bc are each less than n, whence $ad = bc$. Because $\gcd(a, b) = \gcd(c, d) = 1$, $a = c$ and $b = d$. This establishes that the pair $\{a, b\}$ arises from a square-root pair via the Euclidean algorithm method.

b. Follows immediately from (a).

Theorem 7 yields the following algorithm for generating all primitive representations of an integer as a sum of two squares. First, use `SqrtMod` to obtain the set of all mod-n square roots of –1; if there are none, then n is not a bisquare. Then apply the Euclidean algorithm method used in `Sum2Squares` to the pair n and x. The resulting set of primitive solutions is a complete list of all the primitive solutions. Finally, it is a simple matter to go from a routine that generates all primitive solutions to one that generates all solutions. If $n = a^2 + b^2$ where $\gcd(a, b) = d$, then the pair $\{a/d, b/d\}$ yields a primitive representation of n/d^2 as a sum of two squares. Thus gathering all the primitive representations of n/d^2 for each d^2 dividing n and then multiplying each by d yields the set of all representations of n as a sum of two squares. This is what is carried out by the routines that follow.

`PrimitiveReps[n]` returns the set of all primitive representations, `SqrtSquareDivisors[n]` returns the set of positive integers whose square divides n, and `GeneralSum2Squares` (called such to distinguish it from the earlier routine, `Sum2Squares`, that worked for prime arguments) then puts everything together to yield the complete solution set to the sum of two squares problem for n. These routines require `Sqrt-Mod` and all the routines that it requires, and `MiddleRemainder`. Note how the listability of these various number-theory routines makes programming easier. For example, `PrimitiveReps` is applied all at once to the set of integers of the form n/d^2, where d^2 divides n. Also, in `Sqrt-SquareDivisors`, the listability of `Range` is used to generate several ranges at once.

```
PrimitiveReps::usage = "PrimitiveReps[n] returns a list of all
pairs of nonnegative integers {a, b} such that a >= b,
n = a^2 + b^2, and GCD[a, b] = 1."

SqrtSquareDivisors::usage = "SqrtSquareDivisors[n] returns a
list of all positive integers a whose square divides n"

GeneralSum2Squares::usage = "GeneralSum2Squares[n] returns a
list of all pairs of nonnegative integers {a, b} such that
a >= b and n = a^2 + b^2"

Attributes[PrimitiveReps] = Listable
Attributes[GeneralSum2Squares] = Listable
```

```
PrimitiveReps[n_] := Map[{#, Sqrt[n-#^2]}&,
  MiddleRemainder[n, Select[SqrtMod[-1,n], # <= n/2 &]]] /; n > 1

PrimitiveReps[1] = {{1,0}};

SqrtSquareDivisors[n_] :=
    Block[{factorlist = Transpose@FactorInteger[n]},
      Flatten [Outer @@ Prepend[
          factorlist[[1]]^(Range[0, factorlist[[2]]/2]), Times]]]

GeneralSum2Squares[1] = {{1, 0}}
GeneralSum2Squares[0] = {{0, 0}}

GeneralSum2Squares[n_] :=
  Block[{temp = SqrtSquareDivisors[n]},
    Sort[Complement[
        Flatten[PrimitiveReps[n/temp^2] temp, 1], {{}}]]] /; n > 1
```

Some sample outputs of these routines follow. Because SqrtMod is used, the same caveats apply: hard-to-factor inputs and inputs with many distinct prime factors may not lead to any output. Exercise: Perform more extensive checking. Devise a brute-force method to verify the correctness of GeneralSum2Squares for small values of n. Note that given n, a search need only go as far as $\sqrt{n/2}$.

```
PrimitiveReps[Prime[Range[10000, 10005]]]
{{{323, 20}}, {}, {}, {{269, 180}}, {{322, 33}}, {}}

SqrtSquareDivisors[2 3^2 5^2 23]
{1, 5, 3, 15}

n = 2454^2 + 4     (* which equals 6022120 *)
GeneralSum2Squares[n]
{{1838, 1626}, {1962, 1474}, {2266, 942}, {2322, 794},
  {2334, 758}, {2378, 606}, {2446, 198}, {2454, 2}}

Map[Plus@@# &, %^2]
{6022120, 6022120, 6022120, 6022120, 6022120, 6022120, 6022120,
  6022120}
```

```
GeneralSum2Squares[10^10]
  {{80000, 60000}, {84320, 53760}, {93600, 35200}, {96000, 28000},
   {99712, 7584}, {100000, 0}}
```

There is a formula for the number of distinct ordered pairs (a, b) such that $n = a^2 + b^2$, denoted by $r(n)$, which can be used as a further check on `GeneralSum2Squares`. Here we are counting *all* ordered pairs of positive or negative integers; the three types of behavior are illustrated by $r(5) = 8$, $r(8) = 4$, and $r(4) = 4$. The formula for $r(n)$ is obtained from the factorization of n as follows (see [HW, §16.10]): Suppose $\{\alpha_i\}$ and $\{\beta_j\}$ are the sets of exponents of primes congruent to 1 modulo 4 and 3 modulo 4, respectively. Then $r(n)$ is 0 if any of the β_j is odd. Otherwise $r(n)$ is 4 times the product of all the $(\alpha_i + 1)$s.

EXERCISE Define a *Mathematica* routine that on input n, returns the value of $r(n)$. Use your routine to check the result of `GeneralSum2Squares` for some large inputs with many factors. Use the routine to define another function that computes the average number of representations of n as a sum of two squares as n takes on values between 1 and N. Make a conjecture about the behavior of this function as N grows larger. Prove the conjecture (it can be done using only elementary ideas from geometry provided the problem is given an interpretation in terms of the number of integer lattice points in the plane that lie inside ever-increasing circles).

The Euclidean algorithm method for sums of two squares is more general and can be used to find representations of integers n in the form $fa^2 + gb^2$, where f and g are integers, $f, g \geq 1$, $\gcd(n, fg) = 1$, $n \geq f + g + 1$, and $\gcd(a, b) = 1$. Here are the details, as expounded by K. Hardy et al [HMW]; the $f = 1$ case was treated by G. Cornacchia [Cor]. First find all the solutions to $x^2 \equiv -gf^{-1}$ (mod n), $0 < x < n/2$. For each solution x, apply the Euclidean algorithm to the pair n and x and let a be the first remainder less than $\sqrt{n/f}$. Then if $b = \sqrt{(n - fa^2)/g}$ is an integer, (a, b) is a solution in integers to $n = fa^2 + gb^2$, with $\gcd(a, b) = 1$; moreover, all primitive solutions arise in this way. This algorithm is presented, with a proof of its validity, in [HMW].

EXERCISE Extend the routines of this chapter to define `PrimitiveReps[n, f, g]` by implementing the algorithm just described. A solution is given in the Appendix. Here is an example that finds the four primitive representations of 13,904 as $a^2 + 7b^2$.

```
PrimitiveReps[13904, 1, 7]
   {{31, 43}, {73, 35}, {101, 23}, {109, 17}}
```

In 1807 Gauss refuted a conjecture of Sophie Germain that whenever $a^n + b^n$ has the form $x^2 + ny^2$, then $a + b$ also has this form. The conjecture is true for $n = 3$, but Gauss found the following counterexample for $n = 11 : a = 15, b = 8, 15^{11} + 8^{11} = 8,658,345,793,967 = 1595826^2 + 11 \cdot 745,391^2$. Because $15 + 8 = 23$ fails to have the form $x^2 + ny^2$, this example shows that the conjecture is false in the case $n = 11$. It is a bit of a mystery how Gauss found the representation of the 13-digit number in the desired form (see [Mac]). There are smaller examples in the $n = 11$ case with $a + b = 23$. Exercise: Use `PrimitiveReps[n, 1, 11]` to find them.

For a discussion of algorithms for representing an integer as a sum of three or four squares, see [RS]. The numbers that can be written as sums of three squares are those that do not have the form $4^s(8k + 7)$; on the other hand, a famous theorem of Lagrange states that every nonnegative integer is a sum of four squares. One way to get a four-square representation is to repeatedly subtract $x^2 + y^2$ from n until the remainder is a prime of the form $4k + 1$; then the remainder can be expressed as a sum of two squares by the methods of this chapter, which yields a representation of n as a sum of four squares. There are a few shortcuts; the interested reader should consult the paper by Rabin and Shallit [RS]. This technique yields representations of 100-digit numbers in a few minutes.

9.8 Eisenstein Primes

Extensions of the integers are of central importance in number theory, and their in-depth study has led to many results about ordinary integers. Indeed, we have already seen how a study of the Gaussian integers leads to results about representing primes as sums of two squares. More general sets of integers arise from the consideration of the set of algebraic integers in the quadratic field $\mathbb{Q}(\sqrt{D})$, where D is a square-free integer (that is, D has no square factors; algebraic integers are defined in Chapter 10). Recall that $\mathbb{Q}(\sqrt{D})$ consists of all numbers of the form $x + y\sqrt{D}$. An algebraic integer lies in this field if and only if it is a root of a quadratic equation having integral coefficients and leading coefficient 1. If $D = -1$, then the integers in $\mathbb{Q}(\sqrt{-1})$ are simply the Gaussian integers studied earlier in this chapter. In general, if D is congruent to 2 or 3 modulo 4 then the integers of $\mathbb{Q}(\sqrt{D})$ consist of numbers of the form $a + b\sqrt{D}$ where $a, b \in \mathbb{Z}$. However, if $D \equiv 1 \pmod 4$, then the situation is different: the integers of $\mathbb{Q}(\sqrt{D})$ consist of numbers of the form $a + b(-1 + \sqrt{D})/2$, where a and b are in $\mathbb{Z}$. The case we consider here is that of $D = -3$; thus the integers of $\mathbb{Q}(\sqrt{D})$ are precisely those complex numbers in $\mathbb{Z}[\omega]$, that is numbers of the form $a + b\omega$ where $a, b \in \mathbb{Z}$ and ω is the complex cube root of unity, $\frac{1}{2}(-1 + \sqrt{3}i)$. For more background, see [Rie, Appendix 4; Cox, §4A].

One can define a norm in quadratic fields by $N(\alpha) = \alpha\bar{\alpha}$, where an overbar denotes the usual complex conjugation. Because $\bar{\omega} = \omega^2$, the norm in $\mathbb{Z}[\omega]$ becomes $N(a + b\omega) = a^2 - ab + b^2$. In the case of $\mathbb{Z}[\omega]$ the norm can be used in a manner entirely analogous to the proof of Theorem 1(a) (with ω playing the role of i) to show that gcds exist; this in turn leads to unique factorization into primes of $\mathbb{Z}[\omega]$. As before, uniqueness is up to associates, where the units, that is, the invertible elements, are ± 1, $\pm \omega$, and $\pm \omega^2$. The complex numbers in $\mathbb{Z}[\omega]$ correspond to points on a hexagonal lattice in $\mathbb{C}$; indeed, we can identify each element of $\mathbb{Z}[\omega]$ with the regular hexagon of radius $1/\sqrt{3}$ centered at the element. Then, in a manner similar to the procedure used for the Gaussian primes, we can mark the hexagons that correspond to the primes in $\mathbb{Z}[\omega]$, called the *Eisenstein primes*. The characterization of the Eisenstein primes is similar to that of the Gaussian primes; they arise in one of three ways (for a proof, see [Cox, §4A]):

1. Ordinary primes congruent to 2 modulo 3 remain prime in $\mathbb{Z}[\omega]$.

2. $1 - \omega$ is prime in $\mathbb{Z}[\omega]$ [this accounts for 3, since 3 is (an associate of) $(1 - \omega)^2$].

3. Any ordinary prime congruent to 1 modulo 3 factors as $\alpha\bar{\alpha}$ where each of α and $\bar{\alpha}$ are primes in $\mathbb{Z}[\omega]$, and α and $\bar{\alpha}$ are not associates of each other.

The primes of the third type arise from a representation of p as $a^2 - ab + b^2$. We claim that a prime has this form if and only if it has the form $u^2 + 3v^2$. One direction is easy, for if $p = u^2 + 3v^2$, then we simply let $a = u + v$ and $b = 2v$. For the converse, suppose p has the form $a^2 - ab + b^2$.

Then $p \equiv 1 \pmod 3$, so by (3), $p = \alpha\overline{\alpha}$, where $\alpha = a + b\omega$ is prime in $\mathbb{Z}[\omega]$. It follows that α's associates $\alpha\omega = -b + (a - b)\omega$ and $\alpha\omega^2 = b - a - a\omega$ also divide p, whence we can find a representation $p = r^2 - rs + s^2$ where s is even. But then we can set $v = s/2$ and $u = r - s/2$, which satisfy $u^2 + 3v^2 = p$.

Now, we can use our routine for representing a prime as $p = u^2 + 3v^2$ to determine the Eisenstein primes. Simply using `PrimitiveReps[p, 1, 3]` would be inefficient because it calls `SqrtMod[-3, p]`, which in turn calls `FactorInteger[p]`, whereas we will have already checked that p is prime. So it makes more sense to use `SqrtModPrimeShanks[-3, p]`, which assumes p's primality, and then use `MiddleRemainder` to define a routine that returns the desired pair u and v. The following definition does the trick.

```
Representation[p_] :=
  ({u = MiddleRemainder[p, SqrtModPrimeShanks[-3, p]],
    Sqrt[(p - u^2)/3]})                              /; Mod[p, 3] == 1
Attributes[Representation] = Listable
```

As usual, we check the routine before using it further. The value 1,299,709 is the 100,000th prime.

```
Representation[{7, 13, 19, 31, 37, 43, 1299709}]
{{2, 1}, {1, 2}, {4, 1}, {2, 3}, {5, 2}, {4, 3}, {791, 474}}
```

```
Map[#[[1]]^2 + 3 #[[2]]^2 &, %]
{7, 13, 19, 31, 37, 43, 1299709}
```

Transforming the output of `Representation` will yield the two prime divisors of p in $\mathbb{Z}[\omega]$. This is the key step in identifying the Eisenstein primes and is done by `factor` in the code that follows. Other notes on the code are:

- `SetAttributes` is used to make various functions listable; this allows their direct use on sets of numbers.

- Rotations are carried out entirely in the domain of complex numbers.

- A function, `coords`, is used to turn complex numbers into their real and imaginary parts.

■ The units are shown in gray, as was done with the Gaussian primes.

■ The function hexagon[z] returns the vertices of the hexagon that we are identifying with the complex number z.

■ The function associates[z] returns six copies of the aforementioned hexagon; this corresponds to multiplication of an Eisenstein prime by the six units.

```
EisensteinPrimes::usage = "EisensteinPrimes[n] uses hexagons to
generate an image of the Eisenstein primes with norm less than
n^2."

SetAttributes[{coords, factor, associates, hexagon}, Listable]

omega = N[Exp[2 I Pi /3]];
units = {1, -omega^2, omega, -1, omega^2, -omega};
hexagon[0] = N[Exp[I Range[Pi/6, 2 Pi, Pi/3]] / Sqrt[3]]
hexagon[z_] := z + hexagon[0];
coords[z_] := {Re[z], Im[z]};
associates[z_] := coords[hexagon[units * z]]

factor[p_] := ({u, v} = Representation[p]; u + v + 2 v omega^{1,2})

EisensteinPrimes[n_] := (
 realprimes = Flatten[
       associates[Append[Select[Range[5, n, 6], PrimeQ], 2]], 1];
 nonrealprimes = Flatten[associates[factor[
                     Select[Range[7, n^2, 6], PrimeQ]]], 2];
 Show[Graphics[{Polygon /@ associates[1 - omega],
           Polygon /@ realprimes,
           Polygon /@ nonrealprimes,
           GrayLevel[.5],
           Polygon /@ associates[1]}], AspectRatio->1])
```

The output of EisensteinPrimes[25] is shown in Figure 9.2. Problems analogous to the moat problem for the Gaussian primes are open in this case as well.

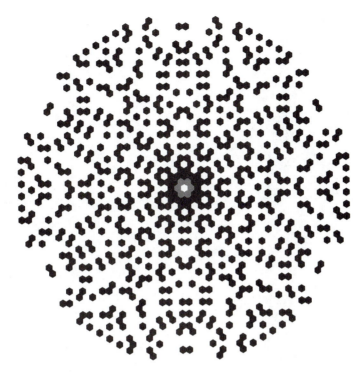

FIGURE 9.2 The Eisenstein primes, that is, the primes in $\mathbb{Z}[\omega]$, having norm at most 625.

10 Additional Examples

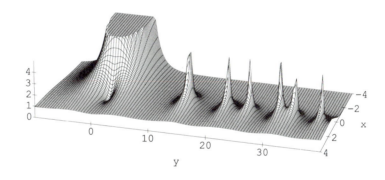

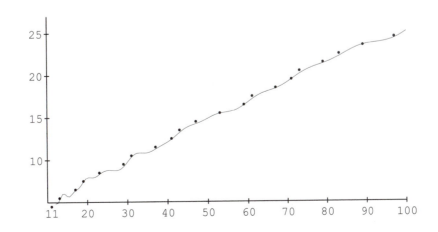

This final chapter contains a variety of *Mathematica* applications presented in a much briefer style than those in the rest of the book. The applications range from the very simple, such as an example of how animations can be used to illustrate the derivative of a function of one variable, to the complex, such as a program that illustrates the proof of the Art Gallery Theorem and another that shows the relationship between the zeros of the Riemann zeta function and the distribution of prime numbers.

About the illustration overleaf:

The surface is a graph of the reciprocal of the absolute value of the Riemann zeta function $\zeta(s)$, which will be discussed in the last two sections of this chapter. The spikes correspond to the zeros of ζ on the critical line $1/2 + iy$. Recall that the global behavior of $\pi(x)$, the prime distribution function, is well approximated by Riemann's smooth function $R(x)$ (discussed in Chapter 1). More delicate information about $\pi(x)$, such as the local distribution of the primes, is determined by the location of the zeros of ζ. If $\pi_0(x)$ denotes the function that agrees with $\pi(x)$ except at prime numbers p, where $\pi_0(p)$ equals $\pi(p) - 1/2$, then modifying $R(x)$ with correction terms for the zeros of ζ yields the function $\pi_0(x)$ *exactly*. The lower graph overleaf is obtained by adding six correction terms to $R(x)$, one for each of the first six zeros on the critical line. The dots represent the points $(p, \pi_0(p))$, p prime. The beginnings of convergence to π_0 can be clearly seen: the graph passes through the first few values of $\pi_0(p)$ and has some horizontal segments agreeing with the step function π_0.

10.1 Animating the Derivative

We begin with a simple routine that compares the graph of the difference quotients of the sine function with its derivative, the cosine function, shown as a dashed line. The step-size h varies from 1 down to $1/10$ in steps of $1/10$. Animating the resulting ten images, two of which are shown in Figure 10.1, shows the difference quotients approaching the derivative.

```
Do[Plot[{(Sin[t+h] - Sin[t])/h, Cos[t]}, {t, -5, 5},
    PlotRange->{{-5, 5}, {-1, 1}}, Ticks->{Automatic, {-1, 1}},
    PlotStyle->{{}, Dashing[{.02, .02}]}],    {h, 1, .1, -.1}]
```

EXERCISE Why does the difference quotient curve look like a slightly shrunk translation of the cosine? [Hint: Use an identity for $\sin A - \sin B$ on $\sin(t+h) - \sin t$.] Generate a similar animation using $[\sin(t+h) - \sin(t-h)]/(2h)$ to approximate the derivative.

Here is a more general routine that accepts the function, x-range, y-range, bounds on h, and number of frames as inputs. The function must be a function of x; ff and fder are used to transform the function and its derivative to functions of t, the plotting variable.

```
DerivativeApproximationMovie[
        f_, xmin_, xmax_, ymin_, ymax_, h0_:1, h1_:.1, n_:9] :=
Block[{ff, fder},
    ff[t_] :=   f /. x -> t;
    fder[t_] := D[f, x] /. x -> t;
```

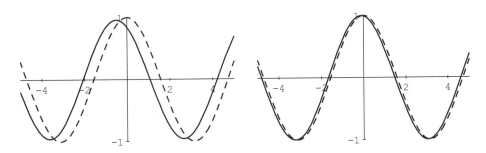

FIGURE 10.1 The difference quotient of $\sin x$ compared to $\cos x$ (dashed); the step size on the left is 1, on the right 0.2.

```
Do[Plot[{(ff[t+h] - ff[t])/h, ffder[t]}, {t, xmin, xmax},
     PlotRange->{{xmin, xmax}, {ymin, ymax}},
     PlotStyle->{{}, Dashing[{.02}]}],
   {h, h0, h1, (h1 - h0)/(n - 1)}]]
```

The first and last frames of the output of the following command are shown in Figure 10.2.

```
DerivativeApproximationMovie[x^10, 0, 1, 0, 30, 1, .02, 10]
```

Another way to animate the derivative is to show a tangent line moving along a function, building the derivative as it goes. For example, Figure 10.3 shows a few frames of such a movie for $\sin x$. Here is some code to generate such animations. The plot of f is stored in plotf and plotder[t] is a function that produces the plot of f'[x] up to x = t; the iterator in plotder begins slightly left of x so that plotder[xmin] will work properly when t is xmin. The DisplayFunction option is set to Identity, which suppresses the output when the Plot commands are called. In the final Show command, this option is returned to the default value, $DisplayFunction. Animations require careful setting of the plot ranges so that the images are properly aligned. In this case, we would like the plot range to be large enough to show both the function and its derivative on the entire x-range. Thus yrange is defined to be the second entry in PlotRange of the plot of the two functions over the full x-range, again with output suppressed. The other graphics operations in

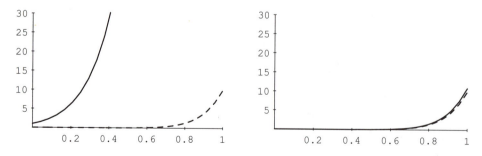

FIGURE 10.2 The difference quotient of x^{10} compared to $10x^9$ (dashed); the step size on the left is 1, on the right 0.02.

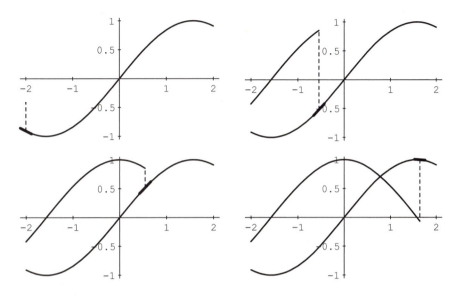

FIGURE 10.3 Four frames from an animation showing the derivative of sin x being constructed as the slope of the tangent line to its graph.

the code that follows are straightforward uses of `Line`. Four frames from the resulting animation are shown in Figure 10.3.

```
f[x_] := Sin[x];
xmin = -2; xmax = 2; delta = (xmax - xmin)/10;
plotf = Plot[f[x], {x, xmin, xmax}, DisplayFunction->Identity]
plotder[t_] := Plot[f'[x], {x, xmin - delta/100, t},
                                    DisplayFunction->Identity]
yrange = PlotRange[Plot[{f[x], f'[x]}, {x, xmin, xmax},
        PlotRange->All, DisplayFunction->Identity]][[2]]

Do[Show[plotf, plotder[t],
        Graphics[{Line[{{t, f[t]} - delta/3 {1, f'[t]},
                             {t, f[t]} + delta/3 {1, f'[t]}}],
        Dashing[{.008}], Thickness[.003],
        Line[{{t, f[t]}, {t, f'[t]}}]}],
    PlotRange->{{xmin - delta/3, xmax + delta/3}, yrange},
    DisplayFunction->$DisplayFunction],
{t, xmin, xmax, delta}]
```

EXERCISE Work the trick for computing the `yrange` into the code for the difference quotient movie and thus eliminate the need for the user to supply `ymin` and `ymax`.

10.2 Billiard Paths on Elliptical Tables ▰▰▰

There is an interesting classical result about the path taken by a particle travelling inside an ellipse and reflecting off the sides as if the ellipse were a billiard table. Of course, if such a particle starts at one focus of the ellipse, it will be reflected through the other focus, and so on indefinitely. And there are also periodic paths that we wish to exclude from the following discussion. But if the particle's initial position and direction do not take it through a focus and if the path is not periodic, then the path it follows will surround either an ellipse or a hyperbola, according as the initial line passes between the foci or not. Moreover, the conic surrounded by the infinite path will have the same foci as the large ellipse. More precisely, there is an ellipse or hyperbola confocal with the ambient ellipse such that each line of the billiard path is tangent to it. An elementary proof in the case of confocal ellipses can be found in [GM, pp. 146–148].

The code that follows produces a billiard path on the ellipse given parametrically by $f(t) = (2\cos t, \sin t)$. The initial positions are given by two t values `t0` and `t1`. The main routine is `newpoint[t0, t1]`, which returns the pair `{t1, t2}` where the line from `f[t1]` to `f[t2]` is the line along which a ball travelling from `f[t0]` to `f[t1]` would reflect; that is, `t2` is chosen so that the angle of incidence equals the angle of reflection (the angle r in Figure 10.4). The computations are straightforward; elementary calculus is used to determine the slope of the tangent. In fact, three slopes are necessary, the slopes of the lines L1, L2, and L3 in Figure 10.4; these are computed by the three functions `slope1`, `slope2`, and `slope3`, which require some special cases to deal with lines of infinite slope and, in the case of `slope3`, some trigonometrical reasoning. Once `slope3` is determined, the new value `t2` is determined by solving the simultaneous equations of the ellipse and the line L3. The `Solve` routine can handle this task since the equations are linear and quadratic, respectively; there are two solutions, and the new one is chosen using `Select`. Note the use of two arguments to the `ArcTan` call preceding

`Solve`; `ArcTan[x, y]` returns the arctangent of y/x, modified if necessary according to the quadrant in which the point {x, y} lies.

```
{a, b}  = {2, 1};
pi = N[Pi];
f[t_]   := {a Cos[t], b Sin[t]};  Attributes[f] = Listable;
ellipse = ParametricPlot[f[t], {t, 0, 2 Pi}];
foci    = {{Sqrt[a^2-b^2], 0}, {-Sqrt[a^2-b^2], 0}};

slope1[t0_, t1_] := Divide @@ Reverse[f[t1] - f[t0]] /;
                                             t0+t1 != 2 pi;
slope2[t1_] := -b Cot[t1] / a          /; t1 != 0 && t1 != pi;

slope3[t0_, t1_] :=
    Tan[2 ArcTan[slope2[t1]] - ArcTan[slope1[t0,t1]]] /;
                    t1 != 0 && t1 != pi && t0+t1 != 2 pi;
slope3[t0_, t1_] := -slope1[t0, t1]    /; t1 == 0 || t1 == pi;
slope3[t0_, t1_] := Tan[2 ArcTan[slope2[t1]] - pi/2] /;
                                             t0+t1 == 2 pi;
```

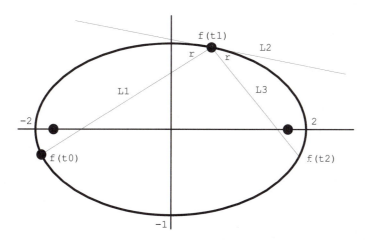

FIGURE 10.4 On an elliptical billiard table, a ball will reflect off the sides so that the angle of incidence with the tangent line L2 equals the angle of reflection.

```
newpoint[{t0_, t1_}] := {t1,
   First[Select[ArcTan[b x, a y] /.
    N[Solve[(x/a)^2  + (y/b)^2  == 1 &&
             y - f[t1][[2]] == (x - f[t1][[1]]) slope3[t0, t1]]],
          Abs[# - t1] > 10^-15 & ]]}
BilliardPath[start_, n_] := Show[ellipse, Graphics[{
      Thickness[.0001], PointSize[.02],
      Point /@ f[start], Point /@ foci,
        Line[f[First /@ NestList[newpoint, N[start], n]]]}]]
BilliardPath[{Pi - .2, Pi/2}, 35];
BilliardPath[{Pi + .5, Pi/2 - .6}, 35];
BilliardPath[{Pi+ArcCos[Sqrt[3]/2], ArcCos[-Sqrt[3]/2]}, 4];
BilliardPath[{Pi, Pi/2}, 8];
```

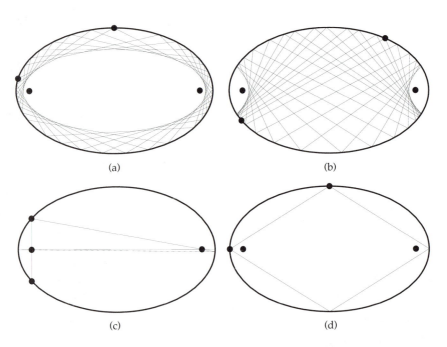

      (a)   (b)

      (c)   (d)

FIGURE 10.5 A billiard path on an elliptical table surrounds a curve that is either an ellipse (a) or a hyperbola (b), unless the path passes through a focus (c) or is periodic (d).

The paths generated by the preceding four commands are shown in Figure 10.5. In the hyperbolic case the reflections alternate their directions at each step; in the elliptical case, the reflections proceed in the same direction.

EXERCISE A loop of the form `Do[BilliardPath[{t0, t1}, n], {n, 1, 20}]` generates an animation that shows a single path progressing along the table. However, there is a lot of redundant work in such an approach, because each call to `BilliardPath` will recompute the entire path. Modify the billiard-path routine so that it produces an animation of a single path without recomputing the trajectory for each frame.

10.3 The Art Gallery Theorem

Consider an art gallery consisting of a single polygonal room having n walls. A theorem that has come to be known as the Art Gallery Theorem states that there is some way of placing Floor($n/3$) guards in the room so that every space in the gallery is seen by at least one of the guards. The theorem was first proved by V. Chvátal in 1975; in this section we shall show how a simple proof found by S. Fisk can be implemented by a *Mathematica* routine that upon input of an n-gon, returns a picture of the polygon along with the placement of at most Floor($n/3$) guards so that the guards see the entire interior of the polygon. This will serve to illustrate how *Mathematica* can be used in both graph theory and computational geometry. An excellent exposition of this area, with many variations and unsolved problems, can be found in the books by J. O'Rourke [ORo1, ORo2].

Before diving into the Art Gallery Theorem, we consider a related problem, namely the generation of a "random" polygon. It is apparently a difficult problem to generate random polygons, or even to define the precise meaning of randomness in this context. Let's be content with simply generating a random-looking polygon. We will try to do so by generating a random walk in the plane, starting at the origin and discarding any choice that leads to a self-intersecting walk; moreover, the final vertex must satisfy the additional condition that the segment connecting it to the origin does not intersect any other segments of the walk. This will lead to a non–self-intersecting random walk, that is, a polygon. Unfortunately, there may come a point at which it is highly unlikely that a successful step will be found. Thus the method yields only small polygons, up to about 17 sides. Nevertheless, it is a good exercise and serves as an introduction to routines that we will need later.

The first such routine is one that determines the orientation—clockwise (–1) or counterclockwise (+1)—of a triangle in the plane. This is done by using the *signed area* of a triangle, which is the triangle's area multiplied by its orientation. The signed area is given by one-half of a 3×3 determinant (see SignedArea). Because we usually need only the orientation, we define a second routine, Orientation, that returns the sign of the determinant. We also define a second case of Orientation to deal with polygons having more than three sides. Then orientation can be determined by finding the leftmost vertex (taking the lowest in case of a tie) and, if it is the ith, simply computing the orientation of the triangle consisting of the three vertices labelled $i - 1, i,$ and $i + 1$. Finding the extremal vertex can be done by sorting lexicographically. More detailed analysis and further applications of many of the routines in this section can be found in [Oro2]. In order to avoid erroneous results because of roundoff error, Chop is used so that near-zero determinants are interpreted as being exactly zero. Chop replaces numbers whose relative size in an expression is less than 10^{-10} by 0 (see page 359 for more on Chop).

```
SignedArea[{{x1_,y1_}, {x2_,y2_}, {x3_,y3_}}] :=
    Chop[Det[{{x1,y1,1}, {x2,y2,1}, {x3,y3,1}}]/2.]

Orientation[{{x1_,y1_}, {x2_,y2_}, {x3_,y3_}}] :=
    Sign[Chop[Det[{{x1,y1,1}, {x2,y2,1}, {x3,y3,1}}]]]

Leftmost[polygon_] :=
        First@First@Position[polygon, First[Sort[polygon]]]

Orientation[polygon_] := Block[{n = Length[polygon]},
    Orientation[polygon[[Leftmost[polygon] + {-1,0,1} /.
        {0 -> n, n+1 -> 1}]]]]           /; Length[polygon] > 3
```

```
SignedArea[{{0,0}, {0,1}, {1,0}}]
-0.5
```

```
Orientation[{{0,0}, {5,0}, {0,5}}]
1
```

We now use `Orientation` to define a function that indicates whether a point lies to the left of the infinite line determined by two points. `LeftOf` returns `True` if the third point is strictly left of the line determined by the first two, `False` if the point is to the right of or on the line.

```
LeftOf[p_, q_, r_] := Orientation[{p, q, r}] == 1
```

Next we define a function that determines whether two line segments, each given by their endpoints, intersect. Two segments will intersect at a point interior to both segments if exactly one endpoint of the second segment is to the left of the first segment and exactly one endpoint of the first segment is to the left of the second. The exclusive-or function allows short coding of this. There is an additional special case that must be dealt with, to cover the possibility that the segments share an endpoint. The case can be covered by defining a betweenness relation for three collinear points, which is done below by using the dot product (to check directions) and vector length (`norm`).

```
norm[p_] := Sqrt[p . p]
```

```
Between[p_, q_, r_] := Orientation[{p, q, r}] == 0 &&
            (r - p) . (q - p) >= 0 && norm[r - p] <= norm[q - p]
```

```
Intersect[{a_, b_}, {c_, d_}] :=
        (LeftOf[a, b, c] ~Xor~ LeftOf[a, b, d]) &&
        (LeftOf[c, d, a] ~Xor~ LeftOf[c, d, b]) ||

        Between[a, b, c] || Between[a, b, d]     ||
        Between[c, d, a] || Between[c, d, b]
```

EXERCISE Check the correctness of `LeftOf` and `Intersect` on several cases.

Now we can turn to the random-walk problem. The following routines accomplish the task in the manner described at the beginning of this section. A random vector of length at most 1 is returned by `randompoint`. The main routine, `RandomPolygon`, starts by setting `walk`'s first step to be one from the origin to a random point in the unit disk; then new steps are generated and checked by the `good` routine, which tells whether a point is good with respect to the current state of `walk`. The final choice must meet an extra condition as explained earlier, which is decided by `goodlaststep`. The counter `j` is inserted so that the program will fail once a certain number of points (the default is 40) have been examined, in which case it returns the number 0. The additional routine `ShowRandomPolygon` displays the polygon in the case of a successful search.

```
randompoint := Random[]*
        {Cos[angle = Random[Real, 2 Pi//N]], Sin[angle]};


good[point_] := And @@ Table[
    !Intersect[walk[[{i, i+1}]], {Last@walk, point}],
        {i, Length@walk - 2}]


goodlaststep[walk_] := And @@ Table[
    !Intersect[walk[[{i, i+1}]], {Last@walk, First@walk}],
        {i, 2, Length@walk - 2}]


RandomPolygon[n_, maxpts_:40] := (
    walk = {{0., 0.}, randompoint}; j = 2;
    Do[While[
        j++ < maxpts && !good[new = Last[walk]+randompoint]];
      AppendTo[walk, new], {n - 3}];
    While[j++ < maxpts &&
      (!good[new = Last[walk]+randompoint] ||
       !goodlaststep[Append[walk, new]])];
    If[j > maxpts, 0, Join[walk, {new, First@walk}]])


ShowRandomPolygon[n_, maxpts_:40] :=
    If[!NumberQ[temp = RandomPolygon[n, maxpts]],
    Show[Graphics[Line[temp]], PlotRange->All]
```

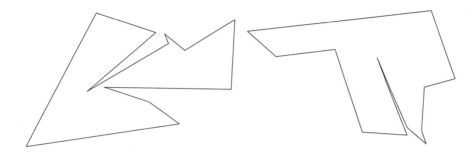

FIGURE 10.6 Two random-looking 12-gons generated by `ShowRandomPolygon` `[12, 50]`. It is difficult to get random polygons having more than 20 sides.

EXERCISE (O'Rourke): Implement the following slightly different approach to the random n-gon problem. Generate a random walk consisting of n points and then check to see if connecting the first and last points yields a polygon. If it does, output the polygon, if not, start again by generating a new walk.

Fisk's proof of the Art Gallery Theorem breaks neatly into two steps. Let's use the term "diagonal" to refer to a line segment joining two nonconsecutive vertices of a polygon, and "interior diagonal" for a diagonal that except for its endpoints, lies inside the polygon. Then the first step of the proof is to use nonintersecting interior diagonals to divide the given polygon into triangles. The second step is to color the vertices by using three colors so that vertices that are adjacent, either by a side or by one of the triangulating diagonals, receive different colors. It follows that the least-occurring color serves as a locator for the guards; that is, simply place a guard at each vertex of the polygon that receives the least-popular color. Then every triangle will contain a vertex at which a guard is placed, and so the guards at these locations will see the entire interior of the polygon. Of course, to turn this sketch into a proof several assertions must be proved. We must first show that the triangulating interior diagonals exist—if this seems obvious to you, try to prove it without reading further. Then it must be shown that the desired coloring exists. We focus first on the triangulation problem.

It turns out that the key fact needed for the triangulation step is that any polygon contains an interior diagonal. Again, this may seem obvious, but a proof is required. Here it is. First choose a convex vertex, by which is meant one for which the interior angle is less than 180°. It is easy to see that such must exist. If v is the convex vertex and u and w are its adjacent vertices, then consider the triangle formed by u, v, and w. If no other vertex lies on or inside this triangle, then u and w determine the desired interior diagonal. Otherwise, choose from those vertices lying on or in the triangle the one that is farthest from the segment joining u and w. It is easy to see that the segment determined by v and this optimal vertex is the desired diagonal.

Once an interior diagonal is at hand, the proof can proceed by induction, using the two polygons into which the diagonal splits the original polygon. The various routines of the implementation are as follows. These routines work properly only if the given polygon is given in counterclockwise order. Thus the first routine ensures that this is the case.

MakeCounterclockwise transforms a polygon to a counterclockwise orientation.

ConvexVertex[polygon, i] determines whether the ith vertex of polygon is a convex vertex.

ConvexVertex[polygon] returns the index of a convex vertex in polygon. It is easier to program the search by starting at the second vertex; because a polygon necessarily has more than one convex vertex, a successful search is guaranteed.

Inside[{p, q, r}, point] determines whether point lies inside or on the triangle {p, q, r}, where the triangle's vertices are assumed to be given in counterclockwise order. Because LeftOf is a strict relation, its negation is used so that the case of a point on the triangle is handled properly.

PolygonDiagonal[polygon] finds the indices of an interior diagonal in polygon, using the technique of the proof of existence discussed earlier. First a convex vertex, polygon[[i]], is found. Then the set of vertices lying on or in the triangle formed by the convex vertex and its neighbors, called invertices, is sorted according to the area of the triangle formed by a vertex in the triangle and the two neighbors of polygon[[i]]. The one with the largest area is the one that, together with polygon[[i]], forms an interior diagonal. The sorting is accomplished by adding

the appropriate comparison as a second argument to Sort. Then
i is prepended to the index of the vertex returned by the Last[
Sort[]] command.

Triangulate[polygon] uses recursion to implement the inductive
proof. A triangle is the base case; the general case is handled by
finding an interior diagonal, splitting the polygon into two smaller
polygons, triangulating them, and then forming the final triangulating set by joining the recursively found diagonals with the initial
interior diagonal. The routine returns the list of diagonals.

ShowTriangulation displays a polygon together with a set of triangulating diagonals. This routine contains the all-important initial
step of orienting the polygon in a counterclockwise direction.

```
MakeCounterclockwise[polygon_] :=
    If[Orientation[polygon] == -1, Reverse[polygon], polygon]


ConvexVertex[polygon_, i_] :=
                Orientation[polygon[[{i-1, i, i+1}]]] == 1


ConvexVertex[polygon_] := Block[{i = 2},
                While[!ConvexVertex[polygon, i], i++];  i]


Inside[{p_, q_, r_}, point_] :=
    !LeftOf[q, p, point] && !LeftOf[r, q, point] &&
    !LeftOf[p, r, point]


PolygonDiagonal[polygon_] :=
  Block[{i = ConvexVertex[polygon], invertices},
  invertices = Select[ Drop[polygon, {i-1, i+1}],
                    Inside[polygon[[{i-1, i, i+1}]]], #] &];
  If[invertices == {}, {i-1, i+1},
    Prepend[
      Flatten@Position[polygon, Last@Sort[invertices,
        SignedArea[{polygon[[i-1]], #1, polygon[[i+1]]}] <=
        SignedArea[{polygon[[i-1]], #2, polygon[[i+1]]}] &]],
      i]]]


Triangulate[polygon_] := {}  /; Length[polygon] == 3
```

```
Triangulate[polygon_] := Block[{diag, poly1, poly2},
    diag = PolygonDiagonal[polygon];
    poly1 = Take[polygon, diag];
    poly2 = Drop[polygon, {1+diag[[1]], diag[[2]]-1}];
    Join[Triangulate[poly1], Triangulate[poly2],
            {polygon[[diag]]}]]

ShowTriangulation[polygon_]:=
    Block[{ccwpolygon = MakeCounterclockwise[polygon]},
    Show[Graphics[
    {Line[Append[polygon, polygon[[1]]]],
      Map[Line, Triangulate[ccwpolygon]]}],
                    AspectRatio->1, PlotRange->All]]
```

Let's test our routines on a polygon, shown in Figure 10.7(a), designed to test several features at once. The search for a convex vertex is successful immediately, at vertex 2. The search for an interior diagonal then runs into a nonempty set of invertices; in this case vertices 5, 7, 9, and 11 are all on sides that interfere with the line of sight from 1 to 3. The sorting of invertices by area will run into a tie for the largest among vertices 5, 7, and 11, which are all at a distance 0.1 from the line joining 1 to 3; thus the search will settle on the last in the natural order, namely vertex 11. Thus the first interior diagonal is given by vertices 2 and 11. The recursion then deals with the quadrilateral $\{1, 2, 11, 12\}$ for which the convex vertex will be the second, that is, 2, and the diagonal will be $\{1, 11\}$ (actually $\{1, 3\}$ after the relabelling that will take place automatically). The case of the larger subpolygon $\{2, 3, 4, 5, 6, 7, 8, 9, 10, 11\}$ will find the convex vertex 3 and then the diagonal $\{2, 4\}$, and so on. The final triangulation is shown in Figure 10.7(a), with labels added for clarity.

```
test = {{1.2, 1}, {0, 0}, {1.2, 0}, {2, .1}, {1, .2}, {2, .3},
        {1, .4}, {2, .5}, {1.1, .55}, {2, .7}, {1, .7}, {2, .9}};
```

```
ConvexVertex[test]                    PolygonDiagonal[test]
2                                     {2, 11}
```

```
ShowTriangulation[test]
```

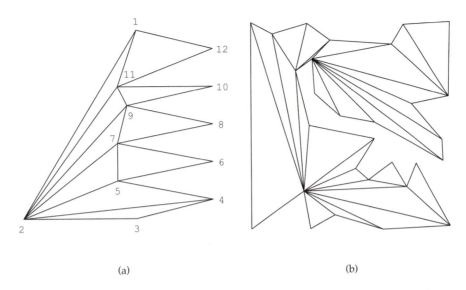

FIGURE 10.7 The result of applying the triangulation routine to two polygons.

One can run the triangulation routine on the output of `RandomPolygon` via `ShowTriangulation[RandomPolygon[n, max]]`. An alternative way of generating input is by using the following code to display a unit square, selecting the square, depressing the command key (⌘), and clicking the mouse on the successive vertices. This forms a series of dots on the screen, which can be copied via ⌘-C and then pasted in as an argument to `ShowTriangulation`. The problem with this approach is that the lines are not shown, so one can easily err and create a nonpolygon.

```
Show[Graphics[Line[{{0,0}, {0,1}, {1, 1}, {1, 0}, {0,0}}],
        AspectRatio->1]]
```

A polygon generated this way is triangulated in Figure 10.7(b).

EXERCISE The `PolygonDiagonal` routine can be made more efficient with some extra programming. This is because the use of `Sort` is unnecessary, and the same result can be obtained using `Max`. In other words, there is no need to fully sort a list when only the largest element is wanted. Eliminate the `Sort` from `PolygonDiagonal`. The same applies to `Leftmost`, but since that is used only once, to determine the initial polygon's orientation, the simplicity of using Sort to obtain the lexicographically least vertex outweighs the time gained by additional programming.

We now turn to the coloring step of the proof. It turns out that a triangulation can be three-colored by following one's nose, or rather, the polygon's ear. An *ear* of a polygon is a set of three consecutive vertices $\{u, v, w\}$ such that the interior of the segment connecting u and w is interior to the polygon. It can be proved that any n-gon, $n \leq 4$, has at least two ears (see [ORo1, p. 13]). In our situation, where we have polygons triangulated by diagonals, it is not hard to see that at least one of the diagonals cuts off an ear. Thus a search for consecutive vertices $\{u, v, w\}$ such that $\{u, w\}$ is one of the diagonals must succeed. Then induction can be used to 3-color the triangulated polygon that remains after the ear is removed and v may then be colored in the way that is forced by the colors of u and w. This leads to a recursive procedure for 3-coloring triangulations, which in turns leads to a routine to locate the guards.

The search for an ear, and therefore the 3-coloring routine, does not need the coordinates of the vertices and diagonals, but only their labels. The routines posn and convert are used to convert the vertices and diagonals from coordinates to labels. Then Color implements the recursive coloring procedure just described, using the integers 1, 2, and 3 as colors. Note how the free color that is to be assigned to the deleted vertex is obtained by subtracting the two colors on adjacent vertices from 6. Color is written so that it can handle any set of vertex labels, not just the labels $\{1, 2, 3, \ldots, n\}$. This is because as the recursion progresses, the labels will be various subsets of the initial set of labels. Exercise: Insert a Print[verts] statement into Color so that all the label sets of subpolygons used in the coloring recursion are displayed. ThreeColor triangulates a polygon, transforms the triangulation from coordinates to labels, and returns a 3-coloring and a properly oriented polygon. Guards takes the output of ThreeColor, determines the least popular color, and generates an image as in Figure 10.8(a).

```
posn[polygon_, diag_] :=
            Flatten[Map[Position[polygon, #] &, diag]]
```

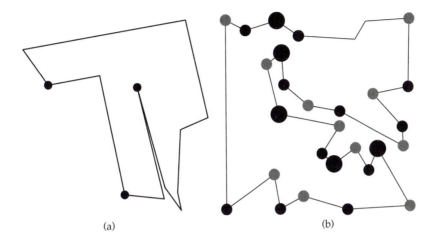

(a)   (b)

FIGURE 10.8 (a) The dots show how three guards can be used to guard an art gallery in the shape of one of the random polygons of Figure 10.6. Can fewer guards do the job? (b) A polygon with 29 sides can be guarded by nine guards; but because the least-popular color in the 3-coloring may occur fewer than Floor($n/3$)times, the program might return a set of fewer guards, as in this example, where six guards (large dots) are found.

```
convert[polygon_, diags_]:=
      {Range[Length@polygon], Map[posn[polygon, #] &, diags]}

Color[verts_, diags_] := {verts, {1,2,3}}  /; Length[verts] == 3

Color[verts_, diags_]:= Block[{i = 1, oldcolors},

    While[!FreeQ[diags, verts[[++i]]]];

    (* preceding finds the ear i-1, i, i+1, since that is
       where a vertex is not on any diagonal *)

    oldcolors = Color[
        Complement[verts, {verts[[i]]}],
        Complement[diags, {{verts[[i-1]], verts[[i+1]]}}]];
```

```
(* preceding deletes vertex i and colors by recursion;
     following colors vertex i appropriately *)

{Append[oldcolors[[1]], verts[[i]]],
 Append[oldcolors[[2]], 6 -
     oldcolors[[2,
       First@First@Position[oldcolors[[1]], verts[[i-1]]]]] -

     oldcolors[[2,
       First@First@Position[oldcolors[[1]], verts[[i+1]]]]]]}]

ThreeColor[polygon_] :=
     Block[{ccwpoly = MakeCounterclockwise[polygon]},
       {Color @@ convert[ccwpoly, Triangulate[ccwpoly]], ccwpoly}]

Guards[polygon_] := Block[{coloring, ccw, colorclass, i},
   {coloring, ccw} = ThreeColor[polygon];
   colorclass = First@Sort[Table[
   (First /@ Select[Transpose[coloring], #[[2]]==i &]), {i, 3}],
                   Length[#1] < Length[#2]&];
   Show[Graphics[{Line[Append[polygon, First[polygon]]],
               PointSize[.04], Point /@ ccw[[colorclass]]}],
                   PlotRange->All, AspectRatio->1]]
```

Guards does not always come up with a minimal placement of guards. First of all, our entire discussion places guards only at vertices, whereas in the formulation of the problem guards may be placed in the interior. Moreover, even with the restriction to vertex guards, the output of Guards is often not optimal [e.g., see Fig. 10.8(a)]. Indeed, the number of guards can depend on the order of the polygon's vertices, since different orderings can lead to different triangulations and hence different 3-colorings.

EXERCISE Modify Guards so that it places dots corresponding to the colors (say, large dots, small dots, gray dots) at each vertex of the polygon. The output of such a routine is shown in Figure 10.8(b).

EXERCISE Modify `Guards` so that upon input of a given n-gon, it tries all n orderings of the vertices and returns the one that leads to the use of the fewest guards.

EXERCISE What will `Guards` do when given a convex polygon? Find a nonconvex polygon of at least 10 vertices for which `Guards` returns a single guard.

EXERCISE For each integer m find an example of a $3m$-gon that cannot be guarded with fewer than m guards.

There are more efficient triangulation and 3-coloring algorithms (see [ORo1, Chap. 1; ORo2]), and the interested reader may want to try programming them in *Mathematica* and comparing their performance with the approach here. The algorithm presented here was just a direct interpretation of Fisk's simple proof. Using subtler theorems about polygons and their diagonals leads to improved algorithms.

10.4 Rational Enumeration

There are many ways to prove that the rational numbers form a countable set. One clever approach is to view a reduced fraction m/n as a number in base-11 notation by giving the digits of m and n their usual base-10 meaning and interpreting the division slash as the base-11 digit for 10, which is denoted by "a". For example, 13/20 becomes 13a20 in base 11, or the integer 19,866. Here is a *Mathematica* routine that combines `BaseForm[a, 11]` with the string manipulation functions `Characters`, `StringJoin`, and `ToExpression` to perform this enumeration, as well as its inverse. Some troublesome cases must be dealt with specially by `InverseIndex`; for example, a number such as 111, which is a1 in base 11 will yield the string "/1", which cannot be interpreted as an expression. Another problem arises from 231, for example, which is 1a0 in base 11 and will lead to a division-by-0 message. These cases are handled by the `If` statements that return `"Failure"`; the division-by-0 message is suppressed by the `Off` instruction.

```
Index[q_Rational] := (
t = Join@@{Digits@Numerator[q], {10}, Digits@Denominator[q]}) .
    (11^Range[Length[t] - 1, 0, -1])          /; Positive[q]
```

```
Index[n_Integer] := (t =
Join@@{Digits@n, {10,1}}) . (11^Range[Length[t]-1, 0, -1]) /;
                                        !Negative[n]


Off[Power::infy]


InverseIndex[n_] := Block[
    {temp = Characters@BaseForm[n, 11] /. "a"-> "/"},
    If[First[temp] == "/", Return["Failure"]];
    temp = ToExpression[StringJoin@@temp];
    If[!NumberQ[temp] || Index[temp] != n, "Failure", temp]] /;
                                        !Negative[n]


InverseIndex[111] = 0


SetAttributes[{Index, InverseIndex}, Listable]
```

```
Index[345/1001]          InverseIndex[66500754]
66500754                 345
                         ----
                         1001
```

```
Index[Range[0,20]/20]
{111, 2563, 2552, 5225, 236, 235, 5214, 10549, 357, 13211, 233,
   17204, 478, 19866, 10538, 477, 599, 25190, 13200, 27852, 232}
```

```
InverseIndex[%]
```
$$\left\{0, \frac{1}{20}, \frac{1}{10}, \frac{3}{20}, \frac{1}{5}, \frac{1}{4}, \frac{3}{10}, \frac{7}{20}, \frac{2}{5}, \frac{9}{20}, \frac{1}{2}, \frac{11}{20}, \frac{3}{5}, \frac{13}{20}, \frac{7}{10}, \frac{3}{4}, \frac{4}{5}, \frac{17}{20}, \frac{9}{10}, \frac{19}{20}, 1\right\}$$

We can see the induced ordering on the rationals as follows.

```
Select[InverseIndex[Range[1000]], NumberQ]
```
$$\left\{0, 1, \frac{1}{2}, \frac{1}{3}, \frac{1}{4}, \frac{1}{5}, \frac{1}{6}, \frac{1}{7}, \frac{1}{8}, \frac{1}{9}, 2, \frac{2}{3}, \frac{2}{5}, \frac{2}{7}, \frac{2}{9}, 3, \frac{3}{2}, \frac{3}{4}, \frac{3}{5}, \frac{3}{7}, \frac{3}{8}, 4, \frac{4}{3}, \frac{4}{5},\right.$$

$$\frac{4}{7}, \frac{4}{9}, 5, \frac{5}{2}, \frac{5}{3}, \frac{5}{4}, \frac{5}{6}, \frac{5}{7}, \frac{5}{8}, \frac{5}{9}, 6, \frac{6}{5}, \frac{6}{7}, 7, \frac{7}{2}, \frac{7}{3}, \frac{7}{4}, \frac{7}{5}, \frac{7}{6}, \frac{7}{8}, \frac{7}{9}\}$$

10.5 Algebraic Numbers

An *algebraic integer* is a complex number that is the root of a monic polynomial with integer coefficients. For example, $\sqrt{2}$ and i are algebraic integers. One way to obtain some algebraic integers is to use Solve to generate the roots of a polynomial of degree 4 or less.

```
x /. Solve[x^3 - 9 x^2 + 27 x - 31 == 0]
             1/3                1/3              1/3                1/3
       1/3  4          Sqrt[-3] 4          4          Sqrt[-3] 4
{3 + 4   , 3 - ---- + -------------,  3 - ---- - -------------}
              2             2              2             2
```

The set of algebraic integers forms a subring of $\mathbb{C}$; that is, the set is closed under addition, subtraction, and multiplication. Moreover, the set is closed under nth roots, where n is an integer. However, it is a famous theorem of Galois—indeed, this is one of the most famous theorems in all mathematics—that there are algebraic integers, roots of some fifth-degree polynomials, for example, that are not expressible in terms of the ordinary integers using $+$, $-$, $\cdot$, and the extraction of nth roots. But if we are given an algebraic integer in terms of $+$, $-$, $\cdot$, and nth roots, we can try to find a polynomial that has it as a root. That is the problem we wish to attack here. For example, the routine we'll develop should, on input Sqrt[2], return x^2 - 2. And given a more complicated expression, perhaps 3 + 4^(1/3) from the preceding example or a much more involved combination of $+$, $\cdot$, and root extraction, it should come up with a polynomial for which the expression is a root.

Let's call our basic routine polynomial, numbering the lines that will be used in the final program.

1. polynomial::usage = "polynomial[alg] returns a polynomial in x
   with integer coefficients for which the algebraic integer alg
   is a root.";

Then some base cases are easy. [Exercise: Verify that the Gaussian integer $a + bi$ is a root of the polynomial $x^2 - 2ax + (a^2 + b^2)$.]

2. `polynomial[n_Integer] := x - n`

3. `polynomial[z_Complex] := x^2 - 2 Re[z] x + Abs[z]^2`

The complex case could be replaced by a case that dealt only with `I`, as other Gaussian integers would be dealt with by the cases that follow. But it is efficient to deal with all Gaussian integers at once. Note that an expression such as `Sqrt[2] + 7 I` does not have its head equal to `Complex`; the `Complex` type is reserved for numbers of the form `a + b I` where a and b are numbers; `Sqrt[2]` is not a number. Experiment with `NumberQ[]` and `Head[]` to familiarize yourself with these subtleties.

The main routine will be recursive and will exploit the proof that the sum and product of two algebraic integers is an algebraic integer. Thus `polynomial[expr1 + expr2]` will request the two polynomials `polynomial[expr1]` and `polynomial[expr2]` and combine them, in a way to be discussed, to get a polynomial for which `expr1 + expr2` is a root. Products are treated similarly. This recursive step is implemented as follows, where `polysum` and `polyprod` are the yet-to-be-defined combining functions.

4. `polynomial[e_ + f_] := polysum[{polynomial[e], polynomial[f]}]`

5. `polynomial[e_ * f_] := polyprod[{polynomial[e], polynomial[f]}]`

There are several proofs that a sum and product of algebraic integers are again algebraic integers (see, e.g., [PD]). The most elementary proof uses only basic ideas of linear dependence of vectors. Although such a proof can be turned into an algorithm, it leads to exorbitant matrix calculations. The best proof from the point of view of computation is one based on the concept of the *resultant* of two polynomials, since the resultant may be computed quickly and, in fact, is built in as `Resultant`. The resultant of two polynomials is defined as follows: Suppose $p(x)$ has degree n and roots $\{\alpha_i : i = 1, \ldots, n\}$ and $q(x)$ has degree m and roots $\{\beta_j : j = 1, \ldots, m\}$. Then the resultant of p and q is defined to be

$$\prod_{i=1}^{n} \prod_{j=1}^{m} (\beta_j - \alpha_i).$$

There is a Euclidean-algorithm-like method of computing the resultant that is quite fast; see [PZ, §2.3.3].

Now, suppose we are given monic polynomials $p(x)$ and $q(x)$. Then a polynomial having as its roots all sums $\alpha + \beta$ where α and β are roots of p and q, respectively, is given by $h(x) = \text{Resultant}(q(t), p(x-t))$. The fact that the function $h(x)$ is a polynomial in x of degree mn follows from a characterization of the resultant as the determinant of an $(m+n) \times (m+n)$ matrix (the *Sylvester matrix*) whose nonzero entries are the coefficients of the polynomials (see [Lan]). To see that h's roots are as claimed, observe that for any x the roots of $p(x-t)$ are $x - \alpha_i$, and so $h(x)$ is $\prod \prod [\beta_j - (x - \alpha_i)]$, or $\prod \prod (\beta_j + \alpha_i - x)$. Therefore the roots of h are all sums of the form $\alpha_i + \beta_j$.

A similar result holds for products; namely, the products of the roots of p and q are roots of $k(x) = p(0)^m \, \text{Resultant}(t^n p(x/t), q(t))$. We leave the verification as an exercise. The formulas for h and k are easily turned into the functions `polysum` and `polyprod`. For lists of polynomials, `poly-sum` and `polyprod` just combine the polynomials using the two-argument case; this is implemented by splitting off elements one at a time and applying recursion. A special function must be defined to return the degree of a polynomial; this is easily done with the help of `CoefficientList[p, x]`, which returns the coefficients when `p` is a polynomial in `x`. The `Expand` instruction in `polyprod` ensures that the returned form is a single multiplied-out polynomial.

```
6. polysum[{p_, q_}] := Resultant[q /. x -> t, p /. x -> x-t, t]

7. polysum[list_] := polysum[{First@list, polysum[Rest@list]}] /;
                                              Length[list] > 2

8. degree[p_] := Length[CoefficientList[p, x]] - 1

9. polyprod[{p_, q_}] :=
     Expand[(p /. x -> 0) ^ degree[q] *
     Resultant[t^degree[p] (p /. x -> x/t), q /. x -> t, t]]

10. polyprod[list_] :=
      polyprod[{First@list, polyprod[Rest@list]}] /; Length[list] > 2
```

Here are some examples. Of course, we should check the answers. In the first two examples, *Mathematica* can do an exact check by substituting a symbolic value for x and simplifying; this yields an exact 0. For more complex polynomials such as those that occur in the third example, a numerical check is much faster, in which case more precision may be required because of roundoff error in the evaluation of the polynomial.

```
polysum[{x^2 - 2, x^2 - 3}]
```
$$1 - 10\,x^2 + x^4$$

```
Simplify[% /. x -> Sqrt[2] + Sqrt[3]
```
0

```
polyprod[{x^2-2, x^2-3}]
```
$$144 - 48\,x^2 + 4\,x^4$$

```
Simplify[% /. x-> Sqrt[2] * Sqrt[3]
```
0

```
polysum[{x^2 - 2, x^2 - 3, x^2 - 5, x^2 - 7}]
```
$$46225 - 5596840\,x^2 + 13950764\,x^4 - 7453176\,x^6 + 1513334\,x^8 -$$
$$141912\,x^{10} + 6476\,x^{12} - 136\,x^{14} + x^{16}$$

```
Simplify[% /. x -> N[Sqrt[2] + Sqrt[3] + Sqrt[5] + Sqrt[7], 30]]
```
0.

Next we deal with exponents. The integer-exponent case is reduced to preceding cases by simple expansion. And a polynomial for $\alpha^{1/n}$ can be obtained from a polynomial for α by replacing x by x^n. Thus, the case of a rational exponent is easily handled by the following two definitions. Because we are considering only positive exponents, a positive query is included in the pattern for line 11. It is omitted in the pattern for line 12, because of the extension to negative exponents via line 15, which uses line 12 for negative rationals.

11. `polynomial[e_ ^ n_Integer?Positive] := polynomial[Expand[e^n]]`

12. `polynomial[e_ ^ q_Rational] :=`
     `polynomial[Expand[e ^ Numerator[q]]] /. x -> x^Denominator[q]`

Lines 1 to 12 form a complete working routine, which we now test with a few examples. Exercise: Substitute `N[r, 50]` for `x` in the following polynomials, where `r` is the algebraic expression, and verify that `0.` results.

```
polynomial[ (Sqrt[3] + Sqrt[2]) ^ (1/5) ]
```
$1 - 10x^{10} + x^{20}$

```
polynomial[ (1 + 19 Sqrt[3]) ^ (1/3) * (Sqrt[2] + 5) ]
```
$33435125491061429479211716 84 + 15746494224976354389332 0x^3 -$
$\quad 1497114925457468151136x^6 - 11961154756028780x^9 + 19292185090369x^{12}$

```
polynomial[ Sqrt[Sqrt[3] + Sqrt[2]] * (5 + I) ^ (1/3) ]
```
$43608742899428874059776 - 88122915739663788605440x^{12} +$
$\quad 18978910372586736952115 2x^{24} - 492839264512061440x^{36} + 208827064576x^{48}$

Note that the routine does not produce a polynomial of minimal degree for which the input is a root.

```
polynomial[Sqrt[2] Sqrt[3]]
```
$144 - 48x^2 + 4x^4$

Although this answer is correct—the polynomial has $\sqrt{6}$ as a root—we can improve things by adding the following special case.

13. `polynomial[e_ ^ x_ * f_ ^ x_] := polynomial[(e f)^x]`

This rule is meant to be invoked before the product rule in line 5. If we simply load it now, it will be placed after the currently loaded rules for `polynomial`. If, however, we place it in the same cell as the main routine, *Mathematica* will use its own rules to decide the ordering of the various cases.

EXERCISE Create a single cell with first line `Clear[polynomial]` and with lines 1 to 13 inserted in order. Execute `??polynomial` and see where rule 13 has been placed. Now change the order by placing rule 13 right after rule 5 (or right before rule 5), reload, and again check *Mathematica*'s internal ordering.

To be sure that rule 13 is examined before rule 5, we could place rule 13 in a separate cell before rules 1 to 12. In the case at hand, however, it suffices to place rule 13 in the same cell, but before rule 5. Thus we renumber rule 13 as rule 4½.

4½. `polynomial[e_ ^ x_ * f_ ^ x_] := polynomial[(e f)^x]`

At this point we should execute `Clear[polynomial]` and reload lines 1 to 12 (including line 4½) in their numerical order. This will cause *Mathematica* to match the pattern `e_ ^ x_ * f_ ^ x_` before the more general `e_ * f_`.

```
polynomial[Sqrt[2] Sqrt[3]]
```
$-6 + x^2$

As defined by lines 1 to 12, polynomial works only on expressions built from integers using +, −, ·, and nth-root extraction. As we have seen in the discussion of the Eisenstein integers in Chapter 9, division can sometimes lead to algebraic integers: $\frac{1}{2}(-1 + \sqrt{3}i)$ is a root of $x^2 + x + 1$. More generally, the set of *algebraic numbers*, that is, roots of polynomials with rational coefficients, forms a field, and we can expand the scope of `polynomial` to return a polynomial, possibly with rational coefficients, satisfied by any algebraic number expressed using radicals, that is, built up from integers using +, −, ·, /, and nth-root extraction. Because line 12 allows for negative rational exponents, an additional line will take care of reciprocals. Adding one more line to deal with pure rationals will complete an extension of the routine to algebraic numbers.

14. `polynomial[q_Rational] := x - q`

15. `polynomial[e_ ^ n_Integer?Negative] := Block[{`
      `temp = polynomial[e ^ -n]},`
      `Expand[(x ^ degree[temp]) * (temp /.  x -> 1/x)]]`

```
r = (1 + 1/Sqrt[2]) / (Sqrt[3] + 5 ^ (1/3)); polynomial[r]
```
$\frac{1}{4096}x - \frac{27}{1024}x^2 - \frac{25}{256}x^3 + \frac{999}{1024}x^4 - \frac{315}{32}x^5 - \frac{877}{256}x^6 + \frac{945}{32}x^7 +$
$\frac{6741}{256}x^8 - \frac{1165}{32}x^9 + \frac{243}{4}x^{10} + \frac{45}{8}x^{11} + \frac{1}{16}x^{12}$

```
% /.  x -> N[r, 50]
```
`0.`

As we have seen so often in this book, it is a striking feature of *Mathematica* that such a complicated procedure can be programmed in only about 15 lines of code. One final comment: If this code is wrapped inside a package, the first line after the context definitions should be `x = Global `x`; otherwise the variable of the returned polynomial will not be simply `x`, but rather `AlgebraicInteger`Private`x`.

10.6 The Riemann Zeta Function

The most famous unsolved problem in mathematics is the Riemann Hypothesis (RH), an assertion about the location of the zeros of the Riemann zeta function $\zeta(s)$. Because the complex function ζ is built in as `Zeta[s]`, we can use *Mathematica* to examine various aspects of this conjecture. We have already met RH in Chapters 1 and 9 where connections with the distribution of primes, the distribution of the least quadratic nonresidue modulo a prime, and the computational complexity of the problem of determining primality were pointed out.

For $s \in \mathbb{C}$, $\zeta(s)$ is defined as follows:

$$\zeta(s) = \sum_{n=1}^{\infty} \frac{1}{n^s} \qquad (*)$$

This infinite series converges only when $\mathrm{Re}(s) > 1$, but the function can be defined on all of $\mathbb{C}$ (except at the singularity at $s = 1$) by the technique of analytic continuation. We refer the reader to [Dav] or [Edw] for more background on the zeta function, including its history, methods for computation, and connections with the distribution of primes (for a brief overview of RH see [Wag] or [KW]). Be warned, however, that ζ does not give up its secrets easily, and a substantial amount of advanced mathematics, mostly complex analysis, is needed to penetrate them.

For integer arguments, the zeta function was studied by Euler, who proved the following remarkable formula in the case of positive even integer arguments: $\zeta(2n) = 2^{2n-1}\pi^{2n}|B_{2n}|/(2n)!$ where B_j is the jth Bernoulli number.[1] In particular, Euler was the first to prove that the sum of the

---

[1] The Bernoulli numbers B_n are rational numbers that can be defined as the coefficients of $x^n/n!$ in the Maclaurin series of $f(x) = x/(e^x - 1)$, where $f(0)$ is defined to be 1. The sequence begins $1, -1/2, 1/6, 0, -1/30, 0, 1/42, 0, -1/30, 0, 5/66, \ldots$. The Bernoulli numbers are built into *Mathematica* as `BernoulliB[n]`.

reciprocals of the squares of the positive integers, that is, $\zeta(2)$, is $\pi^2/6$. We can see these values by using Zeta as follows.

```
Zeta[Range[2, 16, 2]]
```

$$\left\{\frac{Pi^2}{6}, \frac{Pi^4}{90}, \frac{Pi^6}{945}, \frac{Pi^8}{9450}, \frac{Pi^{10}}{93555}, \frac{691\ Pi^{12}}{638512875}, \frac{2\ Pi^{14}}{18243225}, \frac{3617\ Pi^{16}}{325641566250}\right\}$$

A natural question is whether $\zeta(3)$ is a rational multiple of π^3. This is not known, though in 1978 R. Apéry succeeded in proving that $\zeta(3)$ is irrational. In Chapter 8 we pointed out that the probability that two random integers are relatively prime is $\pi^2/6$, which is $\zeta(2)$. This generalizes to: The probability that k random integers are relatively prime is $\zeta(k)$ (see [Sch, §4.4]).

We can generate several sorts of plots to illustrate ζ. For real values of s, $\zeta(s)$ is real, and so we can use the ordinary Plot command. The following commands generate two views, shown in Figure 10.9.

```
Plot[Zeta[n], {n,-10,10}]
```

```
Show[%, PlotRange->{{-10, 0}, {-.1, .1}}]
```

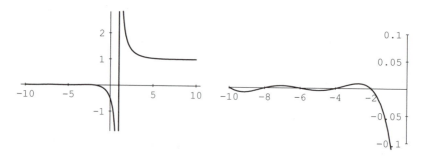

FIGURE 10.9 A plot of $\zeta(x)$ for real values of x shows the so-called trivial zeros, the singularity at 1, and the limiting behavior toward 1 as x approaches infinity.

Figure 10.9 shows that there are zeros along the negative real axis; this can be confirmed by `Zeta[Range[-20, 0, 2]]`. These zeros, whose existence is a consequence of the formula $\zeta(-n) = (-1)^n B_{n+1}/(n+1)$ (see [Edw, §1.5], are called the *trivial zeros* of ζ. There are additional zeros, and it is their precise location that is the question of the unproven and infamous Riemann Hypothesis. In order to get an overview of ζ, we can generate the 3-dimensional surface that is the graph of the real-valued function $f(x, y) = |\zeta(x + iy)|$; an image of this surface forms the cover of the *Mathematica* book [Wol]. Figure 10.10, generated by the commands that follow, shows two views of ζ: (a) is the graph of $f(x, y)$, with the singularity at 1 prominent, and (b) is the graph of the reciprocal of $f(x, y)$, which brings out the zeros more clearly. Because $\zeta(s) = \zeta(\bar{s})$ is true for the values of ζ defined by (*), it remains true for the analytic continuation of ζ; this explains why the graphs in Figure 10.10 are plotted to one side of the real axis. Figure 10.10 shows six nontrivial zeros, all of which lie on the line $1/2 + it$, which is called the *critical line*. The Riemann Hypothesis is the assertion that all nontrivial zeros have real part equal to $1/2$.

```
Plot3D[Abs[Zeta[x + I y]], {x, -4, 4}, {y, -10, 40},
        PlotPoints->{70, 110}, ViewPoint->{8, 1, 3},
        PlotRange->{0, 5}, Lighting->False,
        Shading->False, Boxed->False,
        BoxRatios->{5, 10, 2}, AxesLabel->{"x", "y", None},
        AxesEdge->{{+1, -1}, Automatic, Automatic},
        Ticks->{Automatic, Range[0, 30, 10], Range[0, 4]}]

Plot3D[1/Abs[Zeta[x + I y]], {x, -4, 4}, {y, -10, 40},
        PlotPoints->{70, 110}, ViewPoint->{7, 2, 3},
        PlotRange->{0, 5}, Lighting->False,
        Shading->False, Boxed->False,
        AxesLabel->{"x", "y", None},
        AxesEdge->{{+1, -1}, Automatic, Automatic},
        BoxRatios->{5, 10, 2},
        Ticks->{Automatic, Range[0, 30, 10], Range[0, 4]}]
```

The images of Figure 10.10 restrict the range of ζ to be real by taking absolute values. One way to see more of the complex nature of ζ is to restrict the domain to a line in $\mathbb{C}$ and plot the ζ values of points on the

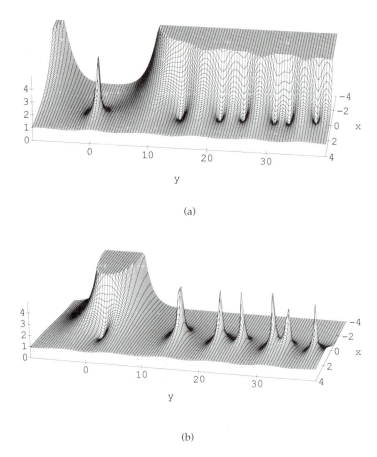

(a)

(b)

FIGURE 10.10 Two views of the Riemann zeta function: (a) shows the graph of $|\zeta(x + iy)|$, with the singularity at 1 prominent; (b) is the graph of the reciprocal of $|\zeta(x + iy)|$. The spikes in (b) correspond to the nontrivial zeros, which, at least for the domain shown in the figure, lie on the line $\frac{1}{2} + it$. The Riemann Hypothesis, considered by many to be the most important unsolved problem of mathematics, is the assertion that all of ζ's nontrivial zeros line up with the first two. It is known that the hypothesis is obeyed for the first billion and a half zeros.

line as points in the complex plane. For example, we may examine the critical line between $t = 0$ and $t = 26$, using `ParametricPlot` to display the ζ values. First we define a routine, `zeta[s]`, that returns the real and imaginary parts of $\zeta(s)$. The output of the following plotting commands, enhanced with some labels and dots, is shown in Figure 10.11. The vertical tick marks were placed by editing the PostScript description of the graphics, which is brought to the screen by unformatting the graphics cell (Cell menu). This could also have been done using the enhanced Ticks option in Version 1.2.

```
zeta[t_] := {Re[temp = Zeta[N[t]]], Im[temp]}
Attributes[zeta] = Listable


zeta[1/2 + I {0,1,2,3,4,5}]
{{-1.46035, 0}, {0.143936, -0.7221}, {0.440546, -0.311646},
  {0.532737, -0.0788965}, {0.606784, 0.0911121},
  {0.701812, 0.231038}}


ParametricPlot[zeta[.5 + I t], {t, 0, 26}]
ParametricPlot[zeta[.5 + I t], {t, 7004.1, 7005.32}, MaxBend->20]
```

The curve of Figure 10.11(a) passes through the origin three times, corresponding to the first three zeros on the critical line. Figure 10.11(b)

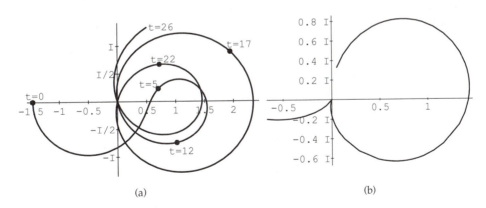

(a)   (b)

FIGURE 10.11 Two parametric plots of $\zeta(1/2 + it)$ in the complex plane; the domain in (a) is $0 \leq t \leq 26$, and in (b), $7004.1 \leq t \leq 7005.32$. The first three zeros of ζ are visible in (a). The curious behavior in (b) was discovered by D. H. Lehmer in 1956. If $\zeta(1/2 + it)$ turns down before crossing the x-axis, then RH would be false. However, there is a crossing as a magnification shows (see Figure 10.13).

shows an apparent zero of ζ, though more computation is necessary to determine whether the curve does indeed pass through the origin. In fact, if the curve ever turns away from 0 without passing through it, RH would be false. A closer examination of this region shows that there are in fact two zeros in the region of the cusp (see Figure 10.13). Such behavior of ζ, that is, a pair of zeros that are very close together, is known as Lehmer's phenomenon, for D. H. Lehmer who discovered the example near $t = 7005$ in 1956. Exercise: Generate a blowup of Figure 10.11(b) near the cusp.

EXERCISE Generate the surfaces that are the graphs of the real and imaginary parts of $\zeta(x + iy)$. Use `ContourPlot` (see example on page 71) to graph the zero curves of `Re[z[x + I y]]` and `Im[z[x + I y]]`.

To focus more clearly on the nontrivial zeros, we can plot the real-valued function $|\zeta(1/2+it)|$. This can be easily done via `Plot[Abs[Zeta[1/2 + I t]]`, which yields the graph in Figure 10.12(a). But it is customary to introduce a smoother function $Z(t)$, which is the product of $\zeta(1/2+it)$ with $\pi^{-it/2}\exp(i \operatorname{Im}(\log \Gamma(1/4+it/2))$. ($\Gamma(z)$ denotes Euler's Gamma function built in as `Gamma[z]`.) The advantage is that $Z(t)$ is real-valued for real t and vanishes for precisely those t for which $1/2 + it$ is a nontrivial zero of ζ; moreover, $Z(t)$ is, for t real, one of $\pm|\zeta(1/2 + it)|$. Thus $Z(t)$ smooths out $|\zeta(1/2 + it)|$. (A discussion of $Z(t)$ and its usefulness in locating roots of ζ on the critical line can be found in [Edw, §6.5].) Note that it does not follow that the graph of $Z(t)$ is simply that of $|\zeta(1/2 + it)|$ with alternate intervals between zeros flipped over the t-axis; rather, $Z(t)$ crosses the t-axis whenever t corresponds to a root of ζ having odd multiplicity. It has been conjectured that all the zeros of ζ have multiplicity 1.

```
Z[t_] := Exp[I (Im[Log[Gamma[1/4 + I t/2]]] - t/2 Log[Pi])] *
          Zeta[1/2 + I t]//N

Plot[Z[t]], {t, 0, 100}]
```

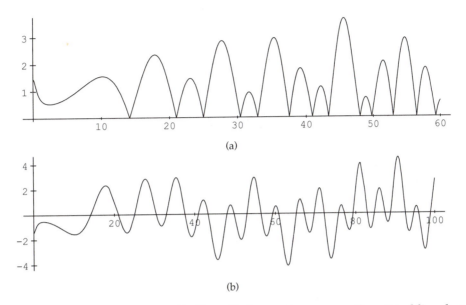

(a)

(b)

FIGURE 10.12 (a) The graph of $|\zeta(1/2 + it)|$ shows ζ's zeros on the critical line, but is not smooth. (b) The related function $Z(t)$ has the same zeros as $\zeta(1/2 + it)$, but is smoother; the graph shows 29 such zeros below $t = 100$.

We can use $Z(t)$ to take a closer look at Lehmer's phenomenon near $t = 7005$. One problem is that numerical error can cause $Z(t)$ to return a value with a very small imaginary part when there should be no imaginary part.

`Z[100]`

$$2.6927 - 1.30377\ 10^{-16}\ \text{I}$$

`Z[10000]`

$$-0.341395 - 4.71179\ 10^{-11}\ \text{I}$$

The relative smallness of the imaginary part in `Z[100]` caused the plotting routine to ignore it. However, larger imaginary parts are not ignored and cause an error in plotting routines expecting real values. The way around this is to use `Chop[`*expr,*` d]`, which turns any floating-point quantities in *expr* having absolute value less than d to zero. `Chop[Z[t], 10.^-6]` provides more control than simply using `Re[Z[t]]`.

Exercise By attempting to plot several constant functions, discover how small the imaginary part of a complex number need be (relative to the number) in order that Plot consider it as being real.

We can now define and plot $Z(t)$ near $t = 7005$; a close-up view resolves the two zeros (Figure 10.13).

```
Plot[Chop[Z[t], 10.^-6], {t, 7004.1, 7005.3},
    Ticks->{{7004.1, 7004.7,7005.3}, {-1.4, -1, -.6}},
    Axes->{7005, 0}]
```

```
Show[%, PlotRange->{{7005, 7005.15}, {-.1, .03}},
    Ticks->{{7005.03, 7005.08, 7005.13}, {-.1, -.02, .02}}]
```

Many more examples of Lehmer's phenomenon are now known, and in some cases Z turns back to 0 after being only a distance of 10^{-7} past the axis. But always Z waits until the axis crossing before turning. Because RH implies that Z has exactly one critical point between successive zeros

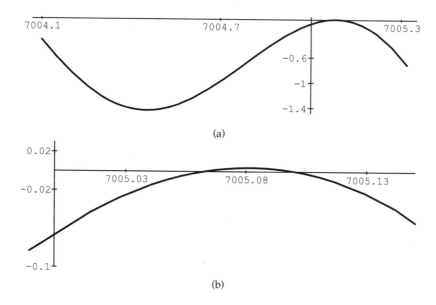

(a)

(b)

Figure 10.13 A plot of $Z(t)$ and a close-up in the vicinity of Lehmer's phenomenon [see Figure 10.11(b)] resolves the two very close zeros of ζ.

[Edw, §8.3], these quick turns may be viewed as near-counterexamples to RH. As observed by H. te Riele, who was part of the team that computed the first billion and a half zeros on the critical line, it seems as if Z and ζ know something that we don't, namely the Riemann Hypothesis!

If accurate values of the nontrivial zeros of ζ are sought, the graph of Z can be used to obtain starting values for the root finder. For example, suppose the first six roots are desired to 20-digit accuracy. First select the graph in Figure 10.12(b), then depress the command key (⌘), click the mouse on the first six crossings, and execute Copy. This places the coordinates of the selected points into the clipboard, and they can be pasted into an input cell. Wrapping First[Transpose[]] around these values yields the t-coordinates of the approximate zeros.

```
approximatezeros = First[Transpose[
     {{14.1745, 0.00813295}, {20.9543, 0.00813295},
      {25.0456, 0.00813295}, {30.4812, -0.00619712},
      {32.936, -0.00619712}, {37.6117, 0.00813295}}]]
{14.1745, 20.9543, 25.0456, 30.4812, 32.936, 37.6117}
```

Now we can add and subtract 0.3 from each of these values and use them in FindRoot to bracket the roots. Using Map allows us to handle all the approximations at once. The default AccuracyGoal setting to FindRoot is 6, which means that it tries to find roots that are accurate to 6 digits. If we want roots to 20 digits, thus matching the other machine-precision numbers in subsequent computations, we have to increase the AccuracyGoal to 20. In the present example it turns out that the machine precision that FindRoot uses in its internal computations is insufficient to reach the 20-digit goal; this can be fixed by increasing the working precision option. Note that the exact value 1/2 must be used, as the use of the machine approximation 0.5 will lead to an error because its precision is less than 30. The high precision will cause some small imaginary parts to be returned; they are eliminated using Chop, as was done for the plot of Z.

```
Chop[t] /. Map[FindRoot[Zeta[1/2 + I t], {t, # + {-.3, +.3}},
        AccuracyGoal->20, WorkingPrecision->30] &,
        approximatezeros]
{14.134725141734693790457251983 6,
    21.022039638771554992628479593 9,
```

```
25.010857580145688763213790926,
30.424876125859513210311897306,
32.935061587739189690662368964,
37.586178158825671257217763481}
```

One way to check the accuracy of the roots is by changing the last digit and checking for an axis crossing by computing Z at the perturbed values. The additional zero digits below force a higher-precision computation; without them the output in all three cases would be simply 0.

```
Z /@ {14.134725141734693790457251983500000000,
      14.134725141734693790457251983600000000,
      14.134725141734693790457251983700000000}
```

$\{-4.95489 \ 10^{-29} + 5.1949 \ 10^{-39} \ I, \ 2.97671 \ 10^{-29} + 2.78131 \ 10^{-39} I,$

$1.09083 \ 10^{-28} + 2.34586 \ 10^{-39} \ I\}$

Because $Z(t)$ is real for real t, the small imaginary parts of the preceding output may be ignored; thus there is indeed an axis crossing between $t = 14.134\ldots19835$ and $t = 14.134\ldots19836$. Hence the first root given by FindRoot is accurate to all displayed 30 digits, even though the goal was only 20 digits.

EXERCISE Find the first 50 nontrivial zeros of ζ to 20-digit accuracy.

10.7 The Influence of the Complex Zeros of ζ on the Distribution of Primes ▬▬▬▬▬

We close this chapter with an example that illustrates the connection between the zeros of the ζ-function and the distribution of the primes. *Warning: Some of the computations in this section take several hours.* As discussed in Chapter 1, Riemann found that $\pi(x)$, the number of primes less than or equal to x, is well approximated by the function $R(x)$ defined by

$$R(x) = \sum_{n=1}^{\infty} \frac{\mu(n)}{n} \mathrm{li}(x^{1/n}),$$

where μ denotes the Möbius function and $\mathrm{li}(x)$ denotes the logarithmic integral, discussed in Chapter 1 and available in *Mathematica* via LogInte-

`gral`; a routine for computing $R(x)$ (in a way that avoids `LogIntegral`) is given in the Appendix. There is much more to the story, however, as $R(x)$ can be modified by various correction terms derived from the zeta function; adding more corrections yields a function that is ever closer to the step function $\pi(x)$. Our goal here is to animate these corrections so as to illustrate the role of the zeros of ζ. Such computations were first carried out by H. Riesel and G. Göhl [RG]. The computations show that although $R(x)$ gives an excellent global approximation to $\pi(x)$, the local variations in the distribution of the primes are governed by the complex zeros of the Riemann zeta function.

We begin with a discussion of an exact formula for the distribution of the primes discovered by Riemann in 1859 and proved by von Mangoldt in 1895. The formula is an exact expression for $\pi_0(x)$, by which is meant the function that differs from $\pi(x)$ only at prime values: $\pi_0(p) = \pi(p) - 1/2$ for primes p [equivalently, $\pi_0(p) = 1/2(\pi_0(p-\epsilon) + \pi_0(p+\epsilon))$]. The Riemann–von Mangoldt formula is given by the following sum (which, as we shall see, is really over a finite set of indices n):

$$\pi_0(x) = \sum_{n \geq 1} \frac{\mu(n) f(x^{1/n})}{n} \qquad (*)$$

where roughly speaking, the function $f(x)$ is the sum of li(x) and infinitely many other terms, one for each nontrivial zero of ζ (a more precise description of f will be given shortly). Ignoring the terms in f that involve the zeros leads directly to Riemann's function $R(x)$, which was studied and graphed in Chapter 1 for x up to 10 million (Figure 1.6). Now, π_0 is a step function and $R(x)$ is a smooth function (see Figure 10.14; Exercise: Use `RiemannR` (in Appendix) and the graphing techniques discussed in Chapter 1 to generate this figure). Riesel and Göhl had the idea of considering a small domain for x, say the interval from 12 to 100, and seeing how the inclusion in f of the terms involving the first 29 zeros—the *correction terms*—will cause the smooth function to transform itself to the step function π_0. If we add in these corrections by considering the zeros one at a time, we can animate the convergence to π_0 and see the effect of the individual zeros. Constructing such an animation is our goal, though we will go a little farther, by considering the first 50 zeros, that is, all zeros with imaginary part less than 145.

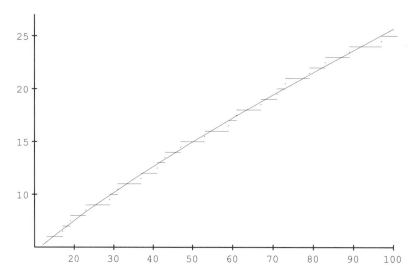

FIGURE 10.14 The step function and dots form the graph of $\pi_0(x)$; the smooth graph is Riemann's prime-approximating function $R(x)$. As $R(x)$ is improved using zeros of ζ, the smooth function is transformed to the step function.

The function $f(x)$ is defined as follows:

$$f(x) = \sum_{n \geq 1} \frac{\pi_0(x^{1/n})}{n}$$

One motivation for this definition is that $f(x)$ can be viewed as a weighted count, where the primes under x have weight 1, the prime squares under x have weight $\frac{1}{2}$, the prime cubes have weight $\frac{1}{3}$, and so on. It turns out that $f(x)$ is a more convenient object of study than $\pi(x)$. Formula (∗) is a direct consequence of the definition of f and a technique called Möbius inversion; moreover, the definition implies that $f(x) = 0$ when $x < 2$, and so the sum in (∗) is actually a finite sum because the value of $x^{1/n}$ is eventually less than 2. Now, the Riemann–von Mangoldt formula is really a formula for f, namely:

$$f(x) = \text{li}(x) - \sum_{\zeta(\rho)=0} \text{ei}(\rho \log x) - \log 2 + \int_x^\infty \frac{dt}{t(t^2 - 1) \log t} \qquad (**)$$

where the sum is over the nontrivial zeros of ζ, considered in order of increasing absolute value, and ei(z) denotes the exponential integral function, which is defined for complex arguments $z = u + iv$, with $v \neq 0$, as the integral of e^z / z along the straight line from $-\infty + iv$ to $u + iv$. This function is built into *Mathematica* as `ExpIntegralEi`. The formula for f is usually stated with li(x^ρ) instead of ei($\rho \log x$), but it clarifies the situation to use ei. Recall that for real x, li(x) is defined to be the Cauchy principal value of the integral of $1/\log t$ from 0 to ∞. In the usual statement of (∗∗), with li(x^ρ) instead of ei($\rho \log x$), li(x^ρ) refers to the analytic continuation of the function li(x^s), where x is a fixed real and s is the complex variable. Now, although li(x) = ei($\log x$)) for real x, this identity will not yield the desired values for complex arguments, because the complex logarithm function will in general not choose $\rho \log x$ as the logarithm of x^ρ, but rather $\rho \log x - 2n\pi i$, where n is such that the imaginary part of the result has absolute value less than π. For further details we refer the reader to the discussion in the book by Edwards [Edw, §1.15]. The main point here is that formula (∗∗) is given in a form suitable for computation by *Mathematica* provided that `ExpIntegralEi` is used for ei.

Our goal is to see the effect of the terms in (∗∗) when they are substituted for f in (∗). In the computations that follow, we will approximate the sum in (∗) using the first 154 terms (the justification of this choice for the computations at hand is provided in [RG], where it is shown that it leads to errors bounded by roughly 10^{-4}). The contribution of the last two terms in (∗∗) is not very much when x is large, but because $f(x^{1/n})$ is used, the lower integration limit is often close to 1. Riesel and Göhl proved that for the computation at hand, the contribution of the integral and the log 2 terms to (∗), that is,

$$\sum_{n=1}^{154} \frac{\mu(n)}{n} (I(x^{1/n}) - \log 2)$$

where $I(x)$ denotes the integral in (∗∗), is sufficiently well approximated by arctan($\pi / \log x$)/π. Their proof uses the fact that $\sum\{\mu(n) : 1 \leq n \leq 154\} = 0$, which is one reason for the choice of 154. We emphasize that the justification for all the computations in this section relies heavily on the error analysis by Riesel and Göhl, and the reader interested in extending these computations must ensure that the error analysis in [RG] remains valid.

Now, because the nontrivial zeros come in pairs, ρ and $\bar{\rho}$, let's enumerate the zeros on the upper half of the critical line in order as $\rho_1, \rho_2,$ $\rho_3, \ldots$ and isolate the contribution of the kth zero to $\pi_0(x)$ by defining T_k as follows:

$$T_k(x) = -\sum_{n=1}^{154} \frac{\mu(n)}{n} \left[\mathrm{ei}\left(\frac{\rho_k}{n}\log x\right) + \mathrm{ei}\left(\frac{\overline{\rho_k}}{n}\log x\right) \right]$$

To summarize, if for fixed x, the infinitely many values of $T_k(x)$ are added to $R^+(x) = R(x) + \arctan(\pi/\log x)/\pi$, then the result is equal to $\pi_0(x)$; keep in mind that each summand may be in error by $1/10{,}000$. Hence our task is to obtain plots of $R^+(x) + \sum\{T_k(x) : 1 \le k \le N\}$ for N up to 50; this will show the effect of the first 50 nontrivial zeros, that is, those with imaginary part under 145, on the distribution of the primes under 100. Note that the smaller zeros have a greater effect than the larger ones, because they yield larger values of ei.

This discussion gives some indication of why the Riemann Hypothesis is related to the distribution of primes. The size of the contribution of the correction term $T_k(x)$ corresponding to the kth zero on the critical line is, roughly, the product of $-2\sqrt{x}/(|\rho|\log x)$ with a cosine function (see [RG]). If RH fails, then there is a root whose real part is greater than 0.5, and this means the square root will become a higher power of x. For a more concrete example, one can try to estimate the number of primes less than 10^{100}. A rough approximation comes from $\mathrm{li}(10^{100})$, which is easy to compute:

```
N[LogIntegral[10^100], 50]
```

$$4.3619719871407031590995091132291646115387572117165 \; 10^{97}$$

Now, without assuming RH, the best known result is that $\pi(10^{100})$ is within $3 \cdot 10^{95}$ of $\mathrm{li}(10^{100})$, so $4.331 \cdot 10^{97} < \pi(10^{100}) < 4.392 \cdot 10^{97}$; assuming RH, however, it can be proved that the error in the approximation is less than 10^{51}, so $\pi(10^{100})$ would be known to be

$$4.3619719871407031590995091132291646115387572 11\ldots \cdot 10^{97}$$

These computations are consequences of results of L. Schoenfeld [Sch].

A simplification in the computation of T_k comes from observing that $\mathrm{ei}(c\rho) + \mathrm{ei}(c\bar{\rho}) = \mathrm{ei}(\rho c) + \overline{\mathrm{ei}(\rho c)} = 2\,\mathrm{Re}(\mathrm{ei}(\rho c))$, for c real. This yields the following expression for T_k:

$$T_k(x) = -2 \sum_{n=1}^{154} \frac{\mu(n)}{n} \mathrm{Re}\left(\mathrm{ei}\left(\frac{\rho_k}{n}\log x\right)\right) \qquad (\ast\ast\ast)$$

Before beginning the computation of the correction terms, we must precompute more zeros of ζ than we did earlier. This is done exactly as before, by using a graph of $Z(t)$ up to $t = 145$ to generate the coordinates of the first 50 axis crossings, whose x-coordinates are then stored in approximatezeros. The same technique used earlier (via Map), with the same precision settings in FindRoot, yields the following list of roots of Z, which is transformed to rho, a list of roots of ζ.

```
zeros = N[Re[t],20] /.
    Map[FindRoot[Zeta[1/2 + I t], {t, # + {-.3, +.3}},
        AccuracyGoal->20, WorkingPrecision->30] &,
            approximatezeros]
{14.134725141734693790,     21.022039638771554993,
 25.010857580145688763,     30.424876125859513210,
 32.935061587739189691,     37.586178158825671257,
 40.918719012147495187,     43.327073280914999519,
 48.005150881167159728,     49.773832477672302182,
 52.970321477714460644,     56.446247697063394804,
 59.347044002602353080,     60.831778524609809844,
 65.112544048081606661,     67.079810529494173714,
 69.546401711173979253,     72.067157674481907583,
 75.704690699083933168,     77.144840068874805373,
 79.337375020249367923,     82.910380854086030183,
 84.735492980517050106,     87.425274613125229407,
 88.809111207634465424,     92.491899270558484296,
 94.651344040519886967,     95.870634228245309759,
 98.831194218193692233,    101.317851005731391229,
103.725538040478339416,    105.446623052326094494,
107.168611184276407515,    111.029535543169674525,
111.874659176992637086,    114.320220915452712766,
116.226680320857554382,    118.790782865976217323,
121.370125002420645919,    122.946829293552588201,
124.256818554345767185,    127.516683879596495124,
```

```
      129.57870419995605099,    131.08768853093265672,
      133.49773720299758645,    134.75650975337387133,
      138.11604205453344320,    139.73620895212138895,
      141.12370740402112376,    143.11184580762063274}
```

```
rho = 1/2 + I zeros;
```

We should also precompute the values of $\mu(n)/n$ that will be needed. The following commands generate the vector of nonzero values of $-2\mu(n)/n$ [the -2 is included because of (∗∗∗)], as well as the set of n for which $\mu(n) = 0$.

```
list = Table[N[MoebiusMu[n]/n], {n, 154}];
MoebiusIndices = Select[Range[154], list[[#]] != 0 &]
MoebiusData    = -2 list[[MoebiusIndices]]
```

The μ computation is quite fast, so the values need not be stored between sessions. The values of the zeros, however, should be saved so that they can be used without having to recompute them. One can simply save a cell containing the definition zeros = {14.13..., ..., 143.11...}, followed by the definition of rho. Finally, the listability of ExpIntegralEi leads to the following short definition of $T_k(x)$.

```
T[x_, k_] := MoebiusData .
   Re[ ExpIntegralEi[rho[[k]] / MoebiusIndices * Log[N[x]]]  ]
```

All the computations in this section are aimed at producing graphs with x ranging from 12 to 100 in 150 steps. The relevant values of T_k can therefore be obtained by

```
domain = Range[12., 100, 88./150]
T1 = T[domain, 1];
```

It takes about two hours to compute these 150 values. They can be displayed as follows (see Figure 10.15, which shows T_1 to T_4, T_{29}, and T_{50}). The highly oscillatory nature of these graphs, especially for small values of x, is a consequence of the cosine function in the approximation to T_k, alluded to earlier. In Figure 10.15 the resolution of T_{50} was improved by using 451 data points, rather than just 151.

```
ListPlot[Transpose[{domain, T1}], PlotJoined->True]
```

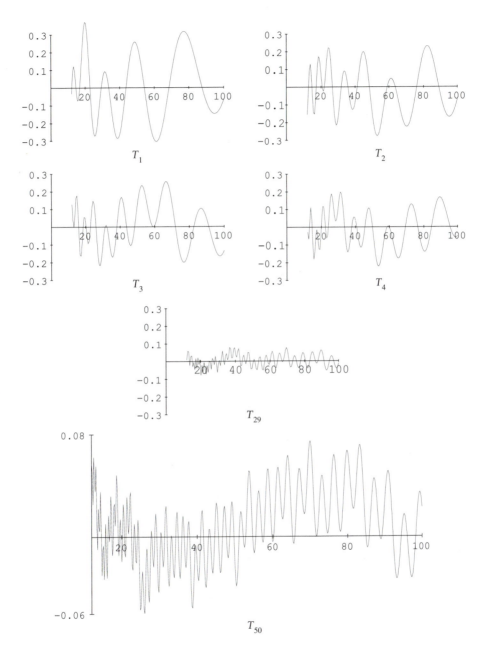

FIGURE 10.15 Graphs of T_1 to T_4, T_{29}, and T_{50}, some of the correction terms in the Riemann–von Mangoldt formula for π_0 in terms of zeros of ζ. As k increases, the magnitude of $T_k(x)$ decreases; in other words, the smaller zeros of ζ have the greatest effect on the distribution of the primes.

Because each set of 151 values in a data list for T_k requires about two hours of computation, one will need to generate this data in small batches. To get an idea of the immense amount of computation required, note that we are generating 50 lists of 151 data points, each of which requires 94 numerical integrals (94 being the number of nonzero values in $\{\mu(n) : n \leq 154\}$)—a grand total of over 700,000 evaluations of the exponential integral. A useful technique for large computations is to have the results written directly to a file. A designation of >> causes the output to be written to a file (overwriting anything that is already there), whereas >>> causes the output to be appended to a file. Thus the following command would place the first four data lists (one overnight computation) in a file called **T.data**. The commands could then be reexecuted by simply changing `start`. After several runs, all 50 data sets will be in one file.

```
start = 1
Do[T[domain, i] >>> "T.Data", {i, start, start + 3}]
```

Once the data points for T_1 to T_{50} are safely computed and stored, they can be combined with the values of R^+ to form the partial sums that converge to the step function π_0. Using the routine for R given in the Appendix, the values of R^+ are easily computed as follows.

```
RiemannData = RiemannR[domain] + N[ArcTan[Pi/Log[Domain]]/Pi]
```

We can now add to `RiemannData` each of the data sets for T_k in turn and thus obtain the desired partial sums. Plotting them using `ListPlot` yields the animation. A neat way to do this is via `Accumulate`. First the 50 data sets are loaded as a single list, `data`. The following command will then generate 50 images. Figure 10.16 shows six frames, with the additional enhancement of dots at the points $(p, \pi_0(p))$. Note how the convergence to the step function π_0 becomes more and more evident. The graph corresponding to 50 correction terms passes through all the prime points and has several horizontal segments corresponding to the steps of the step function.

```
Scan[ListPlot[Transpose[{domain, #}], PlotJoined->True,
        PlotRange->{{10, 100}, {5, 27}}, Axes->{10, 5},
        Ticks->{Range[20, 100, 10], Automatic}] &,
    Accumulate[Plus, Prepend[data, RiemannData]]];
```

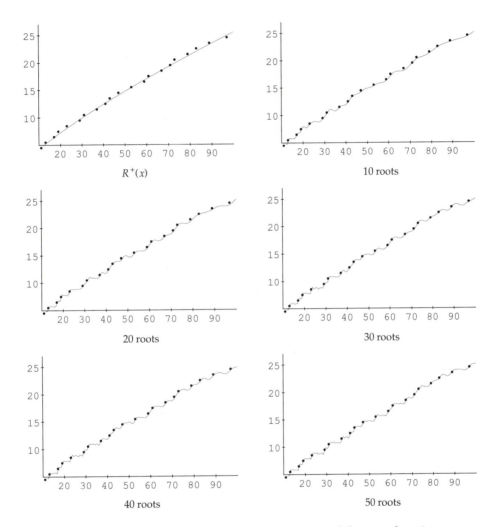

FIGURE 10.16 These plots show how the first 50 roots of the zeta function transform the smooth function $R^+(x)$, which is a global approximation to $\pi(x)$, to the step function $\pi_0(x)$. The dots are placed at the values of $\pi_0(p)$, p prime, $11 \leq p \leq 97$. The 50-root graph shows how the first 50 roots of ζ determine the distribution of the first 25 primes.

This computation reveals the wondrous nature of Riemann's formula and the power of analytic number theory: an extremely complicated combination of almost a million integrals of complex functions yields an approximation to the step function that jumps by exactly 1 at each prime number. Of course, one would not use integrals to find the first 25 prime numbers. But the connection between complex analytic functions and $\pi(x)$ yielded the first proof of one of the most important theorems in mathematics. By showing that ζ has no zeros of the form $1 + it$, Hadamard and de la Vallée-Poussin proved in 1896 that $\pi(x)$ is asymptotic to $x/\log x$; that is, the relative error in using $x/\log x$ to approximate $\pi(x)$ approaches 0 as x approaches infinity. The work of this section also shows the power of *Mathematica*, as an extremely complex computation was carried out using only about 20 lines of programming.

Appendix

Supplementary
Programs

A.1 Chapter 1

A.1.1 Wilson's Theorem Primality Test

The following routine implements Wilson's theorem as a primality test (see page 13). It takes inordinately long for numbers larger than a few hundred, however, and so has value only as a programming exercise.

```
WilsonPrimeTest[n_] :=
  Block[{i = 1}, Nest[Mod[# i++, n]&, 1, n-1] == n-1]
```

A.1.2 An Improved Prime Query

The routine primeQ is a modification of the built-in PrimeQ, as explained in the usage statement. The routine is presented as a package; this means that its variables will not interfere with other variables of the same name that might happen to be in use. Although n could have been protected by wrapping Block around it, there is no way to isolate smallprimes without setting up a separate context. The preamble must be in separate cells, as discussed on page 259.

```
BeginPackage["primeQ`"];


primeQ::usage = "primeQ[n] modifies PrimeQ by first testing for
divisibility by any of the first 1,000 primes; it should be used
instead of PrimeQ when numbers being tested are large"


Begin["`Private`"]

smallprimes = Prime[Range[1000]]
testforsmalldivisors[x_] :=
  (n=1; While[n < 1000 && Mod[x, smallprimes[[n]]] != 0, n++];
        n == 1000)

primeQ[n_] := (n <= 7919 || testforsmalldivisors[n]) && PrimeQ[n]

End[]; EndPackage[];
```

A.1.3 Encoding Messages as Integers, and Decoding Back to Messages

The function encode[message] uses ASCII codes to transform a string of lower- and upper-case letters and digits into an integer. It is convenient to use ToASCII[] − 22 to perform the translation, as that will turn any character to a number between 10 and 99. Well, almost. The one exception is that this translates a "z" to 100. In order to get two-digit codes for all characters, we first replace any zs by "["; the reverse must be done when decoding. encode proceeds as follows: (1) transform the message to a sequence of characters; (2) perform the aforementioned z removal; (3) compute the list of 2-digit codes; (4) turn these codes from numbers to strings; (5) concatenate the strings; (6) turn the resulting string back to a number. Decode's operation is the reverse. See page 22 for sample usage.

```
encode[message_] := ToExpression[
        Apply[StringJoin,
            Map[ToString[ToASCII[#] - 22]&,
                Characters[message] /. "z" -> "["]]]


decode[codedmessage_Integer] := Block[{out},
    out = Characters[codedmessage];
    out = Table[out[[{2i - 1, 2i}]], {i, Length[out]/2}];
    out = Map[Apply[StringJoin, #]&, out];
    out = Map[FromASCII[ToExpression[#] + 22]&, out];
    Apply[StringJoin, (out /. "[" -> "z" )]]
```

A.1.4 The Prime-Counting Function $\pi(x)$

The following definition of $\pi(x)$ as the inverse of the built-in Prime[n] is due to Ilan Vardi.

```
PrimePi::usage = "PrimePi[x] returns the number of primes less
                than or equal to x"

Attributes[PrimePi] = Listable
```

```
PrimePi[x_] := PrimePi[Floor[x]]                    /; Not[IntegerQ[x]]

PrimePi[n_Integer] := 0 /; n <= 1
PrimePi[4] = 2
PrimePi[n_Integer] := Block[{t, diff, m},
    t = Round[N[Log[n]]];
    m = Round[N[LogIntegral[n]]];
    diff = n - Prime[m];
    While[ Abs[diff] > t^2 / (1.16)^2,
        m += Round[ diff / t];
        diff = n - Prime[m];]
    If[diff < 0,
        While[n < Prime[m], m--;],
        While[n >= Prime[m], m++;]; m--];
    Return[m]]                                       /; n > 1 && n != 4
```

A.1.5 $R(x)$, **Riemann's Approximation to** $\pi(x)$

Riemann's function $R(x)$ is equal to the following infinite series [Rie, p. 55]:

$$R(x) = 1 + \sum_{m=1}^{\infty} \frac{(\log x)^m}{m!\, m\, \zeta(m+1)}$$

Because the Riemann zeta function $\zeta(s)$ is built in as Zeta[s], this series is easy to evaluate by using the 100th partial sum. It is efficient to precompute all the denominators into rlist. Then R values can be computed via a single dot product. The following code is due to Ilan Vardi; it gives 20-digit accuracy for inputs up to a googol. For larger x or more accuracy, replace 100 by a value large enough that the last term of the dot product is sufficiently small.

```
RiemannR::usage = "Riemann[x] returns the value of R(x), which
is a good approximation to the number of primes less than x."
Attributes[RiemannR] = {Listable}

rlist = Map[1/(#! # N[Zeta[# + 1]]) &, Range[100]]
RiemannR[x_] := 1 + (Floor[N[Log[x]] ^ Range[100]]) . rlist
RiemannR[0] = 0
```

A.1.6 Counting Primes in a Given Congruence Class

The function `PrimePiModn[x, n]` divides the first x primes into the nonzero mod-n residue classes and pairs each prime with the mod-n count up to that prime. See page 33 for sample output.

```
PrimePiModn[x_, n_] :=
    Block[{i, temp, modlist = Mod[Prime[Range[x]], n]},
        Table[(temp = Flatten[Position[modlist, i]];
                Transpose[{Prime[temp], Range[Length[temp]]}]),
            {i, n-1}]]
```

A.1.7 Counting Primes Mod 4

There are various ways to go about this problem, perhaps using `For` or `Do` loops. However, the following seems to be the most efficient. `Accumulate[Plus, {a, b, c,...}]` forms the list: `{a, a + b, a + b + c,...}`. Hence the following command, which makes use of the listability of `Prime` and `Mod`, produces a chart of the function $\pi_4(x,3) - \pi_4(x,1)$.

```
ListPlot[Accumulate[Plus, Mod[Prime[Range[300]], 4] - 2],
                                    PlotJoined->True]
```

A.2 Chapter 2 ▬▬▬▬▬▬

A.2.1 Trochoid Animation Generator

The code that follows produces a 60-frame animation that shows the generation of the trochoid by a point on a spoke on a rolling wheel. The user enters the radius of the spoke. A value of 1 produces a cycloid; values smaller or larger than 1 produce a curve known as a trochoid. If fewer frames are desired, the final value or the step size of t in the iterator at the end can be changed.

```
r = Input["This program traces the path of a point on a spoke
of a rolling wheel. The radius of the rolling wheel is 1. Enter
the radius of the spoke."]

rr = Max[r - 1, 0]; pi = N[Pi];
cycloid[t_] := {t - r Sin[t], 1 - r Cos[t]};
rotate = {{Cos[theta],Sin[theta]}, {-Sin[theta],Cos[theta]}}
```

```
spokepoints :=
    Table[{t,1} + rotate . (cycloid[t] - {t,1}),
          {theta, 0, 2 pi, pi/4}]
spokes := {Thickness[.004], Map[Line[{{t,1}, #}] &, spokepoints]}
baseline = Line[{{-2,0}, {10.5,0}}];
dots = {PointSize[.006]};
Do[ AppendTo[dots, Point[cycloid[t]]];
    Show[Graphics[{{GrayLevel[.5], Disk[{t,1}, 1]},
                  Line[{{t,1}, cycloid[t]}],        (* spoke *)
                  baseline,
                  spokes,
                  Circle[{t,1}, 1],
                  dots}],
        AspectRatio->(3+2 rr)/(12+2 rr),
        PlotRange->{{-1.5-rr, 10.5+rr}, {-.5-rr, 2.5+rr}}],
  {t, 0., 2 pi 59/40, 2 pi/40}]
```

A.2.2 Epicycloid and Hypocycloid Animation Generator

The code that follows produces a 60-frame animation that shows a circle rolling around another circle (epicycloid) or rolling inside another circle (hypocycloid). For an epicycloid enter a positive r value at the input prompt; $r = 1$ yields two circles of the same size; for a hypocycloid, enter a value strictly between 0 and −1. If fewer frames are desired, increase theta's step size. In cases where the curve closes up exactly after one revolution, for example, when r is the reciprocal of an integer, the animation should be shown cyclically with the last frame deleted. For other curves it might be desirable to extend theta beyond 2π.

```
Clear[rotate];
r = Input["This program traces the path of a point on the
circumference of a circle rolling around (positive r) or inside
(negative r) a circle of radius 1. Enter the radius of the
rolling circle."]

rr = Max[1, 1 + 2 r]; pi = N[Pi]
rotate[point_, theta_] :=
    {{Cos[theta], Sin[theta]}, {-Sin[theta], Cos[theta]}} . point
```

```
fixedcircle = {Thickness[.006], Circle[{0, 0}, 1]}
rollingdisk := {GrayLevel@.5, Disk[center, Abs[r]]}
rollingcircle := Circle[center, Abs[r]]
dots = {PointSize[.006]}
Do[  center = rotate[{-1-r, 0}, theta];
     spoke1 = rotate[{1,0}, theta (1+1/r)];
     spokeline1 = {center + r spoke1, center - r spoke1};
     spoke2 = rotate[{0,1}, theta (1+1/r)];
     spokeline2 = {center + r spoke2, center - r spoke2};
     spokes = {Thickness[.007], Line[spokeline1], GrayLevel[1],
                                            Line[spokeline2]};

     AppendTo[dots, Point[center + r spoke1]];
     Show[Graphics[
     {rollingdisk, spokes, fixedcircle, rollingcircle, dots}],
        AspectRatio->1,
        PlotRange->{{-rr - .03, rr + .03},
                    {-rr - .03, rr + .03}}],
   {theta, 0., 2 pi , 2 pi/60}]
```

A.2.3 Rolling Polygons

The routine that follows generates a 111-frame movie that shows a polygon rolling smoothly along a series of appropriately truncated catenaries
and the curve traced by one of its vertices. The final image in the case of
a rolling square appears in Figure 2.10. This animation uses a lot of memory. For fewer frames, modify the last two elements of the final iterator.
The plot of the linked catenaries is stored in plot, which is then displayed along with the appropriately rotated and translated polygon. The
initial vertices of the polygon are in startpolygon; this list is rotated
and translated as the parameter t increases by the function polygon[t].
The center of the polygon is assumed to move uniformly; this is why the
translational part of polygon is just {t, 0}. Some elementary geometry
combined with an arc-length computation yields the function of t that
gives the appropriate rotation angle.

```
n = Input["How many sides does the rolling polygon have?"]
pi = Pi//N
cr = Csc[pi/n]   (* circumradius of polygon *)
```

```
ir = Cot[pi/n]   (* inradius of polygon *)
a = ir ArcSinh[1/ir]
dots = {PointSize[.0018]}
rotate[p_, t_, center_] :=
    center + {{Cos[t], Sin[t]}, {-Sin[t], Cos[t]}} . (p - center)
plot = Table[Plot[cr - ir Cosh[(x - 2 a i)/ir],
                  {x, -a + 2 a i, a + 2 a i},
                  DisplayFunction->Identity,
                  PlotStyle->Thickness[.001]], {i, 0, 5}];

startpolygon = Map[# + {0, cr} &, Map[{Re[#], Im[#]} &,
        cr N[Exp[I Range[-Pi/2 + Pi/n, 3 Pi/2 + Pi/n, 2 Pi/n]]]]]

polygon[t_] := Block[{loop = N[Floor[(t + a)/(2a)]]},
                        (* loop tells which loop the square is on *)
Map[{t,0} +
  rotate[#, loop 2pi/n + ArcTan[Sinh[(t-loop 2 a)/ir]], {0,cr}]&,
    startpolygon]]

Do[  newpolygon = polygon[t];
     AppendTo[dots, Point[newpolygon[[n]]]];
     Show[
         Graphics[{PointSize[.008], Thickness[.001],
                   {GrayLevel[.75], Polygon[newpolygon]},
                   Line[newpolygon],
                   Map[Line[{{t, cr},#}] &, newpolygon],
                   Line[{{-cr, cr}, {11.5 a,cr}}],
                   Point[{t, cr}],
                   Point[newpolygon[[n]]],
                   dots}], plot,
     PlotRange->{{-cr, 11 a + cr}, {-.2, 2 cr}},
     AspectRatio->(2 cr +.2) / (11 a + 2 cr),
     DisplayFunction->$DisplayFunction,
     Ticks->None, Axes->None],                {t, 0., 11 a, a/10}]
```

A.2.4 Reuleaux Triangle Rotating inside a Square

The routine that follows generates an animation showing a Reuleaux triangle, which is an example of a curve of constant width, rotating inside a square, along with the curves generated by a vertex of the Reuleaux triangle, its centroid, and a point along an altitude that in the initial position, is at the center of the square. The final frame of the animation (where the step size for `t` is smaller than the `Pi/12` in the code below) can be found in Figure 2.11. This animation is a little tricky to program. The Reuleaux triangle itself is drawn with the help of three calls to `arc`, a function that draws a piecewise linear approximation to a 60° arc; `Reuleaux` then pastes the three point lists together and is wrapped inside `Polygon` to get the filled polygon and `Line` to get the border.

The tricky part is figuring out the location of the vertices as the triangle rotates inside the square. The main idea is to start with the Reuleaux triangle inscribed in a square so that one of its vertices—call it vertex 2—is at the midpoint of the square's right side. Let the other two vertices be called 1 and 3, as in Figure A.1. The triangle is then rotated counterclockwise about its centroid; this will move it outside of the fixed square; the proper translation vector needed to return it to the inside of

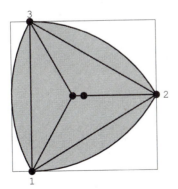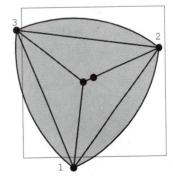

FIGURE A.1 Rotating the Reuleaux triangle about its centroid moves it outside of the square. The correct translation vector to bring it back inside the square is determined, at least for small rotations, by the x-coordinate of vertex 2 and the y-coordinate of vertex 1.

the square must be computed. This translation vector can be determined from the rotated positions of vertices 1 and 2; in particular, $1 - x_2$ yields the x-coordinate of the translation vector (where x_2 is the x-coordinate of vertex 2) and $-1 - y_1$ yields the needed y-coordinate (y_1 is the y-coordinate of vertex 1). So far, so good. But the vertices that get used in this way change as the rotation progresses through multiples of 30°. The vertex yielding the x-coordinate changes as follows: 2, 3, 3, 1, 1, 2, 2, 3, 3, ..., while the y-indicating vertex takes on the values 1, 1, 2, 2, 3, 3, 1, 1, ... And the sequence of ±1s that get used is: (1,−1), (−1,−1), (−1,1), (1,1), (1,−1), (−1,−1), (−1,1), ... Thus the first order of business is to come up with functions that yield these three sequences as functions of the rotation angle, which varies from 0 to 2π. This is accomplished by the function choose, whose output can be reduced modulo 3 to yield the lists of vertex labels and modulo 2 to yield the correct ±1s.

```
choose[Range[0, 2 Pi, Pi/6]]
{1, 2, 2, 3, 3, 4, 4, 5, 5, 6, 6, 7, 7}

Mod[choose[Range[0, 2 Pi, Pi/6]], 3] + 1
{1, 2, 2, 3, 3, 4, 4, 5, 5, 6, 6, 7, 7}

Mod[choose[Range[0, 2 Pi, Pi/6] - Pi/2], 3] + 1
{1, 1, 2, 2, 3, 3, 1, 1, 2, 2, 3, 3, 1}

2 Mod[choose[Range[0, Pi, Pi/6]], 2] - 1
{1, -1, -1, 1, 1, -1, -1}

2 Mod[choose[Range[0, Pi, Pi/6] - Pi/2], 2] - 1
{-1, -1, 1, 1, -1, -1, 1}
```

The additional programming details are straightforward and quite similar to the cycloid animation program discussed in Chapter 2.

```
Clear[t, rotate]
centroid = {1 - 2 Sqrt[3.]/3, 0}
choose[t_] := Floor[.5 (Floor[t / (Pi/6)] + 3)]
```

```
rotate[point_, t_, center_] :=
center + {{Cos[t], -Sin[t]}, {Sin[t], Cos[t]}} . (point - center)

arc[{center_, startangle_}] :=
     Block[{t}, Table[center + 2 {Cos[t], Sin[t]},
                  {t, startangle, N[startangle + Pi/3], 0.08}]]

verts = {{1 - Sqrt[3.], -1}, {1, 0}, {1 - Sqrt[3.], 1}}
angles = {Pi/6, 5 Pi/6, 9 Pi/6};
dots = {};

Do[tempverts = Map[rotate[#, t, centroid] &, verts];
   translate = 2 Mod[{choose[t], choose[t-Pi/2]}, 2] - 1 -
                  {tempverts[[Mod[choose[t], 3] + 1, 1]],
                   tempverts[[Mod[choose[t - Pi/2], 3] + 1, 2]]};
   newverts = Map[ # + translate &, tempverts];
   reuleaux = Flatten[Map[arc, Transpose@{newverts,
                    t + angles}], 1];
   AppendTo[reuleaux, First@reuleaux];
   dots = Join[dots, {newverts[[3]], centroid + translate,
                  rotate[{0,0}, t, centroid] + translate}];
   Show[Graphics[{{GrayLevel[.75], Polygon[reuleaux]},
               Line[reuleaux],
               Line[Append[newverts, First[newverts]]],
               PointSize[.02], Point /@ {
                  newverts[[3]],
                  centroid + translate,
                  rotate[{0, 0}, t, centroid] + translate},
               PointSize[.007], Point /@ dots,
               {Thickness[.001],
                 Line[{{1,1},{1,-1},{-1,-1}, {-1,1},{1, 1}}]},
               Map[Line[{centroid + translate, #}] &,
                                        newverts]}],
      PlotRange->{{-1.05, 1.05}, {-1.05, 1.05}}, AspectRatio->1],
                              {t, 0, 1.99 Pi, Pi/12}]
```

A.2.5 The Cycloid as Tautochrone

The routine that follows simulates a bead sliding down a cycloid under the force of gravity by generating either an animation or a single image that is the composite of an animation, according to a user prompt. The program, which is an enhancement of one discussed on page 58, displays two beads, one falling from the top and the other starting at a user-specified start point. The gravity constant is chosen to be suitable for an image where 15 centimeters corresponds to the width of the image, which is 2π units. Thus the animation can be made completely realistic by setting the frame time to correspond to the user-inputted time increment.

The main part of the program is a `While` loop that increments `t` from 0 to `pi - radius/2`. The upper bound is chosen so that the ball will come to rest exactly against, and not beyond, the stop line; division by 2 is necessary because of the $t - \sin t$ function that parametrizes the x-coordinate of the cycloid. In the movie case, the loop shows a single frame at each pass; in the still case, it simply accumulates the graphics primitives, which will be shown by the final `showstill` command.

```
pi = Pi//N;
box = {Thickness[.003], Line[{{2 pi + .2, .2}, {2 pi + .2, -2.2},
                             {-.2, -2.2}, {-.2, .2},
                             {2 pi + .2, .2}}]};
cycloid[t_] := {t - Sin[t], -1 + Cos[t]};


cycloidplot = ParametricPlot[cycloid[s], {s, 0, 2 pi},
    Axes->None, PlotStyle->Thickness[.0005],
    DisplayFunction->Identity];


options = {PlotRange->{{-.2, 2 pi + .2}, {-2.2, .2}},
           AspectRatio->2.4/(2 pi + .4),
           DisplayFunction->$DisplayFunction};
stopline = {Thickness[.002], Line[{{pi, -2.2}, {pi, -1.8}}]};


showframe := Show[Graphics[{Thickness[.0004],
       Disk[{2 pi-posn[[1]], posn[[2]]},radius],
       Disk[posn1,   radius],
       stopline}], cycloidplot, options];
```

```
showstill := Show[cycloidplot,
    Graphics[{box, Thickness[.0004], list, stopline}], options];


g = 980 2 pi /15;


initial = Input["Enter initial t-value for start time on
                auxiliary cycloid:    0 < t < 3"] //N;
choice = InputString["Do you want the whole movie [movie] or
                    just a single image [still]?"]
inc = Input["Enter the time increment, which controls the
            number of frames generated. Values between
            1/100 and 1/400 are best."] //N


t = time = 0.; radius = .07; list = {};


(* MAIN LOOP BEGINS HERE. The variables posn and t refer to the
case of the bead starting at the top of the cycloid; posn1 and
t1 refer to the user's starting position. *)


While[t < pi - radius/2,
        t =  Sqrt[g]*time;
        t1 = 2 ArcCos[Cos[initial/2.] * Cos[Sqrt[g] time / 2]];
        posn =  cycloid[Min[t, pi - radius/2]];
        posn1 = cycloid[Min[t1, pi - radius/2]];
        time += inc;
        If[choice == "movie", showframe,
            list = Join[list,
                {Disk[{2 pi - posn[[1]], posn[[2]]}, radius],
                Disk[posn1, radius]}]]];
    showstill /; choice != "movie";
```

A.2.6 The Cycloid as Brachistochrone

The code that follows is similar to the tautochrone program in that it produces either a complete animation of beads sliding down wires or a composite image (see Figure 2.13). In this case a bead falling down a cycloid from $(2\pi, 0)$ to $(\pi, -2)$ is compared with a bead sliding down a polynomial curve connecting $(0, 0)$ to $(\pi, -2)$. Moreover, the program could be modified to work for other functions that define parametric curves connecting these two points.

The effect of gravity in the cycloid case is easy because there is a closed form (derived in Chapter 2) for the position of the sliding bead at a given time. For the polynomial case, however, one must resort to numerical approximation methods using the fact that the velocity of a sliding bead at a point (x, y) is $\sqrt{2gy}$ [assuming the bead started at $(x_0, 0)$]. Thus, given the position (x, y) at a certain time, $\texttt{time}$, we can approximate the position at time $\texttt{time} + \Delta\texttt{time}$ as follows. Proceed along the tangent to the curve a distance of $\Delta\texttt{time}\sqrt{2gy} + \frac{1}{2}g(\cos\theta)(\Delta\texttt{time})^2$—the second summand is necessary because of the acceleration that takes place as the bead slides down the straight line—and then use the intersection of a perpendicular line from that point with the curve to determine the next point. The intersection point can be found by using $\texttt{FindRoot}$. Further notes on the code:

- $\texttt{f[t]}$ gives the point corresponding to the parameter value $\texttt{t}$, on the polynomial curve parametrized with its x-coordinate equal to $\texttt{t}$.

- $\texttt{directionf[t]}$ gives the unit tangent vector to the polynomial curve; a special case is needed to handle the possibility that $f'(t) = (0, 0)$.

- $\texttt{d}$ gives the tangent direction; hence $\texttt{Divide @@ d}$ gives the slope of the normal to the tangent.

- $\texttt{posn}$ and $\texttt{posn1}$ give the current position of the bead on the cycloid and polynomial, respectively.

- $\texttt{inc}$ is the time increment, obtained by dividing $\pi/\sqrt{g}$, the total time for the cycloid's bead to descend, by the user-inputted number of frames.

- $\texttt{newposn[\{x, y\}, t1]}$ finds the intersection of the line with slope $\texttt{Divide @@ d}$ passing through $\texttt{\{x, y\}}$ with the polynomial curve. $\texttt{t1}$ is the parameter value of the preceding position on the curve $(\texttt{\{x, y\}})$ and is used as a starting value for the root finder; it must be modified by $\texttt{newposn}$ in the case that $\texttt{t1}$ is 0, since otherwise the root finder, which uses Newton's method, chokes on a singularity. Because of slow convergence near 0, $\texttt{MaxIterations}$ is set to 100.

t runs from 0 to π within the Do loop and is used to compute the position of the cycloid's bead. t1 is the polynomial's parameter; that is, f[t1] gives the position of the bead on the polynomial curve.

To improve accuracy, the new position is computed three times as often as requested by the user, but only the result of every third computation is shown. This is accomplished by the /; Mod[i, 3] == 0, and {i, 3 n} clauses at the end of the code.

```
Clear[i, t, tt]
pi = Pi//N;
norm[p_] := Sqrt[p.p];
cycloid[t_] := {t - Sin[t], -1 + Cos[t]};
cycloidplot = ParametricPlot[cycloid[tt], {tt, pi, 2 pi},
  {Axes->None, PlotStyle->Thickness[.0005],
   DisplayFunction->Identity}];

degree = Input["Enter the degree (between 1 and 15) of the
               polynomial curve connecting the two points."];

n = -1 + Input["Enter the number of frames desired.
               Values between 10 and 30 are best."]//N;
g = 980 2 pi /15; inc = pi/Sqrt[g]/(3 n);

f[t_] := {t, -2 (t/pi) ^ (1/degree)};

directionf[t_] := Block[{v},
If[(degree > 1 && t != 0) || degree == 1,
                          (v = f'[t])/norm[v], {0,-1}]];

choice = InputString["Do you want the whole movie [movie] or just
                     a single image [still]?"];

options = {PlotRange->{{-.2, 2 pi + .2}, {-2.2, .2}},
           AspectRatio->2.4/(2 pi + .4),
           DisplayFunction->$DisplayFunction};
```

```
box = {Thickness[.003], Line[{{2 pi + .2, .2}, {2 pi + .2, -2.2},
                             {-.2, -2.2}, {-.2, .2},
                             {2 pi + .2, .2}}]};
stopline = {Thickness[.002], Line[{{pi, -2.1}, {pi, -1.9}}]};
showstill :=
    Show[cycloidplot, plotf, Graphics[{box, list, stopline}],
        options];
showframe := Show[cycloidplot, plotf, Graphics[{Thickness[.0004],
        Disk[{2 pi-posn[[1]], posn[[2]]}, radius],
        Disk[posn1, radius], stopline}],                    options];


newposn[{x_, y_}, t1_] :=
    FindRoot[f[tt][[2]] - y == -(tt - x) Divide @@ d,
             {tt, Max[t1, 10.^-60]}, MaxIterations->100];


plotf = ParametricPlot[f[t], {t, 0, pi}, Axes->None,
            PlotStyle->Thickness[.0005],
            DisplayFunction->Identity];
radius = .07; posn = posn1 = {0,0}; t1 = 0; d = directionf[0];
list = {Thickness[.0004], Disk[{2 pi, 0}, radius],
        Disk[posn1, radius]};


showframe /; choice == "movie";
Do[ t = pi i / (3 n);
    {x, y} = posn1 + d*inc*(Sqrt[-2 g posn1[[2]]]
                            - g d[[2]] inc/2);


    (* Preceding line computes the point on the tangent line
        that the bead would roll to; the following line sends
        this position to newposn to get the corresponding
        point on the curve *)


    t1 = If[degree == 1, x, tt /. newposn[{x, y}, t1]];
    d = directionf[t1];
    posn  = cycloid[Min[t, pi - radius/2]];
    posn1 = f[Min[t1, pi - radius]];
```

```
If[choice == "movie", showframe,
    list = Join[list,
                  {Disk[{2 pi - posn[[1]], posn[[2]]}, radius],
                   Disk[posn1, radius]}]]    /;
                            Mod[i, 3] == 0, {i, 3 n}];


showstill /; choice != "movie";
```

A.3 Chapter 4

A.3.1 Cantor Set via Intervals

The following code generates the view of the Cantor set shown in Figure 4.6.

```
spawn1[{a_, b_}] := Block[{w = (b - a)/3},
                          {{a, a + w}, {b - w, b}}] /;
          (Head[a] == Head[b] == Rational) || a==0 || b == 1;

spawn1[intervals_List] :=
 Flatten[Map[spawn1, intervals],1] /; Length[intervals[[1]]] > 1;

lines[n_Integer, l_List] :=
          Map[Line[{{#[[1]], n + .5}, {#[[2]], n + .5}}] &, l];
level = 6;

Show[Graphics[{Thickness[.0005],
    Map[lines[level--, #] &,
    NestList[spawn1, {{0,1}}, level]]}],
              Ticks->{N[Range[0,1,1/9],3], None},
              Axes->Automatic]
```

A.3.2 Animation of Cantor Functions

The following code creates images of a generalized Cantor function with parameter p in the set $\{0.01, 0.1, 0.3, 0.5, 1, 4, 10, 100\}$; the case $p = 4$ is shown in Figure 4.8. The images can then be animated.

```
Clear[spawn, f];
spawn[{a_Rational, b_Rational}]  :=
     Block[{w = (b - a)/3}, {{a - 2w, a - w}, {b + w, b + 2w}}];
spawn[intervals_List]  :=
       Flatten[Map[spawn, intervals], 1] /;
                                   Length[intervals[[1]]] > 1;

removedintervals[n_]  :=
       Flatten[NestList[spawn, {{1/3, 2/3}}, n], 1];

connect[{a_, b_}]  := Block[{y = f[a]}, Line[{{a, y}, {b, y}}]];

f[0]   = 0;
f[x_]  := f[3x]/(r + 1)        /;  x <= 1/3;
f[x_]  := 1 - r f[1 - x]       /;  2/3 <= x;

CantorFunction[parameter_]  := (r = parameter;
              Show[Graphics[{Thickness[.001],
              Map[connect, removedintervals[6]]}],
                   Axes->{0, 0},
                   PlotRange->{{0,1}, {0,1}},
                   Ticks->{N[Range[0., 1, 1/9], 3], Automatic}]);

Attributes[CantorFunction] = {Listable}

CantorFunction[{.01, .1, .3, .5, 1, 4, 10, 100}];
```

A.3.3 The Sierpiński Triangle

The following code generates the Sierpiński triangle as illustrated in Figure 4.9.

```
Clear[spawn]
spawn[{a_, b_, c_, a_}] :=
    Block[{ab = (a+b)/2, bc = (b+c)/2, ac = (a+c)/2},
    {{a, ab, ac, a}, {b, bc, ab, b}, {c, ac, bc, c}}];

spawn[l_List] := Flatten[Map[spawn, l], 1] /; Length[l[[1]]] > 1;

Show[Graphics[{Thickness[.001], Line /@
    Nest[spawn, {{0, 0}, {.5, Sqrt[3.]/2}, {1, 0}, {0, 0}}, 7]}],
        AspectRatio->Sqrt[3]/2]
```

A.4 Chapter 5 ▰▰▰▰▰▰▰▰▰▰▰

A.4.1 Chaos Game Using a Universal Sequence

The following code uses G. Goodman's idea of replacing the random choices in the Chaos Game by the entries in a universal sequence. The result is shown in Figure 5.5. For fewer points change the two occurrences of 8 to a smaller value.

```
top = {.5, Sqrt[3.]/2}
f1[x_] := .5 x;
f2[x_] := .5(x + {1,0});
f3[x_] := .5(x + top)

list = Append[Table[0, {8-1}], 1];

Show[Graphics[Map[Point,
    NestList[(   list[[1]] = Mod[list[[1]] - list[[6]], 3];
                 list = RotateLeft[list];
                 {f1[#], f2[#], f3[#]}[[Last[list]+1]] ) &,
            {0,0}, 3^8-1]],
PlotRange->{{0, 1}, {0, .87}}, Axes->Automatic, AspectRatio->.87,
Ticks->{{.25, .5, .75, 1}, {.25, .5, .75, 1}}]
```

A.4.2 Filled Julia Sets for the Real Quadratic Map f_r

```
FilledJuliaSetReal::usage =
"FilledJuliaSetReal[r, meshx, meshy, x,  y, iters] shows the
filled-in Julia set for r*z*(1-z), by using the Escape Time
Algorithm on a meshx-by-meshy grid over the rectangle where x
varies from 0 to x and y from 0 to y. Fourfold symmetry is then
used to generate an image where x ranges from 0 to 1 and y
from -y to y. Thus x should be set to 0.5 to get the entire set.
The number of iterations used is given by iters. A Print
statement in the subroutine orbitcheckreal acts as a
progress checker."

orbitcheckreal[z_, r_, iters_] := (s = z; i = 0;
    If[Re[z] != xold, xold=Re[z]; Print[xold]];
    While[++i <= iters && Abs[s *= r (1-s)] < r0];
    If[i != iters + 1, {},
      a = Re[z]; b = Im[z];
      Flatten[Outer[List, {a, 1-a}, {b, -b}], 1]])

FilledJuliaSetReal[r_, meshx_, meshy_, x_,  y_, iters_] :=
    (r0 = 1 + 1/Abs[r]; xold = 0;
    Show[Graphics[{PointSize[.002],
      Point /@ Flatten[
        Outer[orbitcheckreal[#1 + I #2, N[r], iters]&,
                  Range[0, x, x/meshx],
                  Range[0, y, y/meshy]], 2]}],
    PlotRange->All, AspectRatio->y/x])
```

A.5 Chapter 6

A.5.1 Tree Animations

The routine that follows, which was written by Eric Halsey of the University of Washington, requires the loading of the fast turtle routine from Chapter 6. The commands following the definitions generate some amusing animations.

```
Tree::usage = "Tree[depth, length, angle, ratio] uses the
recursive subroutine, branch, to generate and display a binary
tree with small round leaves at the end of each terminal branch."

depth::usage = "The depth of the recursion of the tree function.
The tree will have 2^depth terminal branches and leaves."

length::usage = "The original length of the trunk of the tree in
the tree function.  This argument determines the overall size of
the tree."

angle::usage = "The whole angle, in degrees, between paired
subbranches of a single parent branch.  This argument
determines how much the tree spreads out."

ratio::usage = "The reduction ratio which determines how much
smaller a subbranch is than its parent branch.";

Attributes[Tree] = Listable

branch[depth_Integer, length_, angle_, ratio_] := (
    forward[length];
    left[angle/2];
    If[depth > 0, branch[depth - 1, length*ratio, angle, ratio],
                AppendTo[points, X]];
    right[angle];
    If[depth > 0, branch[depth - 1,
                    length*ratio, angle, ratio]];
    left[angle/2];
    back[length];)

Tree[depth_Integer, length_, angle_, ratio_] := (
    initialize[];
    points = {};   (* to be a list of dots at the branch-ends *)
    left[90];
    If[depth > 0, branch[depth, length, angle, ratio]];
    finished;
```

```
Show[Graphics[{Line[path], PointSize[0.03],
                  Point /@ points}], PlotRange->All])
```

```
Tree[5, 1, Range[45, 90, 2.5], .8];   (* Tree pushups *)
```

The following command generates a nice animation if the `PlotRange` setting in the definition of `Tree` is changed to `{{-2.4, 2.4}, {0, 3.5}}`. The sequence of frames should be animated in the forward direction

```
Tree[5, 1, 90, Range[.05, .8, .05]];   (* Tree growth *)
```

A.5.2 A Recursive Turtle that Supports a Terminal Substitution, Flipping of the Turtle, and Stack Operations

The following enhanced turtle supports three features that the routine `RecursiveTurtle` presented in Chapter 6 did not: the ability fo flip the turtle upside down, the use of a terminal substitution to be applied at the end of the application of the main substitution rules, and the use of stacks. These enhancements are explained in Chapter 6, along with applications.

The routine is written as a package, which requires that the preamble be in separate cells, as discussed on page 259.

```
BeginPackage["UltraTurtle`"];
```

```
UltraTurtle::usage = "UltraTurtle[recursion, axiom,
terminal:{0,0}, depth, angle, steplength, startposn:{0.,0.},
startdir:{1.,0.}, dim1:1000, dim2:1] returns the image obtained
by applying a turtle to the sequence of movements generated in
depth many rewritings of the axiom. Characters are F, B, -, +,
i (flip), [ (push), ] (pop). Stack operations and a terminal
substitution are supported. If the path will visit more than
1000 points, a larger value of dim1 should be used. The number
of separate paths must be less than dim2. The final turtle
path(s) is in the variable called path, which can be
displayed externally via Map[Line, path]";
path;
```

```
Begin["UltraTurtle`Private`"];

symboltable = {"F" -> forward, "B" -> back, "-" -> right,
            "+" -> left, "i" -> flip, "[" -> push, "]" -> pop};

UltraTurtle[recursion_List, axiom_String, terminal_List:{},
        depth_Integer, angle_, steplength_,
        startposn_List:{0., 0.}, startdir_List:{1., 0.},
        dim1_:100, dim2_:1] := Block[

    {X, U, turtle, rotateleft, rotateright, start, replacerules,
     symbols, i = 0, stack = {{startposn//N, startdir//N}},
     c = Cos[angle Degree]//N, s = Sin[angle Degree]//N,
     count = Table[1, {dim2}]},

start = Prepend[Characters[axiom] /. symboltable, pop];

replacerules[r_List] :=
 Map[First[Characters[#[[1]]]] -> Characters[#[[2]]] &, r] /.
     symboltable;

turtle[left]    :=  U = rotateleft . U;
turtle[right]   :=  U = rotateright . U;
turtle[forward]:=  path[[i, ++count[[i]]]] = (X += steplength U);
turtle[back]    :=  path[[i, ++count[[i]]]] = (X -= steplength U);
turtle[push]    :=  PrependTo[stack, {X, U}];
turtle[pop]     :=  ({X, U} = First[stack]; path[[++i, 1]] = X;
                                stack = Rest[stack]);
turtle[flip]    :=
            {rotateleft, rotateright} = {rotateright, rotateleft};
Attributes[turtle] = Listable;

path = Table[Null, {dim2}, {dim1}];
rotateright = Transpose[ rotateleft = {{c, -s}, {s, c}} ];
turtle[
    Nest[# /. replacerules[recursion] &,
        start/.symboltable, depth] /. replacerules[terminal]]];
```

```
path = Map[Take[path[[#]], count[[#]]]&, Range[i]];
Show[Graphics[Line /@ path], AspectRatio->1, Axes->None,
                         PlotRange->All, AspectRatio->1]]
End[]; EndPackage[];
```

A.5.3 Sierpiński and Original Peano Space-Filling Curves

The following code can be used to generate Figure 6.12. It requires that RecursiveTurtle be loaded.

```
SierpinskiCurve[n_] := Show[RecursiveTurtle[
                    {"X"-> "XF-F+F-XF+F+XF-F+F-X"},
                    "F+XF+F+XF",
                n, 90, side = Sqrt[2.] 2^-(n+2),
                ({temp = ((2^(n-1)6 + 2^(n) -2) side/Sqrt[2])};
(*stepsize*)        {(temp+1)/2 - side/Sqrt[2], (1-temp)/2}),
(*start direction*) Sqrt[{2,2}]/2,
(*path length*)     (4^(n+2) - 1)/3      ],
     Axes->{0, 0}, PlotRange->{{0, 1}, {0, 1}},
     Ticks->{{.25, .5, .75, 1}, {.25, .5, .75, 1}}]


OriginalPeanoCurve[n_] := Show[RecursiveTurtle[
     {"X"-> "XFYFX+F+YFXFY-F-XFYFX",
      "Y"->"YFXFY-F-XFYFX+F+YFXFY"},
      "X", n, 90, 3^-n, {3, 3}^-n / 2, 9^n],
      Axes->{0,0}, PlotRange->{{0, 1}, {0, 1}},
      Ticks->{{.33, .67, 1}, {.33, .67, 1}}]
```

A.5.4 Illustration of a Function from the Interval onto the Square

Once the following routine is loaded, Figure 6.14 can be generated by CantorImage[2 ^ Range[2, 7]].

```
CantorBijection::usage = "CantorBijection[t] gives the value of
a bijection from the unit interval to the unit square based on
```

even- and odd-indexed binary digits. The input and outputs are
base-10 numbers in the unit interval and unit square,
respectively."

CantorImage::usage = "CantorImage[n] gives the path in the unit
square obtained by using straight lines to connect the values of
CantorBijection on {0, 1/n, 2/n, . . . , 1}."

SetAttributes[{CantorBijection, CantorImage}, Listable]

```
base2digits[t_] := Block[{tt = N[t]},
        Map[If[2. ^ -# <= tt, tt -= 2. ^ -#; 1, 0] &, Range[30]]]


CantorBijection[t_] := (
    temp = Flatten@Position[base2digits[t], 1];
    temp = {Select[temp, !EvenQ[#]&], Select[temp, EvenQ]};
{Plus @@ (2^((-temp[[1]]-1)/2)), Plus @@ (2^(-temp[[2]]/2)) } //N )


CantorBijection[1] = {0,1}


CantorImage[n_] :=
    Show[Graphics[Line[CantorBijection[Range[0, 1, 1/n]]]],
        PlotRange->{{0, 1}, {0, 1}}, AspectRatio->1,
        Axes->Automatic, AxesStyle->GrayLevel[1],
        Ticks->Range[{0, 0}, {1, 1}, {.25, .25}]]]
```

A.5.5 A Three-Dimensional Turtle

The package RecursiveTurtle3D implements a three-dimensional turtle that can interpret string rewriting rules. The use of the pitch, roll, and
yaw commands and the implementation of these via matrices is discussed
in Chapter 6, where several examples of the use of RecursiveTurtle3D
can be found.

```
BeginPackage["RecursiveTurtle3D`"];

RecursiveTurtle3D::usage = "RecursiveTurtle3D[recursion_List,
axiom, depth_Integer, angles_List, steplength,
startposn_List:{0.,0.,0.}, startdir_List:IdentityMatrix[3],
dim_:1000] displays the path generated by depth many
applications of the rules in recursion to axiom. The list,
angles, must contain the pitch, roll, & yaw angles in
that order.";
path;

Begin["RecursiveTurtle3D`Private`"];

RecursiveTurtle3D[recursion_List, axiom_, depth_Integer,
     angles_List, steplength_, startposn_List:{0.,0.,0.},
     startdir_List:(IdentityMatrix[3]), dim_:1000] :=

(X = startposn//N; V = startdir//N;  count = 1;
{cp,cr,cy} = Cos[angles Degree//N];
{sp,sr,sy} = Sin[angles Degree//N];

symboltable = {"F"  -> forward,  "B" -> back,
                "&"  -> pitch,    "^" -> pitchback,
                "\\" -> rollleft, "/" -> rollright,
                "+"  -> yawleft,  "-" -> yawright    };

turtle[forward]  := path[[++count]] =
                                X += steplength First[Transpose@V];
turtle[back]     := path[[++count]] =
                                X -= steplength First[Transpose@V];
turtle[pitch]     := V = V.pitchmatrix;
turtle[pitchback] := V = V.pitchbackmatrix;
turtle[yawleft]   := V = V.yawleftmatrix;
turtle[yawright]  := V = V.yawrightmatrix;
turtle[rollleft]  := V = V.rollleftmatrix;
turtle[rollright] := V = V.rollrightmatrix;
     Attributes[turtle] = Listable;
```

```
replacerules =
 Map[First[Characters[#[[1]]]] -> Characters[#[[2]]] &,
          recursion] /. symboltable;

path = Table[Null, {dim}]; path[[1]] = X;

pitchmatrix      = {{cp,  0,  sp}, {0, 1,  0},    {-sp, 0, cp}};
pitchbackmatrix = {{cp,  0, -sp}, {0, 1,  0},    { sp, 0, cp}};

rollleftmatrix   = {{1,  0,  0},   {0, cr,  sr}, {0, -sr, cr}};
rollrightmatrix = {{1,  0,  0},   {0, cr, -sr}, {0,  sr, cr}};

yawleftmatrix    = {{cy, -sy,  0}, { sy,  cy, 0}, {0, 0, 1}};
yawrightmatrix  = {{cy,  sy,  0}, {-sy, cy,  0}, {0, 0, 1}};

turtle[Nest[# /. replacerules &,
          Characters[axiom]/.symboltable, depth]];
path = Take[path, count];
Show[Graphics3D[Line[path]],
   Axes->None, BoxRatios->{1,1,1}, Boxed->False, PlotRange->All])

End[]; EndPackage[];
```

A.6 Chapter 8

A.6.1 Test for Whether Integers Are Pairwise Relatively Prime

```
PairwiseCoprime::usage = "PairwiseCoprime[mlist] returns True
if the integers in mlist are pairwise relatively prime,
False otherwise."

PairwiseCoprime[mlist_List] :=
    Length[mlist] == Length[Union[mlist]] &&
    And @@ Flatten[Outer[GCD[#1,#2] == 1 || #1 == #2 &,
                         mlist, mlist]]
```

A.6.2 The Splitting Algorithm for Egyptian Fractions

```
EgyptianSplitting::usage = "EgyptianSplitting[q] uses the
splitting method to write q as a sum of distinct unit fractions"

EgyptianSplitting[q_] := (
  list = Table[Denominator[q], {Numerator[q]}];
  While[Length[list] != Length[Union[list]], list =
    Sort[Flatten[
        Map[(t = list[[#]];
            If[{#} != First[Position[list, t]],
                {t+1, t(t+1)}, t]) &,
          Range[Length[list]]]]]];
  list)
```

A.6.3 Code to Generate Table 8.2

```
Map[Length[Digits[Last[#]]]&,
    EgyptianFraction[(10 ^ Range[9] - 1) / 10 ^ Range[9]]]
```

A.7 Chapter 9

A.7.1 Shanks's Algorithm for Square Roots Modulo a Prime

```
SqrtModPrimeShanks::usage = "SqrtModPrimeShanks[a, p]
assumes p is prime and returns, via Shanks's algorithm, the
least nonnegative square root of a mod p if such exists,
{} otherwise. It requires the routine Nonresidue"

Attributes[SqrtModPrimeShanks] = Listable
SetAttributes[PowerMod, Listable]

SqrtModPrimeShanks[a_, 2]  := Mod[a, 2]
```

```
SqrtModPrimeShanks[a_, p_] := {}              /; JacobiSymbol[a, p] == -1

SqrtModPrimeShanks[a_, p_] := 0                        /; Mod[a, p] == 0

SqrtModPrimeShanks[a_, p_] :=
  Min[PowerMod[a, (p+1)/4, p]*{-1, 1} + {p, 0}] /; Mod[p, 4] == 3

SqrtModPrimeShanks[a_, p_] :=
  Block[{k = (p - 1)/2, i, L, n, r, s = 1, c, b},
    While[EvenQ[k], k /= 2; s++];
    {c, r, n} = PowerMod[{Nonresidue[p], a, a},
                         {k, (k+1)/2,k}, p];
    While[n != 1,
        L = s; b = n;
        Do[
        If[b == 1, b = c; s = i - 1, b = Mod[b b, p]], {i, L}];
        {c, r, n} = Mod[b {b, r, b n}, p]];
Min[r, p - r]]                                /; Mod[p, 4] == 1
```

A.7.2 Finding Primitive Representations
of n as $fa^2 + gb^2$

```
PrimitiveReps::usage = "PrimitiveReps[n, f, g] returns the set of
representations of n as f a^2 + g b^2, where gcd(a, b) = 1. It is
assumed that gcd(n, f g) = 1 and n > f + g. The routines SqrtMod,
Nonresidue, and CRT must be loaded."

MiddleRemainder::usage = "MiddleRemainder[n, x, f, g] returns
the first remainder r that satisfies f r^2 < n, when the
Euclidean algorithm is applied to n, x."

SetAttributes[{MiddleRemainder, PrimitiveReps}, Listable]

MiddleRemainder[n_, m_, x_, f_, g_] := x /; f x^2 < n
MiddleRemainder[n_, m_, x_, f_, g_] :=
        MiddleRemainder[n, x, Mod[m, x], f, g] /; f x^2 >= n
MiddleRemainder[n_, x_, f_, g_] := MiddleRemainder[n, n, x, f, g]
```

```
PrimitiveReps[n_, f_, g_] := Block[{temp},
   Complement[
      Map[If[IntegerQ[temp = Sqrt[(n-f #^2)/g]], {#, temp}, {}]
         &, MiddleRemainder[n,
            Select[SqrtMod[-g PowerMod[f, -1, n], n],
                  # <= n/2 &], f, g]],
      {{{}}]]                                              /; n > f + g
```

References

Chapter Zero: A Brief Introduction ▬▬▬

[Fay] T. H. Fay, The Butterfly Curve, *Amer. Math. Monthly*, **96** (1989) 442–443.

[Mae] R. Maeder, *Programming in Mathematica*, Addison-Wesley, Reading, Mass., 1989.

[Wol] S. Wolfram, *Mathematica*, Addison-Wesley, Reading, Mass., 1988.

Chapter One: Prime Numbers ▬▬▬

[Boa] R. P. Boas, The Skewes number, in *Mathematical Plums*, R. Honsberger, ed., Dolciani Mathematical Expositions, No. 4, Mathematical Association of America, 1979.

[Gar] M. Gardner, *Penrose Tiles to Trapdoor Ciphers*, W. H. Freeman, New York, 1989.

[Guy] R. K. Guy, *Unsolved Problems in Number Theory*, Springer-Verlag, New York, 1981.

[LMO] J. Lagarias, V. S. Miller, and A. Odlyzko, Computing $\pi(x)$: The Meissel–Lehmer method, *Math. Comp.*, **44** (1985) 537–560.

[PSW] C. Pomerance, J. L. Selfridge, and S. S. Wagstaff, Jr., The pseudoprimes to 25×10^9, *Math. Comp.*, **35** (1980) 1003–1026.

[Rib] P. Ribenboim, *The Book of Prime Number Records*, Springer-Verlag, New York, 1988.

[Rie] H. Riesel, *Prime Numbers and Computer Methods for Factorization*, Birkhäuser, Boston, 1985.

[Ros] K. H. Rosen, *Elementary Number Theory and its Applications*, 2nd ed., Addison-Wesley, Reading, Mass., 1988.

[teR] H. J. J. te Riele, On the sign of the difference $\pi(x) - \mathrm{li}(x)$, *Math. Comp.*, **48** (1987) 323–328.

[Wag] S. Wagon, The Evidence: Primality testing, *The Math. Intelligencer*, **8** (1986) 58–61.

[Zag] D. Zagier, The first 50 million prime numbers, *The Math. Intelligencer*, **0** (1977) 7–19.

Chapter Two: Rolling Circles

[BdP] W. E. Boyce and R. C. DiPrima, *Elementary Differential Equations*, 3rd ed., Wiley, New York, 1977.

[Bli] G. A. Bliss, *Calculus of Variations*, Carus Mathematical Monographs, No. 1, Mathematical Association of America, 1925.

[CS] F. Cunningham, Jr., and I. J. Schoenberg, On the Kakeya constant, *Can. J. Math.*, **17** (1965) 946–956.

[HW] L. Hall and S. Wagon, *Mathematical Roads and Wheels*, forthcoming.

[Lyu] L. A. Lyusternik, *Shortest Paths, Variational Problems*, trans. P. Collins and R. B. Brown, Pergamon Press, New York, 1964.

[Reu] F. Reuleaux, *The Kinematics of Machinery*, trans. A. Kennedy, Dover, New York, 1963 (reprint of 1876 English translation of 1875 original in German).

[TF] G. B. Thomas and R. L. Finney, *Calculus and Analytic Geometry*, 7th ed., Addison-Wesley, Reading, Mass., 1988.

[Whi] E. A. Whitman, Some historical notes on the cycloid, *Amer. Math. Monthly*, **50** (1948) 309–315.

Chapter Three: Surfaces

[AS] A. M. Ash and H. Sexton, A surface with one local minimum, *Math. Mag.*, **58** (1985) 147–149.

[CV] B. Calvert and M. K. Vamanamurthy, Local and global extrema for functions of several variables, *J. Austral. Math. Soc.* (Series A) **29** (1980) 362–368.

[Dav] R. Davies, Solution to Problem #1235, *Math. Mag.* **61** (1988) 59.

[DKM] A. Durfee, N. Kronenfeld, H. Munson, J. Roy, and I. Westby, Critical points of real polynomials in two variables (forthcoming).

[Fra] M. E. Frantz, Interactive graphics for multivariable calculus, *College Math. J.* **17** (1986) 172–181.

[RS] I. Rosenholtz and L. Smylie, "The only critical point in town" test, *Math. Mag.*, **58** (1985) 149–150

[TF] G. B. Thomas and R. L. Finney, *Calculus and Analytic Geometry*, 7th ed., Addison-Wesley, Reading, Mass.:, 1988.

Chapter Four: Iterative Graphics ▬▬▬

[Cha] D. Chalice, A characterization of the Cantor function, *Amer. Math. Monthly*, **98** (1991) 255–258.

[CE] P. Collet and J.-P. Eckmann, *Iterated Maps of the Interval as Dynamical Systems*, Birkhäuser, Boston, 1980.

[Dev1] R. L. Devaney, *An Introduction to Chaotic Dynamical Systems*, 2nd ed., Addison-Wesley, Reading, Mass., 1989.

[Dev2] R. L. Devaney, *Chaos, Fractals, and Dynamics*, Addison-Wesley, Reading, Mass., 1990.

[Gar] M. Gardner, *Penrose Tiles to Trapdoor Ciphers*, W. H. Freeman, New York, 1989.

[Gle] J. Gleick, *Chaos*, Penguin, New York, 1987.

[GO] B. R. Gelbaum and J. M. H. Olmsted, *Counterexamples in Analysis*, Holden-Day, San Francisco, 1964.

[GS] B. Grünbaum and G. C. Shephard, *Tiling and Patterns*, W. H. Freeman, New York, 1986.

[Mau] P. Maurer, "A rose is a rose . . . ", *Amer. Math. Monthly*, **94** (1987) 631–645.

[Nel] D. R. Nelson, Quasicrystals, *Sci. Amer.*, **255** (August 1986) 42–51.

[NH] D. R. Nelson and B. I. Halperin, Pentagonal and icosahedral order in rapidly cooled metals, *Science*, **229** (19 July 1985) 233–238.

[Pen] R. Penrose, *The Emperor's New Mind*, Oxford Univ. Press, New York, 1989.

Chapter Five: Iterative Complex Graphics ▰▰

[Bar] M. Barnsley, *Fractals Everywhere*, Academic Press, San Diego, 1988.

[Dev1] R. L. Devaney, *An Introduction to Chaotic Dynamical Systems*, 2nd ed., Addison-Wesley, Reading, Mass., 1989.

[Dev2] R. L. Devaney, *Chaos, Fractals, and Dynamics*, Addison-Wesley, Reading, Mass., 1990.

[DK] R. L. Devaney and L. Keen (eds.), *Chaos and Fractals, The Mathematics Behind the Computer Graphics, Proc. Symp. Appl. Math.*, **39**, American Mathematical Society, Providence, R. I., 1989.

[Gof] D. Goffinet, Number systems with a complex base: A fractal tool for teaching topology, *Amer. Math. Monthly*, **98** (1991) 249–255.

[Goo] G. Goodman, forthcoming

[LN] R. Lidl and H. Neiderreiter, *Finite Fields*, Addison-Wesley, Reading, Mass., 1983.

[Str] G. Strang, *Linear Algebra and its Applications*, 2nd ed., Academic Press, New York, 1980.

Chapter Six: The Turtle Road to Recursion ▰▰

[Bar] M. Barnsley, *Fractals Everywhere*, Academic Press, San Diego, 1988.

[BP] J. J. Bartholdi and L. K. Platzman, Heuristics based on space-filling curves for combinatorial problems in Eucidean space, *Management Science*, **34** (1988) 291–305.

[BPCW] J. J. Bartholdi, L. K. Platzman, R. L. Collins, and W. H. Warden, A minimal technology routing system for Meals on Wheels, *Interfaces*, **13** (1983) 1–8.

[Dek] M. F. Dekking, Recurrent sets, *Advances in Math.*, **44** (1982) 78–194.

[Fal] K. J. Falconer, *The Geometry of Fractal Sets*, Cambridge Univ. Press, Cambridge, Eng., 1985.

[GO] B. R. Gelbaum and J. M. H. Olmsted, *Counterexamples in Analysis*, Holden-Day, San Francisco, 1964.

[Man] B. Mandelbrot, *The Fractal Geometry of Nature*, W. H. Freeman, San Francisco, 1982.

[Mor] S. Morris, A fractal fairy tale, *Omni*, **11** (Nov. 1988) 124–125.

[PB] L. K. Platzman and J. J. Bartholdi, Spacefilling curves and the planar travelling salesman problem, *J. Assoc. for Computing Machinery*, **36** (1989) 719–737.

[PH] P. Prusinkiewicz and J. Hanan, *Lindenmayer Systems, Fractals, and Plants, Lecture Notes in Biomathematics*, vol. 79, Springer-Verlag, New York, 1989.

[PL] P. Prusinkiewicz and A. Lindenmayer, *The Algorithmic Beauty of Plants*, Springer, New York, 1990.

[Sau] D. Saupe, A unified approach to fractal curves and plants, Appendix C in *The Science of Fractal Images*, H.-O. Peitgen and D. Saupe (eds.), Springer-Verlag, New York, 1988.

Chapter Seven: Advanced Three-Dimensional Graphics

[Ber] G. C. Berresford, Differential equations and root cellars, *UMAP J.*, **2** (1981) 53–75.

[Gro] J. L. Gross, *Topological Graph Theory*, Wiley, New York, 1987.

[Mae] R. Maeder, *Programming in Mathematica*, Addison-Wesley, Reading, Mass., 1989.

[Rin] G. Ringel, *Map Color Theorem*, Springer-Verlag, New York, 1974.

[TF] G. B. Thomas and R. L. Finney, *Calculus and Analytic Geometry*, 7th ed., Addison-Wesley, Reading, Mass., 1988.

[Whi] A. T. White, *Graphs, Groups, and Surfaces*, North-Holland, Amsterdam, 1984.

Chapter Eight: Some Algorithms of Number Theory ▰▰▰

[BS] E. Bach and J. Shallit, *Computational Number Theory*, forthcoming.

[Bai] D. Bailey, The computation of π to 29,360,000 decimal digits using Borweins' quartically convergent algorithm, *Math. Comp.*, **50** (1988) 283–296.

[Bee] L. Beeckmans, Fractions égyptiènnes: algorithmes et équations diophantiennes. Masters thesis, Université Libre de Bruxelles, 1989.

[Ble] M. N. Bleicher, A new algorithm for the expansion of Egyptian fractions, *J. of Number Theory*, **4** (1972) 342–382.

[Bre] R. Breusch, Solution to Problem E4512, *Amer. Math. Monthly*, **61** (1954) 200–201.

[GJ] M. R. Garey and D. S. Johnson, *Computers and Intractability: A Guide to the Theory of NP-Completeness*, W. H. Freeman, San Francisco, 1979.

[KW] V. Klee and S. Wagon, *Unsolved Problems in Elementary Geometry and Number Theory*, Dolciani Mathematical Expositions, Mathematical Association of America, Washington, D.C., 1991.

[Knu] D. E. Knuth, *The Art of Computer Programming*, vol. 2, Addison-Wesley, Reading, Mass., 1971.

[Ros] K. H. Rosen, *Elementary Number Theory and its Applications*, 2nd ed., Addison-Wesley, Reading, Mass., 1988.

[Wil] H. Wilf, *Algorithms and Complexity*, Prentice-Hall, Englewood Cliffs, N.J., 1986.

Chapter Nine: Imaginary Primes and Prime Imaginaries ▰▰▰

[Bac] E. Bach, *Analytic Methods in the Analysis and Design of Number-Theoretic Algorithms*, MIT Press, Cambridge, Mass., 1985.

[Cor] G. Cornacchia, Su di un metodo per la risoluzione in numeri interi dell'equazione $\sum_{h=0}^{n} C_h x^{n-h} y^h = P$, *G. Mat. di Battaglini*, **46** (1908) 33–90.

[Cox] D. A. Cox, *Primes of the form $x^2 + ny^2$*, Wiley, New York, 1989.

[Fla] D. E. Flath, *Introduction to Number Theory*, Wiley, New York, 1989.

[HW] G. H. Hardy and E. M. Wright, *An Introduction to the Theory of Numbers*, 4th ed., Oxford Univ. Press, London, 1960.

[HMW] K. Hardy, J. B. Muskat, and K. S. Williams, A deterministic algorithm for solving $n = fu^2 + gv^2$ in coprime integers u and v, *Math. Comp.*, **55** (1990) 327–343.

[JR] J. H. Jordan and J. R. Rabung, A conjecture of Paul Erdős concerning Gaussian primes, *Math. Comp.*, **24** (1970) 221–223.

[Knu] D. E. Knuth, *The Art of Computer Programming*, vol. 2, Addison-Wesley, Reading, Mass., 1971.

[Mac] N. Mackinnon, Sophie Germain, or was Gauss a feminist? *Math. Gaz*, **73** (1989) 346–351.

[Rie] H. Riesel, *Prime Numbers and Computer Methods for Factorization*, Birkhäuser, Boston, 1985.

[Ros] K. H. Rosen, *Elementary Number Theory and its Applications*, 2nd ed., Addison-Wesley, Reading, Mass., 1988.

[SR] J. O. Shallit and M. O. Rabin, Randomized algorithms in number theory, *Comm. Pure Appl. Math.*, **39** (1986) 239–256.

[Sha] D. Shanks, Five number-theoretic algorithms, in *Proceedings of the Second Manitoba Conference on Numerical Mathematics*, 1972, 51–70.

[Wag] S. Wagon, Editor's Corner: The Euclidean Algorithm Strikes Again, *Amer. Math. Monthly*, **97** (1990) 125–129.

Chapter Ten: Additional Examples ■■■■■

[Dav] H. Davenport, *Multiplicative Number Theory*, 2nd ed., revised by H. L. Montgomery, Graduate Texts in Mathematics, vol. 74, Springer-Verlag, New York, 1980.

[Edw] H. M. Edwards, *Riemann's Zeta Function*, Academic Press, New York, 1974.

[GM] V. Guillemin and R. Melrose, An inverse spectral result for elliptical regions in $\mathbb{R}^2$, *Advances in Math.*, **32** (1979) 128–148.

[KW] V. Klee and S. Wagon, *Unsolved Problems in Elementary Geometry and Number Theory*, Dolciani Mathematical Expositions, Mathematical Association of America, Washington, D.C., 1991.

[Lan] S. Lang, *Algebra*, 2nd ed., Addison-Wesley, Menlo Park, Calif., 1984.

[ORo1] J. O'Rourke, *Art Gallery Theorems and Algorithms*, Oxford Univ. Press, New York, 1987.

[ORo2] J. O'Rourke, *Computational Geometry in C*, forthcoming.

[PD] H. Pollard and H. G. Diamond, *The Theory of Algebraic Numbers*, 2nd ed., Carus Mathematical Monographs, No. 9, Mathematical Association of America, Washington, D.C., 1975.

[PZ] M. Pohst and H. Zassenhaus, *Algorithmic Algebraic Number Theory*, Cambridge Univ. Press, Cambridge, Eng., 1989.

[Rie] H. Riesel, *Prime Numbers and Computer Methods for Factorization*, Birkhäuser, Boston, 1985.

[RG] H. Riesel and G. Göhl, Some calculations related to Riemann's Prime Number Formula, *Math. Comp.*, **24** (1970) 969–983.

[Sch] L. Schoenfeld, Sharper bounds for the Chebyshev functions $\theta(x)$ and $\psi(x)$, II, *Math. Comp.*, **30**, (1976) 337–360.

[Schr] M. R. Schroeder, *Number Theory in Science and Communication*, Springer-Verlag, Berlin, 1984.

[Wag] S. Wagon, The Evidence: Where are the zeros of zeta of s?, *Math. Intelligencer*, **8** (1986) 57–62.

Index of *Mathematica* Objects

Mathematica in Action objects are indexed separately immediately following this index.

Index of *Mathematica in Action* Objects ▬▬▬

Subject Index